Walworth Street

to Wall Street

How an $85 a Week Clerk Became
a $100 Million Investment Banker

A Wall Street Memoir

Pat Scida

ISBN 978-1-64458-780-5 (paperback)
ISBN 978-1-64458-781-2 (digital)

Christian Faith Publishing, Inc.
832 Park Avenue
Meadville, PA 16335
www.christianfaithpublishing.com

Printed in the United States of America

Contents

Introduction..7

Chapter 1: Life on Wall Street Begins.....................11
Chapter 2: The Fix Was In...16
Chapter 3: On the Job: Day 1....................................20
Chapter 4: Old Wall Street..23
Chapter 5: Top Day..25
Chapter 6: If It's Wednesday.....................................28
Chapter 7: How Am I Doing?....................................34
Chapter 8: Working Late and Weekends..................38
Chapter 9: Getting Around and Meeting People......42
Chapter 10: A Raise and a Move...............................46
Chapter 11: The Tubs...49
Chapter 12: Charles Plohn & Co...............................51
Chapter 13: The Plohn Crowd..................................56
Chapter 14: The Home Front.....................................64
Chapter 15: Miracle of the E–Z Book.......................67
Chapter 16: Dees, Does, and Dem............................72
Chapter 17: Hidden Events Unfold...........................79
Chapter 18: Reynolds Securities: DECAB.................82
Chapter 19: The Fall of Goodbody:
            Unmatched Confirmations........................88
Chapter 20: Account Change Methodology Reveals
            Reynolds Securities Back Office Identity.....97
Chapter 21: Institutional Stock Sales Snafu.............101
Chapter 22: Mike L. Comes to DECAB....................107
Chapter 23: A New Broom: Opportunity Knocks.....111
Chapter 24: You Have No Grandma?.........................118

Chapter 25: The Trading Desk..127
Chapter 26: Some Small Coming-Of-Age…and Acceptance......133
Chapter 27: The Papers 141
Chapter 28: Reynolds Bond Department: A Second Look 146
Chapter 29: More Coming-Of-Age: The Early Bird and UITs ...149
Chapter 30: The Regionals Gather in New York 158
Chapter 31: The Acquisition of Phelps-Fenn 161
Chapter 32: The Firm Capitalizes on New Relationships...........166
Chapter 33: My Secret Life 170
Chapter 34: Reynolds Sponsors a UIT.......................................178
Chapter 35: Surprise: A New Alignment....................................182
Chapter 36: Clem Schaefer 185
Chapter 37: The South Shore Bond Club:
             More Clem Schaefer...189
Chapter 38: More Reynolds 193
Chapter 39: The Go-Go Sixties and the Wall Street Vision........197
Chapter 40: The Work and the Market Climate 200
Chapter 41: Life and Money: Looking for Greener Pastures.......205
Chapter 42: The Henry Arbeeny Era: Leadership,
             Inspiration, Change...211
Chapter 43: The New Push for Sales: More Arbeeny 221
Chapter 44: Money, Money, Money…Here.................................228
Chapter 45: But Not Enough Money There................................234
Chapter 46: New Stirrings and a Turning Point 238
Chapter 47: The End of the World..248
Chapter 48: People: Norman, Kondi, Family, Et.al. 252
Chapter 49: Astounding Times, I Thought 263
Chapter 50: Innovation Part I..269
Chapter 51: Innovation Part II...273
Chapter 52: Discovering and Learning My Trade......................276
Chapter 53: Notable Events and A Christmas Party..................280
Chapter 54: 1978...284
Chapter 55: He's Probably Recruiting the Guys in Ketchum.....293
Chapter 56: Reynolds and Dean Witter Merge; Whats
             Going to Happen…?..297
Chapter 57: Settling Scores, I Guess..302

Chapter 58: The Predictable Aftermath 310
Chapter 59: The New Unit Trust Department.....................313
Chapter 60: I Digress: My Part and The Ugly Sheet.................319
Chapter 61: Philosophies, Conflicts, Fixes 324
Chapter 62: Coup de GNMA..330
Chapter 63: Six Million or Seven? Ten, Twenty. That Is
          the Question 335
Chapter 64: Who Are These People? You Have a Family!..........341
Chapter 65: Upheaval Another New/Old Investment 347
Chapter 66: The Regional Sales Co-Coordinators.....................356
Chapter 67: The Talks 363
Chapter 68: Short Term CD Trusts Take Over 369
Chapter 69: New Digs and Continued Chaos..........................379
Chapter 70: Underwriters Distribution Control......................383
Chapter 71: Uneasy Times..391
Chapter 72: A Hundred Million? You're Out of Your Mind 394
Chapter 73: Events Unfold 400

Epilogue...403
Appendix: Fixed Income/Bond Market Primer..........................405

Introduction

When family and friends asked why I was writing a book, I would often say, "Well, in the late sixties, I got a job as an eighty-five-dollar-a-week clerk in a Wall Street firm. Thirty-three years later, I retired as senior vice president and director, so I'm writing about it to figure out just how it happened."

This answer might produce a surprised nod of the head, perhaps form some wide-eyed grimace of approval on faces and a "wow" or a "good for you," and that would be that. My answer was true enough, because I saw myself as a very unlikely candidate for such a unique experience. At twenty-four, with a just barely accredited high school education, I was working at an auto body repair shop. In an attempt to embark on a new career path, I secured an entry-level position as a clerk in a major Wall Street firm. To my surprise, in a little more than a decade, I found myself presiding over the weekly ebb and flow of a twenty-five- to fifty-million-dollar inventory of fixed income securities. Early on, my personal story dominated. However, after a while, the overall experience and back story of Wall Street took over. The parade of people with outsized personalities, the day-to-day mountain of work, its fascinating intricacy and detail, the endless decision making, the small firm-big firm dynamic, the markets and the enormous amounts of capital they represented, the mergers, the deals, and the historical moment of the times all welled up to form a series of essays and reflections, not just on my career, but on the Wall Street experience at large. After showing the material to several former colleagues and friends, I was encouraged to publish them and have come to believe they will interest readers on many levels.

The book approaches Wall Street from the point of view of the worker, not the economist or trader, hedge fund manager, or analyst.

Not that these people don't work or put in long hard hours—they most certainly do—but they bring Wall Street to the public from a gain/loss perspective and a greed point of view rather than one of form, function, and task. Wall Street may appear to be all gain and greed with no other purpose or reason—what politicians and the press often make it out to be. What is forgotten, perhaps taken for granted and rarely projected to the citizenry, is that it would be impossible for the major portion of the public to buy their morning coffee at Starbucks with a credit card, shower with clean water, or commute to work without Wall Street and the credit and equity markets it presides over. More importantly, they have forgotten that in a free society, a capitalist society and civilization like the United States, Wall Street and the work that is done there may very well be the cornerstone of it all. It takes money that is willing to be put at risk to fund the needs of vast and technologically forward-looking populations. It has in this country, at least since colonial times, and that money must be raised, transferred, transformed, managed, and made to perform and, at every step of the way be documented, all of which is a job of work and indeed the laborious task of Wall Street.

The time frame covered is the late sixties to the early eighties and is loosely divided into three sections. I came to Wall Street in 1968, when it was mired in a clerical morass that eventually destroyed a significant number of firms that had dominated the financial services industry since the turn of the century and before. As difficult as these times were for Wall Street employees, a continuing fascination for the business, a willingness to work for next to nothing, and sheer luck kept me employed. The experience of the back office, its politics and the life of a transaction dominate the first third of the book. The middle, (1972–1976) chronicles a transfer to the Municipal Bond Division of Reynolds Securities, a firm of three thousand employees and my introduction to transactional Wall Street (i.e., the markets, trading, and underwriting.) The final third 1977-1981 is concerned with the unprecedented period of high inflation and interest rates leading to a vast movement of capital from the nation's banks to its brokerage firms and the small roll my colleagues and I played therein.

As enormous as Wall Street may be in the trillions of dollars it transacts daily, in contrast, it is small, miniscule in regard to human participation. The number of individuals presiding over, interacting directly and personally with transactions of a significant nature, is a much lesser number than might be imagined.

For example, in the municipal bond industry in the early seventies, new issue volume at the national level (underwritten in New York) averaged two to three billion dollars weekly. It was in the main presided over (underwritten and financed) by no more than ten individuals at the senior level at eight or nine Wall Street firms. Add fifty employees collectively in these firms' municipal syndicate departments and do some division, and you'll come up with each person having responsibility for underwriting an average of thirty million dollars weekly. Multiplying by fifty-two weeks a year will annualize to two billion dollars a year per individual.

Taking this Wall Street head count a bit further, let's say another two hundred to three hundred individuals presided over the taxable securities markets (US government bonds, corporate bonds, and agency securities), add another two hundred participants trading at the major firms and one hundred persons presiding over the major mutual funds buying and redistribution operations, and you have just five hundred to six hundred persons presiding over 90 percent of the credit markets in the United States at the time, some two to three trillion dollars of financing. The same reasoning can be applied today, even with the exponentially larger numbers of securities underwritten. Modern technology has made it so much easier to control inventory, and there are far fewer players (firms) today.

These individuals may be called investment bankers. Generally speaking, investment bankers work at raising money for companies and governments or provide advisory services on mergers and acquisitions and any number of financial activities that move large portions of capital. The type of investment banker we are most concerned with in this book are those employed by the major Wall Street firms to buy and sell or bid on the multimillion-dollar debt offerings that come to the market daily and then resell them to investors. In the mid-1970s, I became an investment banker—one of those five hundred, committing large sums of capital for my firm, underwriting unit investment trusts, and reselling or distributing them to the public though a sales force of stockbrokers, better known today as financial advisors.

Again, this book specifically chronicles the first twelve years of my career from 1968 to 1981. If there is a common thread, it is the people encountered in those years and the tasks our jobs required us to perform, set against the backdrop of the political and economic turmoil of the period—the so-called Arab oil embargo, the Iran hostage situation, unprecedented rises in interest rates and inflation, the New York fiscal crisis, and on and on.

Lastly, a word about the technical side of finance for the general reader, the person who might say at the first hint of a conversation about investments, "I'm bad at finance." Please take into consideration that every business, every discipline, is inherently technical just like any other, from dressmaking to acting to hooking up to your cable network. Each has a particular and perhaps peculiar terminology. However, like any other art or science, the way they work can be explained in a logical and straightforward manner, especially when put forth in an unintimidating conversational style as I have tried to do. As for any remaining worries in this regard, my advice is to read the story and let go of the technical as it is secondary to the story.

Chapter 1

Life on Wall Street Begins

My life on Wall Street began on a brilliant fall morning in mid-October of 1968 on the way to an interview at 80 Pine Street in lower Manhattan, a block or two away from Wall Street and the New York Stock Exchange (NYSE). The phrase "Canyons of Wall Street" came alive for me as I walked through the cold stone and concrete. The sun was shining, but there wasn't a trace of it in the brightly shaded street lined with forty-story buildings as I approached the three steps that marked the lobby I was searching for. Sun or no sun, blizzard or maelstrom, no matter where I was or what I was doing in that time, my life already inhabited a world of bliss. In the immediate past six or seven months, I had fallen in love and become engaged to be married to one Rosalie Scigliano, a woman prettier and smarter than my dreams had ever allowed me to believe I might date, much less marry.

In the months leading to this moment, we discussed our private lives exhaustingly, and if one thing was established, it was my unhappiness at work in my brother-in-law John Moretti's auto body repair shop. Employed there for nearly four years, as is often the case when one works for close relatives, the relationship between John and I had become strained. My sister's husband, whom I dearly loved and who was a father figure to me, nearly thirty years my senior, was a very demanding boss whom I felt wanted more from me than I could possibly give.

My future wife, in the corporate world herself for nearly a decade, understood something I did not—that a clean-cut fellow with a brain could move forward and achieve success in a corporation as long as his head was screwed on straight even if he didn't have a formal education. Rosalie knew people who'd had this experience at her own firm and had worked for a couple of them. After all, she began her own career as a keypunch machine operator and was now an AVP in the Metropolitan Life Insurance Company's Home Office Loan Division. One just had to have an entry point, and mine was provided by Rosalie's boss at MetLife, Anne Ruocco (pronounced Rocco). Anne's brother Mario was a vice president at Eastman Dillon Union Securities, a major Wall Street house and the very person I was on my way to see.

I hopped up three steps from the narrow street into a cool marble-walled lobby and up an elevator to the fifth floor. There was no security desk, just a bronze corporate wall plaque with the words Eastman Dillon Union Securities and under that in capital letters P&S/Order Room over an arrow pointing to a door at the middle of a lengthy corridor. This door or doorway was busy with people approaching from either direction in the ten- or twelve-foot-wide corridor; the comings and goings so frequent that the door itself barely stayed closed for more than ten or fifteen seconds. As my senses were at peak, I noticed in the moment, the people going through the door I had to enter, whether heading out or in, were driven by something more than idle purpose. There was no sauntering down this hallway, no jocular conversation, just serious purposeful determination to pass through. Many of the entrants and those exiting carried papers or clipboards, and all paid attention as they approached because the door sometimes opened with great force and speed from the inside.

A sudden apprehensiveness came over me then. Being early, I decided to hold back before haphazardly entering. Instead I took a position on the far wall, from which I could see the goings on both inside and outside without obstructing passage. The door, when opened, provided a full view inside, while its top half had a window, so there was still a view inside when it was closed. The room was big, with plenty of people moving through a network of corridors formed by rows of desks and filing cabinets. They moved briskly, just like the people going in and out. All with some yet unknown urgency.

"What could be going on in an office that caused people to scurry along this way?"

After a few moments of standing and observing, I became aware of the rush of sound that filled the air each time the door swung open. It was at once just noise, but after a while, I parsed out some of its components. There was an orchestra of telephones ringing nonstop in various overlapping tones. Then, in a lower register, a continuous buzzing and tapping that modulated up and down in overlapping volumes and inflections. I was reminded of the dress-making factory floor I had worked in a few years back, a room full of starting and stopping sewing machines, but this was not a factory floor. Before long, I realized the ringing telephones and the machinery were filtered through a low roar of urgent and charged conversation. The whole thing was quite captivating; these people talking beyond the opening and the ones hurrying around inside driven and animated by the same energy inhabiting the body language of those who entered and exited the space.

New Yorkers carry a certain cosmopolitan bravado with them everywhere they go, but here I was a greenhorn who couldn't put a finger on what was going on. There was tension, excitement and mystery in that corridor and to say it was upbeat at the same time seems odd because these people didn't look like lambs being led to slaughter. Certainly, this was not the atmosphere I expected to encounter at an interview for an office job. I was looking for the long rows of desks and introverted quiet I remembered from the Jack Lemmon film *The Apartment*. Instead, whenever this door opened, I got controlled pandemonium thrown my way, punctuated every couple of minutes by a shriek or a catcall and occasionally the unmistakably explosive sound of a telephone receiver being slammed into its cradle. Gathering my courage, I drew closer to the carnival beyond this doorway but hesitated once again. This time, preventing the door from opening fully.

"Who you lookin' for?" someone said, nudging my elbow. I had been recognized as a stranger in those parts.

"Mario Ruocco?" I blurted out.

"Sure. Follow me. I'll show you where he sits."

13

I entered and was sort of quickstepped across the room past what I later learned was teletype row where the mechanical tapping and buzzing originated and then down a corridor formed by a long row of drab grey desks. On the way, to my left, I noticed a line of longish waist-high metal structures that appeared to be file cabinets turned on their sides and colored the same drab grey as the desks. The first sight of them is a lasting memory because they looked like coffins and oddly enough the people standing around them was a scene reminiscent of a wake. My guide who'd been by this area many times guessed my thinking and said.

"Those are The Tubs, the last stop, where they bury the guys who have trouble handling the action around here."

He was a typical New York wise guy who couldn't resist gybing the tenderfoot he was showing around. I responded.

"Yeah Right," and left it at that.

The room was vast, maybe two hundred feet by eighty or ninety, maybe even bigger, and permanently occupied by at least a hundred people or more and possibly another thirty or forty persons milling around. Wherever there was wall space or a pillar, there was a teletype machine or two clacking away. Their sound was muffled by covers, but when someone opened them to rip off messages, a loud tapping and clacking invaded the airspace. People just talked over the sound. When I was a kid in Brooklyn on Walworth Street my friends and I used to set dried out Christmas trees on fire in the empty lot on the corner. The tapping, clicking, and clacking when the machine covers opened brought me back to that moment precisely when with a rush of flame, you could hear a din of snapping and crackling and then a moment later it was all gone except for the smell. Odd perhaps but my exact recollection at that moment.

I continued to follow my unnamed leader, noticing groupings of desks and tables everywhere with people sitting around them on the phone or talking to one another while others made notations on cards or in books or on clipboards they seemed to be passing back and forth endlessly. The desks were grouped so nearly everyone who sat at one faced someone sitting at another. It looked like some massive card room in which a bridge tournament was being played.

Abruptly, we stopped, having reached a group of half plastic, half glass cubicles located on a back wall. There was a guy standing in the middle of them talking on the phone watching us as we approached.

"That's Ruocco," my leader muttered apathetically and then proceeded with hand signals to announce my presence, walking off without another word. I wondered why he didn't turn to me and say "see ya" or just give me a polite nod. I forgot him immediately though because the man in the cubicles quickly gave me the flat of the hand "wait" signal and mouthed what looked like five minutes, punctuating it all by opening and closing his other hand while cradling the phone in the crook formed between his head and shoulders. So there it was. This was Mario Ruocco, and I had to wait a few minutes.

Chapter 2

The Fix Was In

When he came out of the little wren of cubicles to get me, I noted Mario was tall, maybe six feet two or three inches, broadly built, with salt and pepper hair, a prominent fleshy nose, large hands, and a big white-toothed smile. In contrast to his smile, he had sober grey or green eyes that continually looked out over the vast work floor—for what, I didn't know.

At his direction, I followed his lead through a short corridor to his office and desk where we sat facing each other. He began the conversation by asking about my future wife and congratulating me on my upcoming nuptials, which was indeed very cordial and put me at ease. Beyond that, he got right to the point, explaining there were several low-level clerk trainee positions open with a starting salary of eighty-five dollars a week. That was a very low salary indeed, especially since I was earning one hundred fifty a week at the auto body and fender shop. I was disappointed until, in the next moment, he explained there was plenty of overtime connected to these positions, and if one chose to work it, had to work it in fact, the job was worth better than two hundred dollars a week before taxes and included medical and several other benefits. As for the specific job, there were several departments on the floor that had openings for individuals with good basic reading and math skills. If I wanted the job, he would place me in the spot that needed a body the most when I started.

I suddenly realized it was, as they say, "a done deal," and in that moment, I put it all together. My wife is one of those people who is very much loved once some time is spent with her. This is because of her capacity to be nonjudgmentally friendly to everyone, work tirelessly at whatever she's asked to do, and be loyal in the bargain. Because of the relationship Rosalie had with Anne Ruocco, Mario's sister, for more than five years, Mario, at the request of his sister, was offering me a job, sight unseen and unproven.

If it didn't work out, there was always a civil service job with the Department of Sanitation, the New York City Police, or Corrections Department. Just as suddenly, I became sure if I didn't work out here at Eastman Dillon, it wouldn't be the end of the world for Mario either, barring my embarrassing him in some small way. People probably came and went from this place in droves. He was helping his sister Anne to help Rosalie who had been a good friend and loyal coworker. It's something people do, the fulfillment of an obligation. For my part, my father and future father-in-law were both sanitation workers and made a decent living, raising their families and providing them with a very adequate, if simple, life. I didn't want to work for the city, but if I wasn't able to fit in at Eastman Dillon with Mario, that was my fallback position. Then again, I could always ask my brother-in-law John to take me back in the auto body repair shop, and I knew he would do it, which was actually the more likely scenario if this Wall Street expedition faltered.

Mario spoke again, awakening me from these musings. "Do you think you want the job?"

I accepted the offer, standing and shaking hands and promising I would do my best for him. We agreed I would start on the first Monday in December, which gave me ample time to straighten out my affairs once I got back from my honeymoon. I explained then to Mario how much I appreciated the job offer, that I would do my best to prove his decision to hire me was a good one, and that I was going to do my best not to embarrass him. It was important to pay him this respect in a formal way as he was enabling a change of direction in my life. No matter what the future held, a change and an opportunity that would have been next to impossible without him. After all, what experience or credentials did I have, having been a grocer's clerk, a shipping clerk for a dress maker, and a grease monkey in a garage?

Even if I had a documented resume, would those experiences have been sufficient to get me an interview in the halls of any American corporation, much less one of its top brokerage firms? The interview with Mario now behind me, I proceeded to Eastman Dillon's personnel department where I filled out the customary forms and was told to report for orientation on December 3 at eight o'clock in the morning sharp.

My future wife hailed from our old Bedford-Stuyvesant/Williamsburg neighborhood in Brooklyn. Oddly enough we lived, grew up, just a few doors away from one another on Walworth Street, her at 215 and I at 207. A four-year age difference and my family's move out of the neighborhood when I was sixteen years old prevented our getting to know each other before we'd recently met purely by chance. Our families were paisano, a word derived from the Italian *paese* or "town." Being paisano meant her family and mine had origins in the same town or village in Italy. Particularly, it meant the patriarch of my wife's family, her grandfather, Vincenzo Scigliano, was from a town called Strongoli, the very same town where both my mother and father were born in Calabria on the Ionian Sea in Southern Italy. While being paisano might not have been a terribly important kinship in the old country, it was an important filial bond for immigrants in America. Our families were well acquainted, shared the same culture and customs, and held one another in high regard for good reason.

The Sciglianos had a reputation for hard work, speaking their minds directly, and knowing how to hold onto and stretch a buck, while my own father was considered a man of high principle and a contributor to the common good of the community. My grandfather on my father's side (who never reached American shores) was considered a champion of the poor in his hometown in Italy, and my grandfather on my mother's side who had passed on ten years before had been known as *fadalle*, the Italian dialect word for "apron" as he'd been a well-known shopkeeper and neighborhood sage.

The closeness of the families was borne out by a story that surfaced around this time and was corroborated by aunts and uncles on both sides. The story held that my future wife's grandmother had been a wet nurse for my Aunt Rose, one of my mother's sisters. Now that's close. Fate, it seemed, had arranged a propitious marriage for me.

My mother was fully aware of the reputation of Rosalie's family with regard to money and their penchant for saving and buying multifamily homes. Somehow, she combined that knowledge with the newly found position on Wall Street acquired for her son by her future daughter-in-law into some fortune telling fantasy. I only know this because I heard her declare while on the phone with a friend (no doubt another paisano), in Italian of course: "She's going to make him rich."

Frankly, when she uttered these words, I didn't know what the hell she was talking about, what she meant, or what she might have been referencing. It was one of those statements we sometimes hear from our parents that we just don't understand and write off with a grimace and a few shakes of the head. As children, even adult children, we know our parents often make what appear to be remarks that border on the unhinged. In any case, whatever she was talking about, I gave little thought to. There were more important things to think about and discuss, especially since our wedding was just a few weeks off.

Chapter 3

On the Job: Day 1

On December 3, 1968, a month to the day after our wedding, following a morning of orientation on my first day at work, I knew two things: Wall Street had its origins under a buttonwood tree less than a hundred paces away from our offices, and the firm paid its hourly wage earners for forty hours of work each week, though we worked only thirty-five of them, using one hour daily of the forty for lunch. The first fact referred to the place where wealthy businessmen began to meet in the 1700s to conduct business and money lending, and the other made clear working nine to five was indeed forty hours but the firm lost an hour when we went to lunch. I found out later what it really meant was when we worked overtime, being paid the overtime wage of time and a half per hour began with the forty-first hour worked. Those two bits of knowledge were all I remember taking away from the three-hour orientation other than a book about Wall Street I neither opened nor read until ten years later.

The four or five new employees in my orientation class and I were dismissed around noon and told to get some lunch and report to our respective department heads thereafter. When I appeared in the busy room where I'd met Mario six weeks earlier, I was ordered somewhat gruffly to "take a post," meaning I was to stand near the wall or a building pillar and wait until I was called. There were no seats available.

It was at that moment, waiting to be summoned, I discovered the toxic cloud of cigarette smoke in the room, interspersed here and there by clouds of noxious blue-tinted fumes from the odd cigar or pipe, something I didn't take any notice of on my first visit. Once I discovered it though, I paid no mind to it, although it was a little thicker and stronger here than most places. I was a smoker as so many were in those days and after all those years in a garage where paint spraying, sanding residue and welding fumes permeated the air, a smoke-filled room didn't bother me. Today, it may seem perverse, but smoke from burning tobacco permeated every nook and cranny of these offices accompanied by an ashtray on nearly every desk and window sill. People carried lit cigarettes, even cigars, into elevators, cafeterias, and bathrooms. There was no escape, and no one thought to either. Smoking curbs didn't come into the picture until the late eighties. Again, it didn't bother me as I had a near two-pack-a-day habit at the time myself.

I just lit up and smoked a few Camels, waiting and watching the action all around me. On my first visit, I wondered what could be going on here that caused this continuous fury of activity. This is what a beehive must be like, I thought. It was new to me all over again because between the wedding and honeymoon and painting our new apartment, I hadn't given a thought to what I was coming back to on the job. There was so much activity here. It was like being in Macy's or A&S at Christmas without the festive decor. After a while, a short-ish, broad-shouldered, straight-backed fellow with a bristly mustache and a gruff military bearing came over to me, shook my hand, and introduced himself as Barry McGivney. He frowned a lot, and it was plain to see he had a lot to do and a lot on his mind. After a day or two, I realized he was a really nice fellow, quite gentle in fact, but a guy continually beset by many problems. He explained I would see Mario by the by, and my training was to begin immediately.

"We're really busy and shorthanded right now, and we need to get people trained quickly. I hope you're a fast learner," he said.

Barry then handed me off to one Jack Cohen who would be my trainer. Jack was slight, had dark hair and olive skin, and in a word was affable. He talked a mile a minute, laughing and smiling continually. He seemed to see the world in benevolent good humor. He knew everyone, and they were all "good people" to him, to use the popular expression of the time. He sat me down at the end of a grouping of seven large metal desks, six of which faced each other two by two lined up side by side and were capped off by a seventh desk at the end where Barry sat most of the time and where his boss, a taciturn, swarthy-looking fellow named Lou Perillo, a dead ringer for Leo Gorcey, the leader of the Dead End Kids, sometimes perched. The three or four hours that passed until I quit and went home at about six that evening were a blur of reading trade tickets and trade confirmations and being shown how to check and mark off data on computer-produced booklets. I was introduced to ten or fifteen different people who sat within shouting distance of me or seemed to pass through the office every ten or fifteen minutes to confer about this or that and drop off or pick up documents. Around six I was told to pack it in and to be there the next morning at seven and expect to stay to at least six in the evening on a regular basis. That was not a surprise as Mario had spoken about the overtime.

Chapter 4

Old Wall Street

Every transaction, every buy or sell of stocks or bonds between brokerage firms in the securities industry then and now, must be confirmed in writing by both the buying and selling party to each other. The details of every transaction (stock, bond, commodity, etc.) must be compared to match exactly before delivery of the actual securities three business days after the transaction takes place (in 1968, it was five business days) and actual money for securities is exchanged. This confirmation of the details of each and every buy and sell transaction is the main duty of the P&S or Purchase and Sales Department in a brokerage firm and the function it is named after. While today this activity is exclusively electronic, as much of it was then, that first day of my career, many, many transactions originating in the over the counter (OTC) market were confirmed by way of paper confirmations mailed or otherwise sent to and from the transacting parties.

Archaic to ponder now, the day I walked in the door, at least a dozen clerks were employed at Eastman Dillon, matching trade information with and from paper billings. The area I was assigned to confirmed the details of transactions in stocks with low trading volumes originating in the OTC market. The paper billing itself was called a confirmation or "confirm." It contained the details of the transaction such as what each firm was doing (i.e., buying or selling), the name of the stock, the quantity of shares, the price and the calculation for the total transaction, and the trade date and settlement date (i.e., the date the transaction was made and the date upon which the exchange of money for securities traded was to take place).

Confirmations were also known as "comparisons" because they were used to "compare" one firm's information versus the others, hence my job title "comparison clerk."

When the details on the opposing firm's confirmation matched those on our listings for the same day, the comparison clerk marked the corresponding entry with his initials. Since confirmations were printed in duplicate, the clerk separated the two, kept the top copy for his file, then initialed the bottom copy and stamped it with the firm's official seal and finally sent it back to the opposing firm. This "confirmed" our having received it and, to use industry jargon, was proof of our "knowing" the trade. Sending back an initialed stamped copy of the opposing firms confirmation was standard industry practice and done just in case the confirmation we sent did not reach its intended target.

If there was a mismatch in any detail, the clerk checked the transactions original-tele-typed order (all OTC transactions were tele-typed from the trading floors or trading desks to P&S for processing onto the firms record) to make sure the trade was processed correctly. If found to be processed incorrectly, it was fixed by informing the correction department, another division of P&S. If the trade was found to have been processed correctly, the opposing firm's comparison clerk was phoned to report the problem. Often the discrepancy had already been picked up and was being corrected. Just as often as the problem trades fixed themselves, there were real differences that had to be reported to the traders, the originators of the transaction. In Wall Street parlance, the traders had "executed the transaction" and any difficulty with the trade had to be resolved by the traders. In an ideal world, the traders would then issue orders to change the trade in some way at one or both firms, resolving the problem. The job would have been a piece of cake if all one had to do was check out a few bad trades, but there were many more than just a few problem transactions among the many thousands Eastman Dillon made every week, indeed every day.

Chapter 5

Top Day

At Eastman Dillon, there were 750 to 850 OTC stock transactions daily that were compared with paper confirmations, give or take 50 or 100 either way. Stocks with high trading volume were cleared through an automated system known as the National Over-the-Counter Corporation or NOTC, the forerunner of today's NASDAQ. I was assigned to the sell side of the paper cleared transactions and would get an entire day's sell transactions every other day to shepherd through the labor- and paper-intensive clearing and comparing process just described. This meant on Monday, for example, I would get a printout, also known as a blotter, that noted in alphabetical order the firm's OTC stock sell transactions made to brokerage firms on the previous business day (Friday) that were being cleared with paper confirmations. This was known as "top day." The blotter came with copies of the original teletyped wire transmissions sent by the OTC Trading Desk located on another floor of the building.

The first duty on top day was to compare not just other firm's confirmations to these transactions but also each order transmission to its corresponding notation on the blotter. While mind numbing, this usually turned up an error or two and sometimes more per one hundred trades. Each trader handwrites fifty or sixty trade tickets every day, and keypunch and wire operators type hundreds. Mistakes were inevitable, so comparing the teletyped order to the processed trade blotter turned up errors ranging from price and quantity of share errors to the wrong opposing broker and the occasional trade processed for the wrong stock or the wrong activity (i.e., buy for sell

25

or vice versa). These problems, when discovered, were corrected by handing over the trade ticket with a note describing the problem to the Corrections Desk, another grouping of desks in P&S where problem trades were researched and corrected with cancels and rebookings and other clerical maneuvers.

Some of these were more easily handled by the comparison clerk. For example, when it was discovered a trade was processed for the wrong opposing broker—say, Merrill Lynch instead of MA Schapiro or Dean Witter—the transaction was not cancelled because the error was not one affecting the firm's accounting like an erroneous price or share quantity. One simply called the comparison clerk at the right firm to let them know our confirmation would be a little late but we knew the trade and that our confirmation was typed and sent out.

Next, and this was crucial, the comparison clerk filled out a "change of broker" form in triplicate, sending a copy to "the cage," also known as the Cashier's Department. The word *cage* refers to a department that was/is sealed off to all except those who work there. Cashier's clerks were often behind barred windows like bank tellers because of the valuable nature of what they are handling—in this case, stock certificates. The cashier's job is the physical receipt and delivery of securities and the collection of payment for securities delivered as well as payment for those received. The "change of broker" form notified the cashier to change their own records and deliver or expect to receive the securities in question from a different party than was stated on the original trade date record. There were three or four broker changes of this kind every top day in addition to two or three price corrections. On a 350-trade top day, it usually took until one or two in the afternoon to check the wire transmissions versus the blotter, get all the right forms filled out and sent, plus staple copies to the blotter itself—and not a good day when it took longer.

Top day was rounded off by the receipt of 150 to 200 pieces of mail. The New York Stock Exchange (NYSE), aka the House, has an internal mailing system that provides next-day service for the hundreds of brokers located in downtown Manhattan in close proximity to the exchanges. The mail was almost exclusively made up of opposing broker's confirmations, and most were for the present day's work and many for previous top days as well. Fortunately, mail handlers slit open every envelope, removed and presorted the confirmations according to trade date and buy and sell side and placed them in the appropriate comparison clerk's mailbox aka coup. Thank heaven for small miracles.

Chapter 6

If It's Wednesday

In 1968, when I joined Eastman Dillon, and probably for at least another six months, all trading on the NYSE, the American Stock Exchange (Amex), and the OTC markets was halted on Wednesdays for the purpose of investigating and clearing up unconsummated problem transactions. These were trades (transactions) that were open after settlement date (some for weeks and months); trades for which the details could not be agreed upon by the brokerage firms who had done them. Indeed, often, it wasn't known who the correct broker was; thus, the securities could not be received or delivered, much less fully consummated with payment. Certainly, the magnitude of the problem was enormous if it was decided to close down the exchanges for 20 percent of the workweek.

Trading volume in late 1968 was ridiculously low by today's standards. Daily NYSE volume averaged ten to twelve million shares, but it was double the volume of the early and midsixties, straining the rudimentary systems in place. Similar and even more severe volume increases were affecting the OTC stock market and the bond markets traded over the counter as well. The securities clearing and the subsequent receive-and-deliver function of Wall Street were overloaded—"buried in paper." Massive liability built up because so many transactions remained unconsummated; that is, undelivered and unpaid for. Hundreds, if not thousands, of confirmations did not reach their proper destinations, details were not checked, and name changes were not done properly.

For example, a typical problem situation might occur when the firm sells two hundred shares of ABC for an investor at fifty dollars per share. On settlement day, the brokerage firms pay the investor something less than ten thousand dollars after commissions, with the proceeds being used by the investor to pay for another purchase or otherwise left in place or disbursed to the investor. On that same day, the firm finds it cannot deliver the securities to the buyer-listed (i.e., the firm it sold the stock to because it does not acknowledge having purchased the securities). After exhaustive investigation, no other firm is claiming to have bought that stock. Now, after paying the seller from its own cash reserves, the firm has its own money tied up in a one-sided transaction until it can be paid for when it delivers the stock.

When the stock remains undelivered for three months, it is then "sold out" so the firm could recover its outlay. If the stock was lower in price, the firm took a loss; if the stock was up in price; it took a gain. However, the cost of carrying the stock (interest) had to be considered as well. At the very least, carrying a $10,000 debit at the broker loan rate for three months (say 6 percent) cost $150, not to mention the man-hours spent researching the problem and add to that whatever loss might be taken when the stock was finally sold out. The stock would have to be at least six or eight points higher just to break even. Knowing these circumstances, one can easily imagine what is going on at the opposing firm that bought this stock and cannot deliver it to the client who bought it from them. Now think of these problems occurring at such epidemic proportions that they caused Wall Street trading to halt for a full day each week.

The reasons for the crisis were varied, ranging from a wait-and-see attitude in the securities industry regarding changing its way of dealing with increased volume to a wave of stock and bond issuance in the late fifties continuing into the sixties and a ripple effect of more widespread ownership of stock among the populace over the same period. It was a simple mathematical fact that more stock issuance and more widespread ownership meant more transactions. Part of it was the boom in technology. The industrialized world had discovered electronic data processing in the fifties in the form and usage of super computers. Any number of businesses were being automated from billing and inventory tracking to airline booking, and the preparation of taxes. Small technology firms were capitalizing with underwritings as small as five million dollars, while IBM and Xerox were financing in the stock market and borrowing in the bond market to the tune of hundreds of millions.

Many of the smaller underwritings came with warrants or rights, which were time sensitive securities, giving the bearer the right to buy additional shares at a discount to current markets. An investor buying a thousand shares of Acme Gadget on the IPO received with those shares one thousand rights or warrants that entitled them to purchase additional shares from the company or its agent at a specified price by a specified date—an option in effect. These securities traded in the market as separate entities until their expiration, driving market volume higher. Stock ownership also grew because large and small companies alike expanded their employee stock distributions through various bonus and retirement programs, which in turn expanded brokerage firm account bases, exposing a wider public to the markets in general.

On another front, innovations in the financing of fixed income securities, increased issuance and trading volume dramatically in the bond market. For example, Industrial Development and Industrial Revenue Bonds were very popular in the sixties. Municipalities issued bonds and purchased land or industrial facilities that were in turn purchased or leased by private companies who lent their names and ratings to the municipality. These bonds were usually issued at a premium to the market (higher interest rates). The benefit of such financings was that industry was helped along by the states and cities they chose to locate in, investors got tax-free income, and the local populace were put to work. These financings combined with the many public works revenue bond offerings of the day such as the quarterly borrowing of The New Jersey Turnpike Authority or The Port Authority of New York or Oklahoma Turnpikes and on and on. There were fifty to one hundred or more of these large underwritings a year annually for several years. These issues all had a single characteristic and that was a large 20 to 40 million dollar so-called "balloon maturities" due in thirty or thirty-five years. Because these maturities tended to have a big float (large supply readily available in the market place) they were highly liquid and became known as "dollar bonds" because their value was quoted in dollars instead of yield. This phenomenon of borrowing need and opportunity melded with consumer needs. Federal Income Tax rates during this period exceeded 65% on incomes over two hundred thousand dollars. These higher yielding and very liquid Industrial Revenue Bonds and public works revenue bond offerings became popular with stockbrokers and investors waking up to the fact that there were tax free investment alternatives available to them. Consequently they were distributed to the public in thousands of five and ten thousand dollar lots, contributing still more to the volume of transactions processed daily. Lastly, concerning the bond market, in certain market cycles the faulty notation of early redemption and call features caused the miscalculation of many transaction's resulting in costly delayed deliveries.

The period experienced surges in borrowing by the US Government and Corporations as well, especially the airline industry and the big technology companies among others. The sixties also saw dramatic increases in the issuance of preferred stocks as an innovative method of raising money for corporations that carried a tax benefit. There was also a big surge of public investing in mutual funds in the mid 60's. The result of this boom in financing, securities ownership and increased transaction volume put unprecedented strain on the securities industry's operations and outdated regulatory mechanisms which were ill equipped to handle the increased volume. Collectively even when nothing went wrong the surge in volume during this period put pressure on the clerical function in the brokerage firm as every transaction effected nearly every back-office department including the wire room, the cage, the P&S, data processing and the Order Room.

A consequence of all this volume was clerks like me worked lots of overtime to keep up. I routinely worked seven in the morning to seven in the evening five days a week and often later till nine and sometimes ten o'clock, at least sixty hours a week, and many Saturdays as well. Most clerks took a twenty-minute break at their desks to have lunch. As a reward for not taking an hour lunch break and eating at our desks, we received $1.75 in cash, and when we worked after five to six o'clock, we received a $3 stipend for dinner. This was known as "chop money" and came in quite handy. To put it into context in 1968–1969, a quart of milk was less than a quarter, and you could buy a pack of cigarettes for a quarter as well. A loaf of bread was thirty-five cents, and gasoline was thirty-three cents a gallon. Getting a twenty-dollar food supplement in cash each week was valuable and a great weekly bonus, especially for guys like me who brown-bagged it to begin with. This twenty dollars easily took care of my two-pack-day cigarette habit, gassing up the Pontiac, and a Friday night drink at the local watering hole before getting on the subway and heading home.

By March of 1969, after a few months of handling a couple of top days each week, I had assembled a portfolio of problem trans-actions that resisted clearing up. Some were simply a mess from the beginning; problems that went on and on for a couple of weeks because you couldn't get your in-house trader to reconcile the dif-ference with the trader at the opposing firm and often, as strange as it may sound, the traders would lie. There were many experienced traders who took care of problem transactions immediately once you got them on the phone and informed them. Often, before they even got back to you, the trade cleaned up all by itself, which was notifi-cation enough. But there were a lot of trainees because of all the new stocks and the increasing public interest in the markets. These guys were green and prone to mistakes because of the pressure they oper-ated under and the lack of adequate training. These new guys were often prideful beyond their stations, full of themselves, and arrogant because they were "traders." They had a "who the fuck are you" atti-tude toward comparison clerks who they disdained as perhaps less educated or less sophisticated, take your pick. Some were the kind who, after you brought a problem to them, would say, "Okay, I'll take care of it. I'll get back to you."

But they never did, and no matter how you tried, you couldn't get them on the phone after the initial contact you made with them or, in many cases, they just wouldn't talk to operations people because they had not been taught how to handle or reconcile problems. It seems incredible—hard to believe, I know—but it happened often. If you did by chance get one of these newbies on the phone, they'd say, "Oh yeah, the five hundred tax systems. I spoke to them. They're changing."

The first few times this happened to me, I was so relieved to get an answer to note on the blotter so I could get to the million other things I had to do. Then after a few days or a week, I'd find out no such change was acknowledged by the opposing firm's comparison clerk. I'd be terribly disappointed because the problem reflected on me in my office. I learned after a while to document my conversations with these guys. If you didn't write down who the trader was, when you called them, and what the answer was, you were castigated and blamed for someone else's mess, and it was just a fact of life that the trader's word was trump to the comparison clerk's. Sometime after I got there a special liaison was appointed within OTC who was informed of the problems that were not resolved within an acceptable period of time. She did manage to clean up many problems but she was always overloaded with inquires and tough to get on the phone. For all intents and purposes that liaison position became worthless. I learned after a couple of months that if a problem wasn't resolved after a few days past its settlement I handed it off to Barry or Jack by informing them of its existence and that I had all the paperwork if they wanted to see it.

Chapter 7

How Am I Doing?

After several months at Eastman Dillon, I couldn't remember when I'd been better. I loved my work and new job for many reasons. I liked going there. The room jammed with people, phones ringing nonstop, teletype machines clacking away, and the never-ending stream of cross conversation interspersed with bursts of raucous laughter and hilarious behavior that at first seemed odd and out of place had now become familiar. The hundred or more personalities holding conversation over the din on every subject under the sun to the immediate problems of our work was quite a new and wonderful experience for me. Every topic from bitching and moaning about work, to sports and sex, to books and the vagaries of the market was covered. The talk, coupled with the fast pace of work and learning something new and interesting every day about the market or the business if you were open to it and could handle it made life very interesting. I ate it up frankly and discovered it was my cup of tea. The work itself was simple and logical, requiring basic reading and math skills as Mario had indicated. That it was always at a high volume and fast pace was no bother because I was good at it and kept up easily. I discovered I had a very good memory—in fact, an extraordinary memory—which was very important. If you couldn't remember a problem trade from two weeks ago among the thousands and what you did with it or who you handed it off to, you got the blame for it. If you remembered it and produced the requisite correspondence, you got some respect, and life was easier.

On another level, the work seemed important, and I felt important to be doing it, although many of my coworkers hated it. Multiple hundreds of transactions daily, involving thousands of shares of stock worth millions and millions of dollars, if not billions, crossed my desk every day. It was, to me, a wondrous thing. I felt responsible in some small way for the accuracy with which these transactions were consummated. I felt being responsible for such sums of money was in some way a validation of trust in me, and I developed some pride in myself because of it. Some of the guys thought it was just a drudgery and unimportant and tried to get out of it by discarding confirmations wholesale down the toilets or in the garbage.

Was I naive in these thoughts, stupid to think I was important in some way as an eight-five-dollar-a-week clerk? Would my boss say, "I'll retire to bedlam," as Scrooge said to Cratchit when he wished him a Merry Christmas? Maybe, but I never had that Rambo moment, thinking that even though I got to oversee millions and millions, I was just a nobody. Instead, I felt a sense of wonder and romance about it all. I had read Thomas Woolf's *Of Time and the River* where Woolf reflected on what he felt was the greatness and vastness and wonder of America's teeming masses and its capabilities in the volume of work it could perform and cheerfully at that. Although I didn't think it at the time, in some way, I was realizing and living within what I had read in Woolf's work. Then again, I was the son of immigrants who had bought into this thinking (without ever having read Thomas Woolf or ever hearing or reading the names of all the companies and industries that were represented before me every day). I think now it may have had something to do with a faith and a hope that was built into me, into my subconscious anyway, as the son of immigrants seeking the American Dream.

Trite, you say, and maybe so. If the work was so important, then why didn't the job pay three hundred dollars or five hundred a week instead of eighty-five, a question a buddy of mine often raised. Dissatisfaction of this kind rarely crossed my mind. I had no answer to the question. It was a thrill for me to read the names of stocks and their values every day and to begin to understand, in some small way, the securities business and its manifestation in the great stream of things in the world. I didn't know a stock or a bond from a hole in the ground six months ago or "the Market" in the way I understood it now. Certainly, I'd heard of The New York Stock Exchange (NYSE) or the "stock market," but it was just a name of a thing. The "market" I now discovered to be a dynamic living organism that a few of my coworkers, clerks though they were, dabbled in and talked about as if it was a person, a living force. I couldn't understand or explain it, but it certainly fascinated me.

Everything was good, and so was the money. Overtime was such that I was earning nearly two hundred dollars every week with chop money and more even when I went in on Saturday. My wife was still working at MetLife and earning $165 a week there. With near $350–$400 earned weekly, we lived well and saved a good amount for the inevitable rainy day. Our rent was a mere $112.50 a month.

It's important again to understand the late sixties and early seventies. Wall Street was busy and possibly booming, at least from my point of view, but times were not really that good for a lot of working-class people. College graduates with engineering degrees were taking civil service tests because they couldn't get a job. I had a friend with an engineering degree from a prominent New York school whose father had an executive position high up in the New York City Transit Authority. After graduating an engineer and trying to secure a position in his field, he wound up as a corrections officer working at Riker's Island at $110 a week for nearly ten years before he could get a job using his education. In contrast, for me, lucky to have a high school diploma, the times were good.

Not only was the money good; the show was nonstop. For example, there were two fellows who administered to Amex's contract sheets. While their names have faded out of memory, the spectacle they provided vividly lives on. Contract sheets were computer-generated documents sent to the firm every day, compiling the previous day's trading done with other members of the listed stock exchanges. Cleared trades appeared in one column to the far left—the trades in which all details matched. The open or uncleared trades (whose details didn't match) appeared in several other columns across the page depending on whether they were buys or sells with the clearing numbers of the firms involved. Late one afternoon, a problem on a particularly large transaction was proving difficult to resolve to the point where the two clerks in charge of administering to the firm's Amex clearing process were having a dispute as to how the problem should be handled.

These fellows sat four or five positions away from me to my right and one aisle back. As their arguing got louder, I turned to see what the commotion was, and just at that moment, one of the clerks, the one nearest to me, raised a telephone receiver over his head and was about to crash it down on the other's. At the last millisecond, the other turned, and the blow glanced off his shoulder, though still landing with great force. It was a Three Stooges moment that I still laugh at. A comical scuffle ensued, which was broken up, and the next day, the two were laughing about it as they once again worked together. For a moment, I refused to believe my eyes, but later, when the comedy of it subsided, I understood how in this lowly effort, this seemingly unimportant clerking, in the simple process of clearing thousands of routine buys and sells worth billions of dollars, the tension could get pretty thick.

On another day, I noticed, at the very back of P&S, there was a section of three rows of desks that was called "the Order Room." Technically, the Order Room was not part of P&S, but it was joined to it at the hip because everything that passed through the Order Room was forwarded to P&S for processing. At Eastman Dillon, the two departments were managed at the very top by a single executive. The Order Room housed several small units of employees who conducted business that was somewhat off the beaten path, requiring some special handling (for example, the trading of certain bonds listed on the NYSE) and a unit dealing exclusively with the trading of odd lots on the NYSE and AMEX (transactions of less than one hundred shares) and the two firms that handled such transactions at the time—DeCoppet and Doremus by name.

In the middle of these three rows and separating these small operations was a private, sound-proof, glass-enclosed office that, on rare occasions, rolled back its moving partitions to reveal the luxurious setting in which the partner in charge of operations resided. His name, if I ever knew it, is forgotten. But, wow, when those doors opened and its bespectacled cigar-chomping resident in suspenders deigned to enter the plebian world of the Order Room and P&S, a momentous quiet would descend that must have been what it was like when Caesar addressed the Roman forum. At least that was my thought after I saw those glass partitions part a few times.

Chapter 8

Working Late and Weekends

Though a novice by a long way, I was starting to get familiar with the various smaller departments within P&S. At first, the sheer volume of trades, names of stocks, numbers of shares and billions of dollars were overwhelming. If you've never been exposed to such numbers, there's a tendency to think they're not real or believable. I began to get a better feel for the volume and the numbers because on some evenings, I was drafted by the night crew to help finalize and complete the day's work. It was both an opportunity to learn a little bit more about what was going on and a chance to pick up a few extra hours. Most of the guys in the confirmation and clearance side of the department just didn't want to stay after six. I did, of course, for the money. After all, every hour worked above fifty hours each week was paid at double time or double one's normal hourly rate.

By five thirty or six, nearly all the day's work was in the computer or in "the system," as it was called. By six thirty, at the latest seven thirty, everything had been processed. Frequently, however, the system rejected trades or series of trades, sometimes entire new issues, that amounted to tens of millions of dollars of transactions or a variety of other trades just defied the computer's ability to process them. They were said to have "kicked out." Since the firm's policy was to process all its work every day, these transactions needed to be reexamined to see if some simple solution like a coding error or a calculation could be fixed so they might get processed that night rather than being held over for the following day. This meant the day's tickets needed to be shuffled and rifled through to find the handwritten or teletyped copies of specific trades or groups of trades. This had to be done quickly and required plenty of bodies; hence, the night crew and a few extras like me. Often, a second and a third go-round occurred with the computer rejecting these same trades again or rejecting others. After a while, a decision will be made by the supervisor to leave any repeatedly unprocessable trades out and give the computer the go ahead to finalize the firm's work of that day, meaning that from that final processing, computer runs and blotters as well as confirmations and margin sheets would be printed and this was the final processing of the day for the real money and not just a dry run. After a while doing this, millions and tens of millions became routine and no longer surprising.

There was also good deal of manual filing that had to be done, and several part-timers came in around seven in the evening to help and fill in if the night crew was in need. From what I heard, by eleven o'clock, everyone was gone. The latest I wanted to stay was nine o'clock. I arrived at about quarter to seven in the morning, and twelve to fourteen hours in the office nearly every day was enough for me. Saturday work was not infrequent and often called for by the supervisors, Lou Perillo, Barry, or Jack, when needed. Sometimes it was mandatory, and that was once every three or four weeks when management wanted to go over what were known as "fails" or examine comparison clerk's blotters in detail, usually both.

The word *fail* was short for "fail to deliver" or "fail to receive" and resulted from transactions in which the settlement date has passed and upon which the firm had failed to deliver the physical stock in the case of sales or failed to receive the physical stock purchased in the case of buys. In many cases, a fail to deliver was caused by a fail to receive. These were, for the most part, fails between brokerage firms, not customers, although that was another problem the firm encountered since a fail to receive caused the firm to be unable to deliver the stock in question to the client who purchased it. There were lists of fails, in fact several listings of aged fails, five to ten days, ten or more, twenty, thirty, ninety days, and so forth past settlement. On these Saturdays, a crew came in to look up the trades that corresponded to the fails to try and find solutions to cleaning up the fails and make decisions about them. The original tickets, any cancels and rebills associated with the trades if there were any, were dug up to try and find a solution to the problem and list actions to be taken on Monday. When fails reached the ninety-day mark, a decision was made to "buy in" the stock that we were waiting to receive or "sell off" the stock we couldn't deliver. These were drastic solutions laden with NYSE regulations and documentation, which required monetary reserves in escrow in case of future liabilities. The best thing about buy-ins and sell-outs was that they got problems off the books.

Often on these Saturdays, managers like Lou Perillo and even upper management like Mario's boss, Vinny Dorsa, and others personally went through the previous month's blotters looking for uncompared trades or notations regarding corrections that were not followed up on. On occasion, it was discovered a clerk had made a mistake and had not acted upon a broker name change properly or failed to follow up on a price adjustment. I could understand a detail here and there could be overlooked because it was often so busy that errors or mistakes were easy to overlook especially when the phones were heavy or you became distracted by some other activity like solving some knotty problem or, as is the case with human beings, you got a little careless or lazy. It happened because the job was, for the most part, rote and boring; so endless and repetitive that a detail got past you sometimes. Top day after top day came and went, and the confirmations and paperwork never stopped. Sometimes one just said fuck it and walked away. That was human.

When mistakes were discovered, some of the managers resorted to abuse and humiliation on these Saturdays as a tool to warn us to stay on our toes. Personally, I never cared because I knew others did worse things deliberately and got away with it. I looked at it differently anyway. I could take a lot of punishment on Saturdays for five or six hours of being paid double time and getting a free lunch. Human beings make mistakes, and that was always my answer. One day, I just blurted out, "What do you want from me? If I didn't make a mistake once in a while, I wouldn't be human."

The retort was, "Gwan, git outa here before I…" The sentence left unfinished.

During the winter months of 1969, as I toiled away at my work, I learned much about the world and my work from my coworkers, but through this constant chatter, I began to realize how underinformed I was, in politics especially and the markets and even sports. My reading in those times consisted of my favorite books, mostly Tolkien and the classics and any mystery I could lay my hands on, but I realized after a few months at Eastman Dillon that I would have to take my nose out of those books and pick up the newspapers. If I didn't, I just wouldn't be competitive. My brother had been a reader of the once popular *New York Journal-American*, which I had glanced through on occasion. I began to pick it up and read it on the way home every night as it was an afternoon paper. Before long, I became a regular reader, and after a month or so, I kind of felt in some way like I'd never felt before, informed, perhaps a man of the world. Some sense of self began to take hold. Some sense that I was an individual in the world, and I knew something about it. The fact was a lot of people I knew, most of my social circle in fact, were generally unaware of what was going on in the country and certainly oblivious to the financial markets and politics. My wife's reaction to this when I mentioned these things—perhaps beat my chest a bit about understanding the world a little better —was to say, "Nobody like a smarty pants, so keep it down."

Chapter 9

Getting Around and Meeting People

During all this time, there wasn't much communication with Mario except for a distant wave hello or a pleasant nod when we passed each other or made eye contact. This noncontact was confusing to me, but the body language signaled it was what he wanted. On one occasion in passing, he didn't stop, but he put up the flat of his hand, smiled, and said, "You're doing fine," or some such thing.

Around the end of April, about five months in, Mario came to me one evening around five thirty to say that over the next few weeks, I would be spending time in some of the other departments on the floor, particularly Corrections and then Coding and Figurations.

"Don't worry about being able to do corrections yourself or calculate trades or if your work is checked when they give you something to do. Just get a feel for what they do, and keep your mouth shut." These last words were odd indeed, but that's what he said. "Barry will tell you where to go first and get someone to pick up your work."

A week later, I was assigned to Corrections, and I must say I was baffled by the work they did there. I had no understanding of the difference between customer accounts, trading accounts, and error accounts or cancels and rebills or journals nor how to move transactions between them. In fact, I didn't clearly understand yet there were clients or customers behind the purchases and sales we were making with other firms. In Figurations and Coding, where I went about ten

42

days later, there was so much work and so busy that nobody could talk to me. When I looked over these guys' shoulders, all I could see was a blur of tickets (fifteen or twenty a minute sometimes) seemingly marked at random with two or three numbers or notations. I would learn in the future that these notations told the computer how to treat the transaction as to commission calculation or what business stream the transaction was to be processed through among other things. What was frustrating there was these guys were either unable or unwilling to explain why a ticket might be coded 2–3, 1–2, or 1–9 in its designated coding areas. To make matters worse, the management of both of these small areas within P&S didn't give me the time of day and, in fact, were downright rude.

John Janiak who ran Corrections was a dour guy who rarely, if ever, spoke to me, and it seemed he might just as well spit on me and scowled whenever I looked at him or asked a question. I never really figured out if this was his general demeanor or if I represented something that was repugnant to him. Joe Romagiani the manager of Figurations, or Romy as he was called, kept asking me what I was doing there, who was I working for, and how well I knew Mario. Did I see Mario on weekends? He also had a problem, almost a mania, about the clothes I wore, asking daily how I could afford the suits, shirts, and ties I wore.

The truth was my sister-in-law Clara happened to work at Eagle Clothes, and I was getting 40 percent discounts through her. When I told him this, he didn't believe it and even told me so. I also explained to him in my family, we felt in many ways, "clothes make the man." My father, a lowly city sanitation worker and, in fact, a "street sweeper" on the Lower East Side, and my brother-in-law John, a body and fender worker, always wore coats and ties to church on Sunday, a not uncommon habit at the time, and always changed into dressier clothes to have dinner with the family when they returned home from work. They never ate in their work cloths. This is just the way it was. My brother Dom was very particular about his dress and wore Buddy Lee clothes. When I was six and seven, my mother used to take me to Barney's on Seventh Avenue in Manhattan to buy clothes for me, and in fact, I used to go shopping with my sister in

Manhattan at places like Lord and Taylor and Bloomingdale's. I never knew these were upscale stores for us Brooklyn Italian-Americans until I worked for a dress manufacturer on West Fifty-Seventh Street in my late teens and early twenties. I didn't get that detailed with him, but to whatever I did say, his reply was, "So what?"

I thought he was a little nuts especially when he asked me a few times who I worked for and why I was there. I think he thought I was "a plant" spying for management, for Mario maybe, and so I quickly understood why Mario had told me to keep my mouth shut. The reader might hesitate to believe these stories, but I'm sure I'm not the only person still drawing breath that experienced what I'm writing about at Eastman Dillon.

Besides Romy, Figurations was not short on characters. Nunzio, or Nunzie as he was called, a Figurations desk employee who shaved less than once a week was a grizzled curmudgeonly fifty- to sixty-year-old from Brooklyn. Every other word he uttered was *fuck*, but through horn-rimmed coke bottle–bottomed glasses, in fact, he could code many hundreds of tickets an hour with great accuracy. I remember him more though for the streams of filthy limericks he would often recite. "There once was a girl from Mass who had a poem tattooed on her a…"

Nunzie, to me, was evil incarnate. He whispered in coworkers' ears about this Jew and that nigger and what they looked like to him through his racist mind. He and a guy named Frank were a rotten and evil team. I really had trouble processing this place after a while because there was more ill intent, jealousy, envy, and anger here than all the other places I'd worked in from supermarkets to factory floors to garages put together. I had a lot to learn, I guess.

Another character in Figurations, Wally Walworth, a sallow-complexioned drunk in his fifties, was (amazingly) charged with the calculation of all the bond trades. Despite his boozy and at times vacant demeanor, he was a whiz at it as long as he had only one or two or three drinks in him. Any more than three, and backup had to be called. A rumor had it he was the wayward son of a wealthy Connecticut family who had disowned him for his drunken debauchery. He did his work at times with uncontrollably shaking hands. Whenever possible, he saved as many trades as he could for the late mornings and then the late afternoons after he'd had a couple of shots of Jameson's on his morning and afternoon coffee breaks. This calmed his hands down enough to turn the pages of a basis book and punch the keys on his Compucorp calculator accurately. Wally I could understand. I had worked in a butcher shop when I was a kid with a guy named Tony who was the sausage maker. Tony couldn't pick up a knife, much less use it, in the morning before he'd had two cups of espresso heavily laced with anisette or whatever booze was available. My old butcher friend Tony, the sausage maker, and Wally were both afflicted but both kindly chaps unlike Nunzie or Romy or Janiak who were just plain mean and nasty.

Frankie, Nunzie's buddy, in his late twenties or early thirties at most, seemed to be Romy's de facto assistant manager giving the orders when Romy stepped away. Frankie could have doubled for Phil Silvers, the comedian, when he had hair. He looked just like him, glasses and all, and had a voice even louder than Silvers's signature character Sergeant Bilko. Frank used to go on tirades some afternoons just after four o'clock. He would walk up and down the aisles of the office talking at the top of his lungs about "rats." How "rats who told tales would suffer in the end." "Dirty rats would get cancer and die rat-a-tat-tat." How everyone hates a rat, how they would get theirs, and how they'd be humiliated when the tales they told would hurt their fellow workers. This went on for ten or fifteen minutes sometimes. It was like listening to Broderick Crawford in *All the King's Men*. "You're nothing but a dirty rat."

Talk of "the rat" was prevalent in many places of employ and was about the coworker who told tales or truths about coworkers to management. Whatever was behind all this talk at Eastman Dillon was a mystery to me, but I couldn't believe this spectacle and how management allowed it to go on—middle management anyway. I wondered as well how my fellow workers stood for that kind of treatment at the hands of a misfit like Frankie who was egged on by the evil Nunzie. All one had to do is look over randomly toward the area where Figurations was located, and every once in a while, you would see Nunzie spewing venom into Frankie's ear. Unbelievable, is all I can say.

Chapter 10

A Raise and a Move

The Frankie and Nunzie moments concerned me, but in truth, in these early days, nothing really bothered me. I was too preoccupied with my family and friends to give such BS a lot of thought. We discovered early on in 1969 that my wife was pregnant, and we were very, very happy, as were our families. I had been a hopeless and restless knock-around twenty-four-year-old who drank too much just a year or so earlier, and my wife was headed into her thirties and considered by society and perhaps herself and certainly some in her family as one who had missed the boat, not destined for married life. Our favorite song, or at least one we had strong personal feelings for whenever we heard it, was Dinah Washington's "What a Difference a Day Makes" because from a chance meeting at a New Year's Eve party, our lives had turned in a new direction in so many ways.

Perhaps I wasn't savvy enough either or just too stupid to know or even conceive what might be going on nor did I think Frank rants were about me because I knew nothing and hadn't spoken to anyone about anything. It took me years to figure out that something had to be going on, otherwise why the jaundiced eye from Janiak and the cold shoulder from Romy? Mario was never present during these tirades nor was his boss Vinny Dorsa or Dorsa's majordomo Ori Girand. These guys were all very nice to me. In fact, in May or June, when Barry McGivney got married at the Riviera in Brooklyn, I was invited along with Dorsa and Girand and Dick Kalve from the Order Room. We sat at the same table with our wives. Mario wasn't there, and neither were Romy or Janiak. We had a great time, and they couldn't have been more gracious to me and my wife both socially and after that at the office. After the weekend of the wedding, a sort of kinship developed between these senior fellows and myself that played out in very subtle but noticeable ways. Girand or Kalve who would never have stopped to chat a minute when we passed each other's desks or when our paths crossed when walking around the office now paused a moment to exchange a greeting or a just a "how you doin'?" kind of thing and a momentary handshake. This, of course, was going on during the time I was visiting the other units in the department and may have had something to do with Janiak and Romangiani behavior toward me, but still I honestly didn't know.

Then in late May or early June, Mario came to me again near the end of the day when most of the office had cleared out. I never went into his cubicle except for the day he interviewed me. He would always call me over after five when he stayed late and chat with me standing up over a desk. On this occasion, he told me a twenty-five-dollar raise had come through for me and would commence with the next paycheck in mid-June. This was great news and would translate into a fifty- to seventy-five-dollar-a-week raise as it adjusted the value of the overtime hours I worked. The other thing he said was shocking.

"I'm leaving Eastman Dillon and going to work for another firm," he declared, looking straight at me. I didn't know what to say. "It's probably going to happen in the next few weeks. Nobody knows yet, so don't mention it to anyone."

He then went on to say when he made this move, he'd have a job for me at his new firm and really wanted me to join him. He mentioned there would be a considerable raise in base salary.

"Think about it," he said finally.

I was elated over the raise. Rosalie was going to stop working on August 1 as the baby was due in September. We were saving her entire salary, but once she stopped working, we would need to begin tapping our savings. The raise would limit that a bit. But after a few days of thinking about it and talking to my wife, the news had a sobering effect.

On the one hand, the money was going to be great. A 30 percent raise in my base was a bell ringer. It doesn't seem like much today, but back then, twenty-five dollars bought a week's worth of groceries and more. Mario had promised me when he hired me a raise would be forthcoming in six months, but with all the overtime I was working and how busy I was, I never gave it a thought. As I began to count the chickens that would hatch from this raise, calculating its value based on the hours I was working, the thought of going off to work at another place was not so inviting. Rosalie, more experienced with office politics than me and having Mario's sister Anne in her ear, threw in a few monkey wrenches. "What if the overtime dries up?"

My experience was limited, but I didn't think that would happen. "We never do," was her retort.

Her feeling was it would be better for me if I followed my mentor. I discounted her reasoning. The raise was very important because of the new direction our lives were headed in. Rosalie's salary was going to stop coming in while expenses would rise because of the baby. The raise's potential added fifty to seventy-five dollars to my earnings, while the offered two hundred dollars was roughly what my salary totaled every week now. Staying then at Eastman Dillon, I reasoned, was the right decision. My wife, however, thought differently and persisted in forcing me to think about some of the possible consequences of staying after Mario left, perhaps implied in Mario's messages to "keep my mouth shut" and the emphatically stated "think about it."

With my Rabbi Mario gone, maybe the hostility I detected in John Janiak and Joe Romy toward me due to the perception that I might have been Mario's or, worse still, management's "boy" might flare up. Who would protect me then? Mario was my mentor, and in fact, when I thought about it, many of the guys really resented it, although not so much my immediate management like Barry, Jack, or even Lou Perillo. Mario put no pressure on them regarding me, but the managers of the other groups and the people who worked for them for some reason thought I was getting some special treatment and was a "fair-haired boy." I might have been getting special treatment in terms of the tour of the different departments, but fair-haired boy was a bit much. I began to wonder what else they thought about me. I then got it into my head that if Mario left, they might transfer me to the Tubs, the dreaded Tubs and "the last stop" my early guide to Mario's office said was "where they buried guys who couldn't handle it here."

Chapter 11

The Tubs

The Tubs are Wall Street history and might be considered prehistoric Wall Street history if one wished to take it that far. They deserve some explanation if we really want to explore how the processing of business was handled post 1970–1975. The Tubs, a memorable symbol of old school technology, were three by six feet open bins standing waist-high filled with row upon row of compartments that were packed with IBM punch cards. The IBM punch cards had the physical consistency of a heavy index card. Light blue and red lines divided its surface into sections called fields. The information from orders was punched out onto the cards in the various designated fields. When the cards were fed into the computer, the computer read the information from the punch outs to make computations and produced retrievable data in the form of printed confirmations sent to clients, computer runs, and listings in various forms and formats for the use of every department in the firm. All data entering the computer for tabulation, computation, or notation was carried out at the time using IBM punch cards; there was no entry via keyboard or terminal or scanning as we know it today.

Specifically, the Tubs in P&S contained thousands of IBM cards, which had been prepunched with frequently used information related to the transactions executed on the floors of the New York and American stock exchanges. For example, the firm did three or four hundred trades a day with Merrill Lynch and maybe three or four hundred trades a day in stocks like Telephone or US Steel. Instead of a keypunch machine operator punching out a new card as needed every time a trade with Merrill Lynch or Telephone stock was traded, a prepunched card containing that data was already available in the Tubs. The process worked this way. During the day's slower periods, keypunch operators prepunched these cards and put them into the Tubs to be used later in the day when it got busy. As the day wore on, runners from the floors of the exchanges brought hand-written copies of the firm's transactions called "floor reports" along with copies of the orders that precipitated the transactions. Tub personnel, aptly called "Tub Pullers," upon reading the orders and floor reports, selected the required prepunched cards out of the Tubs and stacked them with the orders and floor reports on a little platform at the corner of the Tubs. Anything on that platform was picked up by keypunch operators who took the material to its next stage in the processing operation, filling in quantity and price information and any special instructions. Tub pulling was backbreaking, pressure cooker work that drove people out if they couldn't get used to it after a month or two. Guys who could stick with the job for more than six months were considered either inhuman, insane, or both.

Once the thought of being on the outs with management if Mario left or possibly being assigned to the Tubs took hold, I stopped worrying about what I was going to do. Mario did leave Eastman Dillon sometime in late June and, a couple of weeks later, called me and offered me a job. I took it. There wouldn't be much overtime except for an occasional Saturday or two a month that paid a flat seventy-five dollars in cash, which was a very cool surprise. On the first working day of July 1969, almost eight months to the day after joining Eastman Dillon, I started my new job as sell-side comparison clerk at Charles Plohn & Co. in 44 Beaver Street, just a few doors down from the famous Delmonico's restaurant.

Chapter 12

Charles Plohn & Co.

My new firm was the largest underwriter of individual new issues on the Street. Cash value was another matter. Over a month or so at Eastman, while I was working the night crew, the firm underwrote three major deals: Tropicana Orange Juice, Sambo's restaurants, and Geno's, the frozen food distributor. These were initial public offerings or IPOs in the current vernacular. There were likely many more, but I particularly remember these names. I don't know if Eastman was the managing underwriter on these deals, but those three new issues probably had a larger dollar volume than all the three-, five-, and seven-dollar stocks Plohn underwrote in a month. For sheer volume of individual deals, Charlie Plohn & Co. was the industry leader for several years. The firm was doing better than 150 deals a year. I remember a small electronics company called Telectro-Mek that came at three dollars, another three-dollar deal called IBI Security, and a magazine called *Scanlan's Monthly* whose first issue cover showed a picture of a forty-million-dollar check that represented its new capitalization through the offices of Charles Plohn & Co. To better place the reader in the time frame of these experiences, the second issue cover of *Scanlan's Monthly* pictured the back view of an enormously fat completely naked man standing in mud in the middle of three hundred thousand people at the Woodstock Festival in upstate New York. Both *Scanlan's* and a beverage company called Yoo-Hoo had been underwritten by Plohn at ten dollars a share. These deals were pumped out at the rate of at least one and sometimes two or three to the week, although the firm's business slowed during my time there as market conditions deteriorated.

Charles Plohn & Co. had a retail sales organization of about 450 brokers in New York, New Jersey, Connecticut, and Florida and catered obviously to a clientele who were trying to make a killing in the new issue market with a smaller outlay than the twenty- or thirty-dollar stocks underwritten by the larger firms. The firm had, over the years, cultivated good relations with the smaller broker dealer community, so it was easy to put together strong joint accounts and selling groups. In the selling of new issues, the term *joint account* refers to the group of firms who band together in a syndicate "at risk" to underwrite and sell a new issue. The firms that were put together in syndicates by Charles Plohn & Co. were generally of the same size or smaller than Plohn, what might have been referred to as second- and third-tier firms in their order of appearance in a tombstone announcement of a major IPO in the *New York Times* or *Wall Street Journal.* The Charles Plohn clientele were the buyers of two thousand to ten thousand shares at anywhere from three to five to seven dollars a share (firms like Wertheim, Herzog, Neuberger Berman, and even Oppenheimer), while the first tier crowd were the buyers of two thousand to ten thousand shares at twenty-five to fifty dollars (the Morgan, Merrill, Goodbody, and Walston & Co. crowd).

Just as the majors believed in their brethren's ability to run a deal, so the lower tier group believed in Charles Plohn. Often the trick in the IPO market on both levels is the syndicate manager's ability to stabilize the market once the issue sold out. If too many investors decide to sell early, the market for the stock will deteriorate, and other holders might get nervous and dump the stock, which could destroy the price completely. Broadly speaking, the market is stabilized by the syndicate manager who puts an open bid into the market if the price of the security declines below a certain level. Stabilization's purpose is maintaining an orderly market and preventing sharp fluctuations for the security due to supply factors. Readers may at this point think that new issue market stabilization was akin to market manipulation. Not so, new issue market stabilization was and is an accepted and time-honored technique and a frequent occurrence. It's important to note too that it usually took place in a fast paced and upward trending market where just a few small boosts set things right. It axiomatic that a robust new issue market requires a strong upward and high volume general market to operate in. Weak markets and low levels of liquidity are not new issue friendly, a market that had been robust and awash with liquidity right up to mid to late 1968.

Charles Plohn had seats on several exchanges in the United States and a seat on a couple of Canadian exchanges as well, so it conducted business with a diverse customer base both inside and outside the country. It could be a correspondent in America for Canadian firms and in Canada for American firms. A correspondent is simply a firm that acts on behalf of another firm on another exchange, in another country or even the same exchange. Because Plohn acted as a correspondent for so many firms because of its different exchange memberships, five and ten thousand share orders for stocks traded on the NYSE and the Amex were a regular occurrence in our shop where they were scarce at other shops our size. The biggest order I saw there was a buy of sixty-five thousand shares of Clorox, a bit more than half of 1 percent of a twelve million share day, a big order indeed in 1969–1970 for a firm like ours.

The P&S at Plohn was of course very different from P&S at Eastman Dillon. Physically, Eastman Dillon's P&S was the size a large catering hall while Charlie Plohn's was more like your Mom's kitchen. A room with a hundred or more people in one, and perhaps ten employees in the other. Controlled chaos in one, and quiet efficiency in the other. Lots of factors contributed to these differences, of course, let alone the sheer size and capitalization of Eastman over Plohn and the volume of business done at Eastman compared to Plohn. At Plohn, there was no order room and no processing center (i.e., keypunch or teletype machines).

Instead Charles Plohn and Co.'s documentation, records, data processing record's and printing was carried out off premises by an outside contractor called RCA. Every night RCA picked up our work (tickets, corrections, journals, adjustments, etc.): in short, everything that was required to be recorded on the books of the firm including its accounting records. In the morning RCA dropped off confirmations, runs, margin sheets, blotters, statements and so on. The working atmosphere was lean, serious, quiet, and quite pleasant. Mario was the manager, and the assistant manager was a good-looking soft-spoken fellow named Mike Losquadro.

The fellow in charge of getting the P&S work ready for RCA day to day was Manny Rodriguez, a good-natured, knowledgeable, hardworking, terrific guy whom everyone liked. Manny had a high pitched gravelly voice that got even higher when he was excited or amused, and it's an understatement when I say we had lots of laughs. There were two senior clerks, Nette and George, who helped Manny out with whatever he had to do whenever he had to do it.

Nette and George handled the correspondence, which is the paperwork that dealt with the record keeping and fee collections from brokers we executed business for on the various exchanges of which we were members. For example, a Canadian firm's purchase through Charles Plohn of three thousand shares of a stock trading on the NYSE would generate a confirmation of course and also a letter asking for special instructions on registration and delivery of the stock as well as stating what our charges would be. Additionally, for expedience and convenience, stock exchange members often used "other members" of the exchange to execute business for them. Firms that regularly acted in this manner were nicknamed "two-dollar brokers" because at one time, they typically charged two dollars to execute a trade. Manny, Nette, and George were kept quite busy in this regard as all of this billing was at first posted and manually calculated, retyped on statements, and mailed at month end.

A young woman, Leslie, no more than twenty-five or so, handled the New York and American stock exchanges contract sheets as well as the NOTC or automated OTC trading, while I handled the confirming of sell side OTC stocks and a fellow with a huge afro sat across from me did the buy side. We called him Linc because of his resemblance to the character Linc on *Mod Squad*, a popular TV show at the time. Oddly, I can't remember his real name. It might have been Alexander. Another fellow, Mario, a Hispanic who always seemed to be half asleep but was as sharp as a tack, did all the bonds. That was it. There were nine of us, and I think if they had to, they could have gotten rid of one of the managers and one of the OTC clerks like me or Linc or Mario and still managed well enough.

They didn't (get rid of us) because the emphasis in the P&S in small firms was not just handling the press of work but also holding to a zero or near zero error policy. Every problem was run down as soon as it surfaced, and nothing was left to chance. When problems went three days (calendar) without being resolved, they were referred to management, or at least management was informed that a currently unresolved trade problem could escalate to a fail by settlement date. Every OTC trade problem with the Street got this treatment, whether it was a thousand shares at three dollars or thirty thousand shares at thirty dollars. This emphasis made for a smooth running, efficient, and trouble-free firm from the P&S side and most certainly from the clearing and cashier's side of the business. Everybody liked it that way, from management to brokers to clients, and the firm was quite proud of it.

Chapter 13

The Plohn Crowd

Charlie Plohn himself was a colorful character, as some readers may remember. On the one occasion that I met him, I had brought a package up to the Syndicate Department in the Pan Am building because they didn't want to wait for the next runner. I was told to take a taxi up, and when I was trying to find the desk, I encountered a white-haired man in his fifties or sixties who appeared somewhat disheveled, confused even (probably distracted more than confused) and not what I imagined a CEO might look like. When I asked him where whoever I was looking for might be found, this old guy said, "Why? Who the fuck are you?"

Now there was some authority in this remark, so I didn't get nasty as I had been warned Charlie could be a cantankerous sort prone to the use of four-letter words and the odds were good I'd run into him up there. I said I had a package of materials to deliver from P&S, and it was needed momentarily.

He said, "Follow me," and led me to the fellow I was searching for, then barked rather loudly to the entire office, "Every c**k s****n' f*****' department in this firm should run as well as the m*****f****n' P & f*****' S department does."

I didn't know whether Charlie just said what he said just to say it or whether it was a reference to the fact that the department did a great job. Mario seemed to think it was the latter when I told him about it. Apparently, whatever trade and stock open fail problems that were extant when Mario got there were no longer in existence. Mario got them cleaned up in short order and had since had a clean slate.

At Plohn & Co., I began to have more contact with Mario both in business-related matters and socially. I was already fascinated with him because of the figure he cut managing the P&S from his cubicle at Eastman Dillon in an impeccable white shirt and tie. Usually, when I looked up from my work, my eyes automatically shifted to where he sat. It was a voyeuristic obsession at the time, observing his body language or simply the movement of his head and eyes when he spotted someone or something on the floor he was interested in. He'd pick up a phone, then wait a few seconds and then, depending on the direction he was looking in, I could pinpoint who he was calling. It was like watching a silent movie when the person he called would sort of come to attention and wave, grimace, laugh, or make some hand signal.

At Plohn, he was never as severe as he'd been at times at Eastman, and it was here at Plohn that my obsession with him led me to believe a fantasy that he knew everything and everyone. It appeared to me he could react without thinking, giving an order or making a suggestion about how to proceed immediately after being apprised of a situation or problem. I was in awe of this when I observed it. On another level, our similar social backgrounds, being Italian and, in my case, first generation, first or second in his case, caused me to identify deeply with him. In a fantasy life, I came to feel I wanted to be him, or at least like him. In effect, become what I thought he was and have his experience, knowledge, success, and business acumen.

Ironically, my own brother Dominick, ten years my senior and right around Mario's age, was doing the same thing Mario was doing at a naval architecture firm called M. Rosenblatt and Son just a few blocks away at 350 Broadway. I didn't know it then, but he was also exhibiting enormous talent, drive, and capability with no more than a high school education. My brother Dom would retire from a very senior position (perhaps three or four steps from the top of his firm) after a distinguished forty-year career with the same firm where he interviewed and was hired at a week after he graduated from Brooklyn Technical High School. I didn't see my own brother's achievement and mentoring value until many years later because there was so much family bickering in the way. Fortunately, Providence had guided Mario into my path.

I'm sure Mario knew I had a great deal of liking and respect for him, and I knew he liked me and my sense of humor and whatever intelligence I might have had. He approached my mentoring from the point of view of harping on work and always asked if I was "up to date."

I admit I lied to him sometimes, but it wasn't difficult to catch up at Plohn even though every day was "top day." The workload averaged one hundred trades a day. Very light compared to Eastman Dillon where two top days a week amounted to between seven hundred and nine hundred trades, and even now with the exchange and trading back to being open five days, it was still only 500 to seven hundred trades a week, eight hundred in a busy week, where it might have been twelve hundred to fifteen hundred or more at Eastman. Even on the odd chances that there could be a thousand trades for me to clear and compare each week, it would still be a walk in the park since there was no checking of trade tickets versus blotters and a much lower incidence of trade problems simply because Manny, the P&S floor manager, had checks in place that kept bad trades to a minimum. The mail was still opened for us, and although we sorted it ourselves, it was no big deal. If I had fifty uncompared trades a week, they amounted to only a handful of problems when the dust cleared, especially with management, Mario or Mike, putting their weight behind problem solving some of the more knotty inquiries. There were virtually no long term problems or aged fails.

The social side of the office was interesting, if not different. At least three days a week, I went out to lunch with my fellow workers. Invariably, we went to a place called the Italian Alps on William Street around the corner from our offices at 44 Beaver. The ground floor had a long bar with a jumble of disorderly tables that customers moved around at will to accommodate the size of their group. In another large room that shared the back wall of the bar, there was a cafeteria-style serving area, behind which a crew of servers dished up all the standard Italian dishes. They called it the Alps because there were two steep staircases to additional dining rooms on the second and third floors. The place accommodated large crowds of Wall Street workers with its relatively good Italian fast food and a glass of wine or beer at reasonable prices. The place was always jammed at lunch and at five until about seven nearly every night.

The Charlie Plohn crowd rarely took advantage of the food, spending most of our time at the bar. On any given day, Mario or Mike, our managers, might be having a drink there at lunchtime, often joined by the director of operations, a great fellow by the name of Tom Francis, and what may be characterized as the firm's personnel director and paymaster, a fellow I knew only as Charlie. Mario, Tom, or Mike Losquadro were usually the buyers while lower-level guys like myself could buy a round once in a while or leave a tip. It wasn't uncommon for George or Nette to join us, and even Manny and Leslie showed up once in a while. No alcoholics here but we were professional drinkers, and those were the days when the bartender bought a round here and there and got compensated for it with a good tip. So the core group wasn't there for just one drink. They didn't leave until the barkeep did his duty, usually the third or fourth round. This almost daily routine made for a mellow office atmosphere on most afternoons with management or at least one of the management team going home early and the place no worse for it. In shops like Charlie Plohn, a lot of the heavy clearing work got done in the morning. In the afternoon, everyone pitched in with any help needed in preparing the present day's work to be sent to the computer processing and tabulating firm, RCA.

At least once and often two or three times a month, tickets to sporting events might come our way; basketball, baseball, and hockey mostly. I frequently got to go to games with Mario and sometimes with Tom Francis who was a big hockey fan and a Bobby Hull lookalike. Hull was a big slap shot goal scorer for the Chicago Black Hawks and Chicago hockey's answer to Bobby Orr in Boston. It was my good fortune that I became a favored guest for these middle-aged and heavily experienced fellows. I'm sure it was because I was married, somewhat mature, had a little life experience, and read the papers cover to cover as they did, even though my paper was the *New York Journal-American*, which was basically an upscale tabloid.

I took for granted then what I would have frowned upon many years later: that they, my own managers, were quite comfortable discussing some of their problem situations with their own management while I was around. They even talked about their subordinate personnel who were senior to me right in front of me. When I asked questions about why this and why that and participated in the discussion, they rarely hesitated to give frank answers. The threads of these conversations were ongoing over days and sometimes weeks, and because I freely participated in them and was up on what stage they were in in terms of policy and decision making in the firm, I was privy to things most, if not all, of my coworkers were not, even Manny, my manager.

I was careful and instinctively knew I couldn't let on about what I knew or heard to my coworkers. One or two of them were often irritated over my being a guest at sporting events and a private dinner here and there, but what was I supposed to do, turn down the invitations? One fellow I heard called me a "brownnose" (a popular euphemism of the time, needing no definition). In any case, while my colleagues saw my association with senior management through a work-related prism, I saw it more as social, a filial, camaraderie of men and a phenomenon of my work life. I had been drinking with my work buddies since I was thirteen; this was just another level. Tom Francis was someone I admired a great deal; a gentleman who helped introduce me to a more polished, more American Midwestern sort of world than, the ethnocentric first-generation Italian American world I had inhabited almost all my life. He even invited me to his home when he had a gathering of friends to watch film of his escapades on a boat, deep sea fishing and catching large tuna. We became friends insomuch as one can be friends over a short period.

Of course, I didn't see that Mario was purposely bringing me on either because he liked me and saw something in me or because I was entertaining. It never entered my mind that these fellows could have shut me down at any time. Perhaps there was some subconscious knowledge within me that these associations would propel me further, allow me to earn more money, but it's hard for me to imagine I looked at myself at the time as someone who might have a career even if I understood the meaning of the word at the time. True to the lower class social strata from which I came, all I was interested in was continuing to earn a living wage to support my family and have some fun along the way. What I did have was a definite inkling that to have encountered these wonderful people in my new line of employ had been a great gift, and I wanted it to continue. Those persons who were somewhat annoyed and perhaps somewhat envious of my associations with management could have furthered their own associations if they had been capable. Not that I knew I was; I just was. Like an Englishman on the British Isles versus a European on the continent, the Englishman knew he was a free man hundreds of years before the European even thought he could be free. I knew my place as an employee but never doubted my social status as a man who could stand equal to the next man. What I mean to say is I rarely felt uncomfortable socially no matter where I was or who I was with.

Occasionally, I visited Mario's home in Brooklyn. One Saturday in August, a month or so after I joined the firm, my wife and I had lunch there with Mario's wife and family. I was amazed at the size and beauty of his home in Dyker Heights, one of the nicest areas in Brooklyn. An indoor barbecue pit in his basement was, to me, the ultimate symbol of status at the time. Complete with powerful exhaust fans, it just bowled me over. Afterward, I visited him several times to help with jobs he had to get done around his house. These offerings of assistance were an excuse for me to hang out with him. Inevitably, we talked about the job, the business, and the firm, and I became curious as to where my next step was.

He couldn't tell me. It was late 1969, October or November maybe, and I had only begun at Eastman Dillon a year before. He said Plohn was pretty strong for a small firm, but the market was the great leveler. He cautioned me about the market and that sudden downturns could mean the loss of jobs for lower-level people. In fact, under the current market conditions, many of the people I'd worked beside at Eastman Dillon were vulnerable. I already knew of several people who had left Eastman since I had who were not replaced. Any of them, he said, would be overjoyed at getting a twenty-five-dollar-a-week raise in base salary or more than double their base salary in a new job as I had with the move to Plohn. The most important thing I could do, he said, was to learn as much as possible about the business and how the clearing function and the processing of business took place so that the ultimate delivery and receipt of securities proceeded smoothly.

Sometime later, I brought a problem to Mario and Mike and was given some advice on how to handle the trader of the stock who was stonewalling me. I did as I was told and persevered with the fellow, telling him the opposing firm insisted they had not agreed to the price change he had told me to expect and they had repeatedly threatened to cancel the transaction altogether. A day or two later, I went back and reported the trade had been fixed. At this, Mario mentioned casually the trader probably didn't want to be "long" the stock in question because of what was happening to the market. The remark went over my head. I didn't understand the term *long the stock*. On such occasions, I became acutely aware of my lack of knowledge, although for some reason, I didn't always ask for an explanation. I hesitated to ask questions. I guess because I didn't want to appear completely clueless despite Mario's continued sermon that roughly stated the most important thing I could do for myself in securing a future on Wall Street was to complete three or four years in as many phases of back office clearing as possible, from comparing trades to coding and calculating transactions prior to processing to researching and correcting problem entries. He clarified this point saying when I understood buying and selling in all its stages and appearances, I would be qualified to do any job I might encounter on Wall Street. "In fact," he continued, "apply for and take any job and subsequently figure out and eventually master it in a relatively short period of time."

When I questioned how I could possibly be able to take a job in any operations capacity, he said something like the following.

"Credits and debits are buying and selling. They correspond to longs and shorts and receives and delivers depending on what point they are at in their passage through the firm, through an account, through P&S, through the cage, and through accounting. In the end, all brokerage firm employees from traders to receive and deliver clerks in the Cage are engaged with one side or the other in any given situation—buy or sell, credit or debit, long or short. As such, Wall Street is very simple. Once you figured out how buy and sell or long and short applied to the position or department you were working in or applying for, you'd be able to function successfully in the job, after that it's just the numbers."

I had some vague idea of what he was talking about, but what I really got out of it was simplistic. That if I paid attention and worked reasonably hard at learning the tasks given to me, I could survive on the Street. I had already decided, unconsciously at first and then later fervently and consciously, that Wall Street was the place I wanted to work for the rest of my life. This decision, conscious or unconscious, did not come with a plan of how I would accomplish what was a wish and fantasy born out of the simple fact that I liked it there. Working on Wall Street, to me, seemed more a social endeavor rather than work. The tasks at hand, the clerical function, the routine documentation and detail work, and the problem solving was ancillary, a kind of sidebar and simply a required prerequisite to be endured in order to support the social interaction with some of the most interesting people I had met in my life to date.

Chapter 14

The Home Front

On Monday, September 9, 1969, Rosalie gave birth to a healthy baby boy whom we named Pasquale after me and both his grandfathers. Just a few months later at Christmas, after less than six months at Charles Plohn & Co., I got an extraordinary bonus (at least I thought it was) of $2,500, equal to more than 12 weeks' pay and nearly $2,000 after taxes. There was good reason for this generosity, arranged we were sure by Mario and Tom Francis. At the time, there was usually a three-month waiting period between jobs before new employer's medical coverage kicked in. Since my son was born during that waiting period between my leaving Eastman Dillon and my joining Charles Plohn & Co., I had to pay most of the medical expenses for Rosalie's hospital stay and the last hundred or so dollars to Rosalie's doctor out of my own pocket. It wasn't that we didn't have the money or didn't realize we would have had to pay. Rosalie worked for an insurance company and was well aware of the prevailing rules. In fact, in those days, most company insurance plans did not pay any costs associated with pregnancy because it was not considered an illness or a malady. Rosalie's former employer, Met Life was one of those companies. The bonus sum, however, amply covered the medical expenses we had already paid, with plenty left over.

My wife has always railed at me about my irresponsibility with regard to money and my being less than careful or thoughtful, myopic in fact, about how I spend it. Once that bonus check was cashed and in the bank, I used half of it to buy a diamond wedding band for Rosalie and left the rest for her to spend or save—whatever she wanted to do with it. Regardless of whether she approved of my actions, it was very important for me to reward my wife with the wedding band she once described to me as something she would have liked. She never said she wanted it nor can I say she seemed thrilled with it. Haltingly pleased is the way I would put it. While perhaps unnecessary as she said and somewhat extravagant, I felt she deserved a beautiful and valuable gift for having gone through a pregnancy, having had a child, and perhaps most important for being the source of my happiness—my very existence, really. The world could admire her through the shiny thing on her finger and me as well for having put it there.

What was money anyway? A vehicle to some sort of happiness and the acquisition of wish fulfillment. I was so heady with my success at coming to Charlie Plohn and at having met Mario and having him as a mentor and friend. Because of Rosalie and Mario, I was discovering myself anew and becoming conscious of a world I'd never have discovered were it not for them. Why not commemorate my happiness with a bauble for my queen? I wouldn't have expressed it that way then, but that's what I was doing.

"She's going to make him rich!" my mother had said that day on the phone talking to her friend Filomena. Of course that invocation was far from my mind, but if it had come to mind at the time, I would have thought her prophesy had come true.

Upon receiving the actual check, my wife delayed taking it to the bank because she wanted to show it to her dad—her beloved Pops. My father-in-law, Pasquale Scigliano, now in his late sixties, had worked for the Department of Sanitation of New York City for twenty-five years, retired, and shortly thereafter had become custodian at a local bank for ten years after that, retiring a second time with another pension. From the time I began to court his daughter seriously, Pops often discussed my job security or lack thereof. He harped at me and more to his daughter that I should seek the security of a city job as he and his son Frank had and as my own father had done. In showing her father my bonus check, Rosalie would be saying, "Listen, Pops. Patty's doing well. He doesn't have to worry about job security anymore. He's got a good job. We've got good money coming in."

We went to her mom and dad's then, and when Pop looked at the check, $1,955 after taxes, he said, "Big deal, $195. You can't even buy a set of tires for the car with that."

Rosalie said, "Daddy, look again. It's $1,955."

Studying the check more carefully then, he looked up at me with narrowed eyes and a scowl and said, "What are they making you do for this money? You're gonna wind up in jail!"

"Pop," I said, "How can you say that…"

The conversation trailed off into my whining explanation of my bonus to no avail, pleading with him to try and understand. So it's hard to win everyone over no matter what you do, but in my own heart and mind, everything was good.

Chapter 15

Miracle of the E–Z Book

It's often no one's fault when things go badly. Sometimes in our lives, we can do better, be more sober, and live smarter, watchful lives so we're more ready for the sharp bends in the road that slam us against unfortunate times. On most occasions, the bad times are unforeseen and happen just when we think everything is going our way. In the fall of 1969, Mario's father-in-law passed away. He had a small contracting business based in a storefront and an adjacent garage on Eleventh Avenue in Brooklyn. A month or so after, Mario asked me to help him one Saturday in cleaning out the place. There wasn't much there—some tools, metal and glass, and lots of old papers. It became apparent the old man had not done any real business for quite some time, or at least it looked that way to me. I don't know what Mario expected to find, but it seemed he and his wife were disappointed. I got the feeling they thought they'd find a strong box full of cash in the desk or the safe. It's not unusual to have these thoughts of people we know because in life, they've given the impression, the appearance, that they were sitting on a pot of gold.

Thanksgiving and the holidays came and went. Little did I know or connect with at the time that the fabulous bonus I'd received of $2,500 and the equally great bonuses I was sure my colleagues had received were actually given at a point when the market was in the midst of a near 10 percent decline in the Dow Jones Index over the second half of 1969.

Intellectually, the meaning and magnitude of a ten percent decline in the market was completely lost on me. I may have understood it numerically, but in terms of its dynamic effect on Wall Street, on the economy, and those members of the populace who make up the market, I didn't have a clue. Things started to get worse, and by February of 1970, the Dow had fallen to about 770 from 870 where it was in June of 1969. Sometime in late January, I remember getting into a taxi after work on my way up to a hockey game at the Garden. The driver said his last passenger told him fifty margin clerks had been laid off at a firm called Dempsey-Tegeler. I never followed up on the story to find out what really happened at Dempsey-Tegeler, a name I knew well because they did so much business with us. Over the following weeks, that cab driver's story seemed to be following me around as I picked up snippets of conversation about layoffs and *headcount reduction*, a phrase I hadn't heard before.

Then a terrible and, at the same time, very curious event occurred. Mario was mugged in the hallway at 44 Beaver Street. He walked into the office at about twelve thirty, battered and bruised about the face and head. His coat was dirty and disheveled as though he had been rolling around on the floor or the gutter. The firm occupied several floors in the building, and it was not uncommon for employees to take the stairs between floors instead of waiting for one of the two slowest elevators on Wall Street (so we always said). Mario had been assaulted and mugged by a couple of guys on the stairwell. Everyone in the office was in shock, kind of mouth open aghast, that such a thing could happen to one of us, although purse snatchings and disappearing property was quite common at the time in buildings like ours that had no security. Some of the management came in shortly after Mario stumbled in. Tom Francis and others took him upstairs. I couldn't help but think how humiliating, how embarrassing, that must have been for him.

By the following Monday, the office had quieted down, and on Tuesday, Mario came in. We, the office workers, suppressed our desire to ask a million questions, and so after a day or two, the event blew over. Not long after, another storm came up, blowing straight at me. In early March, Mario and Mike called me into their office to tell me I was being laid off, and there would be two weeks' severance pay for me included in the next paycheck. Linc, my partner with the afro at the desk across from me, had been laid off several weeks before, and I was doing his work, tellingly reduced from prior times. But even so, I never thought it would happen to me.

Rosalie's words echoed. "No one ever does."

At least no-one as lily white as I was. Not that I was so special, I just never thought it could happen to me. For a few days after hearing this dismal news, a depressed feeling came over me, such as I had never felt before. This new and exciting work environment and social engagement that was so vibrant to me, that I so enjoyed, reveled in, and loved, was slipping away. I stopped working then, let my mail and correspondence pile up, giving it all over to Manny, and just waited for my next paycheck with severance included. I left the place, never to set foot in that building again. I don't remember even saying goodbye to anyone. I wasn't angry at any of my fellow workers. They were all there longer than I was and had seniority—I didn't have a leg to stand on in that regard—but their well-being was none of my concern right now.

My wife was naturally distressed. Who wouldn't be? We had a new baby. My son, Pat, was just barely six months old. Rosalie, however, doesn't panic and was possessed of a feeling at the time, rightly or wrongly, that her life was by nature usually going to be downhill, and the uphill times were simply luck and not the way life really is. She wasn't surprised we were having a downturn. She told me later she thought (secretly of course) things had been going too well for both of us for far too long. Our chance meeting, our falling in love and marrying, my new job success, having a healthy child so soon after we married, dispelling her fears about the difficulties of conception. It was all quite wonderful, she said. But our luck had to change soon, it had to, because that was the way life worked.

My outlook is exactly opposite. Life throws things at you— some good, some bad—and we accept them as they come. There's no bias up or down. It's just life. I had no idea she had such a pessimistic view, and it truly shocked me. We were either boyfriend or girlfriend or married since the first day of 1968, a little more than two years before, but I'd not seen this defeatist and pessimistic side of my wife's mind. And even after I knew it, I have never understood it. In a way, it was a help because she knew, was certain even, that the future was rocky, and so to her credit, she never uttered a complaint because in a way, it was life's destiny to be troubled. But I could never think that way. Life happens, and life's mission is to work it out. That's why God put us here. The alternative is to not exist and to not have been born at all.

The first thing I did after being laid-off was to answer an ad that was in the window of a pizzeria on Nostrand Avenue, a few blocks away from where we lived. Lenny's Pizza, in the person of Joe De Candia, was looking for drivers to deliver pizzas on weekends. A few days later, on a snowy Thursday evening, I began working Thursday through Sunday night from five in the afternoon to midnight and later depending what day it was. Earning nearly $150 in tips and salary that first weekend before paying for gas was quite a surprise. Having a penchant for Lenny's Sicilian, I probably ate a couple pizzas that weekend as well. Had I known the money was that good delivering pizzas, I'd have taken the damn job even before I got the sack and worked the two simultaneously.

I still needed a day job and pondered upon what to do next. I filed for unemployment and got interviewed and offered a janitorial position at a building in the Wall Street area so I could keep an eye open for a position like the one I had lost, so suggested the unemployment office operative.

"Forget it!" I said. I wouldn't even consider it.

Several visits to employment agency offices were disappointing and actually quite depressing since the agencies I visited down in the financial district didn't even ask me to fill out cards for their files. I could have gotten my old job back in the body and fender shop in a minute or pumped gas all day in the gas station of a buddy of mine for a hundred a week, but I held that off. I'd do that when things became desperate or some definitive sign showed me I was destined to go back to my old life, that The Street was not going to be for me. The body shop and gas stations could wait. I didn't want those jobs. I didn't want to get used to making money as a grease monkey again. That would have dulled my desire to get back onto

Wall Street. Giving up so quickly just because some other place could deliver a steady paycheck didn't seem right.

I had had a job as far back as I could remember maybe as young as 10 or 12 years old. I had never been without a job since elementary school and still had one counting the pizza delivery. Contrary to how my wife looked at the world, I felt, in a way, that life, God even, had led me to Wall Street. It was my destiny to be there, and I had faith in the fact that I had not been given this gift only to have it taken away. My family had had its hardships: illness, loss of young lives, but I had never felt they had lost their taste for life or the secure knowledge and faith that a happy future lay ahead for themselves and their families. From a more practical point of view, there were no immediate worries. Rosalie and I had extended families who owned their own homes. We would always be welcome and taken in, if it came to that. Life would go on.

Some time in March an idea began to form. One of the most important tools of the comparison clerk, indeed of anyone in P&S and almost every other department on Wall Street, is a weighty tome known as *the Dealer Book*. Issued annually and published by Dow Jones, it listed every broker dealer in the country in alphabetical order by state. The bigger the firm, the more lines in their listing in terms of naming departments, department heads, and telephone numbers. In New York, because so many firms had a representative office there, Dow Jones published a special edition known as the *E–Z Book*. Its actual title was the *E–Z Guide to Wall Street Brokerage Firms in New York City and Suburbs*. I used the *E–Z Book* almost every day of my employment. I wish I still had one today. I decided to call every firm listed in the book with six lines or more and, after a while, started calling firms with four or more lines because the results were so dismal. There weren't many stones I wanted or could afford to leave unturned. The measure of how difficult these times were (late March 1970) was I received no positive response until I reached the *R*s, the eighteenth letter of the alphabet, near my ninetieth call, before someone asked me to come down for an interview. This alone might have been the miracle of the E-Z Book but there's more.

Chapter 16

Dees, Does, and Dem

Though I don't remember the name of the assistant personnel director who interviewed me, I do remember Reynolds Securities' personnel offices were in 40 Broadway. The interviewer was in his late thirties, taller than six feet, balding, and drifting to overweight like myself. He was wearing a tight-fitting vest and a three-piece brown tweed suit and sat back in his reclining office chair. When he leaned back and spoke I felt as though he was looking down his nose at me. When I confirmed what I'd written that I was earning two hundred dollars a week at Charles Plohn & Co. just a few short weeks before, he scoffed in an arrogant and sneering kind of way, saying two hundred dollars a week was out of the question at Reynolds "if…I got the job." The positions open paid $125 a week with little to no chance of overtime. He was not a nice man, but I didn't react. I was obviously desperate for a job, and this fellow knew they were scarce. Perhaps he caught the scent of desperation. I just took his attitude in stride; there would be no gain in getting my hackles up.

He gave me a large yellow envelope, presumably containing the application I had just filled out and my first interviewer's opinions of me and sent me to the fourth floor of 2 Broadway a few blocks down the street. I was to interview with one Edward O'Donnell, manager of a department known as DECAB that I had been told was part of P&S. It was a short walk, downhill in fact, and a few minutes after giving my name to the security desk, O'Donnell, a thin, sallow, and pointy-faced young man with a mop of straight, blond, movie star–quality hair combed in a conservative pompadour style, came out to round me up.

When I was pointed to by the security guard, he came up to me, stuck out a thin milky white hand, and said, "Ha ya doon? Am Eddy O."

Now I'm from Brooklyn myself and have an accent, although I've never considered it to be very pronounced. Others differ with me and pick up my accent even now. But this fellow who was known as Eddy O spoke some of the thickest Brooklynese I'd ever heard, coupled with a slight speech defect, which had the effect of clipping his words even more than the accent did.

He said "yeh" instead of "yeah," "nh" instead of "nah" for "no," and, not to belabor the point too much, "wudya" for "would you" and "waddaya" for "what are you."

Taking me back to his office, he said DECAB was the firm's Corrections Department, and although it worked closely with and indeed was in close proximity to the firms P&S Department, it was not part of it nor was it managed by the P&S manager. It was a separate and independent department. The acronym DECAB was short for Department of Errors Corrections and Balances. Its location was a cave-like, dingy, dim, smoky, grey room, a little smaller than Charlie Plohn's P&S. It seemed like something out of a Dickens novel. A grouping of eight desks and a line of four and then a couple of others against the far wall with narrow walkways between them surrounded by walls lined with filing cabinets and shelves above them. The shelves were stacked with blue- and red-cloth-bound books of blotters that appeared as if they were going to topple down at the hint of a breeze or a slight push.

I was directed to a chair next to Eddy O's desk that faced outward toward the department and its personnel. I was beside Eddy O, facing away from him answering his questions so everyone in front of us could hear. It seemed at first like it was a trial, and I was in front of a jury. Actually, it was a group interview with plenty of cross conversation, joking, phones ringing, and people walking through and taking time to stop and chat or drop off papers, and every once in a while, someone stuck their head in from the corridor or the front way out to yell something. Occasionally, a street whistle or a loud exclamation or shout could be heard. It appeared I was back at Eastman Dillon all over again.

"Ya fum Brooklin," Eddy said about ten minutes into the interview.

"Yeah. Er, yes, I am."

"Waddadey call ya, Paddy or Patsy?"

"Uh, just Pat is good."

Despite the heavy accents, the kidding, and interruptions, in less than fifteen minutes, Eddy clearly explained he was looking for several corrections clerks, either experienced or trainee and, based on the experience at my two previous jobs, I would probably be a fit for one of them. After the hometown familiarities had been established, I think his exact words were: "Ya probly gonna be a fit fa one or de udder, so ya doan haffta bullshit me bout yer esperience, right?"

"Yes, Mr. O'Donnell. No problem, I understand perfectly."

"Call me Ed."

"Yes, sir."

"Just Ed, no sir."

"Sure."

It took me a few minutes, but it dawned on me quite early in the interview he was telling me I had the job and he liked the cut of my jib, so to speak. I guessed as I was from Brooklyn, "shootin straight wit' no bullshit" was important. I'm sure my body language said I wanted the job badly. I explained, however, the only corrections experience I had was a couple of weeks at Eastman Dillon sitting at the Corrections Desk and only looking over someone's shoulder.

He in turn explained to me Reynolds Securities had fifteen OTC traders about a hundred feet away from where we were sitting, and they alone could occupy a Corrections clerk full time. So if I was as familiar with OTC trading and clearing and its P&S function, it sounded like I was I would get along fine. He added it was especially important that I was used to talking to the traders. The crew in the department could teach me to do corrections in a matter of weeks. The more we talked, the more relaxed I became during this very friendly and frank conversation about my work experience, which was readily listened in on by several of the clerks in the immediate proximity.

"Whaddyatink, Louie?" Eddy said after a while to a heavyset round-headed kid with tight curly hair sitting about five feet away.

"Sounds okay to me as long as he's got some time in talkin' wit' dem trada's. You know how dey can bullshit ya and trow y'off," Louie said. And then to me, he added, "Wherdya grow up?"

"Bedford-Stuyvesant, Dekalb, and Nostrand around there," I said.

"No shit, I'm from Scholes Street. Not too far away."

"Yeah, I know where it is."

"I bet ya do. Wansome koffee? Am goan out for a kintaina."

And so went my interview at Reynolds Securities. Add another two hours or more of banter with some of the other clerks and Eddy O about the way the department operated within their *branch office system*, which was a new term to me, how they communicated with the trading departments, their wire system, which they called Reycom, my work experience, and the common experience for several of us, which was our hometown of Brooklyn.

During this time, I was introduced to all passersby, various and sundry. It was like sitting in front of my grandfather's house on Park Avenue and Spencer Street on Saturday afternoons in summer when everyone in the neighborhood stopped to say hello, chat for a minute or two, swap the local gossip, and find out who the newcomer might be. The only thing missing was the hotdog cart on the corner doing a land office business. It was easy going now because I'd known for an hour I had the job. I'd found a home and wouldn't, for the time being at least, have to leave Wall Street, the new world I'd grown to love that had almost slipped away from me.

Near four o'clock, Eddy filled out a couple of lines on some papers, placed them in the ubiquitous yellow envelope, resealed it, and sent me back to 40 Broadway. I walked the two blocks north as the late afternoon gloom descended and enveloped Lower Broadway. Once there, a young blonde receptionist whom I'd seen earlier congratulated me after opening the envelope and mentioned she would be right with me and if I would please go into the classroom and wait for her to bring in the test materials.

I was stunned. Test material! Had I heard right? Her words left me breathless, as if I had taken a punch to the solar plexus or an arrow had been shot through my neck. I didn't know what to say or do. The blonde was speaking again, but I didn't hear. I was rooted to the spot.

"I have to take a test?" I think I said. "Didn't I get the job?"

"Yes. Yes, of course you did, but the firm has minimum math and reading skill standards that must be met by all employees and verified by a test," Blondie said. Then, I guess sensing my attack of nerves, she added, "Don't worry, it's just a formality. I'm sure you'll be fine with it."

"Wha…what kind of test is it?"

"Oh, just basic math skills and reading comprehension," she said offhandedly.

I hadn't passed a math class or test since seventh or eighth grade. Reading was okay, but math tests were like root canal for me. My high school career had been destroyed by my inability to comprehend any higher math whatsoever, even elementary algebra, much less anything further than that. I was able to get around taking any math until my sophomore year, but geometry was my fourth period class in junior year at Charles Evans Hughes High School on West Eighteenth Street in Manhattan. After a month or two of failing to comprehend and failing tests, I started cutting out after the third period and just not going back. I would simply ride the subways until about noon, hang out in a poolroom until about two o'clock, and then go to my part-time job in a supermarket. Simple math like multiplication and long division was second nature to me, but now ten years later, at the mention of a test, I was frozen. My future seemed to be dependent on what I had failed at so many times—taking a math test.

The classroom Blondie spoke of was a large dimly lit open space lined with cubicles to the right and a far corner piled with spare tables and chairs in a jumble that reminded me at that moment of an old abandoned house. She took me to one of the cubicles and turned on a couple of desk lamps that accentuated the surrounding gloom. Then, handing me a booklet, she asked that I fill out the required information and read the instructions.

"Take as much time as you like to read the sample questions and the instructions," said Blondie. "Call me when you're ready."

After filling in all the standard name and address information, I saw the sample of a reading comprehension question. Two or three paragraphs to read followed by five or six questions to answer. I was to do four of these and move on to the math portion of the test—the part that terrified me. This was a series of interpolations. There were a series of four- and five-digit numbers and then a listing of number groupings. I was to find as many groups of numbers that the numbers in the first listing fell between. There were forty of these, and I would have twenty minutes for the entire exam. If I finished before the time was up, I was supposed to go back and complete a fifth and sixth reading comprehension question.

Blondie called from the next room after about ten minutes with a quizzical tone to her voice.

"Is everything okay, Mr. Scida? Are you ready to begin?"

"Yes please," I said feebly.

Blondie walked in with a timer, set it for twenty minutes, placed it in the next cubicle from me, and flipped a lever to turn it on before walking away toward her desk in the next room.

I was perspiring heavily and worried at one point about getting the booklet wet from the liquid that was pouring down my face and hands—my entire body actually. The buzzer hissed loudly, and Blondie walked in to collect the exam papers.

"Thank you," she said cheerfully. "We'll let you know in a few days." Then, glancing at me, she asked, "Are you okay, Mr. Scida? Are you unwell?"

I really couldn't answer; my throat was like dry plaster and nearly closed. She brought me a paper cup filled with water, and I sat for a few minutes soaked from head to foot with my shirt stuck to my back and my feet swimming inside my socks and shoes. As I got up to go, I felt Blondie watching me from her desk thinking who knows what.

I got home safely, worn out from the day's ordeal, embarrassed, and in some ways ashamed of myself. I resolved never to want something as badly as I had wanted that job. I was pissed off and angry. I had set myself up after the interview thinking I had won the minds and hearts of my interviewers and peers and that getting the position was a completed victory. Instead, I'd turned into a blubbering mess because of that stupid test. I'd never do that again; never take anything that important for granted. What a position to be in—no job, no job benefits, an object of pity. I was angry and miserable, drawing a blank regarding my next move.

At ten o'clock the following morning, Blondie called.

"Mr. Scida, this is…Are you feeling better today?"

"Yes," I said stiffly. "Much better, thank you."

"We were so worried about you, Mr. Scida. You were white as a sheet when you walked out soaked and wet from perspiration."

"I'm fine now, thank you," I said, embarrassed again and steeling myself for the worst.

"Good. Now can you come in on Monday, or do you want to begin the following Monday? New employee orientation is held every Monday at eight o'clock in the morning sharp."

"Ahem, ah, yes, certainly, this Monday. Sure. Sure I can," I said calmly, my heart nearly stopped.

"And Mr. O'Donnell called. He'd like you to give him a call. Do you have his number?"

"Ah, no. No, I don't. Can you give it to me please?"

Here on this insecure note began thirty-one years with Reynolds Securities and whatever firm and corporate name it morphed into over that time. It also marked the last time I ever panicked over a math problem whether I felt I could do it or not. I began to operate under the assumption that I could always figure something out. Some few days or weeks after I had digested this mad incident in which I lucked out qualifying for a job and panicked over a math test, I calmed myself by thinking of Mario's admonition regarding working on Wall Street.

It's not the numbers that are so important. It's the fact that no matter what the numbers are, it's all buy and sell, debits and credits. I took comfort in the fact that if I could understand buys and sells and what they represented, in every way they existed, the numbers that came along with them would get easier to work with too. Thank you, Lord.

Chapter 17

Hidden Events Unfold

In the early weeks of my employment at Reynolds Securities I would learn that about ten days prior to my hiring, a gambling ring had been discovered. One or two of its principals were employed in DECAB and several others in the adjoining Order Room, complete with a direct wire to a bookmaker from the listed bond desk (so the rumor went). Seven employees were let go, at least one of them from DECAB. Had I been more alert on the day I was interviewed, I might have noticed a group of portrait-sized photographs on the wall behind the security desk, of the infamous seven below a sign advising under no circumstances were these individuals to be allowed on the premises. My employment was the result of their transgressions. As the saying goes, "I'd rather be lucky than smart."

More shocking, however, was that not long after I joined Reynolds, I heard my mentor Mario Ruocco left Charles Plohn under highly irregular circumstances. He'd also been hired at another firm and got them to part with over $2,000 in salary advances. However, the last anyone had heard from Mario was a credit card charge at a gas station somewhere in New Jersey. When I called Tom Francis, the managing director of Plohn's operations, he told me the worst cut of all was he now thought the mugging of Mario earlier in the year was faked. What had appeared to him then to have been wounds, he now thought were just dirt and redness from rubbing. He also said the firm had made good the loss from the robbery as it had occurred on payday. The thought crossed my mind that Mario might have been roughed up by loan sharks who he owed money but I didn't mention it. It was a moot point anyway, irrelevant in light of the way things had turned out.

"I loved that guy," Francis then exclaimed.

So did I. Suffice it to say you basked in an aura when you were with Mario. At a ball game, a bar, even in the office, he was always the uncontested magnetic center. He was always cool, in control, and never ruffled. At the same time, one felt he was there to help and bolster you. One had the feeling, maybe it was just me, that with Mario's help, every obstacle could be overcome. For a good while after, years in fact, I sometimes thought I spotted Mario in a passing car or perhaps waiting for a light to change on the opposite side of a roadway. Sometimes I thought I'd caught a glimpse of him at a basketball or hockey game. I was searching for him subconsciously I suppose: and prayed to him when my insecurities got the best of me, that I might find him and that his words would come true.

"Don't worry, kid. After those few months at Eastman Dillon and the time you've put in here with us, there's no job on the street you won't be able to learn. It's all P&S, purchases and sales, debits and credits, shorts and longs, and then the dollars and cents."

I was very distressed when I was told no one could find him. I knew Mario was a gambler on sports, especially basketball and on horses. Like all compulsive gamblers, Mario was seeking that big score, which almost never happens. I realized then that when we were going through his father-in-law's place of business, he was in search of a big score, thinking that possibly his ship had come in. He could never understand why I didn't have good betting tips for him or wasn't interested in them since my wife's brother Frank owned a couple of Standardbred racehorses, also known as trotters or pacers, the horses that pull a sulky and driver. I would go to the track once in a while and enjoy an evening of two-dollar betting, but I never got a thrill from following the sport closely and betting daily as Mario did. On another front my wife and I became estranged from Mario's sister Anne and any small family connection we had with Mario's wife was severed as well. I'm not sure why but I began to think that they might have thought I knew something more about Mario's doings before he disappeared and maybe even his present whereabouts. Again other than that I didn't know what they were thinking. Anne never called me although she spoke to my wife a couple of times before breaking off completely.

Surviving the layoff from Charles Plohn in a dismal market taught me one thing. When you have to save yourself, get back on track and make a new way. You just have to forget about the past and forge ahead. Past mistakes, perceived injustices, insults and slights, and feeling sorry for yourself about ones shortcomings or incapability's or any self-righteousness over them mean nothing. Lucky I may have been, blessed by God as well, but if I wasn't pushing away, being creative, and persevering in some way over my fears, luck and possibly even God would not have had the opportunity to see me through, for indeed God helps those who help themselves. God and the *E-Z Book*, that is.

Chapter 18

Reynolds Securities: DECAB

Reynolds Securities was a medium-sized brokerage firm in 1970 with ninety to one hundred branches and about twelve hundred retail salesmen compared to the larger Merrill Lynch or Goodbody, which were at least triple that size or more. There were most likely another fifty to a hundred institutional salesmen as well. That is, salesman who serviced insurance companies, pension funds, or banks. Reynolds was mainly a retail sales organization that served the public. Its regional strength was in Florida, the south, and the Mid- and North Atlantic states, with a respectable presence in the Mid- and Far West. The firm was a wire house, meaning it transmitted its order flow through a teletype network over American Telephone and Telegraph hard wires known as TELCO in back office parlance (aka AT&T) hardwires. Totally outmoded today but the way it was done then by all the major firms. The company was founded in 1933 with the breaking off of a few scions of the Reynolds family of Reynolds Tobacco fame over a dispute relating to the company's new interests in the mining of bauxite and the manufacture of aluminum in South America.

The Department of Errors, Corrections, and Balances (DECAB), from the perspective of a learning experience, was the perfect place for me to land.

At Eastman Dillon and Charles Plohn, on a smaller scale, I came to understand the interconnectivity of Wall Street firms with one another, meaning that, every day the firms bought and sold from each other and delivered and received from each other thousands upon thousands of lots of stocks and bonds worth billions of dollars. In DECAB at Reynolds, I learned more pointedly that more than 90 percent of the time, when they bought and sold from one another, they were in fact acting on behalf of others. I had some idea of that of course. It wasn't that I didn't know the firms I worked for had private retail clients, as they were referred to. I was one myself as I had dabbled in a trade or two, but the realization that the customer side was so vast was almost a surprise. I never imagined the great quantity of customer-stockbroker relationships, the vast quantity of internal transactions, or the amount of communication that went on between the home office and the branch and the branch office and the product departments, with DECAB continually called upon by both for assistance.

I didn't have a clue that for example, a purchase of ten thousand shares of a stock by the firm might generate fifty or a hundred transactions internally or that a bond underwriting could engender six to seven hundred transactions. I never saw the physical manifestations of that volume because I never saw those listings or computer runs of client transactions. Early on then at Reynolds Securities, it quickly became apparent that there was plenty more than I had imagined to do and learn, that DECAB was immersed in an ocean of doings, and that even more rules of the road and just as many problems, if not more, had to be attended to on the customer side as there were on the street side.

Wall Street is like an iceberg with its trading and investment banking powers majestic above the water, while its bulky mass of detail plods forward below in the form of transaction processing, calculation, accounting, dividend and interest distributions, stock transfer, money transfer, and a myriad of other administrative tasks performed. If you do your operations right, you swim and keep the moneymaking machine above afloat.

In truth I think I might have been slow on the uptake in terms of understanding the ins and outs of canceling and rebooking trades. Instead, I got a more diversified look at the terrain. So instead of cubbyholing into an exclusive relationship with the OTC stock traders, which was the impression I was first given, I got a much more diversified look at the terrain in those first months in DECAB. My training consisted of sitting beside one or another of the DECAB clerks, helping to research trade problems—any kind of trade problem, stocks or bonds. Beyond the research, I was learning to write cancels and rebills and being taught the rules that governed how a listed stock problem was worked and who you talked to for a corporate bond problem. I was also being introduced to people in the Margin Department whose mandate was keeping a close watch over client accounts.

When fixing problems, it was the right thing to do to go into margin and let the clerk who handled the account know a couple of corrections were going to hit the next day—scratch a problem off a margin clerks list, so to speak. I was taken to meet the people in Stock Record, the department where details of the physical location and holder of record of stocks and bonds were kept. I went to the Cage, otherwise known as Cashiers, with Craig Sarch, Eddy O'Donnell's number two. Cashiers, or the Cage, you will remember, is the department that receives and delivers physical stock and bonds. After a few months, I began working on problems on my own with a more periodic spot check of my work.

The atmosphere of the department was interesting. The more closemouthed a clerk might be about the problems they were working on, the more claustrophobic the supervision became. You were expected to talk about what you were working on, especially if you were a trainee, bitch about it even and, in general, openly discuss the communication you were having with other departments and the operations people in branches. The more open you were to the suggestions and experience of senior clerks, the freer you were to tackle any problem that came up and thus you learned. After three or four months or so, I found myself settling in and in close touch with many operations managers and wire operators around the country as well as people in some of the product departments.

A project regularly required by Compliance and Legal was the completion of what were known as "stabilization reports." At least that's what we called them. Requests were constantly coming in for them. DECAB was the emergency backup and clean-up team for any problem or special job that required the documentation of past transactions. One day or week it was Occidental Petroleum, another week it was Pfizer, and another it was Anadarko and a myriad of other stocks and bonds. This week, it was the NYSE, and the next the SEC or our own compliance department that required a list of all transactions between given dates of all stock and option trades in a particular security in a particular state or even in a particular branch done by a specific account and broker. Apparently these outside agencies and our own internal watchdogs wanted to see if there were any patterns to the trading of particular stocks, or at least that was a reason I was given as to why these reports needed to be assembled.

The only place this information existed was in the master blotters that were stored at the firm's warehouse at 49 West Street near the access road leading to Brooklyn Battery Tunnel. There was no microfilm or microfiche yet for this stuff; everything was on paper. There were seven floors lined with row upon row of steel shelves packed with cloth-covered cardboard-bound blotters and rows of storage boxes stuffed with anything from copies of trade tickets to trader inventory cards to carbons of floor reports and handwritten orders.

While I had plenty to do in the office, when the stabilization reports came in for completion, as the new guy, the trainee in the department, they sent me. Sometimes I would be there for days, and often one of the other clerks accompanied me. If we had an inkling we were going to be assigned there, we'd wear jeans. The shelves were eight feet high and in some cases ten. It was easy to catch a pocket or a cuff and tear a hole in your clothing. If I used the word *Dickensian* to describe DECAB's atmosphere, it went double here. Dark and dingy, with rickety ladders and shelves to the ceiling. We had to climb these rolling ladders to get blotters and trade tickets from the top shelves, which were covered with a thick black soot, the residue of the ink and carbon that inhabited the paper. The dust, dirt, and grime of the place was oppressive, and if you were perspiring, it became greasy, thick, sticky, and not easy to remove from your clothes, short of sending them to the dry cleaner and sometimes that didn't work.

Despite the sad working conditions, I liked these little jaunts to the warehouse even though the place felt like you were in some factory or slum. Being away from the office allowed you to sneak off for a two-hour lunch or to BS with the warehouse personnel. Reynolds's copy room and fledgling print shop was at 49 West Street at the time, and I got to know one of the guys, Sam Cuebas, who ran the copy room and eventually the print shop and branch distribution facility for the firm for many years into the nineties. It didn't hurt that there were a few cute girls there whom we liked to chat up a bit as well. I usually bolted out of the office at five on the button on Thursdays and Fridays when driving for the pizzeria and even earlier if I was at the warehouse. I needed the extra time anyway to stop home and wash away the warehouse grime.

That first year or so at Reynolds was just another job for me, a continuance of a journey started a little more than two years before with a now somewhat knowable route or destination. Every few months, someone in DECAB or the adjoining P&S Department moved to Accounting or into Margin or the Cage. A move of this kind was, for me, tangential at the time as no one had ever mentioned anything of the sort, but because it happened from time to time to others, there was a value set upon it in the back of my mind. A hope one might call it, even a fantasy and a daydream at times. In any event, my work now had a broader scope than simply confirming transactions with other firms. I was a clerk in the deep back office, getting a good grounding in the business from some very seasoned people. This sustained continuance of being involved day to day helped me get over being dumped from Charles Plohn and losing my mentor, Mario, possibly the first person I truly ever looked up to and respected other than family. Worse than that, I nearly lost what I had come to love, what in a way nurtured me, the pace, the volume, the people, and the almost daily dump of new knowledge and new variations of old problems. If there was a problem that had to be fixed or a project that had to get done, DECAB got it. Reynolds Operations Management housed across a sort of "no man's land" in one of the outer corridors on the floor were very demanding and, in a sort of roughhouse way, wanted answers and results quickly to whatever was on its minds or at hand.

Coming to work every day, coming to Wall Street everyday even, to what some might have said was "just a lowly back office operations job" was living on an elevated plane and certainly a different cultural experience and social interaction than what many people I knew were involved with on their jobs. Some of my coworkers choose not to keep up, to withdraw to a sideline and just be a clerk, but you could stay in the forefront, interact, get involved, compete, and when you did these things to some degree you directed the course of events. Not that I knew it at the time or would know it for years to come that it was my nature to respond to challenges, volunteer, and be in middle of things, and that in some freaky kind of way, crisis would come my way and benefit me.

Chapter 19

The Fall of Goodbody:
Unmatched Confirmations

The operational difficulties running rampant throughout the financial workplace around the time I joined Wall Street coupled with uncertain markets became a lethal mix for many firms. My former firm, Charles Plohn & Co., was a casualty, going out of existence a few months after I was let go—the fate of many other firms at the time. Just as we have seen in the economic crises of the past several years, size does not matter, and the biggest and seemingly best organizations can be brought to their knees just as the small ones were. This was the case when Goodbody & Co., an old-line, well-respected Wall Street house founded in the 1880s closed its doors and went out of business in December 1970.

Goodbody, then the fifth largest brokerage firm in the country, serving retail and institutional investors alike, was also a wire house and a leading risk taker and underwriter in all of the major businesses from equity (stocks) syndicate to municipals to corporate bonds. In corporate bonds and municipal bonds, Goodbody might have been the retail powerhouse on the Street or close rivals with Merrill Lynch for the top spot. The firm, however, was plagued by operational problems stemming from its inability to promptly deliver and receive securities for its clients and trading partners. It was reported in the press at the time that Goodbody had spent more than a million dollars on an automated cashiering system that failed and eventually brought the firm down.

The problem Goodbody succumbed to, that its new cashiering system was to remedy, was the mitigation of the errors caused by the daily physical movement of thousands and thousands of pieces of paper, namely stock and bond certificates. Stock and bond ownership was evidenced at the time with paper certificates. It may surprise readers under forty years of age that there was no Depository Trust Company (DTC) in 1970 electronically tracking ownership of stock. Stock certificate's were sent back and forth from commercial banks who were the paying and registration agents for corporations to brokerage firms who were the transactional agents for investors who then delivered the stock to investors via the mails. In general investors took delivery of their securities in paper "certificate" form—in "specie" form, to use another term.

These certificates changed hands from brokerage firm to commercial bank and back to the brokerage firm when bought and sold and were delivered to clients through the mail and had to be delivered back and forth between home and safety deposit boxes and attorneys and their safety deposit boxes and so on and on. Certificates were subject to physical damage, loss in the mail, theft, counterfeit, and any other form of destruction and travesty that paper may be subjected to, like being singed by a cigar ash or having coffee spilt on them or otherwise soaked in a flood or burned in a fire.

For the brokerage firms, stock and bond certificates were a huge labor and security issue. Employees who worked in the cage had to hang their coats and leave their personal belongings outside the rooms in which stock and bond certificates were handled and had to show ID when entering the cage from outside and moving from section to section. Employees were provided lockers for pocketbooks, shopping bags, brief cases, and so forth. Why? Suffice it to say, I once witnessed the arrest of two individuals outside of 2 Broadway when they tried to walk out of Reynolds with several hundred shares of IBM stock. Bonds were issued in "bearer" form, presumed to be owned by the person who held them. Temptation to steal was acute. Beyond the personnel problem, there were huge systems, operations, and management issues because the securities were handled and all notation was made by human beings. It was reported at the time that Goodbody had nearly a thousand employees devoted to the orderly movement of this enormous physical volume and weight of paper, and the firm (as it in fact did) was in danger of falling into bankruptcy because of it. The inability to implement the automated cashiering system was, in my understanding, the final blow that sealed the firm's fate.

In December 1970, Goodbody & Co. merged with and was in effect taken over by Merrill Lynch who would in a month or so merge the account bases of the two firms. Merrill Lynch, in the opinion of many at the time, was the antithesis of Goodbody, meticulously managed from top to bottom. People who worked for Merrill were often referred to as soldiers. This was as much a reference to the firm's chairman Don Regan (who would become President Ronald Reagan's chief of staff in the eighties), a former marine who surrounded himself with executives with military backgrounds as it was to a certain mindset at the firm. While the term applied generally to the executive and management corps of Merrill, the staff knew what was meant by the term *soldier*. Like the army and the marines, at Merrill, there was no room for slackers. Employees who weren't ready to sacrifice themselves for the sake of the firm were unwanted.

The Merrill Lynch takeover of Goodbody from another perspective was a great, though unremarked upon at the time, coup for Merrill, which would reveal itself in later years. In acquiring Goodbody, Merrill attached a terrifically talented cadre of middle management skilled in every phase of the financial services industry from accounting to product development. Add to that a savvy, well-seasoned sales force that helped Merrill in the furthering of an already dominant ability to distribute financial product to the public.

The immediate problem, however, that Goodbody's downfall caused in DECAB at Reynolds was an increase in a somewhat obscure operational problem known as "unmatched confirmations." These were client transactions whose confirmations or billings were produced with no name or mailing address; thus, they could not be mailed out, which was the beginning of the setting up of a late payment situation. The term *unmatched* derived from a transaction in an account number that had no matching name or mailing address information in the firm's account database. The problem was obscure because unmatched confirms were an exceedingly infrequent occurrence.

The experience of DECAB showed that unmatched confirms were usually real trades for new clients whose new account information had been late getting into the system the day before. New accounts were set up in the firm's database in New York from information sent over the wire system to a small unit known as, you guessed it, New Accounts, an adjunct of trade processing and the Keypunch Department.

"Big deal," you say. "So a client confirmation (billing) would be a day or two late in getting into the mail. Sooner or later, the information would catch up with itself."

The fact was the problem was a big deal. Confirmations that got to clients late caused a delay in the clients writing or mailing a check to pay for the transaction. If a client did not pay for their transaction by settlement day (remember there were no money market accounts or automatic transfer of funds in those days), the firm would have to pay for the securities purchased with its own money upon the receipt of the securities, either with its own cash on hand or borrowed monies at the overnight "broker loan rate." It's not that one or two unmatched trades a day amounted to much. It was, however, an add on to the general late payment/delayed delivery and pickup problems endemic at the time on Wall Street; part and parcel of the very reason many small firms and indeed Goodbody among others had gone under. If a brokerage firm had to borrow a couple of million dollars every business day at the broker loan rate of 6 percent because of accumulated delivery or late payment difficulties, that amounted to an annual expense of over one hundred thousand dollars, intolerable but unfortunately a cost of doing business that many firms then suffered from. An intolerable problem at another firm, although at Reynolds an anathema to its highly conservative management.

When they did occur, unmatched confirmations got immediate attention, and in December 1970, they happened to be my responsibility. Fixing them consisted of writing a note and having it teletyped to the branch office from which the trade emanated. Addressing the wire to the branch manager hopefully caused it to receive immediate attention. If the trade was known to the branch (because, of course, it could simply be a transmission error from any branch), we asked that the branch send us the client's name and address immediately so we could type the info onto the confirmation and get it out in the afternoon post, minimizing its lateness.

I would then carry the information into New Accounts just to let them know we followed up, and they should have already or would be receiving the New Account information soon. If we were told it was just a bad trade, the problem would take care of itself in that a cancel would be forthcoming shortly, and if it didn't, someone in DECAB would get after it and solve the problem.

When the merger of Goodbody and Merrill Lynch was finally consummated, two things happened. Some Goodbody salesmen who did not wish to be employed by Merrill Lynch came to work for Reynolds. The joke was they had an aversion to becoming soldiers in the armed services of Merrill Lynch, and in turn, many Goodbody clients didn't care to be Merrill Lynch clients for whatever reason. Whatever the case, the migration of Goodbody brokers and clients to Reynolds resulted in record numbers of new accounts being opened daily, dramatically increasing the inevitable flow of data over our wire system.

Oddly enough New York Stock Exchange volume was on the upswing at the time, which meant volume in the other equity markets, the AMEX and OTC, were also trading at increased levels of activity, further increasing the workload over the wire system. In any case, in late 1970 and early 1971, in January through March, DECAB's unmatched confirm problem grew from one or two unmatched confirms every two or three days to between twenty and thirty a day and reached nearly forty and on occasion fifty before the problem was resolved. I was handling the one or two odd unmatched confirm problems before this, so I had the job in its new proportion. In effect, unmatched confirms became my full-time job.

I dusted off a few file racks that were under a desk for who knows how long and used them to organize the unmatched confirms by date and sequential branch office order and then I began writing wires to branch managers. I wrote so many wires and notes to different people and branches with twenty or thirty of these things coming in every day that my right hand would become numb by midday. In cases when a branch might have seven or eight unmatched confirms, I called Long Distance, a no-no in those days. We didn't pick up the phone as easily than as we do now. We were mindful of the expense and the firm's policy, which amounted to "We're spending a fortune with AT&T on a wire system. Use the wire system, not the phone." But the Operations Management crowd didn't feel this way about unmatched confirmations hanging about. They wanted them addressed and in the mail as soon as possible. The trouble with phone calls in this situation was there was a good deal of detail in the relating of the individual transaction and account numbers and on and on. I'd be on the phone for a long time and handwriting omissions or other mishaps while infrequent sometimes compounded the problem. Information in hard copy form was preferable both for us and the branch. Using the phone was troublesome, so I tried to stick to writing the notifications and sending them over the wire and receiving same.

The biggest offenders, if you could call it that, were in Florida, especially our Pompano Beach, Miami, and Hallandale offices, but it was a firm-wide phenomenon. I was writing to twenty different offices a day all over the country, but the bulk came from Florida. Once the information came in, I gave it over to Eddy O's secretary with the confirms for typing and mailing. Lastly, the information was brought into the New Accounts Department just to keep them informed.

When the volume was up around thirty or forty unmatched confirms a day, the problem became a daunting task; shoveling you know what against the tide is an expression that comes to mind. Managers in the branches where the problem frequently occurred were very busy with the activity that was causing the problem; recruiting, interviewing and hiring new brokers. In addition to the attendant tasks of organizing housing within the branch for these brokers, perhaps meeting their biggest clients, procuring business cards while conferring with Legal and Compliance and so on. Even when other branch operatives; assistant managers or secretaries stepped into the breach to help us with the unmatched problems their unfamiliarity with these kinds problems slowed things down quite a lot.

In the meantime, several of the higher-ups in Operations Management began to stop by DECAB to view how we were handling the problem. I and the occasional helper assigned to me tried not to be unnerved by the disparaging looks cast our way and the over the racks of unmatched light blue customer confirmations. They whispered to each other conspiratorially, or so it seemed. It wouldn't be long, they said, before more serious problems and errors causing substantial monetary loss would begin to crop up. They went through the litany of late payment problems I described earlier with Eddy O and anyone who wanted to listen, and in turn, Eddy' O was all over me every day about keeping up until they figured out and implemented a solution to the problem. I stayed late when I could, but there was no overtime allotted to the problem. Frankly, overtime wasn't necessary. We got everything out to the branches every day. The branches were busy, it took time to gather and send us the info, then to type the confirms and so on. It was manual labor all around.

Two or three weeks into this storm, I got an idea. I created a form in long hand that I copied out on the Xerox machine. The wire operators complained it was unwieldy and sloppy, but it saved me a lot of time and effort. When I requested the form be printed professionally and made up into a pad so I didn't have to photocopy the damn things every morning (because the date had to change) or worse write everything out longhand, Eddy' O' followed through very quickly. No one could accuse Eddy O of being slow on the pick-up. This sounds like a simple and logical request and solution to a problem today, but in the seventies, it was a big deal to get pads made up. Just like the aversion to making long distance phone calls, it might be considered wasteful.

"Hey, why waste time and energy and money by taking the time to typeset a pad and send it to a printer to make up thirty pads of paper nobody will use? This problem is going to be over a in a few weeks and then what'll we do with all the wasted printed paper, throw it away?"

I don't think Eddy even mentioned it to anyone. He just wrote it up gave it to me to proof and walked it over to the print shop as a rush job. The form looked and read something like:

To: (branch office wire address)   Date:
Attention: (branch manager name)
From: (P. Scida, DECAB)   Tel:

The following transaction(s) T/D _____
was executed for acct. _____.

Mailing information was not available for this account.

1. Advice mailing information ASAP so we may post the client confirmation
2. Check that New Account data has been transmitted to NY.
3. Advise if you DK (don't know) this transaction, or if another problem exists, let us know ASAP.

Thank you.

                                                    _____
                                                    DECAB, NY

Once we got the form, most of the correspondence was written up and out of the way by eleven before lunch at the latest. If the unmatched that day were particularly heavy, I could recruit one of the other clerks to help out without taking him off other work for more than an hour or two. The form shifted the labor into the wire room that could disperse it among many operators while, in DECAB, it lightened the burden of having to write out the entire message long hand. By the time we finished filling out these forms, information was already coming in from branches, allowing us to turn many confirms around and out into the mail that same day, only a few hours after they would normally have been mailed. Before this, many of them simply piled up and didn't get out until the next day or even two days after their trade date. It also allowed me to get on the phone to push people along in their response to our communications rather than having to take or give detailed information. This faster response time and quicker turn around mollified management and gave them the peace of mind that the problem was being attended to in a timely manner. It got them off DECAB's back, and within two weeks of having printed the pads, I was copied in on a memo, a first for me, regarding some modifications to branch procedure regarding new account openings and trading protocol. In effect, the branch was prohibited from doing a trade in an account number for which new account information had not already been transmitted. Trade traffic took precedence over administrative traffic, which new account forms were considered, and so trades had been getting through but New Account info went in late or the next day. Hence, all the unmatched items.

After about eight weeks, unmatched confirmations went back to the trickle they had once been. It had been an interesting interlude and my introduction to crisis and emergency management. The form we had made up became SOP, and no one, including me, had a second thought about it.

Chapter 20

Account Change Methodology Reveals Reynolds Securities Back Office Identity

There is a reason why some Wall Street firms got along and prospered when the going got tough while others failed. Reynolds Securities was one of those firms that prospered and stayed ahead of the curve. Explaining operations procedure may be boring and pedantic. I'm risking that to tell another Reynolds story, in fact a story that illustrates the kind thinking that kept Reynolds Securities ahead of the curve and devoid of many of the problems other firms encountered.

The fourth floor at 2 Broadway was a beehive, a kaleidoscope of big and small departments carrying on and carrying out tasks and procedures in obvious high volume much the same as Eastman Dillon. Reynolds's back office, however, hummed more like Charlie Plohn's, in contrast to the slash and burn atmosphere I experienced at Eastman Dillon. Reynolds was also a more open and friendly place to work than Eastman, without the animosity, dissatisfaction, and anger exhibited by middle management. The space as well was more accessible in terms of its setup. The Order Room, wire room, and P&S were one huge expanse of space. At Eastman, the adjoining Order Room was walled off behind a petition of file cabinets and was considered a no-man's land for people who worked in the P&S or clearing departments. You could hear the phones slammed down on their receivers regularly and got the feeling that the guys in the order room would eat you alive if you said a word out of the way if you did venture back there. Plenty of practical jokes were played on unsuspecting clerks at Eastman Dillon, exacerbating the feeling to many that the Order Room was a place to stay away from. New hires were regularly sent into the order room with some stupid request. For example, to see the "bond stretcher," only to be dressed down and ridiculed. Early on at Eastman Dillon, I was told to bring in a towel and bathing suit because there was a pool on the thirtieth floor. Luckily, I was warned about the joke, saving myself some embarrassment.

At Eastman Dillon, walking over to Figurations to ask a question was greeted with a cold unfriendliness. At Reynolds, every place was open and everyone respected the jobs people were doing. I have worked in many places on many different jobs and have discovered there is something quite romantic, poetic even, about teamwork and work accomplished and about production and pride in it. Pride in effort extended in a job well done. There was that feeling at Reynolds.

My colleagues probably would have thought me quite insane were I to let on about my romantic view of work and production, but the thousands upon thousands of transactions and the hum of production made it exciting to be part of a group of people trying to maintain control over this vast body of activity that emanated from one hundred different locations around the country. I began to understand, after my adventure with the unmatched confirmations, how varied and complex the activity was, although on some days, it went so smoothly that it kind of put you to sleep and on others, it burst forward with a fierce intensity. One correction that was done hundreds of times a day caught my attention and fascinated me even after watching it happen repeatedly for months. Its execution was so smooth and seamless and, in reality, taken care of in a way that, to me, now embodies the Reynolds way of doing things.

To begin with, because humans touched a transaction from its first "handwritten" ticket in the branch, written up by a salesman to teletyping by a human for transmission and possibly a keypunch machine operator for processing, it's not hard to understand how easily one or two numbers in an eleven-digit client account number could be transposed in the process by any of the humans that had to physically type or write up the transaction. The law of averages dictates that on a busy day, there would be a screw up or two of this kind in most branches and many more at the home office. On high-volume days, anywhere from 150 to 350 of these kinds of mistakes could happen in the firm. If 50,000 trades were done in a day at the firm and a quarter of 1 percent of them were processed in the wrong account number, 125 corrections had to be made over the next few days, meaning each of these transactions would need to be canceled out of the erroneous account number and rebooked in their correct account numbers.

I discovered a big difference in how these adjustments were handled at Reynolds compared to Eastman Dillon. At Eastman, they were just problem trades like any other, and a clerk's time in New York would be taken up with the correction as any other might writing a cancel and a rebill. At Reynolds, they were recognized as a problem that required a more systemized, more automated (as automated as anything could be at the time) response. A system was developed that charged the branch with assisting the home office (DECAB) in writing the tickets that canceled the erroneous entry and processed the good one. As you will see, the processing and notation of the correction was streamlined minimizing the use of time and manpower. Duplicate transactions or transactions with quantity or price problems implied the possibility of monetary loss. Only DECAB was permitted to investigate and initiate corrections so branches did not initiate any correction on their own without the authority of New York. Account number changes, on the other hand, were deemed clerical, placing the correcting of the problem transaction under the responsibility of the branch.

Change of Account or "COC" corrections began with specifically designed paper in the machine on which DECAB received messages from branches. This paper was a triplicate carboned form perforated at its sides so that it could be dissembled. Further its middle sheet was perforated at its center and colored pink. When the COC correction was sent by the branch in a particular format (see below) the perforated pink middle sheet became the cancel and re-booking tickets of the change saving the labor of writing them up long hand. When ripping messages off the machine it was easy to differentiate between the formatted COC request and the inquiry to research other kinds of problems that took a prose form. See an illustration of the perforated two ticket middle form that ordered the change of account.

Cancel Ticket	Perf	Rebook Ticket
	I	
CXL	I	
BUY	I	BUY
5/19/69	I	5/19/69
as/of	I	as/of
5/18/69	I	5/18/69
500 shs	I	500 shs
IBM @ 61 5/8	I	IBM @ 61 5/8
ACCT	I	ACCT
102-44969-2-038	I	102-34469-2-038hus

All the COC clerk had to do was dissemble the form to get at the pink, look up the rebooking trade ticket to make sure it was the same except for the account number, note and initial the blotter entry and the date, and tear the tickets apart and send them into keypunch.

Two clerks processed COCs in DECAB. One was Joe Katz, a grizzled seventy-year-old who had been with the firm forever, in fact a wire operator and order clerk for some of the original partners back in the thirties, and a young Hispanic woman named Brunilda, or Brunie as we called her. She didn't speak much English as I remember, but she had been taught somehow to do COCs and she was a whiz at it. Amazingly, these two sometimes processed one hundred to one hundred fifty corrections a day, in effect the work of six or seven. Deep observation and thinking and the breaking down of operations into minute parts and then redesigning them in accordance with and using the technology available at the time fixed a problem at Reynolds that was costing other firms ten times as much in labor and had unknowable costs in monetary loss when some of these hand written corrections got out of hand.

Chapter 21

Institutional Stock Sales Snafu

After a year, perhaps 18 months in DECAB, mid to late 1971, I was a regular. I hadn't mastered bond corrections yet but I was a speedy clerk at what I knew which was listed trades and OTC. I didn't much care what I was asked to do, and if someone said I had to spend a day or two at the warehouse, I didn't complain even now. I had plenty of leeway around the floor and many friends, especially in options operations where some very cool people worked—Arnie Powel, Jim Cordo, and Charlie Sanicore among others. I can't tell you where they are now, but I can say that for the years I spent in DECAB, these guys were great. We had a lot of laughs, and I used to hang out/hide out a lot in their department and joke around. I also became a guy who could talk to people who were angry, nasty, or pissed off. They could be in a bother for any reason—a bollixed up, screw up of a trade problem, or a missed communication, whatever. I have a long fuse and so took all the weirdos and the people with heavy accents off my colleague's hands. Nothing bothered me. On occasion, major problems and challenges in the processing of business did come along, and tackling them, as we've seen, was DECAB's specialty.

It's difficult to remember exactly what the dates were of this next adventure, although it may have been around the spring or summer of 1971. After the appointment of a new sales manager in the firm's Institutional Stock Sales and Trading Operation, there was a marked increase in business and a corresponding increase in the amount of trades from that department processed in error. I heard it said that between 10 and 15 percent of the trades Equity Institutional was putting through for clients had to be corrected. The mistakes were all over the lot—wrong price, wrong account number, wrong quantity, buys for sells, take your pick. This was an ongoing problem the firm was living with and was causing mounting frustration and embarrassment for everyone connected to the operation. I didn't know what was happening or what the thinking was in the sales area from which the problem emanated, but it was creating quite a stir on the fourth floor at 2 Broadway with the Operations Management Group.

The new sales and business plan for the Institutional Sales and Trading Group was very successful and driven by a gifted sales manager named Al Hansen whom I got to know many years later. He was partnered with a trading manager, formerly of DECAB (several years hence), named Dave Mack. Despite the department's illustrious success, too many of its transactions resulted in corrections (i.e., cancels and rebilling). Increases in corrections of this type often caused worse screw-ups, resulting in the occasional nightmarish tangles of entries occurring in an account because of a mistake made in the processing of a correction. For example, think of a buy of one thousand shares cancelled as a sell. Now the erroneous cancel must be backed out, and the original erroneous trade must be canceled once again. These situations were not uncommon at the time, were confusing and difficult to figure out and often got out of hand. I had seen on several occasions more than 20 entries in an account caused by a single faulty correction otherwise meant to fix a single transaction. There was no doubt that when these situations occurred there had to be some client-firm fallout.

To a great degree I was still a wall-eyed clerk, doing what I was told, often not knowing the reason why. This happens a lot on Wall Street and probably in many other lines of work. The clerk or the sales assistant is told what to do or what to say in certain situations and when particular inquiries are made. He does rote tasks or repeats "stock answers" to frequently asked questions. The clerk really doesn't understand what he's doing or saying or even recommending until one day, after months or even years on the job, things just click. Voila! Eureka even!

This flash of insight happens at a point in time when experience, reading, conversation, training, writing, and the doing of one's job produces the famous "aha" moment that we've all had—the sudden realization and understanding of, in my case and in my future of, house accounting, currency exchange, commodity prices, margin and the calculation of free cash in a margin account aka SMA, selling group, accrued interest lag, and a hundred other things the reader can look up in any financial term glossary. Looking these things up and reading their definitions does not mean we understand them in their practical application. In my experience, one can read these definitions a million times over and not have a clue. It's only when you work with the concepts and they keep coming up every day that they eventually come alive and one's mind, through its experience, becomes disposed to true comprehension and a cohesive understanding of the component within the overall organism. It's also true that even when one understands these concepts, one cannot explain them. That ability may or may not come in time.

For example, I didn't really understand the meaning and purpose of tasks I had regularly performed in connection with securities transactions at Charles Plohn. What I did remember was all orders of five hundred shares or more of listed stocks coming from the branch system, meaning transactions done on the floor of the NYSE or ASE, were screened prior to processing and compared to their corresponding floor reports, which were brought up to P&S by runners throughout the day. I would often help out with this task in the afternoon after my comparison work was done. It was not routine to pick up price and quantity discrepancies between orders and floor reports, but it happened often enough. The floor report is the actual document filled out by the trader on the floor of the exchange upon execution. At Plohn, this checking process ensured almost a flawless daily processing of listed stock trades. Presently at Reynolds, wire operators at our offices on the exchange floors teletyped the floor executions (information taken off the original floor reports) back to Institutional Sales.

After days and days and weeks of correcting these erroneous trades coming out of Institutional Equity Sales, one afternoon, I off-handedly mentioned the screening process at Charlie Plohn to my boss, Eddy O'Donnell. He was standing around near my desk, ripping messages off the machine. I casually mentioned how I used to help Manny Rodriguez out in the afternoons at Plohn matching up customer orders with floor reports.

In a flash, really just a few days later, a second teletype machine was installed in DECAB next to the one on which we received our branch correspondence and COCs. Once installed and tested, we began receiving simultaneous drop off copies of every floor report that was sent to institutional trading from the floors of the NYSE and Amex. When this new flow of traffic was proceeding smoothly, I was given the task of setting up several racks and sorting the reports in alphabetical order by name of stock and chronology of order number and time of execution. It was arranged then with Institutional Stock Trading that all their customer orders were now to be sent through DECAB rather than automatically processed so we would be able to match orders to floor reports and pick up blatant discrepancies.

"Just like old times at Charlie Plohn," I thought,

The day came when the full plan went into action. Floor reports began coming back almost as soon as the market opened. Orders with account numbers, however, didn't start coming in until around eleven o'clock. A typical situation for example might involve floor reports relating to a single order that was consummated with several executions. The order in this case #IN 20 to sell 10000 shares of IBM and the three floor reports relating to the execution of the order and later the three entries that were processed on the firm's books which would also produce confirmations to the client with the details of the transactions. The details below show the floor reports of the transactions done to satisfy IN 20 selling 10000 shares of IBM.

IN 20 Sold 7,000 IBM @91 leaves 3,000
IN 20 Sold 2,000 IBM @90 7/8ths leaves 1,000 and finally
IN 20 Sold 1,000 IBM @90 ¾

As orders came through, I would naturally be able to sort out the correct ones and send them into keypunch for processing. As the day wore on, there were single orders and groupings of orders and floor reports that couldn't be matched. For example, in the case of the order and executions above, I might have orders for an account number to sell:

Sold 7,000 shares IBM at 90 7/8
Sold 2,000 shares IBM at 91
Sold 1,000 shares IBM at 90 3/4

Clearly a mismatch had occurred somewhere along the line. The prices on the 2000 share portion of the order was being put through on the 7000 share portion of the order and vice versa.

The day we went live with this manual report/order match system, we picked up thirty-five or forty discrepancies from the three hundred odd orders executed by Institutional Sales that day. A call was made to Institutional Sales to report each discrepancy found. The wire operators and sales assistants assigned to the salesman and traders researched the problems we passed on to them, and if indeed there was a mistake, they were required to send new corrected orders—a good deal of extra work for these folks and a boatload of embarrassment.

There was an explosively silent reaction to these discoveries. After the first four or five problems were communicated, I fantasized that the phone wires were going to burst into flame. The next day, all the clerks and everyone connected with the processing of these transactions in Institutional Sales as well as the traders on the floor and the sales people went on a kind of special alert, checking and rechecking the details of the orders they worked on. In one day, there was immediate and dramatic results. I mean, if we started checking floor reports against orders on Wednesday, by Friday afternoon and Monday morning, the workflow in the form of inquiries to check on or correct erroneous trades went from a blizzard to less than a flurry. By the end of the following week, the error rate for Institutional Sales transactions fell to less than 3 percent when in recent weeks it had been in the 10 to 15 percent range.

Like the unmatched confirmation problem solved previously, the floor report/order match fix was a momentous event on the floor and got me some recognition. Some of the execs from senior management in operations now, said hello when we met in the halls. I'm sure I developed a little more confidence in myself as far as my work was concerned. In any case, I always looked and spoke and carried myself with confidence, but often it was far from how I felt. I was developing, however, a sort of intuitiveness about work that I may not have been completely aware of. A sort of calmness about things that it was all about getting through the rough spots, and that in this place, at least, in operations on Wall Street, the problems were two for the penny, almost always solvable and the nature of our existence. Again, it's easy to know now and articulate, but then, as I have said and will repeat again and again, at the time, I knew next to nothing, and most of the time, when I did know something, as was the case with my off-handed remark to Eddy'O about screening orders at Charlie Plohn, I didn't know I knew it.

Chapter 22

Mike L. Comes to DECAB

Soon after the Institutional Equity trade problems got fixed, Eddy O'Donnell was promoted to manage the operations on the Institutional Equity Desk at 120 Broadway. I was twenty-eight years of age while most of my co-workers were in their early twenties. The managers like Eddie O and Craig Sarch, Eddies number two were closer to my age. My awareness of the political value and potential personal benefit that might have come from my suggestions to screen Institutional Trading's transactions or organize the process of resolving the "unmatched confirm" problem with a form letter/wire was nil. Neither did it cross my mind that I might have been the catalyst for my boss's promotion to operations manager for the Institutional Stock Trading and Sales Desk and that an added starter for the position had been resolving the unmatched confirmation problem.

As I mentioned earlier, promotion or moving on to greener pastures may have been a fantasy or daydream of mine, but the chance of it becoming a reality I don't think ever crossed my mind. I had enough to think about just hanging onto the job at Reynolds. I dreaded the thought of losing it, as the Charlie Plohn experience was ever fresh in my mind, kept here by the news of a constant stream of firms closing. The Goodbody debacle was joined by the merger of Walston & Co. and DuPont, which eventually failed as Ross Perot was trying to save it from total disaster, proving that Humpty Dumpty couldn't be put back together. Loeb Rhodes and Glore Forgan failed, and Stone Webster was taken over and morphed into Shearson by Sandy Weil & Co. whose crew got the operations right finally. On another front, Eastman Dillon was absorbed into Blythe & Co., which would eventually become part of PaineWebber, not to mention a legion of smaller firms, Charlie Plohn lookalikes falling by the wayside. How I felt after losing my job at Plohn often crossed my mind, especially the fact that I had this job through sheer luck. Had I made the call to Reynolds's Personnel Department a day or two earlier, or later, I might have wound up back in the auto body shop with my brother-in-law John.

With Eddy O'Donnell's move to Institutional Trading at 120 Broadway, Craig Sarch, Eddy's number two, temporarily took over the management of DECAB. Just saying that Craig was an exemplary person is not an adequate description of the man. With Craig Sarch, one knew very quickly that he was a good soul through and through, and besides this, he was, in the estimation of many, brilliant. He had a complete and thorough knowledge of every phase of everything we did in DECAB as well as cashiering, Stock Record, P&S, and the Order Room. In effect, he had a PhD in Wall Street back office operations, and he was articulate, a skill that many operations personnel were lacking. There was no question he didn't have the answer to and no problem he wouldn't help you with within a moment of asking. Craig had an endless amount of patience, good cheer, and a great laugh. He was also a huge hockey fan who often got tickets from the brass, allowing me to see live hockey at the Garden. These were not the lavish evenings I spent with my former Charlie Plohn colleagues but no less welcome or enjoyable. Instead of cocktails at Gallagher's 33 with Mario or Tom Francis, Craig and I went to Tad's Steakhouse where we alternately ate the most tender (it was the luck of the draw) or the toughest grilled steak imaginable and a baked potato for $1.69. The beer was extra. Life was good.

A week or two after Eddy O' moved to Institutional, (it may have been a month or two) Mike Losquadro, one of my former supervisors and assistant manager of P&S at Charlie Plohn, came walking through DECAB with the manager of P&S, Mike De Canto. We greeted each other cordially of course, and although it wasn't explained to me in detail, I learned over the next few days that Mike was either taking or being considered for the job as manager of DECAB. De Canto, a serious, well-intentioned, impeccably dressed man in his sixties had once mentioned to me when he heard I had worked for Plohn that Losquadro, way back when, had been a protégé of his here at Reynolds. A week after our encounter in DECAB, Mike Losquadro took the job, and while we did not become friends away from the office, we got on quite well as manager and subordinate.

Looking back on those days it now makes sense to me that management might want to bring in an outsider like Mike Losquadro. They might have thought that the liaison function DECAB had with the branch offices and the product departments as well as Accounting and Compliance, required a more polished executive. Perhaps they felt that a senior clerk, which was what Craig appeared to be, albeit a genius at the workings of the firm, wouldn't do for the job anymore. They were not willing either to take Craig under their wing and groom him into what they wanted. The gambling incident as well, the very reason I was hired had happened on Craig and Eddies watch had also perhaps left a bad taste in managements mouth. I'm sure Craig was put out at having been passed over for Mike, but he never showed it or said anything about it to me. I think also that management felt DECAB required some changes perhaps a cleaning up of sorts and that a less familiar personage than Craig be employed in this effort.

I had had several confrontations with Mike at Plohn involving my having dropped the ball on certain corrections where some small monetary losses were involved. I thought those incidents might color our present association, but it didn't at all. We were very cordial, and our relationship began with his asking me, quite often actually, who this fellow was and what I thought of him and where this was and where that was. I would run an errand for him or make a call whenever he wanted, and I made it a point to introduce him to my friends in Options Operations, Jim Cordo and company as I thought that they would be simpatico. I had no special projects going on, and because the fellow who acted as liaison to the Municipal Bond Department overseeing their corrections and problems had moved on somewhere, I was being schooled by Craig in the nomenclature and components of bond description and assisting him in doing the bond corrections. The Muni Department was very active, and the subject matter, at least I thought, was complex. I was having a little trouble with the work, and I always made the math a problem even if it wasn't because I didn't have much confidence in myself despite my admonitions to the contrary. In those days, municipal bond calculations were often done using a "basis book," which was a book of mathematical tables (often eight hundred to one thousand pages) used to convert yields to equivalent dollar price and the reverse, dollar price to yield. Bond calculators were expensive and rare outside bond departments, and some firms used a basis book exclusively. The Municipal Bond Departments liaison to DECAB was considered a tough cookie as well, so it was no surprise that I became next in line to work with her. I was sure she promptly concluded I was a dolt after one or two conversations.

Chapter 23

A New Broom: Opportunity Knocks

There was no shortage of characters in operations at Reynolds Securities or Eastman Dillon nor, for that for that matter, at Charlie Plohn. The main difference between the larger shops and Plohn was the tone of behavior was somewhat more subdued, more reserved, at Plohn compared to the outright raucousness that might be tolerated at Reynolds or Eastman. Mike Losquadro, on the other hand, when he joined Reynolds, brought in a sense of decorum those of us already there were less used to. While you couldn't call Mike Losquadro a stiff or straight-laced, his approach to the job was serious without much room for joking around, meaning, for example, that he rarely removed his suit coat, would walk across a room rather than run or shuffle, and would never shout across a room over people. Instead, he'd walk across to speak to you. Because of this attitude, it should have been clear certain behaviors were not going to be tolerated as we shall see.

Six or so months before Losquadro was hired, Brune Aponte, the young lady doing the COCs with Joe Katz had left to have a baby, and a fellow we'll call Mike A. was hired to take her place. Mike A. was in his late thirties to early forties, competent and good at his work. He was also a very funny guy, prone to loud joking, making animal sounds, and various antics. He had a darker side in that he got upset easily when things didn't go his way or when he was disagreed with at length, and at these times, he would frown, sulk, and even talk to himself and stutter before getting over it.

The pattern in which COCs came into DECAB over the teletype was that one found a stack of them to process upon arrival in the morning and then, toward the market opening, they slacked off or trickled in until an hour or so after the opening when they picked up again. Joe Katz never sat idle, so on most mornings after the stack was dispatched, Joe took care of the few that trickled in while Mike A. read the papers. He would spread the *Daily News* or the *Times* across one of the idle desks in the department and scan each page, slowly and deliberately turning them one by one as if he were sitting at his own kitchen table. No one thought anything of it because neither Craig nor Eddy said a word about it or stopped him from doing it. I guessed that was because his job was exclusively COCs and Joe Katz's backup, so when he had downtime, reading the papers wasn't a problem for them.

Well, it wasn't long before for Mike Losquadro told Mike A. straight up, "Get rid of the newspaper."

The first time Losquadro mentioned it, Mike A. asked what the problem was.

He was told, "We can't have management walk through the department and find people reading the papers. They'll think we have nothing to do."

Mike A. replied, "Why? Nobody said anything about it before. Eddy and Craig were okay with it."

"Well, I'm not Eddy or Craig. Just get rid of the newspaper. It doesn't look right," was the coolly delivered retort by Losquadro, and he walked away.

Muttering and sulking, Mike A. disposed of his paper. However, he continued to read the paper whenever he had some downtime in the morning. There was a sort of electricity in the air because additional confrontation between the two Mikes seemed certain.

Joe Katz, Mike A.'s partner in COCs, was a very witty old guy himself with a naturally loud voice who kept things light, rarely, if ever, getting serious, though on occasion, his comic tone turned serious in an instant. He suggested to Mike that the new boss didn't want that anymore, and these days, when management saw idleness, they wanted answers immediately. Firms are going out of business left and right. Mike A. blew him off. I was amazed at this outright defiance and in-your-face behavior. A few days later, Losquadro again told Mike to put the paper away. There was certainly an implication that Mike A was risking his job. The sulking began anew, and the muttering got louder. Mike A. did not hide his anger in any way. If anything, he became openly defiant. I got the feeling Mike A. thought Losquadro would relent and give in, thinking Losquadro would have to accept the circumstances of his new job.

Somebody said he was deliberately trying to provoke Losquadro so that he'd punch him in the nose and then he'd have a lawsuit against the firm. Whatever was in Mike A.'s head, I knew sooner or later, Losquadro was going to come out on top. Within two weeks of Mike Losquadro's arrival, certainly in less than a month, Mike A. was gone. There wasn't much talk about it, although there was plenty of quiet resentment.

"Who the hell was he to come in here and fire one of us" was the refrain. However, the incident faded in light of a new one.

Several part-time workers were employed by DECAB to file everything from order tickets to corrections records and a host of other documents. Some of the part-timers, high school students, came in at two or three in the afternoon, staying three or four hours a day and leaving by eight. The others were postal employees who came in once their shift at the post office was over at five or six o'clock and stayed until ten to eleven and sometimes even until midnight we were told. They were a sort of fixture in the department that one knew were there but took little notice of in the grand scheme of things. I was a bit off balance whenever I encountered one of these guys because I didn't quite know their names or how they belonged there, but their body language had an authority all its own that attested to their right to be there.

Well, leave it to Mike L. to hang around the office until all hours of the night to find out that on most nights, these guys punched in, hung around for an hour or two, and left to put in a few more hours at the post office, stopping back around eleven or later to punch out. Naturally, they were fired, and after a while, an analysis of the work they had been assigned to do was deemed unnecessary. We simply began to bundle and label the stuff they pretended to file in boxes and, when a month's worth accumulated, shipped them off to the warehouse. The news of letting these guys go didn't take long to hit the office grapevine. The incident was another negative stripe on Mike Losquadro's arm alongside the one for firing Mike A. Another for Losquadro's ushering in a sort of "new office decorum"—that serious demeanor mentioned earlier. I'm sure upper management in operations sanctioned this cleanup of personnel, and perhaps knew their minds about it before even hiring Mike L. But to me and my co-workers it was that was transparent and all of this was Mike Losquadro's doing.

Shortly after Mike Losquadro's arrival, long planned systems and hardware installations began to come about in the spring and summer of 1972. Graphic terminals known as Bunker Ramo machines, crude precursors of the PCs and Bloomberg Terminals that populate brokerage and business offices today, were being placed throughout the firm. More importantly, the newest IBM super computers were being installed in New York and linked electronically to the wire teletype systems facilitating direct feed of order entry data into computers, skipping the keypunch-card process for many, many operations. Space required for the data processing departments to expand meant DECAB, which was physically positioned between the combined Order Room/ P&S and the Trade Processing/Keypunch areas, had to move to a different location on the floor to facilitate the modifications.

Moving is always an arduous task, and when crunch time comes, employees are usually responsible for packing up boxes with the contents of their desks (i.e. the materials they work with day to day and their personal possessions). These boxes are then transported by professional movers. In this instance, because we were moving to quarters a hundred feet away, employees were expected to transport a lot of the loose items such as in and out boxes, file racks, bound books as well as some of the smaller office furniture such as chairs and the like. Mike Losquadro, our recently appointed manager in DECAB, as we've described, had not gotten off on the right foot, and so was not able to generate much enthusiasm or help for the move from his rank and file over and above the packing up of their own personal stuff into moving boxes and labeling them.

"Why help management's hatchet man?" was most probably their feeling after Mike A. and the part-timers were let go at the new manager's instigation."

From the firm's point of view, why should it care if people were dismissed over cheating on hours worked or defiance of work rules? It didn't bother me. I was too busy with my own life and work and was not averse to playing by the rules set up by others. I did, however, feel for Mike. In our previous association, despite our differences, I had observed how he (and Mario) agonized over every one of the employees that had to be let go at Charles Plohn, me included. In the Wall Street of that period though, the most respected managers, in a matter of weeks and days, became subjects of ridicule and hate. When the market is going down the drain, everything goes with it—jobs, position, rational thinking, respect, and sensible behavior—when it's really no one's fault but simply the conditions we are forced to operate under. It's also universal that the rank and file want the money and perks enjoyed by management but, in general, have little sympathy, or stomach for that matter, for the duties and responsibilities associated with being the boss or the manager. Not many people want to have to deal with firing an employee from a job as Mike had too. It's not easy, although it is unavoidable at times. It's easier though, I think, to fire someone for cause than it is to lay people off. I agreed with Losquadro regarding the part-timers lying about their hours and even with Mike A.'s refusal to put away the newspapers. I understood his point of view completely. It was a clear attempt at defiance that couldn't be let go. The guy doing it, Mike A., was a great guy and a good worker but just hated change of any kind even though his common sense should have prevailed. My coworkers didn't see it that way or didn't care, to them it was all the new managers doing. Frankly, if I had known about the part-timers cheating, which was known by a few people, I would have probably blown the whistle on them myself. Again, the more larcenous people around scoped these things out, cynically guessing something wasn't right. I of course had a blind spot. As a rule, I always thought most people had honorable intentions and was usually the last to pick up on people's bad intensions.

As far as the move to new quarters was concerned, I was the only person to volunteer to help Mike out besides Craig who had too. I took a Friday night off from delivering pizzas and went in on Saturday morning to help, emptying out a few idle desks and file cabinets and other stuff. I remember pushing wheeled office chairs awkwardly piled with blotters and metal file separators and in and out baskets through the hallways. It got done, and that was that.

Just a week or two after the move, maybe even sooner, Losquadro pulled me aside and mentioned he really appreciated all the help and support I had given him the few months he was there. I thought he was going to give me a raise, and I was touched in a way because even though Mike and I were on good terms, this expression of gratitude seemed to hold great sincerity. It wasn't a raise he wanted to tell me about though. Instead, he informed me of an opening in the Municipal Bond Department for an operations clerk on the trading desk. Further, he insisted there was "no need to think about it."

He said, "Go up for the interview, and if they offer you the job, take it."

When I questioned him about the job, what he'd heard about it, and what kind of people were there, he brushed all my questions aside.

"What's that got to do with anything?" he shot back at me. "These opportunities don't come about that often," he went on. "That's all you have to know." Handing me a sheet of paper with a name and phone number to call on it to set up the interview, he said, "Who knows what a position like this could lead to?"

Riding the subway home that evening, I vividly recalled the last time I'd heard those words spoken. It was when Rosalie told me to call Mario, her boss's brother, at Eastman Dillon a few years back. With a flashing smile and her bright eyes shining, she said, "Who knows what this could lead to, baby?"

That evening, I told Rosalie about my conversation with Mike, and she didn't miss history repeating itself either. We had a good laugh, but it was also a sobering moment because so much had happened since she suggested I call and go see Mario. Later in the quiet evening hours after little Pat was asleep, we continued the discussion, especially Mike's pointed advice.

Rosalie said, "So when will you call this guy in what department was it?"

"Tomorrow. Tomorrow, and its Municipals. Municipal Bonds."

"Mun-iss-sipple Bonds, huh," she said, accenting the word the way some people do, lengthening the middle syllable. "What are Mun-iss-sipple bonds anyway?"

"I'm not really sure, babe, but I think we do a lot of business in them because I see them all over the blotters. I've been doing a lot of work with them lately. They stand out because they're named after every city and state in the country, and I think they're pretty complicated," was my reply.

"That's okay. You'll figure it out. You'll get the job too. Mike is helping you out because of all the help you've given him," she said.

"You think so?"

"Don't be silly, Pat. Of course he is."

Chapter 24

You Have No Grandma?

Each time I thought of my impending interview in the Reynolds Securities Municipal Bond Department, it was accompanied by a slight attack of nerves. When I brought my apprehension to Mike Losquadro, the instigator of the event, he reminded me of how well I had gotten along with the management at Charles Plohn & Co., our former employer. I drew some confidence from Mike's remarks, but Plohn was a much smaller and more intimate place where front and back offices worked more closely and therefore became more familiar with one another. A big firm like Reynolds Securities had a very impersonal feel to it. Unlike Charles Plohn & Co., here at Reynolds, there was something of a barrier between the management of operations and the clerks, so I imagined an even higher wall between the front and back offices.

When I brought this up, Mike said, "Baloney! I never noticed you having a problem making conversation with anyone here or at Plohn, so don't conjure up some imaginary problem that's not gonna happen unless you cause it to happen. Just relax and be yourself."

"Okay. Okay, Mike, I got it," I replied.

"And don't clip your answers down to one or two words either. Just be clear, precise, conversational, and to the point. You want to appear to be intelligent despite what we all know."

All good advice, but I was still wary of the difference in "social class" many of my coworkers in operations seemed to think existed between the front office, sales and trading, and the back office, the clerical end of the Street. Inevitably, the day of the interview came, and when it did, I scrubbed up, put on my best blue suit, and appeared at the duly appointed time at 120 Broadway on the twelfth floor.

My initial contact was one William "Bill" Kondratuck, vice president and comanager of the Municipal Bond Department, whom I'd never heard of or spoken to before. He spotted and waved me in almost immediately as I paused a moment in the open doorway. After a firm handshake and brief introductions, we got right into it. Bill asked no detailed questions about bonds or what I knew about them. How long was I at the firm, what was I doing in DECAB, and what had I done at what other firms was what he wanted to know. This was information I had down pat. Mike L. had coached me, and his advice was to know where I had worked and what I had done and be able to explain why I'd left those places and how I wound up at Reynolds. Easy questions, simple and true facts, nothing to fake, and the result was to put me somewhat at ease.

Next a few remarks about hours and some very generic questions about the properties of bonds that came up briefly and some innocuous social banter. It took less than ten minutes to get comfortable and feel that I'd made a good impression. The next question near floored me.

"How many grandmothers do you have?" Kondratuck asked directly.

"Excuse me…sir?" I replied, following a confused pause. Then I said, "Sir, I'm sorry, I don't understand."

"You heard me. It's a simple question. How many grandmothers do you have?" he said again, looking straight at me.

"Well…er…" I said, still confused. Then seriously, "All my grandparents have passed, and in reality, I only knew one of them, my gran…"

Laughing now with great gusto, Kondratuck, a short, thickset man wearing horn-rimmed glasses is now holding a large fat-fingered hand out in front of my face like a traffic cop signaling me to stop. Smiling broadly, still laughing, cracking up in fact, he says, "Just fooling around, kiddo. A little joke. The last guy we had up here from your neck of the woods called in three times in six months to say he wasn't coming in because his grandmother died, ha ha ha ha, and he had to go to the funeral, ha ha ha ha. I just had to ask the question." He was laughing still and obviously terribly pleased with himself.

For my part, I was still a little confused and didn't know what to think, much less say. I was in a serious state of mind, expecting serious questions, and failed to see the humor in it all, especially since several people at the desks around us were smiling and even chuckling with my interviewer who seemed to be having such a good time. Laughter of course is contagious unless you happen to be the object of it, which I felt at the moment that I was.

I thought, who the hell are these people? I don't mind a joke on me when I'm among friends, but these guys are strangers. Maybe my coworkers had a point about what these so-called "white shoes" thought of us.

Maybe a frown came over my face because Kondratuck, somewhat more serious now, said, "Take it easy, kiddo. No offence, nothing personal, just having a little fun. You get the joke, doncha?" He was smiling now.

"Yes, sir. I guess I do," I think I said, somewhat reluctantly.

Now looking a bit askance at me but still smiling, Kondratuck called out to his comanager, William "Bill" Devlin somewhere behind me and to the right, asking if he wanted to speak to me. I didn't have much time then to think about the grandmother question anymore as I was quickly ushered over to Bill Devlin's desk for phase two of the interview.

Bill Devlin sat at an imperially positioned corner desk from which he could view the entire department he had command over. Devlin, when he spoke, sounded almost exactly like Ronald Coleman, the great movie star of *Lost Horizon* fame, albeit with a somewhat smoky raspy quality to his voice minus the British accent. Devlin enunciated the English language perfectly with great expression just as Coleman did. He even looked like Coleman with silver-streaked slicked-back hair, a lined longish face, and a very neatly trimmed pencil-line mustache. I was never sure in later years whether he affected the Ronald Coleman persona purposely or whether it was natural. In any case, it was appealing, and it never seemed put on or to get old.

Bill wanted to know where I lived and what my father had done for a living. I said I was born in Brooklyn, still lived there, and my father had retired from the New York City Department of Sanitation. Though I quickly added that my brother worked at a naval architectural firm and was a graduate of Brooklyn Tech. I had to show that we peasants were moving on in the world. This mention of my brother Dominick's alma mater drew Devlin out a bit because he said, "That's good. Brooklyn Tech's a fine school." I think he might have told me he was a graduate of Tech as well, but I'm not sure. "Where did *you* go to high school?" he then said pointedly.

"Charles Evans Hughes here in Manhattan," I said and added, "Which used to be known as Textile."

"Yesss," he drawled affectedly. "*Used* to be a good school too."

I didn't respond, although I would have lied and said I had a Regents Diploma if he asked. It was a GED, and I only got it because I went to summer school to finish up several courses required to get it. When I said I lived on Clarendon Road in Brooklyn, he livened up a bit more and said that he had lived for some time or grown up on Farragut Road just a few avenues away. He asked how I got to work (what subway I took) and what parish I was in and told me he'd had been to mass on several occasions at St. Raymond's which was my parish, but he normally attended church in another parish whose name I don't recall.

"What did you do after high school," he said, asking the inevitable question.

I mentioned that I'd attended FIT for a while and worked for a dress manufacturer for several years, but for three years prior to my employ at Eastman Dillon, I worked in an auto body and fender shop owned by my brother-in-law.

"In Brooklyn?"

"Yes, close really. Avenue I and Nostrand."

"Where I see all those taxis?" he was obviously familiar with the turf.

"Right, yes my brother-in-law John had his own shop there just across the street from the taxi company."

After he asked about and I explained in a little more depth how I got from the auto body shop to Reynolds, somehow, we backtracked and got onto cars and driving around Brooklyn and Manhattan. I mentioned I often drove in on Fridays and took the Brooklyn Bridge into Manhattan to avoid the Battery Tunnel toll and parked under the East Riverside Drive near the Fulton Fish Market for only $3.50. He seemed truly amazed at that and said he was going to try it and went on to say he sometimes drove to the city from Long Island the back way through Atlantic Avenue, a route I knew well. He went on to give me the address of the house he had lived in on Farragut Road and inquired as to how the neighborhood was holding up.

The interview with Devlin had become an amiable and friendly conversation between Brooklynites, and in fact, part of me was reeling. All I could think about at this point was this interview with the senior VP in charge of Reynolds Municipal Bond Department was amazingly resonant of my first interview at Reynolds in the bowels of the Operations Division in DECAB a few years back with another Brooklynite Eddy O'Donnell and his hometown crew. It was the old Brooklyn thing again, minus the cussing, the offering of a "kintainer of koffee," and the Brooklyneese.

Suddenly, the interview took a different turn, somewhat more serious, but comical in a way. Bill's next statements were about salary, and I was sure afterward he might have thought I was a complete idiot in spite of the friendly banter we had engaged in a few moments earlier. It stemmed from the fact that I never thought of my salary in terms of annual earnings. It was $145 a week, and I thought of it in that way and always stated it that way.

"We can't do any better than $9,750 a year," Bill said firmly.

Although I was good at ordinary numbers, I couldn't conjure up in my head what my present salary was when annualized or how it stacked up against the $9,750 Devlin was offering. I had never even thought of calculating what my salary was annually. Mine was a week-to-week lower-class mentality. Now, Bill is staring at me and I'm staring at the wall behind him, desperately trying to divide

$9,750 by 52 first and then 24 because that's how many pay periods there were in a year. Drawing a blank my nerves got the best of me I guess, and even if I came up with an answer, I wouldn't have said it for fear of being wrong.

After a few minutes of awkward silence, Bill said rather sternly, "Well?"

"Okay!" I said, quitting my internal calculations and recalling what Mike L., my mentor and chief backer, had said over and over, which I didn't really believe until this "duh" moment.

"If they offer you the job, *take it*."

Visibly annoyed and probably thinking I was an ingrate because I thought the offer wasn't good enough, Bill began shuffling papers and just before I was going to say "that's fine, sir," he said finally, "We'll let you know." Or something to that effect."

It was said in a definitely stern and dismissive tone. I rose thanking him for the time, and we shook hands quite stiffly. Next I walked over to shake hands with Bill Kondratuck before leaving and to thank him too, the mentioning of my grandma's totally forgotten. At my approach, he moved the phone he was holding away from his mouth, and smiling broadly, he shook my hand, saying, "Hey, kiddo, you don't have to call me sir. See you soon."

I had such a powerful desire to pull up a chair. I wanted to hang out and BS as I did in that first interview years earlier with Eddy O'Donnell. Clearly that was out of the question with this crowd. The atmosphere was very different here than at 2 Broadway.

When I got down to the lobby, I bought a newspaper and, with my trusty nineteen-cent BIC pen, scribbled a quick calculation to find out what $9,750 a year translated to weekly. The fact that it was close to $190 a week and represented a near $50 a week raise was flipping great, notwithstanding that in those days, I often earned $200 and more in an extended weekend delivering pizzas.

"Wow, what could the two combined be a year?" I thought, quickly scribbling another calculation and realizing that between both jobs, my weekends delivering pizza and my day job at Reynolds, I would be earning near twenty thousand dollars a year; in the eighteen to nineteen thousand a year range anyway, if I got this job?

There was something then after all to thinking about one's earnings on an annual basis. Twenty thousand dollars a year had a wonderful ring to it.

Even more important, it was plain to see and hear the serious atmosphere in the rooms I had just left. To be sure, there was a certain levity in my interview with the Bond Departments two Bills, but I could feel the drive in the room from the drone of the conversation around me while I was there, along with the ubiquitous ring of telephones and ever-clacking teletype printers. Not that P&S or the Corrections Department I worked in wasn't serious or businesslike, but the roar was different. There were no yells or catcalls in Municipals, no boisterousness, no one passing through stopping to chat idly or asking about the line on the Giants game. At least that wasn't what I had heard. The Bond Department had a different music to it, more formal perhaps, more of a hum than a roar but driven just the same. It was my thing to imagine and give romantic character to the world turning around me, but the truth of the moment was for the first time since Mike had broached the idea of my going to work in Municipals, I began to get really excited about it. The question was whether the two Bills would consent to hire me after that rollercoaster of an interview? I had a strong feeling they would, but there was enough doubt to worry me just a little.

Exiting 120 Broadway and walking back down to Two, I prayed silently that God might grant me this request. It took me about fifteen minutes to get back, but in that short time, a message had been forwarded to my desk, directing me to call Anne Mulaney, the secretary for the two Bills. When I called, she said I had been hired, and I should work out with my boss when I could start. Both Bills had said the sooner, the better.

Mike L. said, "Get out! Go! Pack up your shit and go. Take the rest of the week off and start Monday."

But I didn't take all the time off I could have. Instead I decided to hang out and do as many municipal bond corrections as had to be done and suck up as much advice as I could from my comanager Craig Sarch about municipal bonds in the few days I had left here.

The Operations Division of Reynolds Securities was a sprawling affair that took up the entire fourth floor of 2 Broadway. In my capacity as a corrections clerk, I got to interact with people in the various sub departments around the floor in the Cage, Stock Record, the Order Room, and the Dividend Department. In the few days I had left in operations between the Tuesday of the interview and Friday at the end of that week, the word got around that I was going up to 120 Broadway. While my immediate coworkers were somewhat closemouthed about it, several of the middle-management types, the fellows who managed these smaller departments, made a point of congratulating me and wishing me luck. One or two even came around looking for me to do so. Besides these, there were the old-timers I had come in contact with who were still clerks, albeit senior clerks who'd been with the firm twenty and in some cases near thirty years. While the middle-management crowd patted me on the back and congratulated, the old-timers admonished me, saying things like "Okay, you made it out of operations. Now make something of yourself" and "Gettin' by the interview is one thing, makin' the grade is another."

Another said, "When Joe went up, and he was a bright kid you know, he couldn't handle it and puked out. So watch yourself."

It was like your old Uncle Sam who after hearing you'd gotten 92 percent on a math test asked what happened to the other 8 percent. One woman, Beverly, who had a penchant for poking and even pinching you if you made a mistake or an untoward remark said to me. "Where you're going, they think we're idiots down here. Worse, maybe even animals. It's up to you to show them different. Don't screw it up. You're representing us." Pinch!

The way these folks were talking it was as if moving to work at 120 Broadway was a sacred mission, like being chosen to come forth out of the wilderness into the sight of God. How had I arrived at this point some three or four years after that first job at Eastman Dillon? Actually, I didn't try to answer that question. I never even asked it until a couple of years ago when I began to reflect on my life and career and set out to write this book, and of course, here is the answer.

The cakewalk interview I had had with Mario a few years before this was the same as the interview in Municipals. The fix was in, again. Mario Ruocco, who gave me that first job on Wall Street and the guy I'd worked for at Eastman Dillon and later at Charles Plohn & Co., hired me based on his sister's recommendation and her desire to help my wife whom she loved. Mike Losquadro and other people from operations, I found out later, Mike De Canto told Bill Devlin, "This is the guy you want to hire. He learns fast, and he's loyal and will do what you whatever you need him to do. He'll come up with the answers. It's not rocket science after all, and he's smart enough to use his contacts here to back himself up." I'm sure they added that they'd keep an eye on me as well.

While I had by this time done quite a few corrections for the Muni Bond Department, I still had no idea what municipal bonds actually were, which made me a little nervous, but I comforted myself by invoking Mario's words.

"Don't worry, kid. Once you spend a couple of years in P&S, you'll be fine wherever you go. It's all buys and sells, debits and credits."

On the following Monday morning, I walked into the Municipal Bond Department on the twelfth floor of 120 Broadway at around eight thirty. Everyone in the room was on the phone, from Devlin in his "imperial corner," to a group directly parallel to the doorway, to a few fellows in the back of the room to my left. Kondratuck spotted me as I stood pausing for a long minute in the doorframe. He put his telephone down and walked over to greet me. He guided me over to a seat at the trading desk next to a fellow he said was called John and then, after uttering a few more unintelligible words of greeting, immediately answered a summons that he was wanted on still another telephone. The guy sitting next to me, John Devlin, nephew of Bill, introduced himself, and that was the extent of any formal introduction. By about noon, several of the people around me came over and said hello and introduced themselves. Otherwise, I wouldn't have known anyone's name. Bill Devlin passed to my right a few times and simply nodded.

Chapter 25

The Trading Desk

The room itself was about twenty feet wide by eighty feet long with the business end being the space in front of you when you walked in the door, which was Municipal Syndicate straight ahead and to the immediate right the Municipal Bond Trading Desk situated about five feet away from the wall. (See drawing)

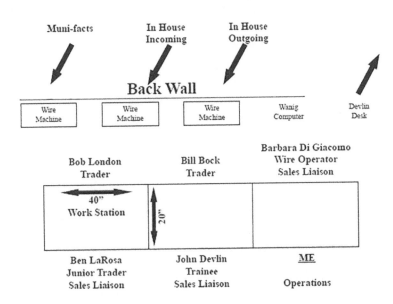

Six position Municipal Bond Trading Desk at Reynold's Securities in the early seventies. Trading desks identical to this one were in use at most firms; at Solomen Brothers or Merill Lynch. They may have had 30 or 40 workstations.

The wall immediately behind the trading desk was lined with several teletype machines. One an incoming machine from the firm; another was called the Muni-Facts machine, which was a wire service that published municipal industry news and notifications and then a machine with a keyboard for outgoing house orders and messages. There was a small table and chair against the Wall that was actually a Wang Computer that I later learned was used to do some very complicated bond calculations related to new issues. Six people were seated at the trading desk including me.

Though referred to in the singular, a trading desk is usually some multiple of desks where some multiple of persons sit, working at various tasks related to a particular line of business or investment product. The word *trading* in its title implies the business conducted by the desk is in previously issued municipal bonds often referred to as the "secondary" or "aftermarket" as opposed to the "new issue" or "primary market." The easiest way to understand this distinction is to compare it to how we buy automobiles. We buy new cars from dealerships who get them from the factory. Used cars on the other hand are a completely different market subject to many different considerations and pressures on pricing due to their differences with new models i.e. age, mileage, accessories, limited inventory of certain models and so on. In a similar fashion conditions in the secondary market for municipal bonds may vary as to lot size, need of investors to liquidate, supply or lack of supply of particular maturities and so on.

The typical trading desk structure is not a bunch of desks grouped together like we might see in back office operations. High speed communication with multiple trading associations is a condition of the discipline, and so a specific physical form for the trading desk has evolved. The physical structure begins with a partition about forty inches high and twelve or fifteen inches wide. Both sides of the partition are lined by workstations of about thirty-six to forty inches in width. Each workstation has one or two drawers, some coops and cubby holes for storage of frequently used forms, and that's about it except for its most prominent and most important component, "a communications turret." This so called "turret" is an electronic telephone receiver; mounted in each workstation and depending on the number of workstations on the trading desk can have a hundred buttons representing outside lines, trunk lines and direct lines to other firms with the ability to support hundreds of calls simultaneously. Trading desks may consist of six rows of these partitions divided into thirty or forty workstations on either side, which you might see at Goldman Sachs or Salomon Brothers, or be as small as the six-workstation unit I was sitting at. The top of the partition is about eye level. When trading desk operatives are seated, they may just about be able to see the tops of each other's head and eyes. However, in most shops, there are so many files and racks and different electronic apparatus sitting atop the partition that the sight of one's opposite is usually entirely blocked unless you're standing.

The focus of attention for me over the next few days and weeks would be Barbara DeGiacomo who sat directly across from me. Barbara was not the best- nor the worst-looking girl around. She was, however, a tall, long-legged, broad-hipped, five-foot-seven or -eight, dark-haired, very curvy, and very sexy young lady of about twenty-five years. I had never seen skirts as short as the ones Barbara wore. Most of the time, she sat facing away from me and the trading desk, furiously tapping away at the wire machine directly behind her, sending orders. When at her workspace, she often curled up in her chair and sat on her legs. The entire effect of this was to make me very uncomfortable. I guess everyone else had become used to the way she dressed and deported herself. In any case, this was a time of feminine rebellion that expressed itself in a good deal of the wearing of short skirts or short shorts to the office. At 2 Broadway, on several occasions, such a ruckus was raised, mainly because guys were jerks, that some of the young ladies were sent home to change.

Dress and looks aside, it became quite clear to me in a day or two that of the fifteen or twenty odd people in the room, Barbara was the busiest. I don't want to be unfair, everyone was busy, but while most people were basically selling or making inquiries or doing some kind of notation, Barbara multitasked, picking up phones, typing wires and orders, tearing off and distributing wire messages, and at the same time answering every question and inquiry put to her.

"So and so is on line 4."

"JJ has bids for Ben."

"Tom at Morgan is looking for Kondi."

Everyone did this, but to me, Barbara did more of it and while doing so seemed to be continually, as was said, tearing messages off the incoming machines, distributing them, and with lightning-fast fingers, typing all the orders and trades done by our office into the system. She was accurate as hell to boot, and of course, when every trade goes by your eyes and through your mind and fingers and you're a serious person, intelligent, and as experienced as she was, you simply know what's going on. In fact, know almost everything that's going on. After a few days, I was in awe of Barbara. I wanted to be Barbara in that I wanted to have her grasp and acuity of the department, I wanted her experience to be in me.

But for all my observation of Barbara, she barely noticed me, and beyond asking a few cursory questions here and there, I had no strategy as to how to proceed. I had no recourse other than to keep watch and lay low. No one was showing me what to do, and so I had to wait for the job to find me. The fellow next to me, John Devlin, talked to me a little about what he was doing, buying and selling, who he was calling, names, who ran the Florida division, and who he was doing business with, this broker, and that broker, and how cool everything was. Some of it I understood, but a lot I couldn't understand because of the manner of his speech. He had sort of a Western Pennsylvania drawl that drew out the endings of words in such a way that I couldn't make out the ends of his sentences, and of course I didn't know the municipal jargon yet, so again I waited.

Watching Barbara gave me an idea that at least I could make myself useful and even help her a little by picking up phones, taking messages, and calling out to people. Walking out those first few evenings, the only thing I could think of was that, I wanted to understand the place like Barbara did. I thought after a few more days, a week maybe, I'd approach her. I'd have to because she wasn't giving me the time of day, and I knew now after a few days that if anyone could map the job out for me, it would be her.

Toward the end of the week, I heard Barbara call my name and say, "Any outstanding money balances in the three thousand account?"

It was like a whip cracking when she spoke. I had no answer, and something, who knows what, perhaps a stupid look on my face, made her realize I had no idea what she was talking about.

"You know that's a wash account?" she asked. "You can't have any money balances in there." And then she said, "What the hell are you doing with the runs you're getting every day?"

I guessed she was talking about the several rolled and rubber banded segments of computer runs that were on my desk every morning.

"Filing them," I replied rapidly, feigning some small authority, finally having an answer that might give the impression I knew something.

"Aren't you checking them?"

"Am I supposed to?"

"Don't say another word. I'll be over," she said with vehemence, at least that's what it looked and sounded like to me anyway.

A few minutes later, she came around to my side of the desk, bent over me, and in a very annoyed whisper, asked me to pull the runs out of the file so she could explain them to me. Oddly, I couldn't focus on what she was saying that first time she explained things to me because I was completely overcome by her perfume, and I couldn't get out of my head what the guys behind me might be looking at as she bent over me and my desk to explain things. I blurted something out like, "Babs, look, I've got a clue now. Let me look at these things and form some questions and then I'll come around. I know you're busy."

"Damn straight!" she said. "Too damn busy to be messing with you," she said and walked away.

Later in the day, Bob London came around, asking to see a copy of the very same three thousand account Barbara had asked me about. I kind of guessed then Barbara had already heard about or anticipated something about the problem Bob was referring to. After he looked at the account, he asked me to cancel and rebook a trade for him. He then asked what I thought of Babs.

"I saw her standing by you this morning. What do you think of that perfume she wears?"

I kind of avoided answering by making out that I didn't understand the question. I really didn't want to talk about someone I hardly knew.

Later in the day, around four when things quieted down, Barbara explained to me the functions of the various accounts. One of which, known as the three thousand account, was used for the processing of transactions in which the department earned no monies. If I noticed any credits or debits in that account, I was to track where they came from, inquire about them, and fix the trades. Cool! There was a road sign I could read and understand.

That night, I mentioned the incident to Rosalie, and she suggested the scent might have been something called musk. Musk had become popular of late and was very strong and off-putting to some. All this stuff was a distraction. The only person who seemed willing to tell me something about the work I was supposed to be doing was Barbara, and I resolved to find out as much as I could from her. That was probably the way it was supposed to go, but since no one told me, it took a while to be revealed.

Chapter 26

Some Small Coming-Of-Age...
and Acceptance

What I ultimately discovered after a couple of quick chats with Barbara and applying what I knew from DECAB and operations in general, I figured out the New York Municipal Bond Department was just another of the firms branch offices, branch office number 90 in fact, whose account numbers began with the prefix 90—90-3000, 90-3024, and so on. The branch transacted purchases and sales with other broker dealers in New York and around the country although the major percentage of its transactions were made with the firm's clients. The departments business passed through four accounts, and it was my job to oversee these accounts for accuracy and, when things went wrong, to fix them.

An integral part of this oversight of accounts was to make sure the balances of inventory on the computer runs were in line with the balances on the traders' inventory cards. The traders bought and sold bonds from The Street and sold them to the firms clients and vice versa. Each time a position of twenty, thirty, five hundred, or even just five bonds was purchased for our own account for the purpose of markup and resale, a handwritten inventory card would be created by the trader and the position or holding, and it's pertinent information would be noted on the card as well as the history of its sale(s). How these transactions played out on the firm's books had to be verified, and the best way was to compare and review the inventory cards against the computer runs every day or two to find discrepancies.

Buys and sells, debits and credits after all. I got it, and I got it quickly and easily. In two weeks, I was generally finished with everything that had to be done by noon and sometimes even by eleven. By the time six weeks had passed, I realized I was the least busy person on the desk and often bored.

I settled into watching the accounts and doing whatever was asked of me, keeping in close touch with Craig Sarch in DECAB who would help me out when particularly difficult problems arose. Contrary to my belief that I still had a good deal to learn, oddly enough, I came to be considered a whiz kid in the department because I got problems cleaned up quickly and even on occasion helped Devlin and some of the salesmen in the department in clearing up niggling situations in their personal accounts as well as some of their clients' accounts. A phone call to Craig in DECAB for some direction on a particular problem or old friends in Options or Stock Record or anywhere in operations usually got the problem straightened out in a day or two.

Within months of my arrival, three at the most, Barbara left Reynolds to join the Muni Desk at First Boston. No one was surprised by her leaving but me. We brought in temporary replacements from the typing pool at 2 Broadway known as the *Z* pool for several weeks until one morning, Bill Devlin told me to call a number in personnel.

"*Me?*" I said to Bill Devlin.

"Yeahs *you!*" Bill said in his best trademark Ronald Colman-esque.

I did so and was told one Kaye Foster, a prospect for the teletype position vacated by Barbara, was available for an interview. I couldn't believe I was supposed to conduct the interview. Well, the young lady was a black girl, clear-eyed, intelligent, as fast or maybe even a faster typist than Barbara, although not as flashy. She was from Brooklyn and about my age and very much like a hundred girls black and white that I'd known in junior high and high school. I told Devlin and Kondratuck she seemed to be okay, very quick and bright, and added, "She wouldn't be doing the phone work Barbara did."

They said, "No problem. You can pick up that slack, right, just like you've been doing since she left?"

"Sure, I guess so."

Then, "If you think she can do the job, it's your decision. Call personnel and give them the approval and tell them to send the papers that need signing."

So Kaye Foster became a permanent member of the department. The little episode was a confidence builder for me.

Time went on. Months passed. While there was most definitely an air of "the Street" in operations, the back office was a sort of rougher, wilder side to life. It was plain that civility and good manners went a longer way at 120 Broadway. I was a natural in that sort of atmosphere, and as a rule, I got along well with everyone.

Bob London was a very nice fellow, and when he wanted or needed something, there was no hesitation. Ben La Rosa was a gentleman, quite amusing, and we interacted well but sparingly. John Devlin was fine to work with. Bill Bock, on the other hand was a pain in the ass. He had a haughty superior way about him that rubbed me the wrong way. He sometimes craned his head and neck back when something was said that he didn't agree with or understand, as if something smelled bad. He did it often and particularly when he was shown a ticket that might have a mistake on it or an unbalanced position in one of the accounts, as if to say. "Me, I made a mistake, moi, you're joking?"

Who knows what the body language reflected in his subconscious. When it was directed toward, me I sort of felt as if his look said, "Who the hell do you think you are? Certainly not equal to me." I wasn't there six months yet but getting on okay, I thought, and if anything annoyed me (nothing did except Bock and only occasionally), I kept my feelings to myself. Bock got under my skin. but I just let it alone until I couldn't anymore because a particularly thorny problem came up.

Bill had purchased a forty-bond block of New York bonds from a broker dealer outside of New York and sold them a day or two later, something that happens a thousand times a day in a hundred firms. The firm, in turn, received the bonds in physically as a block of forty bonds. However, when we tried to deliver them to the party they were sold to, it was discovered they were two lots of twenty bonds each of two different names with the same coupon rate and a one year difference in maturity. Given the problems the Street was having in those days with paperwork, it was a totally understandable and plausible confusion.

In the future, CUSIP numbers were developed by the Committee on Uniform Securities Identification Procedures, under which a unique ID number was assigned to every security, thus eliminating the need to compare different physical characteristics of name or coupon or maturity on the physical certificates, which was a real pain since most of these bond certificates looked so similar. The majority of New York paper for example was printed on buff-colored parchment paper upon which the municipality or authority's crest was embossed in light green. Much of the information was obscure, and one could easily misidentify one security and another with similar information when handling so many different lots, especially ones that were as similar as the two in question.

I went to Bock about it after I got the call about the problem a day or two after settlement day from a fellow named Carmine who worked in the cage. I was ignored along with the problem for a few days. I sort of let it go for that amount of time because sometimes a trader needs to mull a bit before acting, figure out what he was going to do. This problem was particularly a pain for several reasons. There was definitely going to be some monetary adjustment and some loss of revenue. At Reynolds, in operations, these problems, once exposed, didn't stay buried very long. Open items went on weekly reports that were poured over constantly by management, and so I got a call from Carmine every other day about it after a few days passed. I was one of theirs, and they felt I owed them results because their managers were all over them and then I had been going back to operations for help with various problems on a regular basis. Now it was my turn to deliver.

When I went back to Bock four or five days after the problem surfaced and well after settlement date, he said something like, "You take care of it. You're the big operations guy. I'm busy."

He pissed me off. I thought after a while though, "Maybe I had been spreading my expansive personality in a way that rubbed him wrong so he threw out that big operations guy thing."

That aside, the fact was that his answer was illogical. He had to take care of the problem. He had to initiate the activity to fix the problem, not me. He must have known that. I didn't say anything to him though because I wasn't too of fond of the guy, and I just didn't want to get into an open argument with him. Rightly or wrongly, I would lose. Finally, after another call from Two Broadway, I quietly mentioned it to Kondratuck.

The first thing Kondi asked was, "Could you be wrong?"

'I'm sure he knows he has to fix it sooner or later." Then, "It's typical trader blow-by bullshit, just not wanting to take the time and the initiative to fix a problem he caused, own up to it, and take a bit of a beating."

I was immediately annoyed with myself for saying that, but Kondratuck didn't bat an eyelash. He understood perfectly. I didn't mention Bill's ego was as big as a Mack Truck and he thought somehow it was beneath him to have to clean up his own mess, but I didn't have to.

Kondi was a very nice man, considerate of everyone, an undisputed expert in his field, and most amazingly, devoid of ego in any discernable way, which was of course a quality I sensed the effects of even though I neither recognized nor understood it at the time. He could formulate a fifty-million-dollar bid on a bond issue on the back of an envelope in ten minutes, including two phone calls. Another side to him was he would quite annoyingly spend an hour on a five-bond problem, complaining to anyone who would listen, incessantly knitting his substantial Russian eyebrows, going on and on about how details like these have to be cleaned up promptly because they always come back to haunt you. He came around the desk about an hour after I mentioned the problem to him and spoke quietly to Bock about it.

Bock was visibly annoyed at me and showed it with lots of neck stretching, screwing up his face, and the casting of many frosty looks in my direction, but he made the calls to the broker/dealer he'd bought the bonds from and those he sold them to and I did the corrections and the problem was resolved with price and name changes reflecting the reconciliation of the problem. Little problems like these have a complexity all their own, and as Kondratuck said, they do come back and bite you on the butt when they're not taken care of in a timely fashion.

A week or two later, the incident was forgotten and oddly enough I finally felt that I was accepted on the desk and even more broadly finally become a member of the department/family. I had stood up in a situation, got the job done; that is, initiated the fixing of a legitimate business problem. If Bill Bock was bothered by it, he never showed it after that day. Another reason why I felt more comfortable was Bill Kondratuck began to confide in me, often speaking about the inner workings of the department and the people as well. About once a week, he took me into the partner's coffee room across the hall to review any outstanding problems that might be troubling me or that were unsolved to date or that he wanted me to check into. These were ten- or fifteen-minute meetings at most, enough time to drink a cup of coffee. On these occasions, he often spoke his thoughts about the department's problems, its future, as well as what he thought of some of the people. I listened, added my two cents here and there, and was either corrected or nodded at in agreement. I never gave it a second thought except to comment about how good the coffee was.

Immediately behind John Devlin, Ben La Rosa, and myself were a grouping of three desks. One was vacant, and the other two were manned by Bill Kondratuck and Tom Sadler. In a word, Municipal Syndicate, responsible for bidding on and participation in the new issue market for municipal bonds, the so-called primary market. The word *syndicate* refers to the groups of underwriters formed to purchase new issues of municipal securities. Municipalities are continually announcing their need to borrow money along with the precise days and times or deadlines at which they will accept bids for loans of five, ten or a hundred million dollars. These announcements are scheduled on what is known as "The Forward Calendar of Municipal Offerings" and published in the newspapers and many other financial venues including the *Bond Buyer*, a municipal securities trade paper and the Muni-Facts wire service, which was one of the receiving wire machines on the wall behind the Trading Desk.

Based on their history of participating in the facilitation and distribution of these loans in the past, brokerage firms form syndicate groups and collaborate as to what they feel the interest rates should be on these loans based on current market conditions. Typically, the major underwriters in the syndicate meet and formulate the final bid to buy the deal based again on market conditions, orders in hand, market bias upward or downward, and the syndicate operatives intuitive feelings as to how the resale of the loans would be received by the market i.e. large investors traders and the public. The rate schedules, more commonly known as scales, including fees and expenses, are submitted to the municipality on the date and time specified, and shortly thereafter, the municipality accepts the lowest bidder (the bid with the lowest net interest cost to the borrower) and the borrowing process commences complete with the issuance of documents and a final closing, days or weeks later. Almost simultaneously, the brokerage firms in the syndicate solicit orders for the bonds from clients.

Stretching to the back of the room, there was a small institutional sales force: Jim Duncan, Dean Kois, Dick Baldwin (whose father had founded the department), and Jack Hoffman as well as a secretary or two. Institutional clients are banks, insurance companies, foundations, investment advisors, other broker dealers, and mutual funds to name a few. In short, large investors who buy at discounted prices. Commensurately, institutional salesman earn lower commissions than retail salesman (i.e., salesman who deal with smaller private investors). It was a kind sleepy operation in the sense that, except for Jim Duncan, there wasn't a whole lot of business being done by the institutional sales force at Reynolds.

Against the corridor wall and to the immediate left of the doorway was a grouping of four desks, which composed Corporate Syndicate. This unit underwrote and marketed newly issued corporate bonds—bonds or loans made by corporations like Con Edison, IBM, American Airlines, and so on. The group joined syndicate accounts with other firms on the Street, doing business in much the same fashion as municipals. Corporate Syndicate also participated in the underwriting of preferred stocks. Preferred stocks pay a fixed dividend and usually have a priority of dividend payout to investors over common stock and a retirement or maturity date when they go out of existence with a cash payment of principal as do bonds. There may also be a "call feature" written into the issuance documentation (prospectus) that gives the issuing corporation the right to take the security out of circulation at a specified price, date, and so forth. There are also tax benefits to preferred stocks that make them beneficial investments to certain institutions and corporations. Although they are stocks, these characteristics of preference make them similar to fixed income securities and are thus administered to by fixed income departments rather than the equity or stock departments. Corporate Syndicate was managed by Clem Schaefer, a VP with two subordinates, Sandy Hulse and Don Herklotz.

Chapter 27

The Papers

When working on Wall Street in any capacity relating to underwriting or trading, one naturally becomes a student of the market, something that would be a long time coming for me since I didn't have much of a conceptual feel for the term "the Market," much less a tangible understanding of what it was. Certainly not the way people around me understood it, especially the credit markets in which I now found myself embroiled. Most of the people around me had either taken finance as a major or minor course of study at college or had at least taken a course or two on the subject. I had done none of these. I came to the conclusion after a while that the one tool or aid that might help me in this regard was the newspapers.

I noticed everyone walked into the office every day with a copy of the *New York Times* under their arm or protruding from a briefcase. It often sat on their desks until about midday before being dumped into the wastebasket. Others took it home in the evening, presumably to finish reading it or to give to their wives to read. I sometimes noticed one of my colleagues open their paper at midday with knitted brow, perhaps needing to recall some bit of information garnered that morning. I particularly noticed the copy on Clem Schaefer's desk, probably because he sat near the doorway I walked through so often. The paper seemed quite a mess, having been gone through thoroughly, and I noticed it was often bent back awkwardly against its natural fold.

Accompanying the ever-present existence of the newspapers in the office was a comment uttered aloud in various forms at least once and sometimes three or four times a week, usually by Clem Schaefer, that went something like, "What did Janeway say about that?" Or, "Did you read Janeway this morning?" Or, "Janeway said…"

It soon became obvious I had to begin reading the *New York Times* regularly, if only to know what Janeway was saying and because so many people in the office were doing so. It wasn't really something I wanted to do. I didn't want to give up my reading of popular fiction and the odd classic I occupied myself with during the morning train ride. The *Journal-American* had gone out of business by this time, and I just never picked up another newspaper after that. Everyone followed Elliot Janeway's daily market commentary though, and so to be on the inside, so to speak, to be in-group, I had to start reading him too. I was glad I did, and before long, I found that just as my new colleagues were interested, I too became interested in the never-ending saga of the triumvirate of topics that all Wall Streeter's are drawn too—the market, government, and politics.

A year or so later, I dropped the *Times* in favor of the *Wall Street Journal*. It was on the newsstand in the morning right next to the *Times*. It was much thinner usually than its rival, and its front page was laid out in a more orderly manner, in outline form, and still is, which appealed to me. If you've read it, you know business news and the rest of the news are separated and flow in distinct directions, and the journal separated the two. I also gravitated to the quickly-read synopses of articles in both areas on the front page in order of importance and in the format of a comprehensive tables of contents of the day's news, which didn't appear in the *Times* in those days. The writing also seemed more direct, perhaps even more clinical and objective in style, than the *Times*. More educative and less opinion based even then. I don't think I've missed seeing much more than a hundred days of the *Wall Street Journal's* publication in forty-five odd years.

Once I discovered the credit market column in the *Times* and the *Journal*, it became the focal point of my reading—my day even. I read it two or three times every day in those years, weighing every word. Many of the words and jargon that were used all around me in the office every day, words and expressions like *the 05, basis points,* and *scale* were scattered throughout the column daily. *The Fed, GO* for *General Obligation*, and *NIC* which stood for net interest cost, and many, many more expressions were explained in the column for the benefit of the nonprofessionals who might read the column. My colleague's naturally understood these expressions, but I couldn't ask them to explain them. It was too busy, and it took too long to explain because it's not easy to put the meanings of these expressions in a few succinct words, which is precisely what the *Journal's* credit market column and attendant articles did every morning—the literal meanings, in any case.

It took months and, in some cases, years for me to comprehend the true internal and practical, professional meanings of these words and expressions that the *Journal* provided precise rote definitions for. The miracle was I gradually began to get a feel and a context for what was going on around me and what these terms meant within the context of the bond business and the business conducted by the department.

For example, it's easy to understand that an "interest rate scale" is a table of the interest rates created today to price a two-hundred-million-lion bond issue. It takes years to comprehend that the same table of interest rates, on the day and probably for the week in which it was written, within certain "guidelines" can be used to place a monetary value on every existing municipal bond ever issued and currently outstanding with the same credit characteristics (credit rating) regardless of coupon rate or maturity date. Again, when someone says they're going to specifically write a California scale, they are actually saying they are going to write or create a "pricing tool" that "within certain guidelines" (credit rating, lot size, and maturity) can be used to value all outstanding California bonds (billions, if not trillions, of dollars' worth), issued by the state of California.

In time, although I wasn't reading the *Times* or Elliot Janeway's column, I became a repository of the news and someone who could remind another when they asked rhetorically what Nixon or Kissinger said or who's this or what's that or whether Oklahoma is on the forward calendar. I could come up with the answer, and because my source was the *Wall Street Journal*, my perspective on both current events and the business was somewhat different. I am competitive, and frankly, I think I enjoyed having all this information at the tip of my tongue. And all it cost was reading the papers during my forty-five-minute commute.

A second media discovery I made around this time was the *New York Times* Book Review. I bought both Saturday's and Sunday's *New York Times* at the beginning and continued to after I dropped the daily edition for the *Wall Street Journal*. It was rumored that many stories related to politics, finance, and government that were particularly sensitive or controversial were often dumped in Saturday's edition of the *Times* to effectively reduce their exposure. I bought Sunday's edition primarily for the Week in Review section. I had no idea something like the Book Review even existed. I loved books and reading, and after discovering the Book Review, I felt the same pleasure anticipating and reading it I had felt as a child during the summer anticipating the reception of *My Weekly Reader*. For those who don't know the *Weekly Reader*, it was a four- or six-page publication that parents could order for two dollars (in the forties and early fifties), ensuring the reception of an uninterrupted stream of reading material for their children during summer vacations. I'm sure some form of it still exists.

I found the *Times* Book Review informative and useful in several ways. First, simply to be able to take a look at the new books available and get an opinion on them so that I could pick and choose made book buying and sampling a little more precise for me. Second, reading it cover to cover was interesting, amazingly informative, and not a chore at all. It made me an expert on and conversant in America's current reading habits and gave me a perspective on history, economics, politics, management trends, as well as critical review and the arts. Reading the Book Review weekly became a great asset in that people noticed me, were impressed, and remembered me simply because it appeared as though I had read the same books they did or at least knew about them. When pressed, I would admit I had not read the book but only a review, although maybe that happened three or four times in forty years. By the same token, I actually read hundreds of books I would never have known about were it not for the Book Review.

The *New York Times* Book Review section was the college education I never got. It was what made me equal and comfortable standing next to or sitting in the same room with the guys who went to the University of Virginia, Becknell, Stanford, or Princeton for that matter. I have to admit on several occasions over the years, I enjoyed watching some usually sneering white shoe's jaw drop while the boss or the CEO and I animatedly discussed Jane Smiley's last book or the latest popular tome on finance or management.

The only difficulty I faced with all this reading in those early years was it was saved usually until Sunday night and Monday morning because I was always working on weekends. In the case of the Book Review section, it was what I wanted to read first but usually read on Tuesday or Wednesday morning. It didn't really matter much though when I got to it because I always made sure I did get to it before the next edition came out. On occasion, very rarely, maybe once every couple of years or so because of illness or vacation, I missed picking up the Sunday *Times*, and believe me, I mourned those days terribly. I'm happy to say I still read it quite closely.

Chapter 28

Reynolds Bond Department: A Second Look

The work unit I joined was somewhat dysfunctional in that it had been leaderless for several months when I got there. Bill Kondratuck and Bill Devlin were the bosses, the managers so to speak, but the leader had been Kevin Walsh, a gifted trader destined to become a bond market visionary, who'd managed the desk for several years had recently moved on to start a Municipal Bond Department at a firm called New York Hanseatic. He took with him his assistant Sis, Leticia Smiles, whom I replaced.

I didn't know much about Kevin at the time except that he came out of the Reynolds Accounting Department as a trainee perhaps ten years hence and was discovered to have or developed a brilliant grasp of markets and trading and had carved a name out for himself trading large blocks of industrial revenue bonds.

People spoke of him in a way that made him sound like a good leader, and it appeared his leaving left a void of dynamism and leadership since there really seemed to be no one in charge. Bob London was a full-fledged accomplished trader but did not seem to be in charge as a manager, at least one who navigated the course of the desk in terms of risk taking and market decision making. Bill Bock seemed to be still somewhat in the training stages—advanced but still training. John Devlin, still a trainee, and another advanced trainee, Ben La Rosa, handled large block inquiries from the field (fifty thousand to one hundred thousand dollars or more) and helped in working up bids on blocks of bonds as well. Kevin being the gifted trader and manager that he was had the confidence of Bill Devlin. He could manage the desk as he saw fit allowing London and Bock to be somewhat adventurous knowing that under Walsh's watchful eye they wouldn't get into too much trouble. Walsh's leaving then left a void which was not filled.

Bill Devlin, the senior officer of the department, did not seem to have an interest in leading the desk on an hour-to-hour, day-today basis nor were there regular meetings with Kondratuck. As long as they stayed within inventory limits, which I think were pegged somewhere between five million and eight million dollars, they were left alone.

Holding to a fixed quantity of inventory in the amount mentioned was important for two reasons. The first was the five to eight million served as an inventory of bonds for the brokers in the Mid-Atlantic Region to sell to their clients. The New York Muni Desk serviced the 350 to 400 brokers located in New York, New Jersey, Connecticut, and Puerto Rico. The second was holding to a set inventory level made it possible to limit your losses. If interest rates rose causing across-the-board losses of five dollars per bond or thousand dollars of principal value on average, losses would be limited to forty thousand dollars on that day on average.

$8 million principal value X $5 per $1000 of principal value = $40,000

Of course if the market rose in value $5 per bond the gains would be limited to $40000 as well.

The other risk mitigating dynamic that is always in place in a retail operation are daily sales. When you have 300 brokers selling off ten to twenty percent of the inventory daily of the eight million on hand, ($800,000 to $1.5 million dollars worth), that inventory has to be replaced. Theoretically this constant turnover and replenishment of the inventory at current prices diminishes risk. As long as traders diligently stay after the inventory and don't allow individual holdings to get stale (priced out of line with the market) the constant turnover and replenishment is a self-regulating risk abating device within reason. Of course, rapidly changing markets especially to the downside (higher interest rates) might hold up sales in which case losses were taken and in dramatically changing markets when interest rates fell, traders repriced their inventory higher to take advantage of the higher market values.

Besides the New York office that serviced the Mid-Atlantic, Reynolds maintained a network of regional municipal offices in what are known as the major wealth or money centers or those metropolitan areas with the greatest concentration of wealth in the United States. These are Boston, Washington DC, Atlanta, St. Petersburg, Florida, Philadelphia, Pittsburg, Chicago, Detroit, Minneapolis, San Francisco, and several satellites like Lincoln, Nebraska; Seattle, Washington; Huntsville, Alabama.

Generally speaking, these regional offices were mirror images of the New York office that processed many millions daily, most especially in syndicate. Each office employed at least a trader/syndicate expert who managed the office. Some had an assistant trader along with a secretary/operation's assistant. San Francisco and St. Petersburg were operations the size of New York because they serviced major markets that issued large quantities of bonds and had plenty of brokers to service. St. Petersburg, Minneapolis, and Atlanta did especially well in local underwritings. Each of these, or at least eight or nine of them, carried an ongoing inventory of two to three to five million dollars, depending on syndicate involvement—Florida and California a good deal more. Conservatively then, the Bill Devlin/Bill Kondratuck team day to day presided over fifty to seventy-five million dollars inventory at Reynolds in 1972. Formidable I would say for those days and for our size firm.

Kondratuck and Devlin appeared to be a strifeless team during the period under discussion in the management of the one hundred odd people (including institutional salesmen and operations staff) employed by the municipal divisions around the country. Kondratuck was very much respected for his professionalism and expertise in the business. Devlin was a pillar of respect and very good at reading the political tea leaves in the firm and what was going on at other firms as well. Municipals were considered a science and an important cog in the wheel of the firm as well as a big money maker. The regional municipal managers were very competent. Negative comments were rare from any quarter except perhaps about the West Coast in regard to their sort of lackadaisical responsiveness. This was the seventies though. Politeness and respect of one's fellows was still important.

Chapter 29

More Coming-Of-Age: The Early Bird and UITs

By late the spring of 1973, I had become a regular on the desk; well pleased with myself after receiving a bonus amounting to ten weeks' pay just before Christmas, which effectively made my salary roughly twelve thousand dollars a year. I watched deal after deal bang through the accounts and became familiar with the rhythm of the business. By and large, it ran smoothly, with only the occasional fire needing to be put out. Over time, I became confident in my ability to deal with most of the employees in the bond department and was now quite at ease with both Bill Kondratuck and Bill Devlin. As I became familiar with the trading and underwriting processes, my role in them seemed to grow, not so much deliberately but simply as an extension of just being there. To wit, certain experiences have a sort of corner-turning effect on us. We step over a line with them, lose our virginity so to speak, and once we do, they become part of our core. Here are two of those experiences that shaped my future and put me on track to become what I would eventually turn out to be. They are also instructive in that they reveal a great deal about the business of Wall Street in particular relating to municipal bonds and related investment products.

One of the wire services used in the early seventies was known as Muni-Facts. Muni-Facts news service primarily distributed municipal bond market-related information to its subscribers. Today, if it still exists, I'm sure it does in some form, its delivered electronically. It was also a vehicle through which its subscribers could offer securities to each other. A particular service known as the "Early Bird" comprised a sheet of offerings of odd amounts and small lots of municipal bonds at prices relatively cheap to the market. It was published by the wire service at six or seven every morning with information on offerings submitted the afternoon before. The idea of the Early Bird was these were intended to be quick no-negotiation kinds of trades. They were cheap, and if you wanted them, you got them—no quibbling, no counter offers, take 'em or leave 'em. So these small niggling odd lot amounts of bonds were disposed of early on and once and for all without cutting into the time required to deal in the one-hundred-thousand-dollar blocks and more.

We always owned ten or twelve odd lots of this kind because one of the natural occurrences on the trading desk over any given week or two was ten to twenty of these small lots might be accumulated in our accounts, resulting from the traders continually bidding on and buying small lots of bonds from the branch office system. These odd lots were then reoffered in-house. After a week or ten days, those that didn't sell were put on the Muni-Facts Early Bird in what might be called a clearance sale. It's standard practice to clear out inventory that's not selling to make room for inventory that will sell. The consequence of placing these items on the Early Bird for broker/dealers around the country to see was the phone began ringing as early as seven in the morning, just about the time I got in and forty-five minutes to an hour before anyone else did. I rarely picked up the phone when a trader was not present simply because I was not supposed to be talking to anyone in any buying or selling capacity. I wasn't registered (licensed) by the NYSE and thus was prohibited from trading, and there was always the danger, or so I was told, of getting picked off.

Getting picked off happened often to budding young traders early in their careers because they were so in awe of and so nervous about what they were doing that they made mistakes in the offering terms to the trader they were speaking to. The opposite, often an experienced pro, didn't care even if they recognized the erroneous offer or bid. They did the trade anyway, feeling that screwing a young and inexperienced operative was okay and some sort of initiation or rite of passage.

Sometimes these guys just did it for fun and set you up for it. It had happened once or twice to John Devlin who sat next to me and had been quite embarrassing for him. In any case, one morning, I reflexively picked up the phone around ten minutes past seven and experienced something like the following:

"Munis Reynolds, Pat Scida."

"Hey, sport. Orville Hines, Kendle Hebert, Fort Worth. Hey, on the Early Bird, there's—"

"Uh, Orvill, I can't help you, man. I'm the ops guy on the desk. One of the guys will have to call you back."

"Well, listen, sport, uh, what was yer name then, Pat?"

"Yep, Pat."

"Well, listen, Pat. Will ya tell 'em boys, I think one's Bob and the other's Bill, that I called in at about 7:10 a.m. You know, am probly first up." Then he added somewhat testily, "What the hell I gotta do to buy one of these offering anyway? This'll be the third or fourth time in as many weeks, and I keep getting shut out by these guys."

Now the guy's got a little beef and he sounds okay anyway, so I said, "Hold on, let me see what's going on here."

So I go over to the Muni-Facts machine and started shuffling through the morning's messages and finding our offerings. I then got the inventory book out that has a card opened up and filled out for every offering the desk has and went back to my phone.

"Which one you lookin' at, Orville?"

"The 6 Fort Worth's and the 10 Bentonville Arkansas."

"All right, listen, I'm pulling the cards and writing a note, and I'm gonna make sure you're the first call when the traders come in, how zat?"

"Mighty nice of you. You sure I'm talkin' to New York here?"

"Hey, Orv—"

"Jes', kiddin', sport, jes' kiddin'. Appreciate it, really do."

I do exactly as promised. I wrote a note with phone number and name and left it with the inventory cards where it can be seen at the point where Bob and Bill's workspaces meet. When the traders showed up, the phones started ringing off the hook, and I'm involved in something or another. About eleven o'clock, Orville calls and asks for me and wants to know why he hasn't gotten a call yet. It turns out neither Bill nor Bob noticed the note or they ignored it, whatever. It was right in their faces when they came in and now under a pad and folded over. One of the lots was sold to someone else, and the other remained. Bock wouldn't talk to the guy.

"It's your problem. You shouldn't have promised him the bonds, blah, blah, blah."

So I get on the phone and apologize and convince the guy that getting the one lot was better than none and then I wrote the trade ticket selling the bonds to the guy and marked the inventory card with the details and retired it. Period. End of discussion.

From that day on, whenever anyone called in to buy bonds, from the street or one of our branches, and everyone was busy or if a trader was not present, as long as there was no price discussion, I just did the trade, marked the inventory card, initialed it, and wrote the ticket. Screw the regulations. So I wasn't registered, big deal. It wasn't long before I was doing four or five trades a day, and if I was to get called out on it, I could just say since I was told to pick up the slack for Barbara, I was just doing what she did and what I was told to do. I never did a trade where there was a negotiation in price or a block of more than forty or fifty bonds. These were still transactions I would be responsible for if a problem came up, so I didn't want to get too cocky. Thus without much ceremony and no registration with the NYSE, it became routine for me to be executing multiple transactions valued in the hundreds of thousands of dollar range every day. Before long, I developed an easy confidence doing business and talking to people. Traders, syndicate men, management. It became second nature a long time before I ever had any responsibility for trade execution. Consequently, I never had any "nerves" over it whatsoever.

Technically if you weren't registered, had not taken and passed the Series Seven exam you could not transact business, but the rule was broken all the time and it wasn't uncommon in many shops in those days that non-registered personnel; trainees or operations people sitting on Trading and Syndicate Desks executed trades. Even though it was unwise to have such blatant violations occurring in their shops managers were wary of putting forth new people for registration especially those coming from operations departments. The excuse often given was that these transactions were done under the supervision of registered personnel and that was an adequate retort to regulators if necessary. Other excuses given were that the three-hundred-dollar cost for training at Securities Training School and the SEC and NYSE fees were prohibitive. That was baloney too considering the kind of money changing hands on Wall Street every day.

I knew Devlin had been burned a couple of times by guys who took the exam and failed it two or three times. Some took the test and after passing it immediately left for another firm while others failed the background check turning out to be scofflaws or having criminal records. Because of my ethnicity I was sensitive to the feeling that management in general didn't want every Tom, Dick or Pasquale who came along to get into their exclusive club. But once I began executing trades and doing business I stopped hinting about getting registered. Number one I wanted to continue doing the business and I felt that sooner or later someone was going to say.

"Isn't it about time we got Scida registered? He's doing a dozen trades a day."

Another job or group of tasks that I got involved with by default concerned an investment product known as "unit investment trusts" or UITs for short. UITs are fixed portfolios of securities (back then, usually bonds) that are divided into equal parts called *units* and sold to investors as shares of fixed, diversified investment portfolios of securities. Unlike mutual funds, they are not actively managed, commanding much lower fees and expenses. In a way, it was like buying an individual bond in that your fee was up front, and your yield was calculated after expenses with certain reservations (i.e., that your yield was current yield, income divided by price rather than yield to maturity, which was income divided by price and amortized over time).

Municipal Bond Unit Trusts can come to market near and sometimes higher in yield than market yields of bonds of approximately equal maturity and credit quality. This depends on the mix of bonds in the portfolio among other factors. Portfolio diversification, ease of ownership, ready liquidity and professional selection are the features and benefits of the investment that are supposed compensate for the lower yields. In the early seventies, Merrill Lynch underwrote and sponsored a municipal bond unit trust nearly every month or so. It was called the Municipal Investment Trust (MITF) Fund and because Reynolds had been part of the underwriting syndicate in the sixties (when sponsored by Goodbody), there was still some residual demand for the investment in our firm.

Most traders and syndicate men turned up their noses at these so-called "investment products" as they were not individual bonds. These purists tended to avoid doing business in them lest they soil their hands or catch something from them or so it seemed. Nonetheless, because they were considered a bond derivative, they were administered to by the municipal trading desks with the task usually flowing to the junior or least experienced registered person on the desk. On our desk, John Devlin had inherited the job from Ben La Rosa. Now that John had been doing some bidding on bonds and trading odd lots on his own, the job was handed off to me even though I was not registered, presumably because I was doing some trades already. The guys on the desk didn't want to do it, and Bill Devlin let it go because it was small potatoes and his motto was "don't scratch something that doesn't itch." If it's going well and people are good with it, don't mess with it.

The difference with me doing the job was I began to make phone calls to salesmen informing them of the underwritings and the yield expectations, which is what you're supposed to do. Because the traders and budding traders felt these packaged products were beneath them, they tended to take an order whenever they had too but not try to produce business as they might with straight municipals. For one, a unit trust sale might be preventing a bond sale, and as mentioned, the traders saw the investment as unworthy. I can't say I made the calls precisely because I wanted to do the business, but it was inferred to me by the brokers who were doing the business that they would really appreciate a heads up when the next deal was announced instead of having to hear it because some broker from another firm was soliciting their client or one of their clients made an inquiry because they had some money available. In short, I got back to people when I found out a deal was on the way. The result of this communication was whenever one of these municipal unit trusts were underwritten, I would execute two hundred thousand to two hundred fifty thousand dollars' worth and on occasions four hundred thousand to five hundred thousand, whereas the most that had been done previously was one hundred fifty thousand dollars' worth. The structure of the revenue side of this activity was these units were purchased at a twenty-five-dollar discount, all of which was paid to the salesman. So every fifteen or eighteen business days, something between six thousand to twelve thousand dollars of commission was paid into the system by our accounts. After several months of these increased sales, Bill Devlin who was quite fond of nicknames passed by my desk one day and, in his resonant gravelly voice, asked, "How are you getting along with Pierre?"

He was talking about a fellow by the name of Phil Milot, my contact at Merrill who happened to be of French lineage. This was Devlin's way of asking me if everything was okay. Kondratuck, on the other hand, would come by at the end of the month, horn rims on his nose and a cigar between two fat fingers, with a copy of the account and ask about a position in the account if there were any left unsold or a money balance that appeared next to the name of a UIT. We took no inventory in UITs. We bought only what was sold, what we had to buy against orders, so he was just checking me on this, and most of the time, it was either a trade correction or a late arriving account number for which I hadn't written a ticket yet. Sometimes there was a cancel or an inadvertent overbuy of a few units that I might have to get rid of, but that could happen in any syndicate and it was tolerated and understood.

In any case, I usually got a "good job, Boichek" out of it or a pat on the back or he'd just come by with the account in hand and kick my chair a couple of times.

On one occasion, when over six hundred thousand dollars' worth was executed, there were out and out compliments. I was sure "Pierre" was touching base with Bill Devlin just to make sure he thought I was capable and things were running smoothly.

All of this was part of my growth, whether I knew it or not, and part of my development in the understanding of "how business was done," servicing the sales force, and producing and processing business in a way that was so innocuous, so matter-of-fact, that it just happened. I didn't really know I was developing a sense of the market for interest rate and market trends in price and yield and the sensitivity of salesman and indeed their clients to yields as they drifted downward or upward. I just liked doing it and liked the people I was doing it with, especially the guys in the Northern New Jersey offices who were responsible for most of the UIT sales.

Two things should be noted here. Average sales of three hundred thousand dollars' worth of a product no-one really cared about developed one hundred and twenty-five thousand dollars in commissions annually. After about six months of this, Phil Milot informed me Reynolds Securities was now part of the selling group on the deal, and I would now be buying units at a discount of $27.50 but still paying out the $25. The result was for every unit we sold, we would keep a net of $2.50, which would average at the current rate of sales around $12,500. I just did it as part of my job, almost as a reward for being allowed to exist there and stay there. Did I ever connect the fact of the revenue against the ten thousand dollars a year, twelve thousand with bonus, I was earning? Eventually, I would, but it took a while. Call me stupid. Call me ignorant. Naive is probably the best description, but that's the way it was. I just accepted it.

It's also true if I was asked something technical—for example, to calculate a bond's yield to maturity—I was totally in the dark. I was never taught to use the Compucorp machine to calculate yield to maturity or yield to call or, for that matter, and my capabilities with a basis book begun in DECAB had gotten very rusty although by this time that form of calculation was disappearing. I still shied away from these calculations anyway because underneath it all I still had a phobia about my math skills. Fortunately, in most cases the people calling in were just as much in the dark as I was, perhaps even more so. In any case, in regard to UITs, the calculations of yield and other details were hand delivered to me by runner the day the deal came, no calculations necessary. Actually, in the early seventies, we still didn't have fax machines. I took the info down on the phone and relayed it over the phone to the salesman doing the business, and later that day, the official papers, called fact sheets, were hand delivered. It was never even formally written down and recorded except for the writing of the trade tickets. Doing the business, the jargon, the servicing, the good-natured attitude and salesmanship, the calling and the taking of and asking for orders was all done with my own natural God-given enthusiasm, without guile. I was just a guy doing my job.

I have always remembered and related to the famous scene from *Lawrence of Arabia*, in which Anthony Quinn, playing the great Howeitat tribesman and warrior Auda Abu Tayi, extols his prowess to T.E. Lawrence, saying, "And yet I am poor because I am a river to my people."

I was a river to anyone who came in contact with me simply because I was a giver without reservation. Maybe a bit of a jerk, looked at askance by some. I'm sure perhaps somewhat eccentric in some ways because I like to tell jokes and kid around and know a lot because I read so much. But I was and still am, I guess, a giver, and a resourceful one at that. Fortunately, my managers and colleagues had no issues with those qualities and allowed me to be myself.

Chapter 30

The Regionals Gather in New York

In the 1973 movie *American Graffiti*, Wolfman Jack broadcasts a telephone call from a listener who says he's calling all the way from Little Rock, California, and, with a sense of incredulity, says, "Long distance?"

Making long distances calls was still something of a big deal in the seventies, and so was getting on a plane and traveling to another state. When the Reynolds Municipal Bond Department had a meeting in New York (maybe once every two years) of their regional managers, it was very exciting and, for me, a very big deal. The regionals started trickling into the office on a Thursday afternoon, and the air of collegiality that developed was infectious. After a while, I was astonished by the warm greetings of some of these fellows and how several of them gathered around me and after a while, sometimes slapping me on the back and making conversation.

I had not been asked out to dinner that evening and was glad of it since I worked most nights at the time doing inventories for a company called Interactive Inventory Services. I had given up delivering pizzas as my part-time employment and gone to work for Interactive conducting on-site physical inventories of businesses. On Monday through Thursdays (and most Saturdays and Sundays too), I joined a crew of five or six after work, and we would travel somewhere in the five boroughs, usually a supermarket to inventory its stock by speaking the values and quantity counts we encountered into a tape recorder. On other occasions, it could be the shoe department of a Times Square store or Dress Barn or some other retailer. It was an interesting job. Social as well because the crew got along great, and we usually stopped for a bite as a group after the job was done. Each job was worth a minimum of forty dollars and as much as sixty dollars on occasion when the job went past nine or ten o'clock.

In any case, my Fridays were free because retail stores were usually open late. Even if I was working Friday nights, I would have taken off for this occasion because it was important and, after all, I was invited. The entire office trekked uptown to Fifty-Fourth Street and Fifth Avenue to the University Club where the day's earlier business meetings had been held. Cocktails for about an hour and a half and then dinner. I had made a decision to stay away from the booze as I was afraid the body and fender man might come out if he was still in me somewhere. Perhaps it was unfair because everyone else was pretty well oiled by the time we sat down to dinner.

I was also kind of convinced that I might not have much to say or converse about with the group. On the contrary, the conversation was nonstop and quite diverse from the business to politics to family. One fellow, Joe Suski, who was the assistant in Detroit commented to me that I made him laugh all day, and another told Devlin right in front of me it was a stroke of luck that I was able to fill in for Barbara picking up phones and generally helping out and then said that I made Bob and Bill look good. Then one of the guys from Florida, Jim somebody, said Pat is Barbara "without the body or the edge." Everybody laughed.

After dinner, the group retired from the dining room to the bar with some of the New York crowd bunching up at a table for drinks. Tom Sadler, Bill Kondratuck's right hand, happened to be sitting across from me. The chat turned to the business end of the meeting in general, and some of the guys bitched a bit because they felt they were working hard and management didn't see it. When it somehow came time for me to make a comment, I said something to the effect that I didn't care how much work I was asked to do or time I had to put in. I was interested in getting ahead too and making some money. Tom, at this point, said very seriously that at some point, recognition is more important than money. To which I replied, quite seriously and perhaps with Barbara's so called edge, "That depends at what point you are on the salary scale."

Tom looked at me, and I could see recognition of my point come over him.

"You're right, point taken, I'm sorry," he said.

My reply was to scoff and say don't be sorry. It was not taken offensively. I would have never brought it up, but when the subject came up, I couldn't let it go. There were guys in the room saying how Scida was a welcome addition to the place and all, and now I'm sitting with my coworkers, not as an operations guy but an equal, while they are earning four times more than I am. So I got a two-thousand-dollar bonus, big deal. I wore decent suits and had shined shoes but not because of the money I earned at Reynolds.

Tom was from a moneyed family who were friends of, if not related to, John Baker, a senior partner in the firm and a close associate of CEO Tom Staley. Baker might have been one of the founders of the firm as well. I had heard a story that Tom's father and Baker had gone on a safari to Africa to hunt and had bagged an elephant and had one of its legs, toenails and all, made into a waste basket that was given to Tom Staley as a gift. I'm sure Sadler was paid a prominent salary for the time and was looking now for the recognition of becoming a VP. I have an extraordinarily fond memory of that conversation with Tom, possibly because I viewed it at the time as another measure of acceptance. Tom was easy to like, easygoing and very droll. Within a year, Tom left Reynolds, and I saw him on occasion over the years. Wall Street can be defined as the meeting of an endless stream of people you may or may not like but never really get to know for many reasons; the fast pace of the business, turnover of personnel from job to job, department to department and most often firm to firm.

Chapter 31

The Acquisition of Phelps-Fenn

Sometime in 1972, Reynolds Securities acquired the independent municipal bond house, Phelps-Fenn Inc. In the early seventies, the firm also acquired a small West Coast shop called Brush Slocomb and an Arkansas firm called Dabbs Sullivan. I am less familiar with the machinations of the two out of New York firms than I am of Phelps-Fenn. Reynolds had been investing the capital it had raised when it went public in 1970 in new data processing equipment. These improvements boosted the firm's ability to process business, and it followed that further investments were made to increase business (i.e. trade volume and sales). The acquisition of Phelps Fenn was I can only speculate a strategic move to increase the amount of new issues Reynolds could be involved with and to add expertise and qualified personnel to its Bond operation. Phelps-Fenn was an old-line underwriting and trading operation owned by the Byrne family of Pennsylvania. William or Bill Sr., his son Bill Jr., and Uncle Ned were the principals of the firm. They would join Reynolds along with five or six salesmen, a trader, and several operations personnel. I think they came cheap too, because during this time not just the big firms were in trouble, the smaller operations were going under two for the penny. For Phelps a small family owned firm making large capital commitments day to day was getting more and more risky. The Byrne family in this case was risking its private fortune. In later years I thought it was a great coup for Phelps Fenn that all its personnel retained employment and for its principals I'm sure their salaries were considerable for the time.

The bond department at Reynolds was taken completely by surprise. I had the feeling even Devlin and Kondratuck were surprised, though I never discussed this with anyone or knew it for a fact. Certainly the Trading Desk and Tom Sadler did not know a thing about it. It seemed to me anyway as though the event took everyone's breath away when it happened. I was in a unique position to observe because I was invisible as the operations guy on the desk. I can say with some authority, however, that acquisition or merger and acquisition can and does change the course of lives and careers. Anger and resentment are naturally stirred up because it seems quite unfair that some action taken by a remote force totally outside the department just turns your world upside down. Obviously, Tom Staley, the firm's CEO and founder, and his right hand, Robert M. Gardiner, whom I believe at the time was co-CEO, made this trade, and there was no contesting it. Lives changed because many people in the room would not be in the department a year from then, certainly changing things for them and changing things for those employees who remained.

I remember the day it happened quite distinctly, or rather I remember certain events of the day. First of all, it seemed the department was invaded by navy blue suits. Bill Byrne Sr., his son Bill Jr., and Uncle Ned wore blue suits, and so did Bob Gardiner when he came in to say hello. Gardiner's six-foot-four or -five form was impressive as it moved smoothly through the Bond Department's now somewhat crowded space. His commandingly resonant voice (this was the first time I'd heard it) breathed enthusiasm, approval, and encouragement into the room, although I don't remember any of the words he said. Tom Staley, the CEO came in briefly as well. His physicality was not impressive, although there was a definite aura of authority there and a distinct deference paid to it by those present. He was wearing a beautiful gray-blue gabardine suit that was worth at least a month's salary, if not more. Staley did not smile. He simply shook hands with a few people, nodded a bit, and left.

Bill Byrne Sr. was a pleasant enough fellow in his sixties, I guess, who appeared to be flitting around like a butterfly between my end of the trading desk, with Kondratuck's desk behind me and Devlin's desk in the corner to my right.

"Hey, Alligator!" I heard someone say in a voice that was pleased with itself in knowing Bill Senior's nickname from a bygone time. I thought the nickname might have been pretty hip at one time. Had it been dubbed in the present, it might have simply been Gator. It was Jack Hoffman, one of our institutional salesman, another fellow in his sixties. The nickname was apt because Bill's Sr.'s jaw and mouth were formidable and sort of resembled more the trap jaw of a pit bull rather than an alligator, but the reference was there just the same.

I don't know how much Reynolds Securities paid for Phelps-Fenn. I didn't get the impression that they did a great deal of business or that they risked much capital, at least not the kind of money Reynolds put up day to day in the primary markets. Maybe it was an exchange of stock or some cash and some stock. What Phelps Fenn brought to the party was a long history of underwriting municipal issues many of which Reynolds Securities had not been in. Phelps Fenn's underwriting history then instantly became Reynolds history. Coupling this with Reynolds sales force and Bill Kondratucks prodigious skills and leadership capabilities within the municipal community was sure to give Reynolds new standing in the municipal bond underwriting and distribution game.

Within four or five months, the Bond Department at Reynolds, which had grown considerably after the merger with Phelps-Fenn, went to new quarters on the tenth floor of 120 Broadway just two floors below. The new digs were at least six or seven times the size of the rooms upstairs. The area is best described as a series of glass-enclosed offices and open alcoves surrounding a large open area filled by several clusters of desks. The Municipal Trading Desk was now a twelve–work station affair occupied by six or seven people. Bob London was now the only one left from the original group present when I joined the department. Bock was there for a while but later left the firm, Ben La Rosa joined Bill Johnson in our St. Petersburg Florida municipal office, and John Devlin had left as well. They were I think replaced by a trainee and a fellow with some experience. Bill Byrne Junior and a trader called John Caffrey who came over with Phelps-Fenn joined Bob London.

Municipal Syndicate, whose workload doubled because of all the deals it now had to bid on and participate in, was in a large alcove. They had brought on several new people, including clericals from Phelps-Fenn who kept the information flow to Kondratuck moving in regard to the calendar of upcoming loans, what deals were coming up that we could bid on, as well as the history of our participation. Clem Schaefer's Corporate Syndicate Desk added a trader or two, occupying one of the open corners of the room, and the Phelps-Fenn institutional salesmen combined with ours, now a group totaling about ten, and a couple of secretaries occupied a substantial amount of space as well. Bill Byrne Sr. and Bill Devlin occupied a large office as did Uncle Ned. Finally, Kay Foster, our wire operator, now ran a small wire room in the new bond department that included herself, a second full-time operator, Jackie Johnson, and a fellow called Danny who doubled as a runner and sat at a machine to do some transmitting when it got busy. This was the new substantially expanded bond department.

I was at the far end of the office about thirty paces directly ahead from the door in an alcove overlooking Broadway and Trinity Churchyard, which housed the biggest gathering of potheads in the downtown area at lunchtime. My team consisted of Fred Mastermaker, a great young fellow and Vietnam veteran, and an older fellow, Jim Quinn, both from Phelps-Fenn. We handled operations for all departments, including Corporate Syndicate, while I continued to do the UIT business.

Sales volume and trade ticket volume had increased in Municipal Syndicate since Phelps-Fenn had joined us and carried over to Municipal Trading as well who would place orders for entire maturities of the new issues that they believed might be good trading values once the new issues syndication was over. This new prowess in Municipal Underwriting and Trading carried over into the branch office system. Once these new and strengthened capabilities in the firm were recognized by branch managers and regional sales management, the recruiting of salesman from other firms whose expertise and clientele matched the firm's new capabilities in municipals was stepped up.

The acquisition of Phelps-Fenn brought with it, in particular, entry into many smaller local new issues, especially in the local New Jersey market and, to a lesser extent, the Eastern Pennsylvania market, which was a great fit for Reynolds's well-established branches in these environs. Because municipal bonds were the core of wealthy investors' portfolio, access to local bond issues drew the wealthy investors in the area to our firm. If they were not already our clients, they would become our clients. Again, having the inventory attracted salesman from other firms whose business depended on a steady supply of local municipal bond issues.

Chapter 32

The Firm Capitalizes on New Relationships

The Bond Departments move to the tenth floor in 120 Broadway five or six months after the takeover of Phelps-Fenn came at a time when the interest rate markets had been rallying for nearly three years. An upward bias to prices creates a relatively low risk environment and an easier market to operate in. Stable markets and small though incremental rising valuations on previously purchased securities made investors amenable to adding to their portfolios. Twenty-five- to thirty-year maturity investment quality municipals (BAA-rated or better) had come down from around 6.3 percent yield to the 5.25 percent range and stayed near those levels for nearly all of 1973. Rallying and stable markets make for trading and syndicate desk success as they can operate with little fear of losing large sums of money.

Stable markets give traders and syndicate operatives time to sell off inventory without having to mark it down to stay competitively priced. Markets with an upward bias give both the syndicate desk and the trading desk more room to take additional risk. A wire house like Reynolds has another powerful advantage that greatly aids a bond department's success and profitability, which is of course its retail sales force. Reynolds Securities at the time had around one thousand five hundred brokers and maybe another one hundred institutional salesman selling to banks, insurance companies, and other professional investors. The sales force is continually selling to or responding to the needs of their clients and their own desire to earn commissions. The 1970–1973 period was a good environment for brokers for the same reasons it was for the bond departments. Investors were not getting burned. It was also a time when a relatively major segment of the public had not yet invested in stocks and bonds directly for the most part, having stayed in certificates of deposit and bank savings accounts. By the same token, potential investors were willing to listen, and brokerage firms were opening a steady stream of new accounts. Federal income tax rates were very high during these years and being able to explain the benefits of investing in tax exempt municipal bonds was a sure-fire way to open new accounts. The firm, in effect, was firing on all cylinders and expected to do even better, having added the capabilities of Phelps-Fenn.

John Caffrey, the trader who came to Reynolds with the Phelps-Fenn group, had a brother, Larry, who was high up in the chain of command in the Municipal Division at Paine, Webber, Jackson, & Curtis. Paine-Webber might have been a rival of Reynolds Securities if not a somewhat larger and more upscale retail shop. Paine-Webber had been a great connection for Phelps-Fenn since they (Paine-Webber) were capable of taking lots of bonds won in syndicate bids off their (Phelps-Fenns) hands. If you're an underwriter with a poor distribution system (Phelps-Fenn), a large retail operation like Paine-Webber is a great connection to unload bonds and conversely a great benefit to the retail organization, consuming the bonds in this case Paine-Webber, whose sales management capabilities were rumored to be as good as, and probably better than, most of the larger firms on the Street. In short, they had an insatiable demand for municipals, and Phelps-Fenn helped to fill it. Now that Phelps-Fenn had been taken over by Reynolds, its underwriting capabilities were no longer available/ accessible to Paine-Webber. However, another avenue was found by Phelps Fenn to exploit their former relationship with Paine Webber or as some might see it for Paine Webber to exploit Phelps Fenn's relationship with Reynolds.

Paine Webber was a sponsor of a municipal bond UIT known as the "Municipal Bond Fund" or MBF. Every five or six weeks, Paine-Webber partnered with Dean Witter (another large retail wire house with about 2,200 salesman) in the underwriting of a $10 million (or thereabouts) municipal bond unit trust, which they distributed through their combined sales forces, 4,000 to 4,500 stockbrokers. Unit trusts, you will remember, are closed portfolios of fixed income securities, (in later years, stocks were packaged in UITs and the currently wildly popular ETFs are structured UITs as well) with low expenses and a one-time upfront sales charge with no management fees. The "low fee, buy and hold, good quality/diversified portfolio methodology" of UITs was acceptable to bond department managements because it mirrored their own investment conventions and recommendations. Mass marketing UITs, as they were called, might cut deeply into individual retail sales of bonds, but, at the same time there was big money in them and plenty of room to open new accounts with them.

Sponsoring and underwriting UIT's could garner anywhere from ten to fifteen dollars net profit for every thousand dollars of par value underwritten for the sponsors, before sales charges and commission payout. These earnings, known as the sponsors accumulation profit, were derived from the accumulation of the underlying portfolio of the UIT by the sponsors at wholesale prices as an institutional investor. Once the portfolio was accumulated an individual investment company was legally created (the UIT) which purchased the portfolio from the sponsors at or near retail value which constituted anywhere from ten to twenty dollars per bond profit depending on market conditions. Thus, a portfolio of $10 million dollars' principal with an average cost to the sponsors of $975 might be sold to the UIT three or four days after its accumulation for $990 per bond for a $15 per bond profit ($150,000).

Once the investment company has its portfolio in place, a sales charge or markup of 3.5 percent is applied to the unit cost to arrive at the public offering price, the price at which units may be sold to the public.

To summarize, the account of the pricing process as it appeared on page 2 of the official prospectus was as follows:

Unit cost of bonds to the sponsors $975

Purchase price of bonds to the trust	$990
Sales charge	3.5% ($34.65)
Public offering price per unit	$1,024.65
Gross profitability	
Sponsor profit per unit	$15
Sales charge	$34.65
Total	$49.65
X	10,000
	$496,650

Without discussing the complex internal permutations revenue incurs within a corporation, let's say that the Dean Witter/ Paine Webber MBF partnership at the time brought down $500,000 of Gross Earnings each time they underwrote a ten-million-dollar municipal trust. Further if we discounted that half million by $175,000 in hard expenses (legal, accounting, printing) and internal commission expense we'd come up with $325,000 being brought to the bottom line before salaries, bonus taxes and so on. Done ten times a year, that's three and quarter million dollars. Adding Reynolds Securities to the mix and projecting a 30 to 40% increase in sales (3000 to 4000 thousand units) per underwriting would bring the total bottom line to $4.25 to a possible $5.0 million a year with Reynolds share projected to be a million plus. Adding Reynolds to the mix would theoretically spread the inherent risk of portfolio accumulation and put additional pricing pressure on sellers eager to unload bonds. The economies of size and volume would reduce overall printing expenses and trustee fees. Legal and accounting fees encumbered by the trust underwriting would now be divided three ways instead of two. Setting these important business and practical considerations aside, if Reynolds could garner seventy-five to one hundred thousand dollars a month from entry and participation in the MBF Account it would be considered a resounding success for Devlin, the Byrnes and everyone concerned including me.

Chapter 33

My Secret Life

I reveled in my life at work. In the learning, in the relationships with interesting people, in the beginnings of my understanding of a body of knowledge—bonds, the bond market and the securities industry, a body of knowledge that 90 percent, possibly even 95 percent of the population hadn't a clue about at the time—and in the increasingly broad role I was playing in the department. I might not have put it that way at the time, but I was certainly having the time of my life with certain reservations. I was always concerned about where the next bend in the road would take me. I had high hopes of course, but the future was a complete mystery. I wasn't the sort either to try and broach the subject of my own personal interests. I was preoccupied with my work and the day-to-day tasks at hand both inside and outside the office. Inside the office because that was my job; outside the office because I just wasn't earning enough to support my family or my lifestyle.

From the time I was dismissed from Charles Plohn in early 1970 to sometime in 1976, I worked nearly every day of the year with few exceptions. These were Thanksgiving, Christmas, Easter, and Palm Sunday. I worked the Memorial Day, Labor Day, and July Fourth weekends regularly and the better part of most vacations because when I could string a week together on some of these part-time endeavors, I could make some real money.

Aside from delivering pizzas and being a waiter, I worked for an inventory company. For nearly two years, on weekends and especially on paid holidays and holiday weekends, the inventory work became quite lucrative as I led a crew, driving my own car and traveling far and wide to Pennsylvania, Upstate New York, New Jersey, and Connecticut and once during a week's vacation to Michigan. We inventoried everything from parts departments of auto dealerships to plumbing supply distributors, shoe wholesalers, electrical supply houses, and transistor and electrical component manufactures. Every New Year's day, for several years, my firm, Interactive Data Services, inventoried five ladies' undergarment retail outlets located in the Delancey Street area of Lower Manhattan owned by a family of Orthodox Jews. I had never seen so many brassieres in my life.

For a couple of years, I worked weekends with my wife's late brother Frank Scigliano who co-owned a string of racehorses called Standardbreds, often referred to as pacers and trotters. During the week, I groomed one or two nights for Frank at Roosevelt Raceway or Yonkers for fifty dollars a night and double that and more if the horse I was grooming finished fifth or better in the money, as they say. On weekends, I worked on the farm in Muttontown on Long Island where the horses were stabled, doing anything from cleaning (mucking) out stalls to any job I was asked to do like rubbing horses' legs or bathing the animals. Frank had several trailers and a side business transporting animals mostly from New York to the Amish breeders in Pennsylvania and Ohio, and I participated there as well.

Another job I had for three or four months called for shaping up at the *Daily News* plant on East Forty-First Street in Manhattan, shaping up calls for putting your name on a list. If you're called, you work, otherwise you go home. A couple of buddies, Joe Caroniti and Joe Zarzano, and I signed up to work as extras on Friday and Saturday nights. If your name was called, you worked as a helper in the press room, doing anything from pulling the badly folded papers from the printer escalators to carting them away to helping change the plates in the presses, which could severely burn your hands if you didn't wear gloves. This was a pearl of a job that paid one hundred to one hundred twenty-five dollars a night and exceeded two hundred dollars take-home pay for the weekends work, and we always got a couple of hours off during the night for a nap. Remember, this was the early seventies, when that kind of money was difficult to come by. It was short-lived because you couldn't work there more than fifteen to eighteen weekends in a row unless the fix was in for you to get into the union.

The rule was if you shaped up and worked more than twice a week for twenty-one weeks straight, your name was automatically registered in the union membership. Unless you had been designated to be brought into the shop by the powers that be, you were out and off the roster after about fifteen or sixteen weeks at the most. It was a score though to work for a fifteen-week stretch and worth three thousand dollars plus over that period. Theoretically, you could go back several weeks later and begin the shape up process all over again, which took three to four weeks to get your name high up enough on the list so that you were called to work. I never did though because going there just to shape up on those early idle weeks cut into other opportunities to work elsewhere.

As fast as I made money, that's how fast it was spent. Generally, most of the money I earned went to my wife who paid the bills. Rent, utilities, food, car insurance, clothes, shoes, necessities for the kids, whatever. Rosalie ran the checkbook, was a master at it, and I wanted no part of it. At the same time, I spent whatever I felt I had the need to spend.

Money was important to me. Not just to keep me in cigarettes, carfare, and coffee but also to have a drink or a meal anyplace or anytime I wanted, or take a taxi when an extra fifteen minutes to get there on the bus would not have mattered. In this regard, I rarely thought of saving the dollar by taking the subway or a bus. The move to Municipals in a way was not good for me in that my coworkers and associates earned a much higher salary than I did, and in some fashion, I elevated my right to spend as my colleagues might spend. Fortunately, I didn't have the time to go out drinking one or two nights a week as they did, and my wife would always bring me down a peg whenever she sensed I was getting out of line in this way.

When I was working seven days a week, most of the time, I didn't give a damn about saving a dollar because in working those long hours, I felt entitled to be a little indulgent. Life was moving so fast, and I was putting in so many hours that it didn't feel wrong to grab a late-night meal with the guys on my inventory team or a drink with the catering hall team on Saturday night after a wedding job. My wife, on the other hand, was very conservative, to a fault, in my opinion, watching every penny she spent, which was a guilt trip for me when I thought about it. She was certainly critical of my spending habits but backed off a great deal in her criticism I guess because of the time I put in earning the money and the fact of course that I hid none of it from her.

There were other requirements in my life that justified my working these jobs. The table, for example. I came from a family that lived a certain way. As a married man and the head of a household, coming from a traditional Italian background and the home I came from particularly, I wanted my wife to put the foods on the table that I had become used to in my parent's home. Good cuts of meat and veal occasionally. On Saturday afternoons, if I wasn't around, baloney and American cheese sandwiches were Rosalie's choice for her and the kids, but if I was home for lunch, it was prosciutto and fresh mozzarella. Not that Rosalie would go out and buy it either. For her, that would be tantamount to approval of my extravagance. I would have to bring it home, and when I did, my wife enjoyed it too, even though she might not have approved of the expenditure.

My wife, of course, was critical of all the hours I was putting in. I worked as much as I could whenever and wherever I could. Monday to Thursday evenings with the inventory company, Friday night off unless there was something at the catering hall, then all day Saturday and Sunday with the inventory company. And if there wasn't anything there, which was rare, there were always standby openings at the catering hall. It wasn't that she didn't care about money. It certainly came in handy. She was even eking out some savings by this time, but she felt if I was less extravagant, I wouldn't have to work so many hours.

My need to maintain a certain lifestyle, aside from being part and parcel of my personal makeup was tied to keeping my job on Wall Street and some future vague vision of success I fancied awaited me there. At the same time, I wrestled constantly with the fear of losing my position; through merger, through tough times, though I don't know what. The worry was just a presence, an anxiety, there all the time. If I were to put a profile on it now I suspect it was partly a remnant of my dismissal from Charles Plohn & Co, partly my natural insecurity and lack of confidence and partly the whirlwind existence I lived in. The odd thing was that I didn't consider my days, my work in the office, to be work. The other jobs were work, grooming at the race track especially was hard physical work and dangerous considering that half the guys there walked around with smashed and once or twice broken limbs having been kicked by horse's numerous times. Working in the catering hall or at the inventory company or the Daily News plant were all hard-working jobs. My day job at Reynolds in the Bond Department in comparison seemed like more of an intense social pastime and hobby than a job…a pastime that became a vocation that I alone was uniquely qualified for. To my mind no one was as good as I was at helping the traders and the syndicate departments keep their accounts and problem trades at a minimum. None were as good as I was at helping management to run the office. Working those jobs and having that extra money in my pocket helped me to keep up a front, "play the role" goes the old expression and in doing so I held my fears at bey. At the same time, and this may sound strange, in the midst of these insecurities I felt sure that in some way I was going to carve out a permanent niche here, I was going to make it.

So how in the midst of this insecurity does one find hope. Certainly, the continuing flow of events without mishap builds confidence. The old joke about the fellow who jumps off a tall building comes to mind; saying to himself as he passes each story, so far so good. I took comfort in the ongoing activity, the longer things went on the more permanent a fixture I became. I had experienced difficult times before however and come through them and perhaps unconsciously drew a measure of confidence from them. At the age of seventeen, I found a girlfriend and spent all my time and money in pursuing her and her family's higher social status. I became engaged to be married at the age of twenty and broke that engagement a year or so later. That period is such a blur to me even to this day I'm sure I was very immature and after that I despaired of ever finding happiness again. I bound my wounds in work, during the day for a dress manufacturer in Manhattan and nights stocking shelves in supermarkets and then in the body and fender shop. Ten hours a day and a half day on Saturday. I worked hard and drank hard and played hard like a lot of people I knew, but I was not happy. I was going through the motions and having a good time, but something was lacking. The break-up with my ex had thrown me.

My mother used to say about a particular person she knew of, who periodically went through bouts of crying and feeling sorry for herself, "Leave her alone. She has a right to feel that way, poor Christian soul that she is. She's got the blues. Her life's not so easy. She has this heartache or that heartache. God will help her if she prays, and if He doesn't, she'll come around in a few days and make the best of things."

I felt sometimes I might have been that person. I had a decent group of friends such as they were, good-time Charlies but decent people. But as I approached my midtwenties, I felt my life to be unfulfilled. I was unsatisfied. I worked, there was plenty of money in my pocket, but at night, I secretly prayed myself to sleep. Maybe you had to have lived in the fifties and sixties to understand this. Just listen to the music—"My Prayer," "Since I Don't Have You," "Tears on My Pillow." I was supposed to have found a love by then, been married, and working my way toward a family of my own. Had I missed my chance? Falling in love and marrying and having children was ordained for someone with my family background. It was coming through for many of my family peers too because I seemed to be going to a cousin's or friend's wedding every six months. As I neared twenty-five years of age and had not found a mate, I was somehow out of step with the world. I had a job, money, friends but not what my mother and father had or what my sister and brother and so many of my cousins had. I had no purpose, nothing to really live for, and no one to work with toward a future or to sleep and dream with at night.

Then, in the space of a year, I fell in love. More importantly, someone fell in love with me. We got married. I met Mario who gave me a job where I could earn two hundred dollars a week with no dirt under my fingernails, wearing a coat and tie. This was when police and fireman were earning only one hundred twenty-five dollars, if they could get the job at all. In June of 1969, I followed Mario to another firm, and my good fortune persisted in that my earnings stayed the same while my hours were reduced by nearly a third. A few months later, in September, my son Pat was born, and in December, imagine my shock when I received a bonus amounting to near two thousand dollars after taxes. Unbelievably, the firm went down just a couple of months later, but luckily, I was able to overcome that hurdle too, with divine help it seemed.

Now, several years after stumbling onto the job at Reynolds, I had moved up to a new position of some consequence and authority. How could I not believe at this point that if I hung on it was just a matter of time until greater success was going to come my way? It wasn't just that I felt lucky. You may put the book down after you read this, or you may understand what I mean when I say that the good fortune I had on Wall Street and in my personal life during those years I felt to be not luck but the finger of God. What else could it be? I wasn't following a plan I had laid out nor did I have one for the future.

But I had certain convictions. I was convinced that my destiny had to be helped along, and I had to finance the road to success on Wall Street like a lost leader in a supermarket sale. I did it with grooming and wearing good clothes and reading books and the papers seven days a week and with all those part-time jobs, and so what if they boosted my work week to eighty and ninety hours, they put the money in my pocket to play the role I was destined to get in some yet unmade movie. I was fortunate too, healthy and strong, enthusiastic and optimistic, and I simply disregarded fatigue and the grind. I must say as well I was blessed with a wife who stood by me and rolled with whatever was going on.

I know all of this sounds odd, perhaps trite and childish that a thirty-year-old could vacillate this way between fear of failure and a fairy tale vision of success. But I came from a family that had encountered enormous pain and adversity and had only survived and prospered through faith. I couldn't recall any rancor, bile, mean-spirited-ness, or envy toward the world ever expressed in my family, which is quite surprising since my mother and father lost two children to serious disease. My sisters Rose and Marion, one who died from what used to be called infantile paralysis at age twelve, most likely some form of MS, while the other was born with a massive heart murmur and died at age nine. In the thirties, these illnesses were not very fixable no matter what means a family may have had. My mother was forty-four years old when I was born with a club foot in 1943. I weighed fourteen pounds and was sent home after a week while my mother convalesced in hospital for months. I was treated through the years with a series of casts that gradually straightened my right foot enough so that I could walk on my own at age four.

My mother and father lost these two children before I was born, and my sister lost a child, my niece Louise, to Hodgkin's disease in the late fifties. I never met my sisters who died before I was born, but Louise was a beautiful chubby-cheeked little girl who broke our hearts when she passed at age thirteen in 1958. One would think with all this grief, these tragic events my family had endured, that they might have produced a less well-adjusted child than me. I am grateful to my family for everything they gave me, especially their will to go on with faith in the goodness of God no matter what, which they passed on to me.

Chapter 34

Reynolds Sponsors a UIT

I can't put a finger on the exact timing of this MBF 6 underwriting; sometime in mid- to late 1973 is my best guess. In any case, it was around the time or close to when the market began showing signs of deterioration after having rallied since mid-1970. The world was in great political and violent turmoil. In the United States, Watergate was in the headlines every day, and Richard Nixon's thin skin was being punctured daily. The Cold War was in full force, and if that wasn't enough, Arab-Israeli relations were a boiling cauldron with the Israelis in a rickety truce with the Arabs after a hot war with Syria and Egypt and if that wasn't enough the carnage in Vietnam was still raging. Great financial dislocation was about to be born as well because in 1973, the shah of Iran, a huge supplier of oil to the West, nationalized all of Iran's oil production while, almost simultaneously, the Arab oil-producing nations embargoed oil shipments to the West and Japan because the United States and most of the world sided with Israel against the Palestinians.

Oddly enough, in some ways, Wall Street, if one were to visualize it that way, might have resembled a ravaged battleground as well. Old-line firms over the 1970–1973 period, names like Walston & DuPont, Haydn-Stone, Loeb-Rhodes, Goodbody, Glore-Forgan, Eastman Dillon, and Blyth had been blown out of existence for a variety of reasons that included; an inability to recover from poor or lackadaisical management, poor capital management, and not seeing the risk that operations problems posed, and the capital these problems ate up when left unattended. It was a new era fraught with risk, and a conservative attitude was necessary in the management of capital, which contrary to conventional wisdom was not as prevalent as it should have been. Now, smaller firms, managed by brilliant executive teams, saw to the ability to manage their capital and process their business so well that they literally conquered and ate up the accounts of some of the old line firms. The formerly bullish markets of the recent past were experiencing the onset of shaky markets, and at Reynolds, a few bad deals in which heavy losses were incurred along with several washes and a lot of nail-biters foreshadowed the end of the Phelps-Fenn honeymoon.

Into this environment, we brought to market as sponsors with our new partners, Dean Witter and Paine Webber, the Municipal Bond Fund Series 6 or MBF 6 as we called it. About nine-thirty on the day the deal came; and this is a distinct and near-exact memory, a near jubilant Bill Byrne Sr. emerged from Bill Devlin's office to announce to me that our share of the sponsor's accumulation profit was slightly less than sixty-five thousand dollars.

"That sixty-five thousand will cover a multitude of sins," he then said, meaning these portfolio-underwriting profits would cancel losses taken on individual bond positions and syndicate participations off the books. Too bad it wasn't a plus all by itself, but it was better this way than not having it at all.

Because I had been handling the unit trust business with Merrill Lynch, I was put in charge of the distribution, sale, and ticketing of the deal. That and because I knew most of the players who sold the stuff in the branch office system. I had been told to break off my relationship with Merrill and MIT's about five or six weeks before MBF 6 came along. With Merrill, if I got five hundred thousand dollars' worth of orders, that's what I bought—a wash, no position remaining, no possibility of loss, and no problems. Here, I would have something over $3 million (actually $3.75 million worth, 30 percent of the deal of a $12 million deal), and the reality of it was there were only $900,000 worth of orders on the date of underwriting, which I thought was an achievement in its own right. The remaining unsold units after the first date of the offering were priced to the market every day until all units were sold. Were the market to deteriorate, we would incur a loss on the unsold units each time they were marked down. Turning a profit on the unsold units was also a possibility, but overall market conditions were generally not in our favor at the time.

When Paine-Webber and Dean Witter finished selling their allotments three or four days into the deal, they began working on ours, allowing me to sell three or four hundred a day back to them while selling one to two hundred a day in our own firm. I remember the deal going quite slowly and being very painful to me and all those concerned, although we did not absorb much price deterioration, which was lucky.

Simultaneous to the underwriting of MBF 6, we bought three deals as lead manager. I had never presided operationally over running the book on a newly issued municipal bond offering, and the plain truth is that I mucked it up badly. These were three housing finance authority deals (HFAs), two in Florida and one in Ohio. All three deals got off to a slow and rocky start. I was lucky to think of making a few phone calls both in-house and to the Street that helped me out, but the billing was slow and the settlement date was delayed a few days because I was late in putting the order into the Signature Company for the printing of the bonds.

At the same time, Operations Management at 2 Broadway were up in arms because so many bond trades were getting screwed up and not getting fixed as quickly as they should have been. Twenty or thirty bond trades a week (and sometimes more) were failing to deliver or be received on time, but I thought that was simply a matter of the increased volume. It was a bit of a fiasco I admit, but my little unit was managing the sale of MBF 6, managing the lead manager position on several municipal deals while handing the departments corrections. The situation reached a point where I and my assistant Fred Mastermaker and the other clerk who worked for me were overwhelmed. Operations at Two Broadway felt that they had to act and so they sent up a veteran operations guy who'd been recently hired out of the wreckage the lately failed Loab Rhodes. He discounted both Fred Mastermaker, the fellow working for me, and myself and sort of brutally assessed the situation, saying frequently that he "didn't want to cast any aspersions but blah, blah, blah." For my part, I thought he looked at the situation as a way of "making his bones at the firm." I found out later that Operations Management at 2 Broadway wanted to fire me based on his recommendations. Maybe he saw it as a way of getting my job. I honestly don't know.

Luckily, Bond Department management in the form of the Byrnes, especially Bill Jr. whom I talked to quite often, saw I was in over my head. In whatever deliberations that went on, several changes were made. The first thing that happened was all the orders for unit trusts were sent with a drop off copy to operations. We no longer had to proofread and notate tickets. We simply approved the quantities at the end of the day with someone in operations and left all the processing to be done by 2 Broadway. This freed us up to make and answer all the calls from the field about the unit trust business and gave us more time to handle the departments operations, both the current everyday corrections and the cleanup of the aged problems.

As to my termination, I'm sure the Byrnes went to bat for me big time, and I'm equally sure Bill Devlin would have gone along with my firing if that was what it would take to appease the operations people. However, I had made the unfamiliar terrain of the wire house smooth for the Byrnes and their people, helping them with their move and transition. I took care of anything from operational problems to getting their employees set up in their new quarters, showing them everything from how to get office supplies to filling out forms for new business cards. I also staffed my operations units with former Phelps-Fenn employees, one of whom was a useless, totally out of touch old man named Jim Quinn whom we somehow finally placed at 2 Broadway. In fact, at the time, anything that disturbed either the Byrnes tranquility or Devlin's for that matter, from getting a runner to the deregistration of bonds, was my problem to fix, so there was a stake in it for management to keep me around and so the crisis passed.

Chapter 35

Surprise: A New Alignment

Three or four months after the underwriting of MBF 6 and the operations and underwriting screw-ups mentioned, a group of changes came about that literally swept me off my feet. Two Broadway operations took charge, putting their own personnel in place in Bond Department operations. I went into the Municipal Syndicate Department, partnering up with Clem Schaefer who turned Corporate Syndicate over to a new hire and came back into Municipals to manage me and the unit trust sales effort. The numbers (i.e., the money that could be made sponsoring and selling municipal UITs) was too big to ignore once the firm's management began to understand the products implications as a moneymaker. However, they decided to go about it differently than they had been doing. This was the beginning of a new life for me, and I didn't question it in any way. I just went along. I was still consulted on bond operations and was charged with fixing all the operations problems with unit trusts, but my main job was the marketing, sales, and service of the firm's unit trust business.

I think we were underwriting MBF series 8 or 9 when Clem and I moved in with Municipal Syndicate. Whichever it was turned out to be the last unit trust underwriting Reynolds participated in with the Paine-Webber/Dean Witter group. Once that connection was broken, we joined the Merrill Lynch group as sponsors and underwriters of the Municipal Investment Trust Fund, otherwise known as MITF. While I was not privy to any discussions leading up to these decisions and events, eventually I would come to understand the reasoning.

The firm had not been ready for the risk associated with three- to four-million-dollar commitments in unit trusts nor was its sales organization able to handle consecutive underwritings of this volume no matter how rich the rewards would be in underwriting and accumulation profits the department and the firm could garner from them. There was potential, however, to make a good deal of money selling unit trusts, and partnering as a sponsor with Merrill Lynch at 10 or 12 percent of their trusts, which averaged twenty million dollars, Proceeding this way would be less of a burden at present and give us time to build up our sales. Norman Schevey, who headed UITs at Merrill, had been a syndicate partner with Reynolds when he was with Goodbody and remained a good friend of Clem's. An added starter was our sales force, generally speaking, was familiar with the MITF product as it had been featured in the firm several years before (early to midsixties) and had continued under my own management until recently. Clem and I, then, were a new creation, an adjunct of the Municipal Bond Department called Unit Trusts, formed for the purpose of marketing what was essentially a new though somewhat familiar product to the firm.

The other occupants of the space were Bill Kondratuck and Mike Fitzsimmons. Mike had replaced Tom Sadler as Kondi's number two. The space we were in, an alcove you might call it, was actually the space of three private offices with the partitions removed to form perhaps a thirty-foot-by-fifteen-foot deep space. Fitzsimons and Kondratuck occupied desks just behind Clem and myself.

Kondi, hardworking, quick thinking, businesslike, and pleasant most of the time, was always very, very busy. The schedule of deals had picked up immensely with the combining of the Phelps and Reynolds bidding histories, and the need for money by municipalities had picked up dramatically as well.

Mike Fitzsimmons, Kondratuck's new number two, was an amazingly well-organized, well-spoken, and articulate in a very measured Old World way, professorial, and I mean Cambridge or Yale or what I imagined those to be, and a real contrast to the streetwise brawler types who were common in the municipal business. While there was some interaction between us, we were definitely two separate teams involved in selling two very separate though related entities. We might have a laugh here and there together at some passing phenomenon, but we really didn't have a great deal of interaction.

In any case, here I was, working in close quarters with three guys who were experts in the art of the interest rate market and underwriting fixed income securities, namely municipal bonds. They had a hand in the creation of and oversight of hundreds of millions, no doubt billions, of dollars' worth of loans in the form of bonds. They understood the rules and the laws they were required to abide by and handling the attendant risks. They had the fearlessness and personal fortitude and the stomach to take that risk on their shoulders and into their minds and hearts and souls. Believe me, when you carry a twenty-million-dollar position, you do it mind, body, and soul. Knowledge is a terrible thing. I say this because it was not until I worked in this room with these men that I understood what it was to take risk. To say I want three or five million dollars' worth five or six times a week and then be personally responsible for the ownership of all or diminishing quantities of that inventory over a week or two while the market is moving sideways or against you. By the same token, this was their business, and they took risk like rolling off a log. I was fortunate to be with them, to be able to listen to them, and learn from them.

Chapter 36

Clem Schaefer

My new partner, Clem Schaefer, had been at Reynolds Securities since the early sixties and possibly even the late fifties. By the time we began working together, we had known each other for a few years, but beyond telling a joke occasionally or comparing some notes on a news story, the most interaction we'd had was when problems came up in his trading accounts. I had been balancing them and making corrections for his Corporate Syndicate operation since the move to the tenth floor. Now that we were working together as partners, we got a little closer. Clem had been hired on at Reynolds as a sales trainee in the firm's Brooklyn office. After graduating from Oceanside High School on Long Island, he attended Becknell University in Pennsylvania. At first, he wanted to make his entry point into Wall Street at the corporate finance level. He told me about one particular interview with Dominick & Dominick, an old-line investment banking shop founded in the 1870s, where he was told on several occasions he did not meet their requisites because his father was a butcher. Social standing was still quite important then. Suitability for employment in finance required a familiarity with professional money on a high level through breeding or family connections or business association or through parents and relations.

This is simply the standard the old-line firms had. If JP Morgan or Morgan Guaranty, First Boston, Dominick & Dominick, or Lazard were going to have you work with or pursue the likes of the presidents and CEOs of the major corporations in the United States, then you had to have certain pedigree's that went along with drinking out of the right glass and using the right fork and maybe some country club affiliations that went along with living in New Rochelle or Greenwich.

Clem would often joke about what some of the more "high born" people in our profession might think of us, about our acceptability in polite society, as I was a former grocery boy and he a butcher's son.

When we had to attend some social event like the graduation of a training class or one of the firm's charitable events, he would jokingly say, "Don't let 'em know we broke down the fruit stand and rolled up the awning before we scrubbed our fingernails and put on our Sunday clothes. They're not crazy about fruit venders and butchers up there."

After being turned down by the white shoe investment banking firms First Boston, Morgan Stanley, and the aforementioned Dominick & Dominick, Clem decided to go the "retail firm sales trainee route" and was eventually hired as a sales trainee in Reynolds Security's Brooklyn office. In the late fifties and early sixties, the training programs of the larger firms were three-month affairs where prospective stockbrokers got a thorough grounding in the securities industry while studying for the Series 7 exam, which made them legally qualified to sell securities. Once he'd secured his Series 7 license, Clem prospected for new accounts but did not have a great deal of luck. It takes a certain kind of individual to say over and over and over again, "Can I put you in for a thousand shares, or will it be two thousand?" or "Will you be taking twenty thousand dollars' or fifty thousand dollars' worth of these New York State Thruway Authority bonds?" and not be nonplussed when the client or prospect says no, then go back in and ask for a lower amount immediately thereafter or the next day. Truth be told, I don't think I could have made it myself as a commission salesman either. Clem would often say you had to be a taker to be a salesman (read as stockbroker), but you had to be a giver to be a marketer. Salesman needed to be brazen and pushy as well as enthusiastic and service-oriented and immune to rejection. This was not a requirement of the in-house service/marketer position. The sales force was a captive audience that wanted to hear from us, as opposed to investors who had to be convinced, cajoled and sought out. In-house service and marketing operatives however had to be service oriented, as well as knowledgeable and resourceful enough to get the answers to questions that were not common knowledge. Enthusiasm was not a requirement per se, but went a long way in making the operative effective. Marketing and liaison operatives in a brokerage firm only had to be service-oriented, enthusiastic, and knowledgeable of course.

Clem did eventually have some success selling municipal bonds. Their conservative nature dovetailed with his own conservative bent, making him comfortable with and enthusiastic about them. So selling municipal's put him in touch on a regular basis with the Municipal Bond Department, which led to his encounter with the Long Island crowd that inhabited the municipal business at the time. Bill Devlin who ran Municipals at Reynolds was a Rockville Centre inhabitant, which was just a stone's throw from Oceanside where Clem lived. Jim Duncan, the leading producer (salesman) in Municipals, went to high school with Clem and starred on the Oceanside High School basketball team that Clem also played on. Once these associations developed, it was just a matter of time before Clem would join the Municipal Bond Department.

The ensuing years up to the early to mid-sixties Clem spent learning the municipal trade in both the underwriting and trading forms and then taking on the project of starting up a Corporate Syndicate Department operation circa 1968–1972, give or take a year either way. During those years in Municipals, Clem became a member of a group that might have been called "the young lions" of Reynolds Securities. This was a sort of "in crowd" of up and comers that formed a "litter of cubs" that Reynolds Securities management, in the persons of Tom Staley and Bob Gardiner, might call upon to shepherd important sectors of business or operations of interest to the firm. This included Jim Bach and Vona Hopkins who ran mutual funds in the sixties to seventies, Ray DiRussa who was the manager of the firm's flagship New York office at 120 Broadway, Dave Mack who started the Equity Institutional Sales Operation, and Hyder Haynes who ran Equity Syndicate for many years among several others. Howard Dean Sr., the father of the former governor of Vermont, was a partner in the firm and a close confidant of Robert Gardener may have played a leadership role in this group.

I must emphasize I don't know much about the goings on of this period because it was before my time. My view of that time is rendered from what Clem told me during the years we were associated with one another. I met Clem in 1971–72, when I was brought into the Bond Department from DECAB, several years after the upswing in the underwriting of preferred stocks and corporate bonds in the sixties brought the firm to the conclusion that it should mount a meaningful sales effort in this area. It was logical that Clem, the member of the "in crowd" hailing from the Municipal Bond Department, should head the operation, and it should be housed physically on Municipal Bond Department real estate.

Chapter 37

The South Shore Bond Club: More Clem Schaefer

Harking back to Clem Schaefer's management of Corporate Syndicate, it's important to know Clem was a planner and a thinker. He rarely did anything by the seat of his pants, and that when he was chosen for the job, he must have had good reason to believe he would succeed in mounting an effort in the preferred stock-corporate bond area for Reynolds even though it was not his trade specifically. My theory as to why Clem took the job and why he might have been confident in his ability to achieve success was his membership in the South Shore (South Shore of Long Island) Bond Club. Unlike the Municipal Bond Club of New York and many other such organizations around the country, the South Shore Bond Club (SSBC) had no charter, no president, elected board, or formal meetings nor dues or public agenda. In fact, it never even had a name as far as I knew until I dubbed it as such in my notes. The club existed nonetheless, meeting informally twice a day on the Main Line of the Long Island Railroad, which traversed the space between the Town of Babylon in Suffolk County and Penn Station in New York City or the LIRR Atlantic Avenue Station in Brooklyn, either one just a twenty-minute subway ride from Wall Street. The club met in small groups in the morning at various times on varying trains with larger more raucous sessions held in the bar cars that left Penn Station or Atlantic Avenue in Brooklyn between five twenty and five thirty-five for the evening commute home. Considering the amount of business that undoubtedly transpires on the golf course, it should come as no surprise that billions of dollars' worth of bonds were priced and traded on these rails annually.

I never became a full-fledged member of the club as the business track I was on was unit trusts rather than pure fixed income. I didn't take risk in the market the way these fellows did, and I didn't do business directly with any of them as Clem had in both of the "bond lives" he had led—the first in municipals and the second when he got into corporates. I could and did discuss the broader markets with these guys, but unlike other members, I couldn't take several million bonds off their hands or sell a million to them either. UITs were priced by an independent evaluator, Standard & Poors. The South Shore club members were traders or syndicate-oriented, purists as it were.

I knew all the members, however, and as Clem's friend and number two, I was always welcome in the presence of club members whether on the train, at lunch, or any other Street function. I attended meetings of the club from time when I took the LIRR to or from Rockville Center instead of Oceanside, which was my regular commute. Morning meetings might be casual discussions about the days newspaper headlines or subdued incisive conversation about the new issue calendar: which deals would be easily sold, what firms were likely to stay in what deals, who would drop out and who had orders for particular maturities. Some gave up information willingly while others probed for it. I'm sure Devlin, nicknamed the Duke by club members, imparted whatever he heard on these mornings to Kondratuck.

Another big topic of conversation might be who owned what in the secondary market and what kind of bid it would take to buy this or sell that block of bonds or where there might be an order for them or even who might be interested in holding on to five or ten million for a week or so until some inventory might be disposed of. This was called parking bonds and not common practice or playing by the rules but none the less practiced by some. Make no mistake, friendship easily turned to a kind of blood in the water shark mentality when it became known that one of their number might be choking on a couple of million bonds that had to be cleared out. The term "all is fair in love and war" certainly applied here.

Evening meetings were less serious although one could tell at a glance who might have had a gloriously profitable day or one filled with pain and loss. At evening meetings, one could observe every manner and type of drinker, from the guy who nursed a scotch and water for the entire forty-minute trip to Rockville Centre, to the nasty drunk who'd be picking a fight after downing a few, to the one resembling the Jackie Gleason character known as Charlie Bracken the Loudmouth, complete with off-color, loud, and often uncouth embarrassing remarks. Any night had the capability of producing a couple of hilarious practical jokes or someone being sick or so loaded that they missed a stop or slept their booze off riding to the end of the line. On other nights, you might pick up on the threads of an incisive conversation about the business or the philosophical writings of Descartes. At any given time, the group might break out into spontaneous song or someone would render a Shakespearean soliloquy. Make no mistake, notwithstanding a good deal of their behavior, these were not stupid men by any stretch of the imagination, one or two had been educated at some of the finest schools in America.

Evening meetings might end abruptly as members in the bar car on the train that came out from Brooklyn might have to change trains at Jamaica (the Long Island Railroad's East-West hub) to get to their destination, while members in the bar car on the train that came out of Manhattan might have to change as well. The ride from either station took about twenty minutes to reach Jamaica. The change required the commuter to cross a platform and board the train at an adjacent platform. On occasion, the change necessitated crossing the platform and walking through the train on the next platform to a third train across from the one just traversed.

Friday nights proved to be the most perilous and, at the same time, the most comical, bordering on the insane. On Friday, the imbibers were prone to let go completely, not that they didn't let go during the week. It was just Friday nights were often out of hand because the drinking began at lunch. The dangerous part took on a sort of hilarious tone during the three to five minutes spent in

Jamaica watching the stupefied club members navigate their way across the platforms to the trains that would take them to their final destinations. The spilt drinks, the blind leading the blind, the runs and stumble back for forgotten packages or briefcases and the frantic backtracking, the confused and disappointed body language displayed when the bar cars of adjacent trains were offset, the near falls, and on occasion, the forlorn or blank looks on faces when trains left guys stranded on platforms sometimes coatless and hatless but with drink in hand. These sights, though infrequent, when they occurred were alternately comical or pathetic depending on my frame of mind when I witnessed them and tempered by whether I had had a drink or not myself.

Most of the club members were in the municipal business. However, prominent among them were two leaders in the corporate bond business. Bill Marlin, whom Clem called a "genius," headed the Bond Department at Bache & Co. and an older gentleman from Rockville Centre named Larry Keating who had managed corporate bond trading at Goodbody and possibly the entire corporate bond operation at Goodbody, which was thriving in the early and midsixties. Bill Marlin and Larry Keating were leading figures in the corporate bond industry of the time and, as such, were always seeking to mitigate risk through broadening their distribution network. They eagerly let Clem into deals and supplied him with bonds and preferred stock, which in effect, amounted to making him a success in his new endeavor at Reynolds and at the same time, if one chose to look at it this way, amounted to the de facto annexation of the Reynolds Securities sales organization by Keating and Marlin. Why not. It was profitable to all the firms involved, and Clem was one of their own, a favorite son of Long Island and a fellow SSBC member. And if we don't know it by now, distribution is the key to mitigating risk no matter where you come from or who you are.

Chapter 38

More Reynolds

Much of Clem Schaefer's attitude and outlook on business was informed by the years he headed Corporate Syndicate and the years before when he ran with the up and comers—the young lions of Reynolds as I called them. His distaste for the political infighting that often took place above the middle management level became very apparent to me. Perhaps I am putting it too strongly, but I think Clem was very put off by the lengths to which people would go (*depths* is perhaps the correct term) to get ahead, achieve success, and be looked upon with favor by ones superiors and, at the same time, very much disappointed by the behavior of some of his superiors as well.

I thought working directly for Bob Gardiner and, by default, Tom Staley made Clem privy to the pain of being accepted or rejected or simply put out in limbo by the rulers of the firm. Today, despite all the talk and the public outcry against CEOs, there is much more public exposure and transparency vis-à-vis the top echelons of large corporations. The CEOs are in the spotlight, people go to the press or write tell-all books, private communication via email and text is much more vulnerable to exposure than a crumpled note tossed into the wastebasket, and so untoward behavior has had to modify or run the risk of being exposed. Large corporations continue as oligarchies run by CEOs and boards of directors, but in the sixties and seventies, the doors were closed. The public could only surmise how tough and cutthroat and possibly cruel life was in the boardroom. Sometimes a play or movie came out about it like *Patterns* with Van Heflin and

Everett Sloan and *Sweet Smell of Success* with Burt Lancaster and Tony Curtis. These showed the ruthlessness of the boardroom and the rich and powerful, but the depictions were very remote from a life that, at least, I imagined although they made for great drama and entertainment.

I don't want to make it sound like there was a torture chamber anywhere at Reynolds, but Clem once told me about his having to turn his back and walk out of a room to make a statement regarding the fulfillment of previously agreed upon employee bonuses. Paltry sums compared to the money being made by his department much less the firm. He said he lived in fear for nearly a week after that, thinking he was going to lose his job. On another occasion, during a management meeting in North Carolina, he was invited to the home of Tom Staley for a private luncheon where a number of new business ideas were presented by several employees sitting at the table. He witnessed, as he put it, the "tearing to shreds" of one of the presenters by Tom Staley. I think Clem himself was always fearful of the embarrassment of being on the short end of one of these dressing downs. He would sometimes say when discussing upper management, especially Tom Staley, "These are not nice people."

Indeed, I was told if I ever got a call from TF (Tom Staley), I should put him on hold and immediately find someone in management to talk to him. On one occasion, I did get a call. We had been up and running on the tenth floor for several months, and it was very busy at the time. There were stretches during the day when everyone in the department both in Trading and Syndicate were on the phone for extended periods of time. If you were on the outside trying to call in, it could, be quite frustrating. Apparently, Staley bought a one-hundred-thousand-dollar lot and wanted to ask Kondratuck a question. He finally called my extension, the operations number, I guess out of frustration. Just the tone, the rancor I heard in his asking for Kondratuck, tipped me off to who it was. I just said, "Hold on sir," and went and got Kondratuck.

It was explained to me later that TF wouldn't think twice about firing someone of lower status if he got answers he deemed unsatisfactory.

Thomas F Staley was an enigmatic figure to me and many others because his reputation for sternness, meanness and intolerance in contrast often didn't fit with one's personal encounters with the man. A few months after I was brought into the bond department at 120 Broadway, I found he was standing beside me waiting for the elevator on the 12th floor. I think our eyes met and I nodded casually and politely to him. I had no idea who he was although there was an aura of authority about the man and you couldn't help noticing especially how well dressed he was, even in shirtsleeves. A moment later, alone with Staley in the elevator waiting for the doors to close he turns to me and quite boisterously says,

"Did you read the good book today?" Then when I didn't answer, he repeated it even more emphatically and a little bit in my face. He appeared as if he was a bit part character in a Faulkner play. "Boy!" he says. "Did you read your good book today?"

My answer, and the only thing I could think of, was to say, "I'm a Roman Catholic. I go to mass on Sundays and observe the rules of being a good Christian, but no, I didn't read any scripture today."

We were down to the lobby by this time, and he said something like, "Well, that's fine, young man. That's a good answer, boy," and walks out. Just like Bob's your uncle, as the English say. I myself walked out of the elevator after him and have remembered the incident all my life.

Some referred to TF as Lefty because he would often reach out to shake your hand with his left hand as if he were putting his hand out to be kissed like a cardinal or a king. The flip side of Lefty was another persona characterized by his oft repeated remark, "I'm just a salesman."

He would ask when encountering product area personnel or salesman in the field what their best sales idea today was, and once recited, he would in turn postulate one of his own and then ask what your next best one was; actually Clem and I co-opted this technique several years later and conducted sales meetings with this theme.

I heard a story about TF that took place on the Metro North rail line upon which he commuted to his home in Scarsdale when he was in New York. One evening, he found himself seated near or behind two gentleman talking about a deal that they had been talking to Merrill Lynch about, which had apparently been turned down. After having heard something of their conversation, he apologized for interrupting, handing one or both a card with his name and number on it with a second name and phone number handwritten on the back, suggesting they call that person at Reynolds Securities. When asked who he was, he replied, "Oh, I'm just a salesman there."

Looking at the fine figure TF cut, even as an old man, one could not mistake his polished demeanor and the personal magnetism he radiated for anything as common as the word *just* suggested. I'm sure the two fellows he encountered on the train that evening saw through his act. The deal (I was told) they were pitching was called Barnett Bond Banks of Florida, and its first installment was twenty million dollars, and indeed, I think several of them were done in the late sixties and early seventies, as they were all over our trade listings at the time I joined the firm in April of 1970.

Tom Staley may have deprecatingly referred to himself as 'just a salesmen," but I learned, actually gradually came to the realization, everyone is a salesman of some stripe on Wall Street, whether you were selling bonds or stock or your idea to sell more bonds and stock or your plan to get others to sell more bonds or stock (read as mutual funds, annuities, commodities, managed money, or whatever else the firm was interested in selling at any given time). In late 1973, early 1974, Clem and I partnered up. Clem, already a salesman and marketer/marketeer, and I would become one sitting alongside him. Our clients being the sales force we marketed to and served.

Chapter 39

The Go-Go Sixties and the Wall Street Vision

The failed go-go mutual fund era of the 1960s was a subject that Clem brought up from time to time in discussions about the mass marketing of investments and investment products other than individual stocks and bonds. The go-go era was a period during which an enormous public interest in the stock market, and to a lesser degree the credit markets, translated to big money being made by the large Wall Street firms and several independent mutual fund operations located in New York and Boston. This expansion of sales and stock ownership through mutual funds caused the ensuing market collapse of the late sixties to cut across a greater cross section of Americans than ever before. Not as many as there are in the market today but big enough to cause plenty of press by the standards of the time. There were no TV business networks at the time that might have prepared the public for the risks they were taking. For many Wall Street operatives, it was a golden chance that failed. Others took a more derisive tone because the losses incurred on a broad scale led to so much bad press directed at Wall Street. The fixed-income crowd was especially annoyed because the public tarred them with the same broad brush it painted the equity crowd with.

Clem, while in the second camp, had strong convictions regarding the benefits that investing could provide for individual investors. He, along with many others, was very much interested in finding the solution to resurrecting the public's enthusiasm for investing despite past experience. This concern is less important today because of the widespread participation of both the public and the press in all things financial. However, in the sixties and seventies, when the country's still somewhat naive middle class was first burned by the market, the public anger and disappointment of clients directed at the brokerage firms and their brokers who had sold them these securities was very deeply felt.

There was lots of blame and anger to go around on both sides—the poetic license and good old boy salesmanship of the salesman/stockbroker and the wanting to believe that markets go up forever on the part of the investors. Investors have short-term memories, especially of their own greed, and greed is often the very emotion or character trait that stockbrokers play on to make sales. By the same token, the rules regarding disclosure of risk were nearly nonexistent. Within the firms, the sales forces screamed to management about the lack of due diligence, timely notification, and buyer-beware attitude. Many salesman lost books of clients that had taken years to build and had to start all over again. The phenomenon of the go-go sixties and the huge public interest and buying wave of stocks and mutual funds it engendered fascinated Clem and many others. The many books written about the period are testament. The potentially enormous appetite the public could have for investments and, in turn, its revenue producing potential was something Clem didn't just talk about. There was a great driving force within him that he would eventually instill and enliven in me.

I would eventually understand Clem believed, knew instinctively, that Wall Street would again have the opportunity and the ability to market and merchandise to the public's enormous appetite to invest, especially in fixed-income securities. It would be fair to say he dreamed he could be instrumental in making that happen while making his own fortune in doing so. This is the identical dream Colonel Sanders had when he drove around the country cooking Kentucky Fried Chicken from the trunk of his car or any other spirited entrepreneurial idea from the Olivieri brothers in Philadelphia inventing the "cheesesteak sandwich" to Jeff Bezos or Mark Zuckerberg and no less legitimate.

The problem that was continually pondered upon then was the delivery of an investment product that could provide a competitive rate of return and exhibit ongoing and dependable safety of principal characteristics and liquidity in both rising and declining markets. Clearly, after the go-go debacle, it was thought that equity mutual funds (composed of stocks) were not the answer because of the way they fell apart when markets deteriorated. It was true that bonds put into mutual funds did not hold up well in declining markets. Even when the underlying portfolio of a mutual fund was said to be closed end, that it couldn't be traded, the funds liquidity often suffered because shares were traded based on the supply and demand for shares rather than the aspects of their underlying portfolio. The other problem in mutual funds was the constant erosion of principal caused by the application of management fees and expenses, meaning every year anywhere from 0.5 to 1.5 percent of the value of the securities was taken by the investment manager.

On the other hand, Clem was fixed on the idea that unit trusts (as opposed to mutual funds) was a better way to invest for the American public at large. He felt that unit trusts were a better structured bond, made stronger by diversification while continuing to maintain the integrity of a bonds fixed stream of income and fixed maturity value, which had a direct impact on liquidity and stability of income.

Unit trusts, from Clem's point of view, could be believed in and relied upon to perform adequately well in the market, just like individual bonds. Of course nobody cares when the market is on the rise or when interest rates are steady or coming down, but the relief provided by par or" fixed maturity value" value and a fixed income is precious breath to an investor and great consolation when the market is headed south (i.e., when interest rates are rising). In Clem's way of thinking, unit trusts were an answer and a pathway to bringing back all those disappointed mutual fund investors and making a lot of money while doing so. For my part, I was just learning. I did not see so deeply into the merchandising mindset Clem and his "young lion" counterparts understood. I was, however, beginning to understand the quite beautiful symmetry of bonds and would eventually become as fervent and as enthusiastic a believer as my new boss was.

Chapter 40

The Work and the Market Climate

By the end of the year, the small department Clem and I formed would be selling two additional investments besides the municipal product known as the MITF. We joined Merrill Lynch in sponsoring the Corporate Income Fund and the Corporate Income Fund Preferred Stock series. The first, the Corporate Income Fund was composed BBB or better rated corporate bonds, anything from Con Ed to Delta Airlines to IBM and Canadian Hydro Power and several hundred others. Investors in lower tax brackets, small institutions and pension accounts, and plans protected from taxation were candidates for the purchase of corporate bonds. The Corporate Income Fund Preferred Stock Series, composed of stocks with fixed dividends, had a special tax benefit to corporations. Only 15 percent of the income from this portfolio was taxable to the corporate holder at that time. The three investment products formed a lexicon of investments that a broker could offer to a variety of investment requirements that came about among his clients and prospects.

The sort of half-hearted, not fully thought out entry and venture into the joint sponsorship of a Unit Trust with Paine Webber and Dean Witter now became a seriously managed joint sponsorship with Merrill Lynch in not just one product but three separate investment vehicles.

The days became quite busy indeed learning the various aspects of the new trusts we were offering and explaining them to an ever growing base of brokers who offered them to their clients. There was a constant flow of calls, questions, situations to navigate, and decisions to be made, and I, the ex-body and fender mechanic, was in the thick of it.

Bill Kondratuck and Mike Fitzsimons who comprised Municipal Syndicate just behind Clem and myself were no less busy than we were. We were not involved with each other's work per se, but because of our proximity to one another, we were very much aware of the ease or difficulty with which our work proceeded. We were both slaves to the interest rate market, the individual calendars of upcoming new issues in each of our markets, and the information about them that was required to be digested, sometimes formally listed, pondered upon and acted upon, and finally delivered out to the sales forces for consumption and sale. Being in Municipal Syndicate in our little office enclosure brought us very close to intense market decision making in a shaky market. Mike and Kondi put their marbles on the line every day, a few million here and a few there, and we did the same. It's something you learn—to work doggedly to sell off your risk, to swallow hard and move on, to call on every ounce of your strength and mental resource and then move on to the next deal and the one after that. Within this maelstrom, the phone never stopped from about eight-thirty in the morning to four-thirty in the afternoon when it slowed somewhat. I think that some people in our business, and this is an observation of a 30 year man as opposed to a cub in the business 5 years, become blase" about risk. A kind of "the firm knows what business they're in, what can happen to its capital, they're not children." I would see this in the future and it just was in total contrast to the careful and prudent way I learned to conduct business during the period we are now discussing.

Not long after, Clem and I got together, the effects of the Arab oil embargo began driving inflation and interest rates higher. The unemployment rate had exceeded 8 percent and was on its way toward 9. The cost of nearly everything consumed rose because of the dramatic increases in the price of petroleum and petroleum-related products. Everything from toothpicks to cleaning supply products to fuel costed more because the price of oil was rising. As a result, municipalities anticipated higher expenditures and a normally scheduled loan from a state or a municipality of $100 million was increased to $130 million simply because budgets were growing due to higher prices for goods and services.

There was also a big push going on in the development of major urban areas in the United States, which was a by-product of HUD (Housing and Urban Development Administration) legislation put forth and passed in recent years. These two dynamics put great pressure on the interest rate markets, especially the municipal market. The calendar was filled with multiple states, towns, and counties coming to market to borrow $100 million to $250 million to finance housing projects. It was not uncommon to see two or three HFA deals each week: New York State Housing Finance Agency; Rochester Hill; Rochester, New York; or Fort Worth, Texas, HFA; and many, many others. Tack on the New York City Urban Development Agency and Battery Park City Authority and the beginnings of the Washington Public Power Deals, a monster of a power plant financing in the Pacific Northwest later known as WUPPs, and frequent market visitor Puerto Rico, and you had had a hurricane of activity in our little office space almost every week, not to mention the elephant in the room at the time. New York City, which would soon enter a near fatal state as a viable, solvent municipality.

As far as investors were concerned, in this climate, it was true rising interest rates were decreasing the value of the bonds they already owned. However, as yields rose, it was prudent to commit some new monies to secure these high yields, and so we did some business both in straight bonds and unit trusts. Increasingly, investors in bank certificates of deposit (CDs) were becoming aware that high quality municipal bond investments, both in individual bond form and unit trust form, were delivering astronomical taxable equivalent yields. Meaning if you were in the 50 percent tax bracket and bought $10,000 worth of a 7 percent CD, you earned $700 and the government took 50 percent or $350, leaving you with $350. If you bought $10,000 worth of a 7 percent municipal bond earning $700, you kept the entire $700. That meant you would have to earn a 14 percent taxable return to equal the yield value of the 7 percent municipal bond—obviously an impossibility.

By early 1974, New York City GOs or general obligation bonds were coming to market to borrow $250 to $300 million quarterly. The term GO means "the borrower is pledging its full faith and taxing power" to the payment of the interest and principal of the loan." At this time, the shorter maturities of these New York City loans, the one- to five-year maturities, were commanding yields of 7, 8, and 9 percent tax free with lower yields for longer term maturities. When short-term bonds are higher yielding than long-term bonds, the phenomenon is referred to as an inverted yield curve. When yields are plotted on a graph normally lower short-term yields give way to higher longer-term yields and so the graph line moves diagonally across the graph from the lower left to the upper right. An inverted yield curve in which short term interest rates are higher than long term rates is not normal and means specifically that during that time the New York City yield curve was abnormal and portended fiscal crisis. (See the accompanying Illustrations)

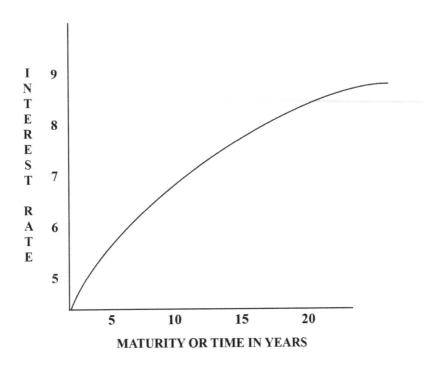

MATURITY OR TIME IN YEARS

Normal or Positive Yield Curve
Short-term securities maintain lower
interest rates than long term securities

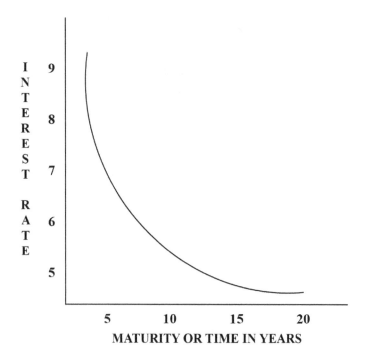

Negative Yield Curve or Inverted Yield Curve
Curve maintaining higher short-term
interest rates then long-term rates

(Illustrate here normal or positive and negative or inverted yield curves from municipal definition)

Chapter 41

Life and Money: Looking for Greener Pastures

Early in 1974, my wife and I and our four-year-old son and year-old daughter were living in the apartment on the second floor of my mother- and father-in-law's home on Clarendon Road in Brooklyn. My own father had passed in April at the age of eighty-four. I felt his loss deeply in that I had only just begun to appreciate him, in a mature way, after I got married. Before, I had seen him as a loving and benevolent though restricting figure, especially from my fifteenth or sixteenth year onward as he was near seventy years old when I was fifteen. The gap in our ages made it difficult for me to reach a true meeting of the minds with my father, although I have since realized what an extraordinary man he was. My mother, a larger-than-life figure to all, not just her children, died about eight months later in December 1973. My life was a whirlwind then because of the amount of time I spent working in both full-time employment in the Bond Department at Reynolds and in the several part-time jobs I worked for extra money. It saddens me to say it, but I think I was so busy that the deaths of my parents did not put a great burden of mourning and sadness on me at the time. It's not that I didn't love and admire them. I just didn't have the time or inclination to think about it too much then.

My wife's parents by then were thinking of selling their home in Brooklyn where we lived. Their oldest son Joe was by now living on Long Island in Rockville Centre. Their other son Frank, the race horse driver/trainer whom I worked for, was planning to leave Brooklyn as well to move to a small farm in Yaphank, also on Long Island in Suffolk County where he would eventually move his small string of Standardbreds. My wife and I were making noises as well about moving because the neighborhood schools were not terribly appealing to us, and we could not afford parochial school for my son who would be five years old in 1974. It turned out my in-laws bought a house in Oceanside, not far from their son in Rockville Center, and we moved there with them in May 1974. We took the lower floor as a rental. In effect, my wife and I would be charged with the care of my in-laws into their old age and in turn their home provided housing for us. We paid rent of course.

During this transition from Brooklyn to Long Island I had been working Clem over for a raise. I was now earning around fifteen thousand a year having secured a two thousand dollar increase on the anniversary of my first year in the bond department, including a ten or twelve-week bonus at year end. Another eight thousand or so was coming from part-time sources. Good money for the time however our expenses automatically jumped with the move to the island. Beside a modest increase in rent and the generally higher cost of living in Nassau County the cost of commuting on the Long Island Railroad came to about a hundred and fifty dollars a month or close to two thousand a year. In fact, that was what I was looking for, a 15 to 20% increase in base salary would provide an ample enough increase in take home pay to deflect the new commuting costs. It was I realized a big expectation but a reasonable one I felt especially because Clem agreed to make that request for me in writing.

It was not in Clem's power however to grant the raise as he was not in charge administratively, Bill Devlin was. Bill had to grant me the raise and I was relying on Clem's lobbying to smooth the way for me. At some appointed time, I think it was a Friday afternoon, I was supposed to go in and see Bill. When the day came my stomach did a flip when my internal data-bank harked back to the day of my interview with Devlin when we had first discussed what my salary would be. Kondratuck who was always in my corner had secured my first raise, but in the back of my mind I knew that Devlin was a tougher sell and a bit more temperamental in these matters. I was sure in one thing however, that both Clem and Bill being Long Islanders realized how my recent move there had dramatically increased my expenses. Still I would proceed with caution.

Bill was usually in a good mood, and so was I. Clem had assured me he had been talking to Devlin for several days about our meeting. It was Friday morning and the meeting had been set for that afternoon at which time I presented myself at around one-thirty.

"Hey, Bill. Clem said you were expecting me."

He waves me in and then says, "You again?" Standard Devlin, of course, and he's shuffling papers, looking kind of cross. I just kept quiet, and in a minute or two, he says, "We're bringing you up to twelve thousand dollars a year."

I said "Bill," and in that moment, I looked at him directly and saw he had half a bag on. He'd been drinking at lunch, as I knew he often did, as we all often did. I can't really recall what I thought then. I just froze for a moment, got hold of myself, and conquered my disappointment, thinking, "Don't be a jerk. Don't argue and get yourself in trouble." So I said something like, "Jeez, Bill, you hear Clem calling me. He's such a pain in the ass."

And Bill laughs and says, "Yeahs, hic, he most certainly is. Go scratch his itch."

I walked out of his office quite annoyed, angry, and without any knowledge of any raise in salary, which I was really hoping for—desperate for, in fact. Clem was apologetic. The lasting feeling that came out of that meeting was I felt slighted, insulted. After all, the raise was overdue and a sore spot with me especially since after being in the place nearly three years, there was also the sore spot of my requests to get registered still being turned down. I got a note in Bill's hand a few days later that I would receive a three-thousand-dollar raise. Of course, I was always cordial with Bill before and after that incident and often enjoyed a joke or humorous observation with him. Nonetheless, I never forgot that incident. It's just stuff one remembers. Ironically, in years (the midnineties) to come, working for Brian Devlin, Bill's son, I would be responsible for a major wave of salary increases to the second tier trading staff of the firm's municipal bond division.

Our trading desk had direct lines to twenty or thirty broker dealers and bond departments around the street, and several of them had legs on the phone consoles in syndicate where Clem and I sat. When some of these lines buzzed and trading couldn't pick up, Clem or I picked up if we were free and relayed the message. One of these lines was to aforementioned Paine, Webber, Jackson, & Curtis, a firm much like Reynolds although probably a bit larger.

"Bobby! Back to Carey at Paine," bellowed loudly was usually enough to get someone's attention. The guy whose name you mentioned usually acknowledged it with a nod if he was able to make eye contact, and if not, you might see a hand and arm raised. Once you shouted out the message, your responsibility had been fulfilled.

Clem had a good friend at Paine-Webber named Alan Blair who managed the unit trust sales operation there. Allan had come to Paine-Webber via Blyth, which actually was known at the time of the take-over (or merger with PW) as Blyth-Eastman, one of my former firms, Eastman Dillon, having merged into and otherwise now amalgamated into Paine, Webber, Jackson & Curtis. This fact is just another reminder of the ways firms had gone out of existence in the relatively recent past. Once in a while, Allan would call to talk to Clem, arrange a luncheon, or we'd call to purchase some MBF units for brokers in our firm who had clients who wanted to add to their MBF positions. I got a good feeling the few times I spoke to Allan myself, and he'd even said I should pop up to their office sometime. I got an idea after a while that Blair wanted me to get in touch with him privately. My loyalty to Clem made me ambivalent about it all. Clem and I were quite a good team by this time. He trusted me and I him, and we got along well. After a while of course I began to realize that Allan, Clem's so-called friend was actually wooing me and planning to poach me away from Clem, supposedly his friend. I got the message then through a third party that there was an opening for me at PW and then on a chance encounter on the direct line Blair asked if I could talk. The result of the conversation was cordial and positive with the next move on my part to send Allan a resume. It took me about a week to get the resume together, then typed accurately and sent over.

A few days later, I got a surprising call from Carey Wiseman, the manager of Paine-Webber's Muni Trading Desk. He said he'd seen my resume on Allan's desk quite by accident, and he thought it would be a good idea to hold up on things for a while.

"You can't tell anybody about this. That I called you," he said. "Not even Allan. There are going to be some changes around here in a few days, and you might want to hold off on your decision until then."

I knew Carey, of course, from picking up the direct line every once in a while when he was on the other end. How you can say you like a guy or trust a guy from a casual pick-up every now and then is hard to say, but I did, simply from the humanity and cordiality he displayed whenever he was on the phone. And anyway, there wasn't a big rush. I had gotten the raise I was hoping for, and in a way, I welcomed the stall. I was sure I was doing the right thing by checking the job market out, but I was also a little scared about changing jobs. My two previous firms were no longer in existence, and even at these early stages of my career, I had some understanding of Reynolds Securities staying power.

And then again I was very busy and had begun to wonder how a possible move to Paine-Webber would play out with my part-time work life. Sooner or later, I would have to talk money with Blair, but I was still kind of naive and shy about the subject. On another front, my wife's brother, Frank, around this time was on the card almost weekly at either Roosevelt or Yonkers Raceway. He had a pretty decent (but crazy) colt called Lee Fall that finished in the money quite often, and he needed me to groom especially with this horse because I was used to him and vice versa. Clem, on the other hand, was pretty easy about me walking out around four o'clock when I had to, and so I used to drive in on race days and leave as early as possible, usually getting to the track by a quarter past five in plenty of time for the first race, which went off at five minutes past eight. I never told him where I was going, but he knew I was working at the farm on weekends with horses although I don't think he picked up on the fact that I was grooming at the track on the days that I left early. These grooming jobs were important because they paid a fifty-dollar bill for grooming (about six to eight hours), a hundred if the horse finished in the money (fifth or better), and several hundred more if he won or came in second or third. On almost every other weekday night except Friday, I was still doing inventory jobs as well. While I didn't forget about the possibility of moving to Paine-Webber, acting on it got crowded out a bit because I was so busy. I said I was busy, but the reality of it was I was going crazy with my only night off being Friday unless we raced.

Then within about ten days of my conversation with Carey regarding my resume and staying put for a while, it was announced that Henry Arbeeny, head of Fixed Income at Paine-Webber, had been hired by Reynolds Securities to manage all of Fixed Income. This was a major turn of events for the firm and all of its fixed-income employees, and if I hadn't completely decided yet whether to look for an offer from Allan Blair or not, it was certainly important to hang back for a while to see what this Arbeeny guy was like.

Just after it was announced, moments later in fact, Carey called me to say something like, "Look, Scida, Henry is a terrific boss and a great guy. Check him out for a while, and see what you think. You can always pick up where you left off with Allan, and if you do wind up leaving, you won't have any regrets about how things might have turn out had you stayed there."

"It makes perfect sense to me," I replied and thanked him.

When I put down the receiver, I sensed some kind of commotion to my left in the direction of the doorway to the department. I couldn't see because of the wall, but in less than a moment, Henry Arbeeny was walking by with a big smile on his face. I don't remember who it was who was introducing him around, but we shook hands and he moved on. The phones were ringing off the hook, and I settled into business as usual as though Carey had never called or Henry had never walked in. We do make our own success or failure to a degree, and some of it is luck and some of it the result of our prayer's. Often, we look far and away for greener pastures, and sometimes they come to us of their own accord. Then it's a matter of recognizing them.

Chapter 42

The Henry Arbeeny Era: Leadership, Inspiration, Change

Henry's stepping into the room was meaningless to me. He was just another boss. I had no history or prior knowledge of him with the exception of a luncheon at the Banker's Club the year before. Bill Devlin asked me to tag along as some question or point of information might come up in their discussion regarding our cosponsorship in the MBF. A few days before the lunch, he mentioned we were having lunch with the "Camel Driver," referring to Henry's Lebanese descent—offensive today but acceptable in those days. Beyond a handshake and an unsmiling nod, we spoke not a word. He appeared to me at the time as a hulking barrel-chested man, quite imposing and intense, seated three or four spaces down at the end of the table across from the more diminutive yet no less imposing Devlin, both smoking incessantly, as most of us did in those days. Luckily, George Charlton, a member of the South Shore Bond Club was there. George ran the Municipal Bond and Unit Trust operation at First Michigan and was a Rockville Centre resident as well. I remember thinking after a while that Devlin might have set it up that way, inviting Charlton to lunch to keep me amused while he sat two spaces away from us, quietly chatting, negotiating, and plotting perhaps with Arbeeny.

Clem was kind of agog at this development—Henry joining Reynolds as director of Fixed Income. He liked Henry I think, knew something of him, but was skeptical of what the outcome might be. I learned over the next day or so that Henry was the brother-in-law

211

of Bill Marlin, another previously mentioned member of the SSBC, probably its leading member, a drinking buddy of Clem's, and one might say even a mentor. Bill Marlin and Henry Arbeeny were in fact married to sisters. Henry also rode the LIRR, having lived early in his tenure on Wall Street on the South Shore of Long Island in Babylon. He'd since moved to Plandome on the North Shore. I could not see Henry as a full-fledged member of the SSBC because he wasn't a clubby, chummy sort of person in any way and was quite reserved and abstemious almost to a fault. He once said to me at a business dinner or cocktail party that he made it a practice not to have a drink until ten o'clock in the evening. That way, he could be sure the boss and other senior officers had had a few themselves or had left. The practice assured he would keep his wits about himself long enough that he wouldn't get into a mess with either too much familiarity or speaking out of turn without thinking. While such sentiments mirrored my own to some degree, after hearing them articulated by Henry, they became a piece of advice that I followed for years until it became habit.

I cannot of course say with absolute certainty, but I thought Clem's thinking and opinion of Henry was shaded to some degree by what Marlin thought of Henry. Certainly, there was an aura of high-mindedness and aloofness about Henry that was very apparent, and I understood this attitude on Henry's part. Many people who have been raised under the influence of Old World, or shall we say European customs and manners, as I have (certainly Henry's Lebanese Maronite Catholic background qualifies in this regard), are at the very least uncomfortable if not contemptuous at times of what my mother would have called the "Merican" or American sense of familiarity and assumption, which would extend to drinking and carousing in public. Personally, I chalked it up to the man's seriousness and sense of appropriate behavior and decorum. I dare say many members of the SSBC would have reacted (and Clem would definitely not have been in this group) with a resounding, "Who the hell does this guy think he is?" when asked about Henry.

As far as I knew, Henry had been a Strategic Air Command pilot and retired a lieutenant commander from the US Air Force. Before retiring, he taught at the Air Force College in Japan. All of this he had achieved after being admitted to Officers Candidates School (OCS). After retiring from the Air Force, his brother-in-law Bill Marlin aided him in securing a position on Wall Street, and the rest was history. I have no knowledge of how long it took Henry to become director of Municipals at Paine Webber or what stops he had made along the way, although I venture to guess it had something to do with respecting the chain of command, rigorous following of orders, application of the latest cutting edge management skills, and the aggressive pursuit of advancement in rank. This included the exploitation of every opportunity afforded him by his brother in law Bill Marlin and his (Henry's) association with if not left handed membership in the South Shore Bond Club. Whatever it was, Henry was now at Reynolds Securities as head of Fixed Income. There were two additional distinctions I learned about Henry that predisposed my opinion of him. He had had very little college prior to entering the service, and he'd grown up in Brooklyn. In some ways then, some might say, he and I might have been fabric cut from the same bolt.

As I said, Clem was sort of in shock and skeptical at Henry's appointment, and as his partner, he shared his feelings with me, which amounted to, "Henry could be gone in six months."

Henry was too much of an idealist and an intellectual of sorts. Wall Streets Fixed Income Divisions, at least the ones he (Clem) was familiar with, were not run on rhyme and reason, much less the logic of civil people. They ran at the whim of men like Devlin and Marlin who were brilliant in some ways but not able managers. Men who could be ruthless and unkind and at times crude ruffians in their appeasement of their superiors.

It turned out a few weeks prior to the announcement of our new chief joining the firm, Henry had had run into Clem on the street in front of 120 Broadway. Henry must have pumped Clem for all he was worth about the department, the people he worked with, and the business we did while at the same time gauging where Clem's own heart was. Notwithstanding that aloofness just mentioned, Henry was also a great charmer and a good schmoozer. Gardiner and Staley might have suggested to Henry during their discussions that for the most professional and honest insider's view of the bond department, Clem would be the guy to talk to, and I'm sure Henry stalked the building's entrance until he saw Clem. There was no indication of course that Clem had been a party to Henry Arbeeny joining Reynolds, but Clem was the right guy to talk to because his heart was pure, he had no ax to grind and no animosities, and above all, he was a very serious guy and a pragmatist.

On another note, it was conceivable that the Phelp-Fenn acquisition had perhaps born less fruit than Tom Staley and Bob Gardner thought it would. There we were in the midseventies at the end of the Nixon-era government-imposed price controls and the Nixon presidency. It was also the era of gas lines and inflation heating up to as high as 11 percent depending on whose charts you looked at. Though it had grown, Reynolds Securities Bond Operation remained somewhat of a backwater when compared to Merrill Lynch, Smith Barney, Kidder-Peabody, or Bache & Co. Even some of the smaller retail operations like Edwards & Hanley were hitting more of the fixed income hot buttons than we were. Reynolds, for a wire house, with more than one thousand five hundred brokers was not pulling the revenue or the market share it felt it should be drawing.

In Municipal Syndicate the new issue business had picked up as mentioned and led to the hiring of a third underwriter, Henry Howard, and a young fellow by the name of Bob McTiernan, out of operations as a trainee. The firm's unit trust business was steady if not the pie in the sky situation the Phelps-Fenn crowd envisioned when we joined the Paine-Webber account. Corporate Syndicate had grown, thanks to Clem Schaefer, from next to nothing in the late sixties, and now Joe Goodnicht, Clem's replacement, had been brought in to take it to the next level. Among other things, I don't think Gardiner or Tom Staley quite knew how to manage Joe and his team into living up to its potential. Something was lacking in the sales management side of the business and the overall management of all the businesses that would be listed under the fixed income heading.

Dare I say Devlin was too old and maybe Kondratuck too much the scientist rather than the manager and maybe even not tough or pragmatic enough or enough of a visionary for the scope of the job. Clem could have had a shot at the job, but I'm sure he didn't want it given what the job was. The person who took it had to be tough, a little ruthless, with a stomach for frequent confrontation and an astute political awareness, and though Clem could be all of these from time to time, he did not want to be them all the time. Henry's job, Director of Fixed Income within Henry's vision of what the department had to become and the way he attacked it, was carried out in a kind of 24/7 way. Again, that term was not as ubiquitous as it is today, but it became clear to me Henry devoted his every waking moment as far as was necessary to the forward progress and success of his new firm's fixed income division.

It should be mentioned there were certain capabilities in place at Reynolds that were the envy of other firms. There was an excellent sales training model developed by the great mentor and trainer Glen Givens and several devoted followers. The firm exhibited high retention of its home trained sales force, which flourished and remained loyal to the firm. This was common knowledge on the Street as many firms benefited from our program because so many of our less successful trainees who took somewhat longer to develop were often hired away by other firms knowing that the quality of their training gave them something to work with.

The firm's new era of operations, that had begun with a near ten-million-dollar investment in the early seventies (when I was still in DECAB) in new super computers and software, was continuing with the programming and development of systems capable of handling the volume of transactions that both Tom Staley and Bob Gardiner predicted was ahead of us. It doesn't seem quite clairvoyant today to have predicted that volume on the NYSE would one day exceed 100 million shares (let alone a billion plus) but when Tom Staley began saying it in the early seventies when the volume was actually twelve to fifteen million shares, many dismissed the thought as an absurdity.

Whatever their musings about the future may have been, it appears now Tom Staley and Bob Gardiner knew they had to grow the fixed income business because the stock market was going nowhere. The DOW would close in 1974, barely above six hundred. They knew also making the right choice with regard to an individual could be quite successful. Reynolds was just another player in the options business (a big commission revenue source) until they brought Leroy Gross to New York in the late sixties. The options business was fraught with problems, not the least of which was client suitability as investors and brokers could wipe themselves out if not held in check. When they put Leroy Gross in as head of the Options Department, they put in a powerhouse of sales and a guy who backed up the business with some of the best operations and backup people in the business. Gross opened the front door, so to speak, by inspiring brokers to be better and to know more about the investments they recommended to clients and prospects. He admonished brokers to be more thorough, harder working salesmen, to ask for larger orders, and to build solid books of clients that would stay with them for a lifetime. At the same time, he covered the back door with a solid trading, operations, and compliance team to manage the mechanics. I think when Staley and Gardiner hired Henry Arbeeny, they felt they were taking steps to duplicate their success in options with an equally successful hire to lead Fixed Income. At least it looked that way to me.

The level of risk in this venture was quite different than it was when they built the options business. Yes, options were traded and there was some risk, but nothing like the capital commitment required by the fixed income business. A daily inventory requirement of thirty to forty million in the secondary market and near that in municipal syndicate and corporates if not more. Such risk provides great opportunity as well as perilous loss if not handled in the proper way. A ten-dollar price adjustment for example, a point in bond lingo, might adjust the value of a fifty-million-dollar inventory depending on its credit quality and maturity variation three hundred to five hundred thousand dollars either way, not a game for people with queasy stomachs.

In relation to where I was sitting with Clem and the way Clem described his talks with Henry about our work, it was clear that they saw eye to eye. Henry's attitude about the UIT business and how it augmented the bond business was much more than a stopgap that might cover up or make up for the multitude of sins theory that Bill Byrne Senior had remarked upon. In fact even such a mild statement as that might have been considered cavalier by Henry or at least an incomplete thought. I think it's safe to say from Henry's point of view, the unit trust business and its profitability was not a license or an excuse for adventurism in the taking of risk in other sectors.

Many, countless even, changes came down the line over the next few years at Henry's instigation. In my opinion, the cornerstone of Henry's program and what I bought into was an overall attitude and program that amounted to "what he could do for me in exchange for what I could do for him and the firm." Henry's shtick was there was money to be made and a goodly amount of it for the people out on the floor of the fixed income division, not just the managers or the executive corps but also the soldiers who doggedly picked up the phone, doled out the information, did the research, and wrote the tickets hour after hour and day after day. That the money to be made was in exchange for working hard, paying attention to the policies of the department and the firm, keeping a civil tongue in your head, being loyal to both the department and the firm, and doing everything in your power to increase business. Implicit in this promise was that Henry was the guy up front, working with the firm to get you your bonus, timely reviews, and raises. It was a given that the firm was all-important because it was not the trade (the industry) that most often rewarded us and made us successful both in the pocket and in power and promotion but the firm. The more successful we made the firm, the better off we would be, and though it was not mentioned very often in those days, the higher the price of the stock would go. Early on, this was the very thing Clem could not buy into. Clem had a deep distrust of upper management and was skeptical that Henry could handle them in regard to making good on their promises. Yes, do this and there will be bonuses and, yes, a review and a raise every year or two, but management had the right to break their promises and agreements at whim. And if you didn't like it, you could leave. This was Clem's experience and proven because the street was filled with people in responsible positions who had trained at Reynolds but had to go elsewhere to get the money that their capabilities were actually worth.

Leaving this reluctance to believe in Henry aside for a moment, let's look at one of the first changes or innovations made. Within weeks of his arrival, Henry hired over from Paine-Webber a very knowledgeable bond-savvy young woman, Linda Andrews, perhaps in her thirties at the time. Linda was a lady and brought the gentleman out of those men around her who were capable of being gentleman. She was well-spoken, had a great attitude, personable, demonstrative, service-oriented, patient and helpful. From the standpoint of the broker in the field in touch with high net worth clients who had business to do or a desire to increase their business in municipals, Linda was someone whose help and advice they wanted to enlist. While it was the trading desks job to work with salesman, the traders were very busy, tending to their risk positions, formulating bids on bonds that brokers wanted to sell internally, and making bids on blocks of bonds externally to reoffer in-house. The traders leaned toward dealing with the salesman in house who knew bond market jargon and got the message on the first go round. The broker who was not familiar with market jargon or the quick give and go of the trader just never got to first base in fulfilling the potential he might have had with some of the bigger clients being served by other firms in his locale. These clients might take your call, but if you couldn't get them twenty-five or fifty thousand of the latest state or local offering, you were useless to them. Linda changed the face of the trading desk with her attitude and her willingness to work with salesmen in the field and anyone, novice or expert, inside or outside the firm, to get business done.

What Linda brought to the department and the firm at large might be better understood in the story of a salesman in the Peoria, Illinois, branch with a connection to a ten-million-dollar account that he's doing the occasional options or stock trade with but little else. He's frustrated because he knows even though he has a great relationship with the account, his lack of knowledge in municipals doesn't allow him to get past first base with the guy. He can't sell him bond one and someone else at another firm or two is getting the lion's share of his business because they can service the major portion of the investors account—his municipal portfolio. Whenever he's tried to learn something about municipals, to find a way to do a trade, make the account take notice of his firm's prowess in the municipal arena, he's been frustrated by the busyness of the trader, the jargon thrown at him, and the general disdain he feels the traders have for him because of his lack of knowledge. Embarrassed by his lack of savvy in the area, he avoids the subject with the client.

Enter Linda Andrews. She might make the time to speak to our salesman in Peoria for ten or fifteen minutes on end, he could ask her the same questions two or three times without getting his head bitten off, and when Linda promised to call him on an upcoming new issue that his Illinois account might be interested in, she kept the promise, which was manna from heaven to the salesman. Often a call to a municipal bond buyer with price and yield ideas on an upcoming new issue will garner a pre-sale order. Just imagine the confidence builder getting such an order might be when this salesman could barely get this client to answer the phone three months ago. She'd suggest that the broker ask for a copy of the client's portfolio in the event that an opportunity to sell something out of it (at a fat profit of course) came along. With this kind of competent, patient, and diligent service available on the desk, business begins to get done where it didn't exist before. This is how you get business done for a salesman, how you win over a sales force, and how you give the confidence to a salesman, like the one we're discussing, that is finally comfortable with the one "big fish" municipal investor he had and how you get him to go out and find another and recruit him as an ardent product and department loyalist. The development of this kind of service and liaising with the sales force had a major effect on business and the persona of the department vis-à-vis the sales organization.

On the unit trust front, Henry sat down with Clem and said he wanted increased sales in unit trusts so we could petition Merrill Lynch to increase our underwriting percentages in the product lines, meaning the more consistent an increase in sales, the more of a chance we would have of raising the percentage we would receive of the sponsors accumulation profits and underwriting fees. He laid out his plan to Clem. "I'm going to reach out to the regional directors around the country and ask them to include the unit trust underwriting and product information prominently in their communications with their managers and in their sales meetings and advise their branches to do the same."

The firm's regional directors oversaw the branches in the various regions of the country. For example a fellow named Andy Carol in South Florida and Mel Wright in the Mid-Atlantic and so on. These regionals managed the branch managers, oversaw recruiting, communication, real estate rental, leases, property management, legal and compliance, and the million other duties involved in the employment of two hundred fifty to five hundred people in five or six states. While it was a given that branch managers and in turn brokers were charged with maximizing sales there wasn't a constant product push that came from headquarters in New York in those days, at least not at Reynolds. Emphasis may have come on Mutual Funds at one time and on individual underwriting's here and there and when there was, it was the Regional Managers who were contacted and who then initiated the push. In later years regional managers hired regional sales managers to orchestrate individual organized sales in the regions. The flip side was that if Henry was successful (there was some skepticism), we, Clem and I, had to step up to the plate on the servicing side because Henry's initiative was bound to increase call volume and demand for information. In effect, Henry and the regional directors would push the branch managers and the sales force toward us, and we had to be ready for them.

The stakes we were playing for at this point were on average something in the vicinity of a sixty thousand to seventy thousand dollars payoff for the department and firm each time it sponsored, underwrote, and sold two million dollars' worth of long-term municipal investment trust units and twenty-five to thirty thousand dollars each time we underwrote a corporate bond or preferred stock trust. In effect, one and a half to two million dollars on about forty deals a year, and these were early days in an endeavor that would eventually double and even triple our current production. In these years and in these times and place, with municipal syndicate behind myself and Clem and the endless stream of unit trust after unit trust underwriting, bonds and the securities industry became my life's work and fascination.

Chapter 43

The New Push for Sales: More Arbeeny

The new push for sales made it necessary for Clem and myself to sharpen up our act both internally with our own sales force and externally with the sponsor/syndicate member relationship. It's one thing to just fill demand as the orders materialize and wholly another to push for and anticipate what maximum sales are going to be, take down the maximum amount of product and back it up by ticketing it all in a timely manner and then transitioning immediately to the next deal. We could not have more than $150,000 (150 units) worth of a deal left over once the account closed, that is when the lead manager determined all the underwriters and sponsors had completely sold out their commitments. If you had larger amounts unsold on hand, your managing underwriter was sure to find out. Dumping your excess inventory on the Street after the deal is closed will get back to them via rumor or gossip or on the occasion of a new deal being announced. Weaker indications of interest will give you away. In-house, having leftover inventory, will make the sales force lazy regarding presale and getting indications of interest in on time for new deals. The only answer was to work hard to step up sales.

As Henry started his push with the regional managers, Clem and I went from a kind of casual, take it easy, the buyers will come attitude to more of a pressure cooker approach. The regional municipal offices around the country were charged with helping us put the word out on new issues by announcing their details (date, yield, price parameters, and so forth) to each branch manager or designated product coordinator in the branch. The branch had the option of phoning us in New York or the regional municipal offices with questions regarding how the security worked among other details. In this regard, we had regular Monday afternoon conference calls with the municipal regions, and on request, we began doing educational/promotional conference calls to branches. The municipal regions were charged with going back to the branch managers or product coordinators a second time, requesting some idea as to a number of units that they expected to sell. These so called "indications of interest" or IOI's were relayed to us in New York. These indications of interest along with the tempo of incoming calls, the feeling or the intensity we sensed both from incoming calls and our regional municipal people's opinion of the veracity of the indications and our own defined sales goals, all factored into our decision as to what we would go in for. That is, the formulation of a number of units to take down from the lead sponsor, Merrill Lynch, on the particular offering.

While we usually went in for less than the branches said they were going to sell, we awarded whatever the branches indicated for as part of an inventory control strategy. When the issue was priced and orders began to flow, we pulled back the inventory the branch office system was working with. For example, the system might have indicated it was going to sell 5,500 units ($5.5 million), while we had real inventory of 4,000 units ($4 million). When we pulled back the extra 1,500 units that we'd allotted into the system, the appearance would be given that the deal was moving faster than it actually was. This technique usually had substantial impact as it gave the appearance to salesman and branch managers in the field that the deal was selling out at some velocity, which led them to become more efficient in all aspects of the sales process from prospecting to showing and recommending the product to their clients and closing sales more efficiently. Execution of this technique required a good deal of phone work on our part and on the part of the municipal regions. We also devised multiple wire station codes so that a single teletype code form wire could send a message to an entire region of offices or all the municipal regions. The way we handled the ebb and flow of inventory vis-à-vis our sales force plus the internal push from the regional directors got the product off the ground in the firm in a much broader manner than before.

These sales efforts by Henry, the regional directors, branch managers, Clem and I, and our regional people effectively pushed the stockbrokers, and in effect the firms contact with the public on the subject of the product especially the municipal trust. This new awareness now created a movement with a mind of its own. In response to the management push branches began to develop sales programs on their own. For example, they requested approved letters to send to their established client bases about the product. These letters would be sent specifically to investors with large cash balances in their accounts as well as investors that brokers were sure had caches of money in bank savings accounts. The next step was to systematically phone these investors following up the mailing. Did the client read the letter, didn't he or she want to improve the production of their savings, earn tax free income, earn a higher yield and so on? As these programs got under way branch managers pushed for results, talked up successful sales and imposed sales quotas as sales began to pick up. Once brokers see other brokers succeed its game set match. One of our branch managers, a fellow by the name of Ron Maci, in the Washington DC area started a sales program that spread to many branches. He placed a fifty-unit (approx. $50000) quota or sales goal on each of his trainees.

Generally, trainees are salesmen in their first three years with the firm. They are preoccupied in these first three years with building a book of clients. If they succeed in building a book in these three years, say opening ten or twelve new accounts each month, they will succeed in the business. If not, they will sink and eventually drop out. This branch manager then in imposing this quota, forced the trainees to use the product as a prospecting tool, making phone calls, so-called "cold calls" to potential clients, engaging them specifically in conversation about the benefits of earning tax-free income. Investing in tax-free municipal bonds was still a new concept for many, many investors at the time. Once the trainee qualified the investor as a bona fide prospect for tax-free income, the trainee would introduce the municipal bond tax-free unit trust as the vehicle to invest with.

On another front, Henry began to bring institutional salesmen into the firm both in New York and around the country in an effort to beef up sales of fixed income to professional investment accounts, insurance companies, unit trust and mutual fund buyers, banks, and investment advisors. He hired Bob Holly in New York and gave him the specific task of selling bonds to the UIT underwriters like Merrill, Paine-Webber, Van Kampen, and Smith Barney. Along these lines, Henry hired a couple of very high pressure New York salesman who covered New York and vicinity broker dealers as well as some retail. One was Steve Ratner who bore a strange resemblance to his namesake, and the other was called Stan Beckerman. They could have been called Hose and Super Hose because spending the day being hounded by them to amend your price to meet a sale or a bid felt like you were being beaten with a rubber hose. These guys sold bonds and knew where bonds were and could get them for you for a price. They were sharp on the market and worked everyone over, client and in-house trader alike. They weren't very well liked, but they certainly made things interesting and did a boatload of business.

The added business, and sales effort required larger and larger risk commitments. Increased marketing and sales and the hiring of additional sales people, especially institutional sales, has a natural effect on inventory. It has to increase to meet demand, and at the risk of being too simplistic, it increases day to day risk. Needless to say, Henry wanted to keep a close eye on inventory and wanted his charges around the country, the regional municipal managers, to keep an even closer eye on inventory. To wit, Henry wanted (*demanded* is a better term) to know by eleven to eleven thirty every morning what the entire firm's municipal bond inventory was. These were days when you just couldn't look at a computer screen and know how many millions of bonds the firm owned. There was a listing printed every day of all positions in all firm accounts called "the accume." It was the size of two Gutenberg Bibles, very unwieldy and very difficult to read. Until someone thought of getting operations to customize and print a specific daily run for Henry, the way he got an accurate count was through a message sent via the wire system from every regional municipal office to a single individual in New York who was charged with compiling the report and giving it to Henry by about eleven o'clock every morning.

Some of the regions like Florida, Chicago, Washington, and Detroit were always on the money, always on time or even early. Others needed to be chased. Atlanta was just a bit lackadaisical, and San Francisco was always behind the eight ball because of the time zone difference but on the other hand were always in early (by the clock) but lazy as well as resentful that they had to report in the first place. I knew this firsthand because the guy who compiled the report daily was a friend of mine, Bob McTiernan, who had been brought into Municipal Syndicate as an operations clerk from the Mutual Funds Operations unit at 2 Broadway. The report used to drive Bobby crazy and me as well when I had to help him out with it. By eleven, we had most of the data, the names, and quantities of each issue held, and a bottom line total amount of bonds held by the region with their value rounded to the nearest thousand. The report given to Henry was composed of the cuttings of the wires sent to us which we taped onto legal-size paper with totals for each region and a grand total calculated by Bob or myself. If you got in to Henry by 11:30, everything was cool. If it was later, you had to endure Henry's jaundiced eye as he walked into the department to see what was holding it up.

As sales volume increased, the regions were granted commensurate permission to increase inventory on hand. However, Henry introduced a new component to the inventory report—the age of the position. He wanted the report divided by how long the bonds were held—under five days, five to ten days, ten to fifteen days, and fifteen to twenty days. The demand was based on the theory that if something isn't selling, the trader must find the price level at which it will sell and move it out, making room for new inventory that was more currently priced. Henry made you face the truth and live with the demons of the business. In this case, cut your losses, don't give them the opportunity to grow, don't wait for someone else to do it for you, recognize the position was a turkey by the time it was ten days old, and get rid of it in fifteen before Henry had to call you out on it. Of course we're talking about $150,000 blocks and higher at a minimum.

In this same venue, Henry built a relationship with the Accounting Department. My experience when I was the Trading Desks operations clerk was the traders always fought with accounting and blamed accounting for blindsiding them or so they thought, while Devlin and Kondratuck took accountings word as gospel. But Henry welcomed them in, lunched or met with the head of accounting regularly. Regular dialogue and discussion pertaining to profitability and the liability of the inventory on a week-to-week, even day-to-day, basis began under Henry. The way it used to be was Accounting got its rocks off by reporting to management about the lack of concern for the P&L by the fixed-income crowd. Of course accounting was silent when there were gains and simply reported the figures on those occasions. Henry took the job and responsibility of reporting fixed incomes profits and losses to management away from the accounting department. Accounting now reported to Henry, and Henry reported to management in a timely fashion. It became Henry's job then to tell Stretch we're going make money or we're losing money or breaking even this month. These kinds of management controls were believed by many (Clem included) to be applicable and workable in the tangible industries like manufacturing and services but not in the business of Wall Street.

Henry, facing the reality of having to do business in bad and good markets, strived and succeeded in achieving profitability in both markets through the application of management principles and management technique (i.e., reporting, accountability, open and frequent communication, and incentive), no doubt concepts he'd experienced in the military and probably his wide reading on the subject. Management, namely Tom Staley and Bob Gardiner, found it almost difficult to imagine such dependability, and competing managers found his style exasperating in that it drew constant attention from upper management. Most important among these, he once said to me, was the management of his own managers, his superiors, standard operating procedure today but relatively unknown then and totally unknown on Wall Street at least in most firms.

As to operations, Henry invited Irwin Menchel, SVP and director of operations, to the table through regular meetings and luncheons with the question being, "How can we make your job easier Irwin?" We never had an operational problem, debacle, or communications breakdown ever again after these meetings began. The point is that when lines of communication open and mutually beneficial ground rules are set, the table is cleared for a successful outcome for all the parties involved.

The development of these new alliances that formed between Fixed Income, Accounting and Operations were all the more interesting because of a rumor that floated around for a while. While the rumor was never confirmed it alleged that the interest income earned in Municipal Bond Department trading accounts as a rule was funneled off into operations accounts to defer costs incurred by operations for overnight borrowings on delayed deliveries among other things. A six percent bond earns sixteen cents a day. A firm that holds forty million dollars' worth of bonds over night every night of the year at this rate (6%) earns about $6500 of interest each day. The collection of this money occurs in the day to day calculation of accrued interest based on the settlement date of purchases vs the settlement date of sales. That's more than $2 million a year. I'm sure this policy was in place since time immemorial. I'm also sure that Tom Staley and Bob Gardner were probably unaware of it or had forgotten it. I don't care who the CEO is, when that kind of money is found, the CEO wants to look into it to see if he's getting his fair share of it or in fact to see if he can claim it for himself and the firm's general coffers. Some said that Henry got the job at Reynolds because he found that money. Again, I don't know how true it was but I think right from the beginning these departments realized that they couldn't trifle with Henry the way they did with me or the traders.

Chapter 44

Money, Money, Money...Here

In the final quarter of 1974 and into early 1975, Clem and I were busier than we'd ever been. Business had picked up on both the municipal and corporate trusts because of rising yields and several other factors. Within several months of the new initiatives in marketing and sales of MITs and the Corporate Income Fund and Corporate Income Fund Preferred Stock series, we went into high gear in terms of how busy we were and the amount of sales and ensuing revenue being produced. We added two new items to the product line.

The firm's greater strength was in the east, so it was to be expected that this was where the response would be the strongest. The more consistent sales came from Florida (with nearly twenty branch offices) and then the Washington DC and greater New York area including New Jersey were second. We had a strong following in upstate New York and in several Massachusetts branches. The municipal regional office in Atlanta gave us great penetration into Georgia, North Carolina, and Alabama as well through its satellite office in Huntsville. The numbers tapered a bit west of the Mississippi with the better part of the volume out that way coming through Chicago. What business there was to be done in the Far West and the southwest came on the individual response from brokers and branch managers who paid attention to the announcements of deals that came across the wire. As yet, there were no computer terminals or electronic communications other than the teletype wire system we had in place.

Notwithstanding the new organized sales push in place, we must again underline the fact that yields were near 7 percent on municipal unit trusts in 1975 when they had been in the 5 to 5.5 percent range just two years before in 1973. This was tremendous incentive for investors who became very receptive to these opportunities, especially those invested in CDs at the bank. On the other hand, the availability of yields such as these would engender great cause for criticism by management if we were not doing the business. We worked very hard to sell the product, and in early 1975, our monthly sales were in the following range:

$5.5 million to $7 million of municipal units,
$3 million to $4 million of corporate units
$2 million to $3 million of preferred units

I realize that these numbers are broadly spread, five to seven million in municipals, three to four in Corporates and so on. I don't want to exaggerate or minimize the business we were transacting. If we look at the numbers from the minimal point of view they amount to $100,000 being earned from portfolio accumulation, the bulk of which came from municipals. Another $250,000 of commission production of which the firm paid out forty percent to brokers ($100,000) and kept sixty ($150,000.) After all expenses were paid by the account manager, settlement checks and remaining cash in our accounts amounted to another $75000 a month. That's a minimum of $325,000 a month net, close to $4.0 million annualized at a minimum. The term unbelievable is bandied about these days in relation to a slice of pizza or a touchdown catch. Considering the kind of money they were paying me and the fact that we were just two guys, Clem and myself, and it was just the mid-seventies, if you want to call something unbelievable it was us.

Another big reason why the unit trust business flourished was because Clem and I were good at it. We had become a solid team, and I emphasize that we were very, very good at our jobs. The phones rang steadily from about eight-thirty in the morning with a short hiatus around noon if we were lucky and then on to around four in the afternoon when it tapered off. It was not unusual for the phone to be ringing sporadically when we left at five to five fifteen. We picked up the phone diligently, answering the same questions over and over, always with an upbeat, enthusiastic, and encouraging attitude. This came natural to us because I think we both loved people and loved to kid around, so the atmosphere was always light. Greeting people who call courteously, who are in effect perfect strangers to you, is a powerful ice breaker and an important confidence builder in the callers who doubt themselves because their calling from Mobile, Alabama, or St. Charles, Missouri and have the impression that their talking to some big Macha from New York who doesn't have the time of day for them and might just as well spit on their shoe as talk to them civilly. When these callers were made to feel welcome, they opened up more readily to what is really on their minds. This was an era of skepticism, and Clem was very much aware of it and didn't hesitate to fill me in on why so that I could understand the task at hand. Again, it was the go-go growth stock/momentum investing/mutual fund era of the sixties that had blown up on investors and brokers alike in the bumpy markets of the sixties and the below 650 performance of the Dow Jones in 1972. Even though we were selling fixed income, brokers wanted reassurance that a blow up wasn't going to occur again. No one could guarantee markets. However, answering questions with clear and patient explanations of how unit trusts and underlying securities in the portfolios worked and lived in the market instead of the terse "yeps" and "nahs" usually served up on trading desks gave brokers background information that could be turned into talking points and repeated to clients. For my part, I was still in my formative years, getting a practical education on the "theory, purpose and use" of various securities and the theory of their arrangement in a portfolio. Of course this education was biased to bonds and fixed income securities, especially to municipal bonds and earning income that was/is free of taxation in various ways. You might say I was becoming a "muni-guy" a specialist in municipals, but I was also well on my way to becoming a generalist as well because of the other products that were incorporated into unit trusts, like corporate bonds and preferred stocks.

Of course it helped our attitudes that every call that came in could be considered a potential sale, but it helped even more that we were both the sort who didn't mind the constant contact with people. There is often a low threshold for anger or a hard exterior that develops in people who deal with a public every day. We see it sometimes in a nasty postal clerk or at the Motor Vehicle Bureau or in a bus driver. I saw it in municipal bond and corporate bond service people who felt that the brokers should know all the idiosyncratic details of bonds and fixed income securities. We were sure a good deal of business that might have been done in straight bonds came to us because of our patience. What we did was listen to brokers talk about the potential sales they were working on and answer questions about some point of information in regard to the security and how it functioned in the marketplace. Why did it take three months for the first income check to be received? Can the investor use the security as collateral for a loan? Can the investor take delivery? Can the investor register the securities in one name and send the income to another? Are there any trusts without Puerto Rico bonds in them and so, on and on; possibly ad nauseum to some? Maybe there was something wrong with us, but we answered these questions repeatedly, if not enthusiastically as if they were being asked for the first time.

Because we were so busy and the business was so profitable, Henry allowed us to bring in a new hire. Carlos Rodriguez from White Plains or New Rochelle, New York, a recent college graduate, a nice kid, and an athlete, in fact a Rugby player, and as I would see often in future, a typical Clem hire—bright, aggressive, an athlete, and willing to work hard for the opportunity to get a starting position on Wall Street. Carlos, of course, was very unlike me in that I never even knew that a place like Wall Street or a job in a Municipal Bond Department existed much less had a plan since my late teens to secure that job. I think Carlos had been recommended by Henry Howard who was now working with Kondratuck and Mike Fitzsimmons in Municipal Syndicate. I thought as well he may have been acquainted with the Byrnes in some way. There seemed to be a New Rochelle connection there.

Around this time, a Henry Arbeeny directive ordered that anyone working on a business desk for six months or more, even remotely connected with executing a transaction for the department, needed to take the Series 7 exam, also known as the NYSE's Registered Representatives exam. The two immediate beneficiaries were Bob McTiernan and myself.

For my part, I had been begging Devlin and Kondratuck on and off for years to get the department to sponsor and allow me to attend Securities Training Corporation for classes and preparation to take the Series 7. I had discovered it was easier to pull a giraffe's tooth than it was to get the firm to sponsor you, especially if you had come out of operations. Any guess I might make as to why this was a problem for that generation of management might sound like sour grapes and a claim of victimization, so I kept my mouth shut, although my heart leapt with joy at Henry's pronouncement on the subject. Doing the work and the study was a different story. During the months I was studying, attending classes four nights a week, I often thought of just packing it in. First because it cut into my part-time work at the inventory company. Then I would daydream about asking Clem if I could delay taking the exam for a few months. It was a grind for me and in some ways quite rote and boring, and my fear of taking tests often surfaced.

After about five weeks, the class began to dwindle, and when I realized this, I wondered what kind of reception these folks who dropped out got from their managers. The idea of having to go back and tell people I'd dropped straitened my back to the task. Failing the exam, God forbid, was more honorable I thought than dropping out. Henry kept tabs on us as well by asking how we were doing when he passed by your desk or encountered us in the men's room or in a corridor, and I instinctively knew his question was not casual. He was asking how the studying was going. He also worked on you through your manager who asked for updates on what stage of study you were at and when you thought you'd be taking the exam. When I noticed Clem put it in his Day-Timer every Wednesday to question Pat about Series 7, I knew Henry was behind it.

Henry was, of course, way ahead of previous regimes on the subject of registration with the NYSE. I heard him say several times that if you weren't registered, the brokers doing business with you would (if they found out) feel you were not even made to know the minimum required about the securities business that they had to. So in a way, it was the blind leading the blind when you were advising them. The second point was if any legal or regulatory problem arose on a transaction or series of transactions or there was any accusation of impropriety involving a nonassociated (that is, nonregistered) individual, the firm and the department would almost automatically lose standing in the dispute if not lose the case altogether or not even enter into a dispute for fear of embarrassment.

Chapter 45

But Not Enough Money There

On the home front, by the summer of 1974, as mentioned, we moved to a house on Magee Place in Oceanside on Long Island, a small dead-end street less than a half mile from my wife's brother Joe. It was a cozy five-up and six-room down house known as a mother-daughter with a massive full basement and garage and plenty of backyard. The move and purchase of some new furniture and decorating plus the new expense of commuting on the LIRR had severely depleted our savings. The raise I had secured had been spoken for as quickly as it was received every two weeks. The small inheritance my mother had left when she passed in 1973, about $2,500, was a big help but gone. I was driving a 65 Chrysler Concorde at the time with a little over a hundred thousand miles on it, which I had unexpectedly had to pay $550 for after literally running my 64' Pontiac Bonneville into the ground delivering pizzas. One night several months before we moved, the driveshaft under the car disconnected with the front end, stopping the car abruptly as it dug an inch or two into the pavement.

Several months before Christmas of that year, I was sure my 1974 bonus, which was payable around January 15, 1975, would be at least ten weeks' pay and possibly more, but I was strapped for cash with the holidays coming in December. Because there was so much activity from the pickup in business, I told Clem I needed to come in on Saturday to check over the inventory cards and clean up details and problems. He okayed it, and I was able to pick up a cash disbursement of fifty-five dollars at least twice and sometimes three Saturdays a month. A couple of weeks before Christmas, I popped into Chase or Chemical Bank (I don't remember which because I always had a personal loan or two outstanding with either one in those days) to fill out an application for a personal loan of $750 or $1,000, whatever I could get, the purpose of which was to make the holiday for the family.

That first Christmas living on Long Island, we spent Christmas Eve in Brooklyn with my family as we had been doing since we'd married in 1968. Early on at my parents home, and after they passed at my sisters, just upstairs in the same house…Rosalie's family didn't make much of "the Eve" as we called it, food or celebration wise so it wasn't a bother for her family, that its favorite daughter and baby sister was absent. She would be home on Christmas day for their festive meal and gift-giving. The politics and social dynamics of Italian American families in regard to where married children and grandchildren spend the holidays can be anger filled, causing the beginnings of life long feuds. There was no such doings in our families. My family had a big celebration on Christmas Eve with all the typical seafood dishes and gift-giving that began after a drink at midnight that lasted often until three or four in the morning. But leaving Brooklyn at two-thirty in the morning for Long Island for a forty-five minute trek home and then facing the task of then putting our own children s toys together for Christmas morning turned out to be too tiresome to think about the following year for Christmas 1975.

A year later while I repeated the same ritual a few months before Christmas of making the rounds of the banks to close out short term loans and take new ones my wife began to make some changes to the way her family spent Christmas Eve. Since we left Brooklyn and were in a way starting anew Rosalie wanted to begin to build her own family tradition, celebrating the Eve, "La Viel e' Natale," as the Italians say, also known as the Vigil of Christmas in her own home. Rosalie convinced her mother to spend Christmas Eve in our house. That is to say on the first floor where we lived rather than upstairs at my mother-in-law's.

In past years, my wife's home was relatively quiet on Christmas Eve compared to mine. While both families celebrated the poor shepherds of Galilee waiting for the birth of the savior with a traditional seafood dinner, at my wife's home, it might be spaghetti with onions, fried flounder filet, and potato croquettes, while at my family home, it was a flashy affair beginning with a fancy cold seafood antipasto, onto linguini with calamari, and continuing with mounds of fried shrimp, baked lobster tails, and the grilling of eels in the backyard among other things. My good wife, despite her dim view of my outrageous spending habits, made for me and her family that second Christmas on Long Island the holiday I was accustomed to and perhaps to her own chagrin the Christmas Eve she had become used too. Included in this new tradition were her two brothers and their children and several of our closest friends. Of course, part of the loan mentioned above financed the meal and I'm bound to say we still celebrate Christmas Eve on Magee Place in Oceanside, the sit-down dinner now a buffet because there are usually more than twenty-five persons in attendance.

When the twelve-week bonus came in mid-January, the near $2,500 after taxes had a big chunk go to paying off one of the outstanding personal loans. That was a direct command from my wife, and the remainder went into Rosalie's general fund. I don't really know if I had a true realization of the pressure I was under at the time. I just moved forward and tried not to think about the possibility of some impending day of financial reckoning. Work was busy, home was busy, Saturday was a work day for me often in the office if I could justify it, and after that when I could get it some inventory work. I would take a Sunday with the inventory company as well or with my brother-in-law at the horse farm. There was a hiatus from study at Securities Training for the holidays, and in January, I blew school off once a week to groom because the colt was winning or consistently finishing "in the money," and these nights were worth a lot of money to me.

During the period I studied for the exam, I drove down to Howard Beach in the morning, taking the subway into Manhattan instead of the LIRR. The primary reason was to study. The exam was a 250 true-false, multiple choice affair, plus a couple of multifaceted questions or story situations you had to answer in essay form. Given my fear of tests, I decided to use my commuting time to advantage by going over questions in the one-and-a-half-hour subway ride each way on the A train. It didn't hurt that I saved a few bucks as well not having to pay the $125 LIRR fare for a few months.

The teaching methodology at STS was for instructors to spend time in the classroom on the items that had to be taught like how to read and interpret a research report or how to calculate SMA, which is a margin accounts credit line. Additionally, reams of questions appearing on previous exams were handed out almost every night along with the answers. Between the two forms of study, I managed to pass the test on a cold Saturday in January. I remember sitting in the Blarney Stone after the exam on John Street or on Broadway with Bob McTiernan and a couple of other guys, drinking beer and eating sandwiches while watching an NFL playoff game. I'm almost sure the Steelers were playing, but we were numb and some of us thought we'd blown it, but as we learned during the following week, we'd both passed with average grades.

This was an immensely important event for me. I was now, for want of a better term, a made man on Wall Street by virtue of the fact that I'd gotten a passing grade on the NYSE's Series 7 exam. Being approved and licensed by the NYSE to sell securities was membership in the exclusive club that I thought Bill Devlin among others was trying to keep me out of. Out of a working population of 150 million in the United States, maybe there were 150,000 who were registered with the NYSE. That was a pretty exclusive club, I thought. Then there was perhaps my own personal most important reason to be registered. If I lost my job at Reynolds, at least I would qualify to get work in some other firm as a desk jockey on a unit trust desk or as a stockbroker. Whatever, I had passed the RR's exam and I had been admitted to the community, and no one could kick me out any more unless I screwed up. I was a registered representative and could represent investors as a financial advisor.

Chapter 46

New Stirrings and a Turning Point

Though our business in unit trusts had picked up considerably since Henry's arrival and because of Henrys reaching out to the regional people, Clem remained skeptical of Henry's ability to be successful in managing risk to suit upper management. I, on the other hand, much less experienced in dealing with upper management and not as yet having formed the opinions I am now writing with, responded to Henry's leadership wholeheartedly. Besides responding to the clarity of his communication, which came at you in several ways and what I perceived to be the logic of his thinking, I felt a sort of kinship with him. There was, in fact, a certain zeal about Henry and a righteousness that reached out to me. Perhaps I am easily led, naïve, and just not a skeptic. Perhaps I want to believe that everyone is sincere. Whatever he was and I am, in any case, seemed to gel. I also felt simpatico with Henry because I had several Lebanese friends who I knew to be very good people and I was a fan of the Lebanese poet Khalil Gibran. There was as well I think a great deal of sentiment directed at the Lebanese and Lebanon because in recent years there had been a struggle for a free independent government in that country that was stopped with the terrible assassinations of several charismatic leaders. Consciously or unconsciously I think these personnel feelings caused me to lean in Henry's direction.

The second form of communication came through in very clearly written memos putting, forth both firm and departmental policy in a way that stated both what the policy was and the reason for it. I cannot emphasize enough how well-written and deductive these missives were. Any question or doubt as to whether the troops were informed about the rules under which we were made to operate could have had no standing whatsoever.

The third form of communication was, as they say, up close and personal. Every two weeks or so, usually on a Friday, Henry would come out on the floor with a container of coffee in one hand and an ever-present cigarette in the other to chat with the troops, usually making a stop at every business desk. Of course sometimes you were busy and couldn't talk, but Friday after lunch was the right day for it because things did wind down.

The subject was always business, peppered with some light joking around but always straitlaced, with little raucous behavior and no cursing or dirty jokes. Henry also deprecated his favorites knowing they could take the joke from him and others who may have thought ill of them enjoyed seeing them made fun of. Inevitably, whether talking to a desk manager or a worker, the process of doing business came up and the obstacles one faced along with it. He steered you in this purposely. The amazing thing was he would ask what you thought should be done about this or that problem, and he might say, "That's a good idea. You should do it." Or if he was talking to Clem or a manager, he'd say, "Lets meet on Monday and talk about it." Again, if he were talking to an underling like me, he might say, "We have to think about that. Tell Clem to ask me about it."

The best part of it was if you didn't mention the conversation to your boss, one of two things would happen. Your boss would come back to you a few days later with, "What the hell were you talking to Henry about that you were supposed to remind me about? Goddamn it! Whenever you have a conversation with Henry, I want to know about it."

Worse still, the next time, Henry himself might remind you of the conversation, saying, "Did you ever tell Clem this or that? He never mentioned it to me."

You could be embarrassed easily in these situations because it's easy for the inexperienced employee to say the wrong thing, but for the most part, these conversations had a positive effect. Henry was coaching and teaching, building morale and instilling confidence in us, no doubt something never seen before on Wall Street except maybe across the street at Merrill Lynch. These sessions were also about straightening out peoples thinking in terms of interpreting events and explaining department and firm policies. Depending on what might be going on in the market or the department or a new hire or an article in the papers, the conversations would always verge on business and management, again the market, trading and selling, inventory control, use of interpersonal skills, regulatory policy from the NASD or the MSRB or the SEC even, or competing products in the firm, personal advancement, and any number of topics related to work and business, never sports or woman or entertainment although sometimes a book one might be reading came into the discussion. These sessions, while casual, were serious and were viewed by the troops in different ways. Some of course took them at face value, businesslike and positive. Others thought them too direct and felt they were being put on the carpet in some way.

"Yeah, he's making people feel good, but when the chips are down, will they get paid? Will they get raises?"

Yes, that was one level of thinking, which eventually did happen. But on another level, a level that is sometimes difficult to distinguish because people see progress and change in themselves as self-wrought rather than influenced by outside sources. I know I began to change; I became more thoughtful and disciplined in my thinking, especially when it came to opening my mouth and speaking or acting impulsively. While I cannot speak for the entire crowd in the Bond Department, my interpretation of Henry's message was: to be successful, one had to be more serious about the job, find ways to increase business, try to realize what your strengths and weaknesses were and work on the weaknesses while capitalizing on your strengths. If an individual wished to take it that far it was not a problem at all to make suggestions and follow up on your ideas and convictions. Once I realized this I felt that Henry was there not just to successfully manage the firms business and the department but also to make me more successful too. As I began to listen then more carefully, certain things Henry said have stayed with me.

"Any person of reasonable intelligence can learn any business in two or three years, but after two or three years of learning and immersion in that business, real success and advancement in business is dependent on the individual's people skills."

Another thing Henry would say

"Whether you like or dislike someone should not prevent you from working with that person for the good of the firm. After all, no one is asking you to invite them home to dinner."

Another saying I took to heart and practiced throughout my career was

"I never made an impromptu speech I hadn't given fifty times before."

Meaning if you were at a trainee luncheon or a branch office dinner and asked to give some impromptu remarks as the representative of your department, you had better be ready (i.e., prepared with something polished in your back pocket). In this way, you would be prepared and appear professional rather than appearing to fumble or worse say something untoward.

In later years, I ran into Henry one day feeling and perhaps looking very down. When he inquired about what was wrong I said that I was backed up with several problems that had to be tended too, which interfered terribly with my routine. I explained or rather complained of the situation saying that it was not an infrequent occurrence; that in fact something blew up and needing emergency tending to, almost every day. At this point Henry tells me to stop by his office the following morning for a chat. Now I want to kick myself because I think I've let myself in for a lecture. I bring Henry a coffee and a danish the next morning and he begins by joking that the firm is not paying me because I'm good looking, far from it. He goes on to say that I'm being paid because I have experience, know the business and can be trusted to conduct business with the firms best interests always in mind, and to do so under the stress and duress and the pressure that is part of being at risk on an hour to hour day to day basis. To wit, he says, my problem is one of attitude and personal philosophy. Further he says, you must come to work every day with the sure conviction in mind, that you're going to have ten problems of a near insurmountable nature that day and every day. That beside your daily routine these problems are going to have to be solved and overcome. Once you convince yourself of this, once your mind is tuned in this way, your problems and your stressing over the burden you complain of now will cease to exist. He further explained that if only two or three problems surfaced a day, I'd have had an easy go that day and if things really got out of hand, well, I'd have had a tough day.

"How do you think a general in battle gets through a day? Think about it, and think about how Eisenhower or Patton got through their days." He went on to recommend a famous biography of General Eisenhower that I may have bought but don't remember ever reading.

In a way with this little tete-e tete, Henry turned my life around because I began to understand what my job really was, that I was a manager with authority to change and fix things. That I had to have the strength of my own convictions. Indeed I began to lose my fear of what could come up in the day to day routine. As far as the sayings I mentioned above I memorized them and wrote them out longhand often ten and twelve times and even fantasized situations in which I would act upon or act out these precepts successfully. Where could you get this kind of advice anyway?

I used to watch him in these Friday afternoon conversations from across the room and observe people drawing upon his knowledge and advice and willingness to give it while he, at four or four thirty or so, would walk off the floor to his office, passing by my desk, not so much as if he were exiting purposefully but appearing as though he had completed a task or accomplished a mission so to speak. Obviously, it was a job of work, and I surmised he would be tired from it. Who wouldn't be after performing and lecturing for two or three hours straight, drinking three or four cups of coffee, and smoking half a pack of cigarettes if not more?

Naturally, I thought all of this was very positive and exciting, and I loved it when Henry stopped by to talk. Even though he was talking mostly to Mike Fitzsimons or Clem most of the time, I managed to get in a quip or a comment here and there, it felt good, and somehow, I thought Henry liked me but I didn't really know or just couldn't tell. My self-confidence was still wanting and I had a tendency to overthink everything, especially when it came to the favor of my superiors and double especially with Henry because he had secretly become my idol. Clem still felt it was just a matter of time before the market blew things up and upper management would cave in on Henry, but it was also quite clear Clem was beginning to warm up to Henry. Obviously, Henry did not have the problems Clem had with senior management. He managed his managers, while Clem had become personally demoralized by their behavior. Years later, I found out Henry recommended almost immediately after coming to Reynolds that Clem get a raise, and in this memo he (Clem) was copied on and which I stumbled on years later in a file, it was mentioned Clem Schaefer is "clearly a person upon which the future success of the department is dependent upon."

One night, toward the fall of 1975, I stayed late to do some catching up on paperwork and to check out a few unresolved trade problems. I was helping the operations people as usual with some of the trade foul-ups as a means of putting in for overtime and continuing to come in on Saturday once or twice a month for the extra cash. It happened that Henry had also stayed late for some reason that evening, and he came walking past my desk without noticing I was there. You couldn't see the space Clem and I worked in unless you passed the solid wall to our left and then only if you turned in that direction. I saw as he walked by that he didn't notice I was there because he didn't turn, so I shuffled a few papers signaling someone was behind him. He heard, turned, and spotted me and then came over, sat down next to me in Clem's chair, took one of my Winston's out of the open pack at the edge of my desk, and lit up. After a minute or two of small talk, he said, "You know you have to make up your mind."

I was a little puzzled with this remark and replied, "About what?"

I can't remember Henry's exact words, but it went something like, "You have to make up your mind about what you're going to be committed to. Traders, salesmen, and investment bankers on Wall Street, Wall Streeters, even prospective ones, don't look to do operations work to make a few hours of overtime pay. Nor do they run out at four in the afternoon to go to a second job."

I was aghast and quite embarrassed. I felt a flush coming on, but it subsided as Henry continued. He went on to tell me my employ at various outside jobs was no secret among my coworkers. He said he required a commitment "from me" in order to get a commitment from management "for me," meaning if I wasn't going to devote myself fully to the profession I was in, I had no chance of being rewarded for the work I was doing. Don't you realize that your counterparts on The Street, people doing the same work your doing are making a lot more money than you are.

Henry Arbeeny, the first person after Mario I'd ever thought of as a personal hero and mentor, sat before me and went on to pay me several compliments and at the same time scolded me for not having the presence of mind to understand my own abilities both on the technical side of things but also in my social skills and managing my work. He said in his travels around the country and through management circles, people always asked after me and commended my work. He intimated I demeaned myself before others with half the talent I possessed because they knew that as long as I continued along this course, I would never get ahead or amount to anything. I was at once elated and laid low.

My rejoinder was to explain, and this was the truth and what came to mind that I had never really felt until recently, in fact, since he had come to the firm that management had any confidence in me at all. I mentioned also that my outside activity should in no way be considered disloyal to him or the firm. I was entirely engaged in these things to make money.

His answer, "You devote all of your time and energy to this job and let me take care of the money. Do you need any clearer an indication of my confidence in you and of management's confidence in you?"

This little talk to say the least was an odd and off-putting experience, and when it was over in eight or ten minutes at most, Henry stood up, shook my hand, and bid me goodnight. I must have sat there for another half hour mulling it all over and sort of stunned. I had been complemented grandly and been told I was an idiot by the boss all within a ten-minute period. I called my wife to tell her about it while it was still fresh in my mind. Rosalie has never been very interested in my work. I think she got tired of my constant chatter and obsession with markets and trades and new deals and talk of millions when she struggled with hundreds. She just stopped listening to me after the first five minutes. Despite what she may have thought, what she knew or didn't know, what she did say was right on the money.

"Well, it seems Henry really likes you because he sounds sincere and you like him and believe in him. No one has ever spoken to you like this before, so you have to believe in him for a while anyway, even if it's just to see if he comes through."

There was a Chock Full O'Nuts restaurant on the corner of Cedar Street and Broadway diagonally across from our building. Almost every day, I went down around ten o'clock for a container of coffee and one or two of their cream cheese on date nut bread sandwiches, and on this occasion, the day after my talk with Henry, I bought a second container and a sandwich for Henry and stopped by his office on the way back to my desk. Normally, you couldn't just walk in on Henry, but he wasn't on the phone and Angela, his quite charming secretary, didn't gate me so I just walked to the doorway and stood there for a quiet moment. When he looked up and saw me in the doorway with the two Chock full O'Nuts bags, he waved me in, and I walked to his desk and handed him the coffee and said, "Whatever you say, Henry, you have my commitment. If you need anything, just ask, and thanks for the advice."

245

Henry rose from his chair, smiled (not a rare occurrence but not something he did often), and said, "Don't mention it, Scida."

Henry and I had many little talks over the years in which I learned a great deal, and I brought him many containers of coffee. I was always a pretty thickheaded guy who didn't pick up on the mission sometimes when it was first introduced, but there was none that I remember more vividly than the one I've just described. It gave me great confidence and a feeling that I'd arrived despite what I felt were my shortcomings of little formal education, being somewhat socially outcast especially on Wall Street as a bit too ethnic, an Italian American, and somewhat obese.

I groomed several races over the next month until my brother-in-law was able to find a replacement. I would only go out to the farm or track after that for recreational purposes with my children. At the inventory company, since I was part of a regular crew that always worked together, I waited a while for my boss, a great guy by the name of Sid Branson, to find a replacement in the crew for me and after a while I stopped calling in for assignments.

Sometime later, toward the end of the year, I went to the Chemical Bank around the corner from 120 Broadway and took a two-thousand-dollar personal loan. With Christmas on the way and the cessation of part-time work, the ready cash was needed. It would get us through the holidays without any discomfort while giving the new situation some more time to ripen. What the hell, it was only money. Money was all around me, and it dripped from every word I uttered or wrote, so what was the difference if I owed a few thousand or a few hundred. Instead of leaving early for part-time work, I began attending sales training program prospecting clinics. I knew one of the brokers, Jeff Retaliata, who helped sales training out in these sessions. I volunteered to buy dinner, which amounted to a few pizzas and soft drinks, and spend a few hours with the trainees who wanted to try prospecting with municipal unit trusts. Product departments rarely, if ever, did such things in those days. It became a trend actually that probably is still being done today.

In mid- to late January of 1976, I received an $8,500 bonus as well as a talking to about a salary adjustment later in the year. We use the word *awesome* today to describe a cup of coffee or an egg cream ascribing an overwhelming attribution to a soft drink. What can one say then about a windfall of $8,500 in 1976? Words fail me in any attempt I might make to describe the awe I felt at those pronouncements, the wondrous and overwhelming feeling that came over both myself and my wife in the days and weeks following this event. The bonus immediately put us on solid ground financially and the promise of a raise in my base considerably brightened prospects as I had earned close to twenty-four thousand dollars that year without counting any part-time wages earned.

Chapter 47

The End of the World

I began to understand and feel connected to the risk associated with the weekly calendar of offerings. Clem and I managed two municipal trusts a month simultaneously working off corporate and preferred stock deals at the same time. No sooner would one close than another was announced. Behind us, Muni Syndicate, in the persons of Mike Fitzsimons, Bill Kondratuck, and Henry Howard, shepherded through an inexorable flow of municipal bond offerings, municipality after municipality looking to borrow $250 million or $130 million or $500 million. New issue after new issue came and went, and if you weren't careful about what you bought, what deals you stayed in, and how many bonds you took, you could get hurt. The calendar of new offerings was an unstoppable steamroller that we faced and priced and ran before frantically, week after week after week.

A regular occurrence in 1974 and from my earliest days in the Bond Department was the quarterly borrowing by New York City. You could set your watch to it, and our New York City branches were good for ten million dollars and more in sales on almost every deal. But in early 1975, when Wall Street refused to bid on an issue of short-term New York City notes, a strange and alarming crisis erupted. Controversial statements made by the mayor and controller of the city and several other issues regarding city employees arose in the press that simply destroyed the market for New York City bonds including those of the state as well. While the city did not default, its troubles and ministrations first to shift blame and then to set its affairs right had ripple effects. The markdown in prices of outstanding New York City bonds and related New York State bond issues was severe. The phenomenon effected every bond issued by the state or city or authority in the state from direct obligations of the state of New York, to dormitory authorities, bridge and tunnel authority issues, and the issues of the NYC Water Authority and Housing Authority among others.

The markdown had a profound effect on outstanding unit trusts because a typical twenty million-dollar MIT portfolio was composed of twenty-five to thirty percent and in some cases forty percent New York related issues. Maybe as much as two million NYC's and another two million of New York State issues of various names such as NYS Dormitory Authorities or Triborough Bridge and Tunnel Authority and so on. Puerto Rico bonds were in all trusts, perhaps as much as two million dollars of par value because they're bonds were exempt from income taxes in all states. The problem with that was Puerto Rico paper got marked down in sympathy with New York paper. As a rule, one could say that forty to fifty percent of all existing long term unit trusts outstanding of all the major underwriters was marked down by fifty percent. This amounted to a $250 to $300 markdown per unit. In effect a very typical investment in fifteen units at a cost of around fifteen thousand dollars was now worth eleven thousand dollars not including any general market deterioration.

The reaction by investors, meaning individual retail investors, to the heavy losses in valuation of New York City bonds and related issues was varied. Many simply sold out and took losses, while others held on, working on the assumption that no matter what the state and the federal governments rhetoric, they were not going to allow New York City to default. Still others had definite convictions that New York City would not default, and there was a great deal of money to be made by scooping up as many of these discounted bonds and unit trusts as they possibly could at bargain basement prices.

New York City bonds themselves and bonds that were direct obligations of the city such as the New York City Urban Development Authority and Battery Park City Bonds were at the lowest bargain basement prices. These were 7, 8, and 9 percent 20–30 year bonds redeemable at $1,000 and trading as low as $450 to $500 a bond. Investors bought these securities directly from the street at a five-dollar fee per bond. These transactions were processed as direct purchases from the Street as the firm did not wish to appear as if it recommended these securities. Such trades were known as agency trades as the firm was acting as agent for the investor. New York State bonds such as New York State GOs or New York State Dormitory Authority or New York State Power Authority bonds were also trading at bargain prices in sympathy with NYC Paper. These however, were not in danger of default, and thus the firm acted as market maker continuing to buy these bonds and offer them to its clients interested in taking the risk. Nice profits were incurred in this business.

Because the New York Trading Desk was so busy at the time, Henry asked Clem if we could help out in servicing the retail sales force in all the particulars regarding sales of these distressed New York–issued securities. Besides the buying of direct obligations of the city, there was demand for certain bonds that the Trading Desk didn't want to position because their prices were just too volatile. These were the aforementioned Battery Park City Bonds and New York City Urban Development Authority. In addition to these, the low coupon bonds issued in the fifties and early sixties, when long-term (twenty- to thirty-year) municipal bond rates were in the 2.5 percent to 4 percent range.

In particular, there were loads of bonds outstanding that came to market to finance the building of the New York State Thruway that were trading at the time at twenty to forty-five cents on the dollar during the one or two years that the New York debt panic/crisis was full blown. These were called New York State Thruway Authority Guaranteeds. An investor could purchase (and many did) one hundred thousand dollars face value of New York State Thruway Guaranteeds, 2.75 percent bonds due in 1985 for thirty thousand dollars. Such an investment would deliver $2,750 a year of tax-free income until 1985 and then be cashed in for $100,000 with the final coupon payment. These transactions often produced yields to maturity of 20 percent plus, tax free. I personally did two or three of these trades a week of ten or fifteen bonds and some as big as ninety and a hundred thousand dollars of par value. At the same time it must be remembered that these were bearer bonds. Bearer bonds needed no name registration. The person who showed up at the bank with bonds to cash them in at maturity received their principal value no questions asked to leave or disclose the name of the individuals cashing in the loans. In effect, these transactions in their entirety were tax free. In the case mentioned, a seventy-five-thousand-dollar capital gain over ten years was garnered with no taxes paid. I probably spoke to several hundreds of people about these deeply discounted bonds and helped to execute hundreds of transactions many in the fifty to one hundred-thousand-dollar face value range and never bought a single bond for myself. For good reason of course, I just never had the disposable cash to invest.

Chapter 48

People: Norman, Kondi, Family, Et.al.

After my encounter with Henry and the subsequent raise and bonus came through, there was plenty of time to become more involved in the business. Paying attention, for example, to the underwriting process, the legal, accounting, and printing aspects of the unit trust business. Each new issue of unit investment trusts or mutual funds for that matter has a formal closing attended by the sponsors lawyers, accountants, and members of the managing sponsor's firm and the joint sponsors. This event is akin to the closing one might have at the buying or selling of a piece of property. Every new issue of securities, whether it's a bond, a stock, or a mutual fund at its onset, its birth if you will, has a formal closing of some kind.

These closings were a combination of routine business proceedings as well as social occasions for cosponsor employees. There was work to be done in the proofreading of various sections of the final prospectus like the portfolio and any new material being added to the boilerplate (the prospectus' basic or standard language) by the attorneys, which I tried to participate in when I attended. The numbers are gone over by the accountants and footed several times to avoid error. During these proceedings, a buffet meal was often served. In addition part of the group might go out to dinner after the closing with transportation provided home by taxi or limo for the attendees ostensibly at the printer's expense. In those days, it wasn't uncommon to have dinner at some of the finest restaurants in town like Four

Seasons or the Sign of The Dove or Giordanos no doubt one of the perks of killing yourself with tension and pressure ten hours a day. At least I saw it that way.

These dinners, buffets, and cab rides home might have been the excesses of my Wall Street experience, the three martini lunch come working dinner. Perhaps there were other perks that Clem and Norman Schevey might have enjoyed. I don't know and didn't care to know at the time. In those days, I was one of those guys who was always "on," meaning I was almost always thinking about the business and work and thought everyone else was too. I began going to closings maybe once a week or every ten days and usually left for home when the crowd was going out to dinner. I didn't want to put myself in the position of getting wasted and making a fool of myself or worse going out with some of the guys and participating in activities I didn't want particularly be involved in. Not that I knew for sure anything was going on. Clem might go to two a week, and some guys went to every single one, relishing the free food and booze. After all, it was a free dinner and plenty of booze if that was your thing and there might be a party after the party so to speak, but I rarely even thought of those things, much less participated after the buffet.

If you went to closings though, you had to endure Norman Schevey who was a sarcastic, even one might say sadistic, all-around rotten, nasty individual. Brilliant, yes, but very rough on people he thought were using him and the product's prowess for making money without contributing to the overall benefit of the product, the business, and the account in general. This may have seemed a benevolent boorishness on Norman's part, as if to say he was only working over some of the hangers on who were simply there for the ride. To this, I say, "No, emphatically, no." Norman's behavior was something out of the movies, often mean, cruel, and demeaning and meted out to everyone except a select few.

Clem warned me about him, and I was always on guard not to speak out of turn. At closings, about six-thirty on most occasions, the first pages from the prospectus that required thorough proofreading came out. Printers' assistants handed out proofs to about ten to as many as fifteen people sitting around a huge conference table. Each person at the table would read a paragraph or two, and the reading would move around the table like at an AA meeting. Once early on, when it was my turn to read, I looked up before I began and Norman, staring at me, said, "Who the fuck are you?"

"Pat Scida," I said. "I work for Clem Schaefer at Reynolds."

He paused for a moment and then said, "Fuck you, fuck Clem Schaefer, and fuck Reynolds, and just watch your fucking step."

I don't remember what I said. I think nothing. I just went on and read. Later, I thought I should have said thank you and was later thankful that I didn't, but I just went on and read, had something to eat, and was in a car riding home at eight or eight thirty. The next morning, when I mentioned it to Clem, he said it was just Norman keeping up his reputation.

"He loves us."

"You coulda fooled me," I said.

As I began to go to more closings, I would go out to dinner if the plan was to go out to a hot restaurant like Giordano's or the Four Seasons, but I stopped going after a while because Norman usually went too and he was always beating somebody up. Guys never learned. They tried to be nice to him by making small talk, sucking up to him by asking ingratiating questions. When you did this, you were just asking for it, and in some way, this spectacle became the main event—the feature of the night. Not that I wouldn't speak at all. A lot of Merrill Lynch people were at these dinners and when the talk revolved around facts, sales ideas, and the market and sales forces, we were all on common ground. It was when you veered off and tried to ingratiate yourself that Norman pounced on you. I just tried to kept quiet, enjoy the food, and participate in the conversation. These guys, whether lawyers or accountants or just Wall Street operatives like myself, were smart guys, and the conversation about markets, current events, and business was top shelf. But it was just much too uncomfortable sometimes. You had to watch your words all the time because Norman, if he was in a mood, needed no excuse to vilify anyone. To my way of thinking, here were some of the greatest meals in the city reduced to an aggravating, indigestion-producing nightmare. I would rather have gone to the Market Diner on

West Street for a greasy hamburger and fries and enjoyed it instead of being subjected to this childish behavior at the Four Seasons that left you with a belly full of agita.

In January of 1976, I received a bonus that literally bowled me over—$8,500, something more than $5,000 after taxes—and in April, shortly after my sixth anniversary with the firm, my salary was raised to just shy of $22,500 a year. Taken altogether, almost five times the $6,500 ($125 per week) I started at when I was hired at Reynolds by Eddy O'Donnell in 1970. I became an assistant vice president that year when officer elections were published in late summer. Of course, I felt pretty hot about myself and no longer thought of my job on Wall Street as transitional. I was there to stay. I was good at my job, and my attitude, energy, and enthusiasm had a positive effect on the people around me. I don't know if I knew these things at the time. I was just being myself. I came from an Italian family where, in most cases, there exists a zest for life and an overarching enthusiasm that everything is going to be either good, okay, or better than okay. What I did know, what I felt very deeply, was I had Henry alone to thank for recognizing whatever talents I had and rewarding them. Clem and I got along, and no matter how grateful I have to be to Clem for teaching me everything he knew, I just didn't think it and in fact it didn't feel like Clem was the protagonist of my rewards of salary and position. While Clem was all about the business and getting it right and getting it done as indeed Henry was too, Henry was also very much about people, their particular value to the organization, and their loyalty both to him and the company, department, and so forth. Henry after all thought enough of me to say, "You have to do this and that in your life, and I'll make sure you're rewarded."

Maybe Clem didn't have the power or didn't think he had it or just didn't see the need or just didn't have the inclination for being this kind of a mentor. For me, Clem was my direct boss, my manager, but Henry was my mentor and benefactor, and on another level, Henry, after all, was another guy from Brooklyn, which was kind of unbelievable when I thought about it. Another overachiever from the old neighborhood in a long line of them, stretching from Woody Allen to my own brother Dom to Walt Whitman to Al Capone to

Fabiano Caruana who was a chess grandmaster. Henry just happened to go to the Air Forces Officer Training School, eventually becoming a lieutenant colonel in SAC and an instructor at SAC in Japan and another Brooklyn guy influential in my career beginning Mario Ruocco, Eddy O'Donnell, and Bill Devlin. The question has occurred to me a thousand times.

"What would have become of me had I not run into these guys from Brooklyn?"

The first real casualty of Henry's arrival at Reynolds was the resignation of Bill Kondratuck sometime in 1976. I'm sure Bill felt that at some future time the legacy of heading up the municipal operation would fall to him once Bill Devlin retired. These hopes were dashed after a while by the arrival of Arbeeny and led Kondratuck to finally accept a long standing offer from the management of Macdonald & Company, the great Ohio-based retail regional firm. He left to head up their municipal operation and possibly their entire fixed income operation. It's possible Kondratuck would have got the head of municipals job at Reynolds had the firm not had greater ambitions for their Fixed Income Division and simply waited around for Devlin to finally retire, but when Arbeeny was hired, Kondi, I think, was personally offended and perhaps hurt and just didn't want to be there anymore. Events in a career swing the right way or the wrong way, meaning whether Kondi was right or wrong for the job or got the job that he always thought he was going to get or secretly pined for and didn't get are very difficult to bear for a sensitive and essentially good, openhearted person like Bill Kondratuck to recover from—a fellow who cares about and tries to do the right thing all the time. It's better to be a little ruthless, I think. You don't get hurt as much.

In any case, Kondi, like me, was not, in my estimation anyway, politically cunning as Henry was, as Clem was. The difference between Henry and Clem was Henry had the stomach for the game. Some people are made for having the savvy and thick skins needed for political infighting. They maintain an ability to recover from untoward events that affect others in a very personal way. I think for Kondratuck, having not gotten the job he wanted and thought was rightfully his combined with a couple of errors in judgment under Henry, might have made life at Reynolds just a little too difficult.

A particularly embarrassing situation for him occurred on the heels of a big Port of New York Authority deal that fell apart. We were handed several millions of a thirty- or forty-million-dollar float of thirty-year term bonds known as Port 5.80s in bond speak, meaning Port of New York and New Jersey Authority 5.8 percent of 2015. The deal came at the very edge of a big sell-off and Kondratuck chose to trade the allotment of bonds himself, rather than turn them over to an experienced dollar-bond trader like Bob London. Being so emotionally involved in such a situation almost never works out well. He looked a little pathetic and disappointed sitting out on the Trading Deck. I don't know what the eventual turnout of the Port 5.80s was, but it was good though that he had an out in McDonald & Company's long standing offer to join them. With that kind of offer, who needed the aggravation at Reynolds anyway.

People and the memory of the events they were connected to slipped into my own personal history and became a subconscious store of events no less relevant to me than the history of countries, wars and civilizations. I had a fascination with the nonstop passage of people in and out of my life. There is no other place where people disappear or are forgotten faster than Wall Street. People, events, heartfelt human connection, and camaraderie, anger at one another and overcoming obstacles and problems become yesterday in twenty minutes, and feel like they happened last year in less than a week. No business travels faster than the money business, especially in the underwriting and trading functions in which a nuance can change one's perception of the immediate world. People, their personalities, good and bad deeds, got lost and forgotten in a snap of the fingers. These writings are simply an attempt I think to make sure they were real. I had been writing since high school and about this time I began to write about my job experiences if only to preserve them from being blurred out by the speed with which they occurred.

I used to kick myself around, thinking I should have stayed more in touch with Kondi, but soon concluded there wasn't enough time, that there were so many, too many, obligations for me to fulfill between work and home and extended family. There wasn't much time for anything else, and I wasn't the kind to stay in touch with the solar system—what they call a networker, I guess. The work was my world. The task at hand before me was more important to me than the periphery of people. Reynolds in-house became my home, my family away from home, my passion, my only other loyalty besides kith and kin, and if you were out of this mainstream, I forgot about you.

******

My father-in-law, also named Pasquale, passed away in the spring of 1977 from a heart attack and stroke on a sunny Saturday morning. He was seventy-five years old. We were lying in bed and heard a thud upstairs. Before my brain processed the sound, Rosalie instinctively knew something was wrong. She jumped out of bed, running to Pop's aid upstairs. He died several hours later in the hospital. It was very sad. I had grown to like him despite his gruffness and jumping to conclusions. He was a devout man in his way, very fond of his daughter and wife and great with my children, a pretty good trombone player, a fisherman, and a guy who could fix anything from a leaky faucet to a lawn mower that wouldn't start. I was quite upset over it while Rosalie kept her composure and repeatedly reminded me to be careful about upsetting our children. Pat was close to nine and Nancy would be six in August.

Since moving to Long Island a couple of years before, and before that for a few years when we were still in Brooklyn, Rosalie and I had been my in-laws' caretakers. I had, as I said, grown to like Pop, my father-in-law, and to have enormous respect for my mother-in-law as my own mother had. My mother had been a contemporary of my father-in-law, living just a few doors away from his family when they were children and just a few doors down from my wife's family on Walworth Street until I was sixteen. I remember him stopping by the gate in front of our house every so often for a chat with my mother, often in the native dialect of the hometown in Calabria. My father-in-law was born in the United States. His father, however, had been born there, and it was the language spoken in his home when he was a boy.

I don't think Rosalie and I ever put a lot of thought into how much we'd been through in regard to the loved ones we'd lost since 1968 when we met and got married. These events just washed over us, and we simply bore them just like everyone else does. By the time we were together 4 years my mother and father had passed away, then Rosalie's father as well as my sister in law Clara. Clara was Rosalie's sister in law, Frank's wife, a lovely gentle woman who suffered from chronic heart disease discovered in her twenties. Over the same period there were at least five other deaths during those years and maybe more. Uncles and Aunts on both sides of the family. Older people yes, in their seventies and eighties but larger than life figures who we felt very close too. We were products of the old Brooklyn neighborhood where we grew up in the shadow of these people before the diaspora of the Italian immigrant population to more suburban locals. They weren't remote or vaguely familiar aunts and uncles who lived in Massachusetts or New Jersey: you met Uncle Sammy and Aunt Mary in church on Sunday and Aunt Lizzie and Uncle Dominic or Aunt Rose and Uncle Nick came over for coffee on Sunday night and on occasion stayed late to play cards and have a late supper.

I was quite familiar with my wife's side of the family because as I mentioned earlier Rosalie's family and mine were from the same town in southern Italy. In the US my mother had grown up a few doors away from my father in law and his sisters and they had been quite friendly. Two of Rosalie's aunts, Mary and Lizzie and another Aunt Rose often came over to visit my mother during the week, I would find them at my house at least once a week when I got home from school sipping coffee and chatting away. Their husbands were childhood contemporaries of my father, who had grown up in Strongoli and then migrated to the US as young men. My grandfather, my father's father was an overseer on the land of a local aristocrat and landowner and since my father worked with his father from a very young age he knew or was familiar with most of the local families and their family names. At least one Sunday a month and sometimes during the week one of these uncles or any one of a number of men or woman in my parents social circle would show up with a letter from a relative in Italy that he wanted my father to read and respond too. My father had the equivalent of a fifth or sixth grade education garnered from a sympathetic officer when he was in the army in Italy. He could read and write fairly well in Italian and get along in English. Rosalie's uncles, the older ones, Uncle Nick Varino or Uncle Dominick Cotrone for example were completely illiterate as my own mother was.

In those days the dead were waked for two and three days and in the case of aunts and uncles we went on all three nights and then to the funeral mass and then to the cemetery. We watched our parents and aunts and uncles grieve for family members as well. We got through it all by sharing the burden of grief amid our duties to our extended families but our children I think saved us from any real despair. We knew we were living for their happiness and progress in the world. Our instinct was to protect them from the pain of loss, so we compartmentalized the hurt in our lives, pushing it into little corners of our consciousness. Not forgotten, never forgotten, but to be remembered in quiet moments and at that point in the mass on Sundays when we are called upon to remember the dead. Then there is the memory that comes out of the blue, like a bolt of lightning, when we suddenly remember the approach of a birthday or an anniversary. I went through a period of about ten years after that time, having masses said for the dead on their birthdays or at Christmas. We also made visits to their graves, which I often did with my mother-in-law and still do with my wife.

The memories of those who had had left us came up as well around the times of baptisms and first communions and birthdays, at athletic events and Boy Scout and Girl Scout events and meetings, and church socials that we hoped in some way our parents were looking down upon. The dead were remembered especially when we packed up the kids, bought fifty dollars' worth of cake, and trundled off to Brooklyn to visit Rosalie's Aunt Jay or my Aunt Rose, Filomena or Francis. We went to Rosalie's Aunt Rose and Uncle Chic as well in Howard Beach. On the kids' birthdays, we deliberately staged big weekend events so we could get the older folks who didn't drive picked up and brought out for a day of celebration with lots of food and drink and fun and reminiscing. I saw these times as little victories in life that defeated and diluted the personal loss and sadness we carried around, helping it to fade even deeper into the recesses of my mind at least. My wife might have toned these events down a bit, but I think she deferred to me because she knew how important I felt they were. Then again, they were built around the children, and that made it worth all the work and expense.

******

The other phenomenon I recall and wondered about so often over the years, if only to myself. Some of the most mad and passionate lovemaking of our lives took place on those evenings, returning home from wakes and funerals. I don't really know why, except for the possible need to escape from reality, totally immersed in the deep passion that we had for one another, for our own lives, to have twenty or thirty minutes in complete abandonment of the world and the troubles we left there if only for a little while.

The office sent flowers to the funeral home where we waked my father-in-law. No one from the office came to the wake, and it didn't bother Rosalie or me that they hadn't. Henry called offering his condolences and told me to take as much time as I needed. A few days later, Angela, Henry's secretary, called, reiterating Henry's suggestion that I take as much time off as was necessary. I got the feeling from these little quips of conversation that Henry was very conscious of the passing of emotions both negative and positive. He didn't want me, a guy who was never down, to come in to the office if I was feeling down. I remember thinking, was sure of the fact, that he felt that feelings of loss, negativity, and hurt could be spread just as easily as upbeat ones could. This astounded me because it was a new discovery in how deeply observant Henry was, how very much like my own people he was, and how very much I liked him.

******

After Kondratuck left, I'm kind of lost as to who came into Municipal Syndicate, because by this time Clem and I and Carlos had moved out to a spot on the floor. In a period of about six months more or less, Scotty Marlin, Bills Marlin's son came into Municipal Syndicate along with a fellow named Cross who came over from Merrill. Mike Fitzsimmons left for I don't know where as did I think Henry Howard. Carlos left for a spot at Bank of California and Clem then hired young Jean Alexander. Jean was born and raised in Rockville Centre, an old Long Island aristocracy stronghold as Clem called it, the next town over from Oceanside where I lived. Jean's father was the town clerk in Rockville Centre at the time. Jean herself was a gracious, beautiful, and poised young lady who worked her way through the day in a seemingly effortless, calm, and kindly manner. She seemed mildly amused at the goings on around her and the antics of myself and Clem while getting everything she had to get done and more. One might try to define this young lady's graciousness and poise by comparing her to images of Grace Kelly or Audrey Hepburn, realizing however that they were acting and Jean was the genuine article and a Notre Dame graduate too. Jean brought out the best in a couple of guys who knew how to be gentlemen when they had to be when a lady was around. Henry said Jean made Clem and I look better than we were by 200 percent.

Chapter 49

Astounding Times, I Thought

I said to Clem one day, "Corporate history can be more important (is more interesting I think) than world history." Clem flipped out completely when I said that. He was a history buff, and I know he thought I was a jerk for saying things like that. Yes, romantics may be given to overly idealistic and somewhat frivolous thought. However, what I meant is the proximity of an event to the individual can determine the importance of the event to that individual. D-Day is an important historical event, I agree. However, being in the midst of a five-year wave of major Wall Street firms closing their doors combined with the near financial demise of New York City with its debt selling for as little as forty cents on the dollar was much more important to me than D-Day because it happened in my wheelhouse, involved me even. I was in the midst of it. Not to mention the fact that in 1970, I was earning $125, and my earnings had increased five or six fold and more since then.

Maybe I wasn't smart enough, hadn't got enough higher education, or wasn't cynical enough to be distracted by politics or history. I was so impressed by the near financial destruction of New York City and the shunning of Puerto Rico's entire body of debt, not to mention the Washington Public Power Authority's default on two billion dollars of debt that it crowded everything else out. The Washington Public Power debacle was the borrowing title of the Bonneville Public Power project in Washington state. It was known among traders as WHUPP's and later monikered as WHOOP's by the press. I hated the term WHOOPS because it made light of what was really a very serious event for the financial markets, the underwriters, and the investors. At the same time, I was personally involved day to day with the underwriting and sales of million upon millions of dollars' worth of securities. How could I not be in awe?

Interest rates turned and began to decline in late 1976 and into 1977, business became quite steady if not a heavy flow despite the events mentioned. At Reynolds, the sales force was growing although I'd be hard pressed if I had to put a number on it. In the not too distant future technological advancements in the ability to track massive quantities of data would soon make possible some very practical and very popular investment innovations that would dramatically boost sales. For the present, in our firm, the municipal bond and corporate bond investment of choice were the municipal bond and corporate bond UIT. Henry had relentlessly promoted the UIT to every corner of the firm, including senior management, and the executive committee that fixed income investment through unit trusts was the only logical choice for retail investors.

Around this time, Henry wrote a single sheet "For internal use only" document, listing and defining no fewer that fourteen aspects or features of the unit investment trust structure, beyond the inherent benefits of the underlying security that was being invested in. It was a grand sort of position paper reduced to a compelling one- to two-minute read about suitability and a definition of what unit investment trusts were, followed by a table illustrating the fifteen features mentioned. It was also typical Henry, powerful and logical and mowing down any opposition real or imagined. I could not find an original copy with the original prose portion still attached, but I had reprinted the point-by-point features in many branch office distributions. Here is one:

FOR INTERNAL USE ONLY

A Unit Investment Trust is an alternative means of investing characterized by its underlying security. Suitability is key.

Consider the appropriate trust in relation to an investor's financial capabilities, sophistication, tax status, investment objectives, and other relevant suitability factors.

Additional Aspects	Municipal Unit Trusts	Corporate Unit Trusts

1- Diversification............As a means of spreading risk

2- Indepenent Evaluation....................................

3- No Liquidation Charge.................No sales charge upon redemption or sale in the secondary market

4- Flexibility...............................Ability to purchase unusual amounts (i.e. 1, 3.17...100)

5- Flexibility.........................Ability to sell (liquidate) odd amounts at same price. No odd lot penalty

6- Flexibility............................Ability to sell unusual amounts or pieces of a block of units.

7- Flexibility....................Ability to sell off odd amounts at the same price as a round lot

8- Minimal Initial Purchase..........................1 unit

9- Registered without the usual disadvantages of a registered bond

10- Ongoing Involvement......Sponsor, Trustee, Evaluator

11- Participation............................In issues often not usually available: private placements, negotiated issues.

12- Ease of Ownership........Safekeeping, annual statements, ready quotation, no coupon clipping

13- Prospectus....................Each Unit Sale must be made through current prospectus

14- Tax Swaps............Units lend themselves to convenient exchanges for other units taking advantage of tax loss.

Clem thought it was overdone, pedantic, a bit much, especially in the many permutations of flexibility. I disagreed. Investors complained bitterly about the evaluations and bids on their individual bonds, and stockbrokers were on the receiving end of this complaining. The material in this paper hit home. What I liked best of all, however, was the prose part of the sheet that defined a unit trust as "an alternate means of investing in a security characterized by its underlying security."

"I know that," Clem said.

Maybe so, but then no one had come up with that simple statement before. It defined and framed the UIT in its truest sense because unlike a mutual fund, using a unit investment trust as an alternative means of investing did not change the fixed income nature of the investment itself as a mutual fund did. You retained par value, you retained fixed income, and the underlying portfolio was not and could not be sold off or added to or traded except in strictly specific circumstances. The phrase "characterized by its underlying security," made clear that in corporate bond or municipal bond unit investing trust was indeed investing in an alternative very much akin to the actual real thing. In a mutual fund no matter what the underlying fixed income investment was the mutual fund turned the bond into a stock. At the time it was something that people really cared about.

The firm, from management to branch managers to brokers loved this document, although I don't think it would have survived compliance and legal scrutiny by the mid-90's and beyond. It was much too explicit and it may be a moot point to say that it wasn't vague enough for modern compliance and legal standards. The document for one thing affirmed the investments features and benefits (its practicalities) and verified, perhaps even justified in a way the investments popularity at the same time. Not a good mind set when it comes to investing because there are so many things that can go wrong. At the same time the products revenue producing capability was I'm sure addictive to the firm. Fifty to one hundred thousand dollars of gross revenue to the firm, depending on whether a municipal, corporate bond or preferred stock trust, or some other permutation of one of these was underwritten. The profitability came in some combination of portfolio accumulation gains, underwriting fees, and commission retention. Without burdening the reader with too much detail lets say that a $4 million municipal commitment would garner perhaps $45,000 net from portfolio profits, another $15,000 in fees and another $40-50,000 in commission retention and a corporate bond issue of a similar size would garner roughly 60 % of the what a municipal deal would. The likes of Bob Gardiner and the executive committee had no problem with Henry's push on the product, and in fact, many invested in in it themselves. We, Clem and myself, were depicted by Henry as the gurus of unit trusts backing up Henry's claims. In effect, we killed ourselves day in and day out to service the sales force in such a way that rarely engendered a complaint on any level. We were the ideal backup for Henry, and the truth is Henry unceasingly mentioned our names all the time. This was another line in Henry's management manual. The more Henry deprecated himself and extoled the virtues of Clem Schaefer, Pat Scida, and Gene Alexander to the firm management, the bigger Henry became.

The more than adequate profitability we earned as a sponsoring partner of the Merrill Lynch Unit Trust Account was a tremendous backstop to the risks inherent in running a bond department. Managing both facets of the total operation well; made for great results when things were going your way and a passable result when the market went bad. Remember Bill Byrne Sr.'s remark about UIT underwriting profits covering a multitude of sins. That Henry had perfected the art and that it was a deliberate and working strategy, keeping management fat and happy in good times and not terribly unhappy in bad times was to me unquestionable and to Clem the stuff of myth and heroism, something that early on he believed to be impossible for Henry to pull off. In Clem's way, he loved it though. While from the first moment Clem had been loyal to Henry, he had also been terribly skeptical of Henry's ability to pull off an amiable and fair-minded relationship with upper management at Reynolds, but by now, he had become an admirer, although at times I was sure he was shocked. Henry, despite his toughness and deviously political thinking, strategizing, and charm, often appeared to be too brash for Clem's taste. Clem was an incurable pragmatist and a minimalist, and generally critical of grand schemes that were intellectually reasonable but to his (Clem's) way of thinking, on a practical level impossible to implement. Around this time Henry had begun to approach management with a plan to pay bonus's semi annually and at some future time quarterly. In addition Henry had drawn up a proposal to put in place a firm wide format and policy for the timely review of personnel vis a vie employees personal performance review, promotion and wage increases. Needless to say Clem was simply stunned at how naïve Henry could be, not realizing on most occasions how unbelieving he had been about so many other proposals Henry had made and were accepted since he'd come to the firm. In any case what Clem did acknowledge was that Henry protected us, we could do no wrong and woe be tied to anyone who might attack us, from in the department or outside of it.

Chapter 50

Innovation Part I

In 1976–1977, and well into the 1980s, 90 percent of the population of United States and possibly 95 percent and more of the world's population didn't know anyone with a cell phone or a personal computer, and an even greater number, if that is possible could not conceive how these two instruments would affect their lives in the future. Realizing the truth of the last statement, it should come as no surprise that in the midseventies, other than social security and pension benefits, one could not invest in a security that could deliver regular and even monthly payments of income. Some mutual fund payments were made monthly but were notoriously uneven as income ebbed and flowed with the quarterly payment of stock dividends and semiannual income from bonds. Brokerage accounts could be put into monthly payment mode, but again, payments would be uneven for the same reason. A thousand dollars this month because a bond made a payment, nothing next month, and a hundred and forty the month after from a stock dividend, and unevenly on and on. The introduction of a security that would, after a three- or four-month waiting period, deliver dependable, regular, and even payments of income monthly was a big deal. A very big deal indeed.

Investors who previously went to the bank or cashed a check to supplement income or otherwise depended on investment income for their subsistence could now make new investments or convert current investments to a municipal or corporate bond unit trust that would pay regular, even monthly, payments of interest income. Mom or dad might be relieved of the task of running grandma or grandpa to the bank two or three times a month or perhaps eliminate the need to send junior, at veterinary school in Granada, a check every month. The securities could be set up in such a way that the unit trusts trustee bank would automatically send an interest check anywhere the client designated.

Monthly payment of income from our municipal, corporate, and preferred stock funds became quite popular almost immediately and swayed many investors who had previously said they'd stick with their CDs or straight bonds. The introduction of monthly income also led brokers to canvas their accounts and cast an even wider prospecting net because of its appeal. Sales ideas abounded because monthly income could be used not just for personal income but to defer electric or gas bill or even mortgage payments. If savings were in place, they could be moved into investments that could supply the monthly income to pay them.

A larger than life illustration of the importance of this innovation presented itself some six months after the Municipal Investment Trust First Monthly Payment series was underwritten. We were in the midst of taking orders for the tenth or twelfth monthly payment series. I randomly picked up the phone one afternoon only to find the great Robert Stovall on the other end. Bob was, at that time, Reynolds Securities' head of Research, as well as its market guru, public face, and spokesman. Stovall was also a regular or soon would become a regular guest and commentator on WNET's *Wall Street Week* with Louis Rukeyser. Bob had a deep and resonant radio announcer-narrator voice with the kind of inflection that implied that if "Bob Stovall said it, you could depend on it." We had spoken from time to time, and occasionally he put in an order for unit trusts, usually municipals. On this day, however, his mood was skeptical. He asked if the first few underwritings of the municipal monthly payment series had begun making monthly payments yet. These early trusts had a three- or four-month waiting periods before enough income was received into the trusts current account to facilitate regular and even monthly payments. Remember, bonds pay semiannually, so an escrow had to build in the trusts account before payments could commence.

"Are they operating smoothly?" he asked.

"Why wouldn't they, Bob?" was my retort.

I went on to explain that there were some questions regarding the holding period and the way accrued interest was calculated, that is, how the investor is compensated for the earnings over the waiting period, but otherwise everything is running along smoothly. There were very few complaints, and I told him so. He went on to say a customer of his had seen several ads in the *Times* over the past few Sundays and had been asking about them.

"Bob, that's not unusual," I said. "We've had plenty of response to these ads. Brokers are having great success with it, and clients have become very enthusiastic about it, especially after the checks begin rolling in. They do complain a bit about the three- or four-month waiting period. However, most investors understand the idea of building up an escrow. But what's the big deal. There is a six-month waiting period to get a bond payment."

"I don't doubt or depute that," he said, "but has anyone given you a million dollar order yet?"

"You're kidding."

"I wish I was. This guy scares the hell out of me. He wants to make this investment purely on the convenience of receiving monthly income."

After asking several questions about the client and his finances, I asked the following question. "Would you feel the same way if he wanted to buy a million bonds? You know, a million straight municipals?"

No, of course not. He already owns nine or ten million dollars' worth of municipals.

"What in God's name do you think he's doing? It's the same thing, isn't it? Just another million bonds for him. Lots of people buy the trust instead of straight bonds or buy both."

"I know that, but a million dollars' worth?"

"You say this client's got big money, why does he need the income on this block of bonds sent monthly?"

"He doesn't need it for himself. He has three daughters, none of whom are in New York, and he says he's constantly being bothered to send a check to San Francisco or wire money to Paris or New

Mexico. So he wants to put a million dollars' worth of these in his account and redirect a third of the income to each of his daughters every month. Can we do that, keep the units in his name and split the income three-ways?"

"Yeah, I'm pretty sure we can, but I'll double check."

"What a country!" Bob said and then, "Listen, he may not go through with it after all."

"I won't be surprised if he does," I might have said.

Less than a week later, Bob called with an order for 990 units that came to a bit over a million dollars, a transaction earning a commission of something in the area of $27,000 for Stovall. I don't remember which trust it was or what the yield was, but just for the sake of putting an end to the story, let's say the income was $62.50 per unit annually. Since the investment income was to be divided equally, each 330 unit block earned $20,625 (330 X $62.50) and would pay $1,718.75 monthly once the waiting period was up and regular even monthly payments commenced. Now, knowing that an investor of this caliber was willing to drop in a million dollars, helps one to imagine what an important development and what a hit regular monthly income was among rank and file investors. Monthly income from unit trusts was an important innovation, and its usefulness in the management of an investor's money cannot be stressed enough.

Chapter 51

Innovation Part II

There was another leg to the monthly income innovation. For many investors, the introduction of monthly income posed a dilemma. Investors, especially those who were not retired, did not need the monthly income and did not necessarily want to own an investment that paid income monthly. Today's sophisticated money market accounts, by-products of everyone's investment account like Merrill Lynch's vaunted cash management account, which was the very first, or Dean Witter's AAA account that sweep all loose income into a money market fund would not be introduced until 1978–1979 and would not become commonplace until the mid-1980s. Indeed, investors might view monthly income entries into their brokerage account more as an annoyance than a convenience. This was still a time when investors went over every entry in their account just as they would balance a check book every month.

The solution to the problem was the setup of an automatic reinvestment account that provided what Andrew Carnegie and Albert Einstein no less called the eighth wonder of the world—"compounding." In our case, the unit trust sponsors set up a municipal bond mutual fund for the sole purpose of receiving monthly income payments from Municipal Investment Trusts units as well as a Corporate Bond mutual fund to accept monthly payment from Corporate Income Fund units. Now if you didn't need the income, every cent earned together with every dollar invested was employed in the earning of additional monies every day of the year. Ask yourself what better benefit you could provide for your money, the money earned by the sweat of your brow, than to have it at work daily, earning more money.

Again, generally this benefit was available in mutual funds, but mutual funds were not a viable investment alternative at the time. They were still viewed unfavorably because of their lackluster performance in the sixties, and since the market had been backing off, their yields were not competitive with unit trusts. On another plane, the yield to maturity calculation of individual bonds theoretically implied a compounded value that was never achieved unless the investor did what we were doing—placing every semiannual income payment (in this case, monthly payment) into a tax-free investment the moment it was received. To put a finer point on it, $25,000 invested in a savings account at the bank, compounded quarterly at 5 percent, will have an end value in 10 years of $41090.49. Left uncompounded, its end value at the end of 10 years would be only $36,500. That is a difference of nearly $4,600 or close to 50 percent more income. Imagine the same $25,000 invested at 6.5 percent tax-free unit trust compounding at 5 percent tax free monthly, which were the prevailing rates at the time or an 8 percent corporate bond trusts income compounding at 6 percent.

The concept of compounding was universally understood and important to investors because they were savers before they became investors. I knew and understood the concept perfectly. I vividly remembered from childhood the Friday afternoon ritual of my father bringing home his meager paycheck and my mother then accompanying him to the bank where they cashed it, always leaving five or ten dollars of it in their savings account. The Friday every three months, when interest earned for the previous quarter was posted in the bank book, was always a sort of red-letter day because that interest payment was now theirs and added to their previous balance.

In the same way that compound interest in their savings accounts was a valued aspect of saving money the monthly interest income and reinvestment programs we introduced were an astounding success. Monthly income for its utilitarian usefulness and reinvestment for delivering a procedure to channel income and ultimately convert it into additional principal. The vessel used to collect income until its eventual conversion into additional locked in principal was (is) a mutual fund because mutual fund shares are easy to create and redeem at low cost. Typically, a twenty-thousand-dollar unit trust investment at six percent took a year to accumulate enough income to purchase an additional unit of par value guaranteed to return a fixed value at maturity. Investors received monthly statements of accumulated income in the reinvestment mutual fund and brokers received notifications when client's reinvestment proceeds exceeded one thousand dollars.

The reception of a notification that a clients reinvested income was sufficient to purchase an additional unit was a signal to the broker to call the account and convert (liquidate) the mutual fund shares and purchase another unit. In reality, it was a signal and a pretense to call the client and ask if there were additional monies to invest besides the reinvestment accumulation. Most brokers waited for the accumulation to reach two thousand dollars before calling and there were instances when clients initiated the call to purchase an additional unit. In any case the program worked and perpetuated itself. Some brokers dedicated themselves to programs of selling one hundred thousand dollars' worth of UIT's every month for the specific purpose of reinvesting the proceeds. After a year or two these brokers had several clients to call every month to convert their reinvestment monies and ask for additional monies. Of course, each time an investor converted reinvested income and/or added monies it effectively accelerated the accumulation of monies for future purchase of principal, good for the investor, good for the broker.

Suffice it to say that the program of monthly income and the reinvestment alternative was a self-perpetuating sales machine that was not just popular with brokers but became popular with investors. I must add that this enormously successful investment program, procedure and device must be put down to Norman Schevey's drive, creativity and vision as well as the atmosphere at Merrill Lynch that made such innovation possible. It's appropriate to mention here that Norman Schevey and one of the greatest investment franchises ever assembled (MIT, CIF the very account we are discussing) came to Merrill Lynch via its takeover of Goodbody and Co earlier in the decade. Oddly enough Norman Schevey was once employed by another defunct brokerage firm called Ira Haupt and Co. In 1963 Goodbody took over Haupt's bond business after the SEC closed Haupts doors due to it's involvement in the great Salad Oil Scandal.

Chapter 52

Discovering and Learning My Trade

Business was booming. The product had taken a firm hold in the branch office system for many reasons. The sales force had accepted the investment and was selling it enthusiastically. Branch managers had their rookies prospecting and were hiring brokers away from other firms who did business in the product. It's SOP in the securities industry to offer a broker from a rival firm a fifty or one hundred thousand dollar bonus to migrate to another firm today these offers run into the millions. If the broker is confident that a large percentage of his clients will follow him to the new firm and that he can continue to comfortably conduct his normal business in the new firm he'll do it. The practice is alive and well today although the stakes and the bonus' are much bigger. Taxes were still very high and the public was being educated aggressively on the subject of earning tax exempt income. In addition the innovations of monthly income and reinvestment were deemed enormously practical and salable and were instrumental in winning brokers over who had not been interested in the product before. In addition the Sponsors introduced several variations in the product. An intermediate term (15 year maturity) was introduced both in Municipals and Corporates for investors less willing to invest long term. A hybrid Corporate Bond-Preferred Stock Trust was introduced as well. By this time I had gotten approval to for several prospecting letters and had them distributed to the sales force and we had finally gotten approval to employ the printer in copying some of Merrill Lynch's sales material with our name (exclusively) on it as we had not put together an in house marketing operation yet.

On the selling and marketing front, my natural enthusiasm and willingness to serve made me quite popular with the brokers, trainees and journeyman alike. Clem was a protagonist within the sales organization and was "proactive" fifteen years before the phrase became popular. I had after a few years become his twin. Within our work-week, in the midst of the onslaught of incoming calls we each tried to make two or three particular telephone calls. These were to branch managers for a general chat and then we'd get down to specifics by asking which of the salesman in their branch should get a pat on the back for doing the business, (there were no sales listings in those days) and which salesman in their office we should call who may have the potential for increasing or doing business in the product. Some of the names we knew and others we didn't. We made the calls, answered the questions, got suggestions, picked up and gave out sales ideas and made sure guys knew they could always call us in NY for any reason whatsoever. We kept a log of who we called and when and jotted down the details as best we could. We never completed a full round of calls in a branch more than two or three times a week but the process was very effective as the feedback that came back through our regional municipal offices and regional managers among others was always positive.

In any case the business was coming in over the transom, with deals opening and closing in a day or two. It was a perfect time for me to learn my trade. Under Clem's guidance I began to go in for larger and larger take-downs. In this work it's the process and the feel for the process that eventually shapes an instinct for accurately predicting how much one can sell, specifically how much a sales force of 1800 to 2000 stockbrokers (salesmen and saleswoman) will produce through the time that the security is estimated to be available. For example one might say I want 5000 units (roughly $5 million worth) of the $25 Million being underwritten and in doing so, one is saying "I will be able to sell them in the two or three or four days that it will take for the entire twenty-five million to sell out."

Merrill Lynch in the person of Norman Schevey tracked sales very carefully and built new issues based on previous performance.

Despite this, Merrill often very selfishly scrimped on, and shaved other sponsors allotments when they misjudged their own sales organizations performance. Thus, besides communicating with and reading the vibes being given off in my own sales organization I had a kind of cunning psychological war going on with the people at Merrill. I had to signal them early, as to when I felt that my take-downs were going to increase by 500 to a thousand units (five hundred thousand to a million dollars or more) so that if and when I didn't get it I could claim that I gave them ample notice. In addition when I knew they were cheating I had to say it, in a polite way of course, because all of this stuff went back to Norman for sure, but again I had to make them understand when they weren't giving me the allotments I asked for, and was entitled to, based on past performance I was giving that feedback to my superiors. As mentioned I had a decent relationship with Schevey but I couldn't go directly to him on such matters, that was Clem and Henry's province. Years later I began to get the feeling that my reads of my own sales force influenced them in reading theirs. Years later, when ticketing became automated the people who worked for me were often shocked when I could predict sales at any given time before getting an automated read. The only thing I can say is that one gets a feel for the process. The next question is, exactly what is the process and what are you reading?

There are many sign posts to read, some in your face and others subtle. For example, what is the reaction in the sales force to the announcement of the new issue vs. the last, especially to the yield and any change in the yield from the previous issue. What kind of (presale) order flow do we have, before any kind of firm price ideas have been announced? What is the current market psychology, meaning what is the public and the sales forces perception of the market and its direction, up or down, positive or negative?" Has it changed in any way recently? How are the indications of interest coming in and what has been the trend of actual sales versus indications of interest. Have the phones picked up in New York and do we feel an uptick of enthusiasm in peoples attitude or are we bouncing along normally? What regions (branch offices) are making a special push and are there any large orders in the wind or in hand. Many brokers just don't put their

278

tickets in until a real price and yield are announced which begs the question. What sense do we have of what the ticketing follow-through will be (weak, strong) once the deal is priced. Not that every one of these questions is asked out loud or overtly, again it's the feel that one gets from the process, from picking up the phone and making calls around the sales organization to picking up the phone and having random conversations, again, getting a sense of what's going on. I have often compared this work to that of the vintner or the coffee roaster who uses his senses of taste and smell to make decisions.

I rarely went in for a take down without discussing or informing Clem of what I was thinking and going in for, although Clem always deferred to me and waited for me to make a mistake before being critical. Thank God there weren't many mistakes. Getting your boss and partners support in this work is very important with the kinds of numbers we're working with, it's not an easy burden to carry alone. At the same time there was a separate dynamic in play. There was an overall goal to raise our share of the underwriting and portfolio profits and the only way to do that was to increase sales. The more consistently you sold twelve or fifteen percent of the units underwritten the more you made the case for getting twelve or fifteen percent of the portfolio and underwriting profits. Clem and Henry went to a long lunch with Norman every ten or twelve weeks to discuss our rank and position in the account among other things and to negotiate upticks. A few days after these meetings Clem and I usually had an evening meal out to discuss what had gone on at these meetings and occasionally I'd get called in by Henry and Clem just after or the next day to hear of a policy shift or I'd be told to carry on some follow through in my discussions with the people I worked with at Merrill. I am naturally aggressive, however my aggressiveness in those days was jet-fueled by being in on what transpired at these meetings. I realized years later it was all part of a plan. Arbeeny pushed the sales organization through the upper levels of management, he and Clem schmoozed and negotiated with Norman for higher percentages, and they filled in and motivated the feisty aggressive kid to push and motivate the sales force and to manipulate the sponsors from his end. Truly I loved every minute of it.

Chapter 53

Notable Events and A Christmas Party

Between 1975 and 1978, there were several extended two- to three-day long business meetings held at the Harrison House Conference Center in Great Neck on Long Island. There were staggered attendance schedules so business could continue uninterrupted at the office. The meeting opened with a luncheon at noon on Thursday and ended with a Saturday morning wrap-up session. These were weekends in which Henry made several presentations both in writing and from the podium in which he submitted a rough picture of where we were, what had been accomplished, where we had fallen down, and what we were going to attempt to accomplish in the next six to twelve months. Department managers spoke as did representatives of the legal, compliance, and operations division of the firm. These were meetings in which we got our proper due diligence lectures, which would be documented to the regulatory bodies that we were informed of the legal and compliance tenets that were applicable to our business. In addition to the in-depth descriptions of the problems we faced as our business grew, the meetings promoted the growth of the individual. Some of the handouts were decidedly scientific in the sense that they discussed time management and the role of leadership and management skills in career development.

Municipal bond and corporate bond personnel were mixed with representatives of the Legal, Operations, and Compliance departments for the purposes of creating an overall better understanding of various aspects of the business and the firm. The municipal operatives especially were notorious for living in a vacuum. Over all, the meetings were designed to recharge the groups' batteries and inspire and bond us. In addition, guys played tennis, golf, went swimming, and at night, shot pool. The meals were great, and there was plenty of booze to grease the skids of camaraderie.

Henry's influence had fully taken over by this time. All the departments within the Fixed-Income Division, Corporate Bonds, Municipal Bonds, Unit Trusts, and GNMAs were running at optimum levels of efficiency and profitability. The department coalesced nicely as people worked hard, got paid, and seemed to be advancing their careers. There was a movement to get the firm to begin to pay bonuses on a semiannual basis, and even a quarterly bonus was mentioned at one time. Henry was a star in the firm although he continued his appearances out on the floor nearly every other Friday or thereabout.

I can't say I remember the actual place where the Reynolds Securities' Bond Department Christmas party was held in 1977. In reality, it may have been the entire firm's New York Christmas party. I don't rightly remember. What I do remember was it took place in a huge room somewhere around the Wall Street area. There were still plenty of seedy, beer-smelling back barrooms and low-ceilinged basements around the Street at the time. There were two incidents that evening that remain in my memory. Several hours into the party, when everyone was pretty well-oiled, a tall, curvy, and somehow familiar looking blonde with a coy, mischievous look on her face walked up to me rather unsteadily and said, "Hi, Pasquale. Remember me?"

Nobody called me Pasquale at work and then I suddenly realized she was the young lady (woman now) who administered the math aptitude tests in personnel the day I interviewed with Eddy O'Donnell six or seven years ago. The very same person I called Blondie who so graciously inquired as to how I was feeling and who'd called and told me I was hired. Before I could get a word out, she kissed me in a way that made me respond, although in what seemed like a flash, she broke off. In that moment, I must say I experienced quite a thrill. She smiled then and said, "Call me. You know where I am." Then she wished me a merry Christmas and gave me a cheek-to-cheek hug and walked away again putting one foot carefully if not unsteadily in front of the other.

Clem was standing next to me and asked who she was. He'd always had a keen, indeed a salacious interest, in tall blondes. Then again, who doesn't? I also remember one of the guys in Corporate Bonds who worked for Joe Goodnicht, a trader named Bob I think, slapped me on the back and said, "Way to go," rather loudly.

I never called her, although I saw her more than several times over the years, passing in a corridor or the lobby of whatever building we were in at the time. Sometimes we said hello and sometimes not. I honestly think she was so loaded when she got to the party. She might not have even remembered doing what she did or maybe she became embarrassed by what she'd done. I think now she might have wanted to get out of personnel at the time and thought I might help her because I was an individual, or so it seemed, of some provenance. Whatever, it was just one of those things that happen to us that stays in the mind forever.

The other incident occurred earlier in the evening as I crossed through the crowd ferrying drinks. I felt a pair of hands grip my shoulders and then heard an unmistakably familiar voice say, "I don't care where he's going, but I'll follow him there anyway," or something meaningless in that vein. There was no mistaking that voice. It was Bob Gardiner. When I put the glasses down, I turned and stuck my hand out to wish him a merry Christmas. He took mine and said, "The same to you and your family, young man," flashing his famous smile. Then he continued in a more serious tone. "Henry talks about you and Clem all the time. The way you work and run your business. I hear a lot of good things from the managers and the regionals too. Keep up the good work."

I think I managed to blurt out my appreciation for his compliments in the form of a "thank you very much, sir, and merry Christmas" before he moved on into the crowd that always gathered around him in public. I knew Stretch Gardiner to say hello and briefly shake hands when he visited the department. I once met him in the lobby of 120 Broadway and ventured to mention how much it meant to the people down in the department when he stopped in for a few minutes, to which incidentally he did not respond. There were also several dinners honoring Bill Devlin at various restaurants before he retired, which Bob attended, where we perhaps nodded hello in passing. But there was never much of an exchange as there was here. It was Christmas and the time for such talk, but needless to say, I was pleased with the notice from on high and stayed high from both of these incidents throughout the holidays.

Chapter 54

1978

Nearing the 2000 broker mark, Reynolds Securities was not as big a firm as its major competitors, Paine-Webber, EF Hutton, or Dean Witter. It was not so flashy a Wall Street place; perhaps viewed as the journeyman of the crowd plodding along not so spectacularly but putting one foot before the other quite steadily. Certainly, it was noted for its training program, probably the number two on the entire Street and certainly in the top three. It progeny remarked upon and present all over the Street, a tribute to the great Glen Givens, our director of training. Certainly, there was also a tradition of salesmanship that started with its founder, Tom Staley, and a long record of profitability, which the firm coveted and mentioned publicly at every turn. That might have been the outside look. Inside, there was a great familiarity of personnel on all levels of management and throughout the sales organization that radiated through the firm from top to bottom.

There was a great spirit of cooperation and loyalty to one another and to the firm. It's possible that my own romantic spirit conjured this up, but it appeared quite clear to me right from my beginnings in DECAB that there existed within the firm a palpable and identifiable tradition of service. This tradition manifested itself in anyone from clerk to manager to executive taking a call to help anyone anywhere in the firm to aid in the fixing of a problem. The operations division under Irwin Menchel had an enormous reputation for improving efficiency and working conditions both for its own purposes and the firm at large. In our case in Unit Trusts, we mirrored the firm. The salesmanship, the service provided to the sales organization, the reliability of the product and its availability, all had an impact. To say Reynolds Securities was a close-knit firm at that time and place in 1977 would have been an understatement.

At the end of 1977, I received several notes and cards from regional managers and branch managers congratulating me on becoming an AVP and several others from the same sources thanking me for working with trainees or for working with brokers in the field. I had become a minor figure on the recruiting end of the business with branch managers in that they would send as yet unhired brokers from other firms to spend a half hour with me to talk about the kind of service they could expect if they came to Reynolds. Again, another activity that put me in a favorable light with the sales force at large.

The new year, 1978, barreled in. We were doing business at a breakneck pace. Gene Alexander had left us, and we hired a guy by the name of Ed Miller. Eddie was a really good kid, quiet, very attentive, and someone who took his work very seriously. I think he was terrified at first by the sums he was dealing with and summoned all the concentration he could muster in doing his job. Clem used to watch him, often remarking on his concentration and intensity with his prominent jaw set hard and eyes almost bugging out of his head. But we also had a lot of laughs. Eddie thought Clem and I were nuts as our brand of humor was kicked up a notch from what he'd been used too.

Eddie took the secondary market over completely. It could no longer be handled as a sideline since so many new trusts had been underwritten in the past two years. The work was labor-intensive and detailed. Good records had to be kept, and the phone rang incessantly for quotes on trusts held by clients. Remember, this was before automated input and information on demand. In addition, tickets had to be written by hand. There were also standing orders to keep track of, for example, an investor who owned twenty units of the seventh monthly payment series and might want to purchase five more from the proceeds of his reinvestment account. We kept a file of these orders, and when we spotted a sale that fit one of these orders, we worked it out. In addition, a very lucrative business was being done in the execution of transactions in the secondary market which were known as "tax swaps."

Investors who had purchased securities that had declined in price because interest rates had risen or for any other reason were entitled under federal tax laws to take those losses as tax deductions on their income tax returns if those losses were recorded by the sale of the securities. Remember that New York City bonds and related New York issues as well as Puerto Rico issues were still out of favor and depressed in price, and these securities were present to some degree in most of the municipal bond unit trusts in existence at the time. Tax laws stated realized losses were applicable against capital gains and a limited amount of ordinary income, but the case was often that investors did not necessarily want to sell the securities outright and take the loss, they simply wanted to record the loss for the purpose of declaring and deducting it from ordinary income or capital gains.

This was done through the simultaneous (same day) sale of the security the investor held (recording the loss) and purchase of another similar security; similar though somewhat different in price, differing as to makeup and further to investment quality, easy requests to meet when exchanging portfolios of differing yet similar securities. Ideally, the purchase or buy side of the swap would be consummated with the seller adding no new monies to facilitate the purchase. Thus, if a client owned 25 units at an original cost of $1,010.00 per unit ($25,250) and sold them at $800 per unit ($20,000), ideally the buy side should be executed a little less than $20,000, producing a tax loss of roughly $5,250.

An enormous amount of work went into these transactions as proceeds had to be calculated by hand, and daily, sometimes hourly, inquiries had to be made to see if suitably priced units had come into inventory at Merrill Lynch. When they did turn up, they were reserved for a half hour or an hour ("taken firm" in street parlance), which gave us time to contact the broker for approval, and lastly, buy and sell tickets had to be written. The truth is when swapping was in full swing, we often held inventory away (units that were sold by our clients) from Merrill, which was against the rules, but it made our search for swappable units much easier. The tax swapping service was a great benefit to investors and created a commission for the broker and additional profitability for the house. I had little to do with them, however, as I had my hands full with the new issue operation. Clem, on the other hand, had a real knack for doing these trades and enjoyed doing them. He liked the mental exercise, I think, while piling up a heap business (i.e., profits and commissions).

With an extremely active new issue market, selling near eight to ten million dollars in unit trusts every week to ten days, an active tax swapping operation on top of a very busy secondary market sales and service operation, there was no doubt we had come of age. There could be no doubt that our operation was the centerpiece of the fixed income division.

Sometime in June or July, I was approached by Clem and Henry and asked, told in fact, that I would be attending the firm's Pacesetter outing in October of that year. The outing was an all-expenses paid weeklong trip to Sun Valley, Idaho, for the top 150 salesman in the firm (and their spouses) as well as a select group of New York product department personnel.

Though Clem had been on one or two of these fabulous trips, he was decidedly not too fond of them and not interested in going to this one. He was not a good traveler, meaning going on a trip of this sort was not his idea of having fun. From another point of view, Clem was simply not into the social side of a weeklong event of this kind. Getting dressed for dinner two or three nights of the week, going on a hayride or a hike, or making small talk at breakfast five mornings in a row was just not his glass of beer. Clem's tie came off at five o'clock, and it was all he could do to keep his shirt tail inside his pants after three in the afternoon. Not that I was any better, I'd never done anything like it, but of course I was keen to do it and quite proud of having been asked. And I had a wife who would very adequately cover the details and keep my shirttail tucked in as well. The other thing was Clem did not enjoy the domestic company of woman. Woman were much too demanding in the sense I think of the decorum one had to keep around them, perhaps the small talk one had to make, and the general demands woman might make on men in the ebb and flow of socializing, especially the moneyed and sophisticated homemakers one met on these trips.

My opinion was that it was all Henry's doing as was the comment at the Christmas party by Gardiner. It was a habit of Henry's to continually mention the names of the people who worked for him in what he called "key positions" to members of the executive board and encouraged them to call these people for investment advice if they required it, or anything else. Then at the end of the year, when he listed Pat Scida for a ten- or fifteen-thousand-dollar bonus, no one would be surprised. In fact my 1977 bonus, received in January of 1978 was $17500, an astounding figure that put Rosalie into a new Pontiac. Funny though, a new car was the height of prestige and a dream come true for my wife. For me after three years way back when, in the body and fender shop, I drove an old station wagon that I changed the oil and spark plugs on myself. One Saturday morning Clem came over for breakfast and found me in my driveway putting in new brakes. He thought I was crazy, "Don't you have a mechanic," he said, and then "what the hell are you doing with such an old car, what do you do with your money? He was even more baffled when Henry and I once had a detailed conversation about installing a sprinkler system in our lawns because it turned out that we had both done it ourselves. All he could say was "you guys from Brooklyn!"

I felt deeply that the bonuses and raises came from Henry, and that being a representative of the department at the upcoming Pacesetters trip was Henry's doing, not Clem's. Sometimes I just didn't know what Clem thought of me. We had a strange kind of love/hate thing going on and a rivalry. A rivalry that, in later years, I began to think Henry stoked. Henry was a fabulous guy but not above pitting contenders and competitors against one another. It's just another way to increase production. As I said, Clem and I were business partners, friendly rivals, and competitors with little time in between to let the darker forces dominate because we were so busy with the pace of the work and the driving force of Henry Arbeeny. My dominant feeling at the time, however, was we were responsible for the success of a tremendous business endeavor, but Clem felt I was lacking in some way and at other times, I worried I was being unfair and that it was all in my own mind. Be all this as it may we, human beings cannot help being who and what we are. We don't have much choice in how we are wired.

One incident that sticks in my mind involves one of Clem's old crowd at Reynolds who came to work for Henry. There are tons of administrative duties in any division of a major brokerage firm, ranging from correspondence with joint underwriting partners to maintaining a working knowledge of the firm's policies and those of the regulatory bodies and on and on. Jim Bach was a pleasant enough fellow on the surface but someone who never seemed to be saying what he was thinking. In Jim's presence, I was always reminded that I was a product of the great unwashed, and he was not. He never said anything to that effect of course, but he made you feel you didn't belong. He would say, "You're good at this. That's why you're here," as if to say, your being Italian, only a first generation American, almost a foreigner, with no college and a lower class background would generally preclude you from being here. What he meant was you really didn't belong here, and if it wasn't for this capability, you wouldn't be here. At least that's the way he made some people feel. I wasn't the only one who got these vibes from Bach either. Ted Pavick a colleague for many years who had worked for Jim, mentioned something to this effect to me on several occasions several times.

Jim spoke with a Connecticut Yankee drawl that came off a couple of shades down from Jimmy Stuart. I knew Bach had administered the mutual fund business in the sixties, but I had no clue as to what he was doing before he came to us. I used to think Gardiner got tired of having Jim around on the twelfth floor, so he palmed him off to Henry. But the truth was that Henry could not do the admin and manage the division at the same time. There was an incident, inconsequential and unrelated to Jim's personal demeanor, that illustrates the rivalry that existed between Clem and myself.

Several months after the already mentioned Reinvestment Program begun, some correspondence came through from Merrill regarding certain expenses relating to our share of the cost of setting up the reinvestment vehicle and that by the same token, there would eventually be revenue that would flow back to us. Thus an account at our corresponding bank had to be set up for dispersing and receiving monies for this purpose. Reynolds Securities policy stated that such accounts had to have names, and such names had to have their defined purpose on file both in our department and in Accounting.

Jim, true to form for an admin guy, placed great store in getting these account names to be reasonably meaningful came by the desk one busy morning, customary sheaf of papers in hand, and told me the story about having to name the account. It is my nature to shoot from the hip. I often hit my target and just as often miss it. Reacting in this way, I said, "How about Re-Vest or Rey-Vest, capital R-E-Y for Reynolds for both Reynolds and reinvest." After saying that, I thought, "Wow! Cool!" and said, "Right, Jim! There would be no mistaking that moniker for what it is, right, Jim?"

At this, Bach took a step back, looking like he witnessed a crime. He then gave me this sort of incredulous narrowing of the eyes look while his head and neck bent sideways. Talk about body language. "Did you know about this?"

"I don't think so," I replied."

"Are you sure?"

"What do you want from me, Jim? You asked me a question, and I gave you a suggestion. Is this a test? What's going on?"

"Nothing, Pat. No, nothing. This is fine. Fine, thanks." And then, "That's a great talent you have, you know. Henry told me to ask you."

"What the hell are you talking about, Jim?"

"Henry said you would come up with a name for this thing in a minute, and he was right, but I wasn't sure if he told you about it beforehand."

"Okay, Jim, I gotta pick up a phone here. Good. You need anything else, just come and talk to me."

I was annoyed. The guy asked me for help, he told me what he was working on, I suggested something he liked, and then he questions whether I'd been informed beforehand. If it were someone other than Jim, it wouldn't have bothered me, but you never knew what Jim was thinking. Around this time, and perhaps why Clem may have been annoyed at me, I had a small sign on my desk taped to a metal desk organizer. It was quite cryptic in the sense that it was simply a sheet from a three-by-eight yellow pad that had the word *CREATE* written in heavy marker on it. On impulse, I had haphazardly jotted the word down, put a piece of tape on it, and thumbed it up. The reason being that I had just read the book *The Entrepreneurs* by a guy named Robert Sobel and had become fascinated by the seemingly routine though creative business decisions (at the time they were made) by now famous and, dare I say, iconic American entrepreneurs. The book fascinated me with several stories that I fancied might similarly occur in my own life.

For example, Cyrus McCormack's reaper was an inferior machine to most of his competitors' models. However, because he employed farmers as his salesmen to go out and talk to other farmers as opposed to his competitors who sent engineers and mechanics, McCormack's company lead the way in sales of the reaper. Hence, we think of the reaper as McCormack's invention.

In the same way, Sam Goldwyn owned several hundred large wooden picture viewing boxes with cranks that the viewer turned to view more than five hundred still pictures so that the figures in them appeared to be moving. Hence, the term *moving pictures*. These viewing machines are now sometimes seen in amusement park arcades. When rents rose for above-ground storefronts to show these earliest of moving pictures, he began showing them in empty basements in Brooklyn and Manhattan, which he rented very cheaply, charging pennies to use them. Before long, all the still picture sets had been viewed so many times that the public grew tired of them and business dropped off. When Goldwyn looked into it, he found plenty of out-of-work actors from both New York's Yiddish theatre and Vaudeville and decided to begin producing his own movies, and that was the beginning of what eventually became the movie industries Metro-Goldwyn-Mayer.

There were ten or twelve stories in the book that sang to me that I could one day come up with an idea or an innovation that could make me a millionaire. Hence, my "CREATE" sign and reminder to myself to think freely, to think out of the box so to speak, which probably wasn't even an expression at the time. Unknown to me, however, was that Henry loved it and had mentioned it to several people. He never commented on it to me, but his sending Jim to me was in a way a comment on it.

When Jim came around a few days later with an official memo on the naming of the "Rey-Vest" account and its purpose that Clem had to sign, he went on and on about it a little too much and Clem snapped at him with a testy "Knock it off already" remark. I knew Clem had viewed and listened to the entire exchange between Jim and myself.

When Jim said, "What's the matter?" Clem got up and left.

Jim looked at me, and I just shrugged and said, "I don't know."

The truth was I did know, and when Clem seemed to get angry about these things, I alternately gloated and got sad. Clem and I had a love-hate relationship going on for a long time, but it was also true that a good deal of this stuff could be chalked up to Henry because Henry as I said earlier, pitted people against one another purposely. Competitiveness even among partners was good for production.

Chapter 55

He's Probably Recruiting the Guys in Ketchum

I didn't care if I was second choice from Clem for the Pacesetter's meeting. It was an acceptance of me and an appearance in what Clem and I used to joke about as being "the polite society" of the firm. It was an overt and unmistakable sign of advancement and the natural continuance of an existence that I could never have imagined in my wildest fantasies ten years before. The heroic daydreams of my childhood, of building bridges and cutting down endless forests, became reality in a new form. Instead of wielding an ax, operating a derrick or a steam shovel, I wielded a pen and drove a telephone as I moved enormous sums of money and investments in the creation of unspeakable profits and commissions, simultaneously influencing the success of the firm and the very salesmen who would attend this meeting. My head spun with these thoughts, bringing me high at once and then low again in awe of it all.

Rosalie and I had never left our children before for any great length of time, and I mean never more than a few hours to go to a wedding or a funeral, and now here we were going to almost the other side of the United States for six days. My mother-in-law, Helen, and her cousin, coincidently someone we called Aunt Helen, stayed with the kids, and my wife's brother and sister-in-law were a stone's throw away in Rockville Centre if they were needed, so we were fairly confident that they were in good hands. It was late September to early

October, and our children, Pat age nine and daughter Nancy age 6, were in school. How bad could it be, getting them out in the morning and feeding them and bedding them down at night?

We flew out of JFK to Chicago on Saturday or Sunday morning and, once there, switched to a Salt Lake City flight on whose check in line and boarding lines I recognized around me many voices of people I spoke to regularly. Not the faces mind you but the voices. The trip began there for me, with my meeting in person people I'd spoken to on the phone for years. My wife, Rosalie, was excited for me, but she tends to be shy and quiet in these situations when meeting new people, not being any sort of an extravert at all. Although she loves to travel, especially to resorts like Sun Valley. In reality, the happiness over our good fortune and excited anticipation about the trip, combined with her beauty, produced a radiance in her that spoke for itself. Truth be told, when most of these guys got a look at my wife's beauty, their estimate of me rose even higher. At least that's how I think about it. My wife has always made me look good.

Once in Salt Lake City, we switched again to a Conair 440, which took us up to more than eight thousand feet above sea level, finally landing in Hailey, Idaho. We were then put on buses and driven to the Sun Valley resort, passing through Ketchum, Idaho, population forty-one, which oddly enough had a Dean Witter branch office that we passed on the way. Apparently, there was enough money up there to justify a satellite office of a major firm. We changed for dinner, and I can only say that evening was the beginning of one of the best vacations we've ever gone on to this very day, meaning perhaps that how good a time one has is probably a state of mind. I had only been on one real trip or vacation of any kind up to that time, and that was our honeymoon in Aruba. That first night in Sun Valley, we had dinner in a restaurant on the resort grounds that had the biggest wedge of a log I had ever seen aflame in the biggest fireplace I had ever seen in my life, and everything was up from there.

I enjoyed that week immensely, spending a great deal of time with a fellow named Harry Brown and his wife, Ursula. Harry, a long-time Reynolds employee, was mainly a commodities specialist with several large accounts of his own and in partnership with many other brokers in the office, handling commodities for their larger accounts. He had worked for the major portion of his career in the downtown office and had just, a few years before, moved uptown. We hit it off with Harry and his wife right away as we were New Yorkers and had much in common, having similar working-class backgrounds and having left our similarly aged children at home with relatives and being first timers on a trip such as this. Harry had heard of me, and I had heard his name a few times as well. That was enough for us to feel at home with one another.

The business meetings for employees and their wives if they were interested were held on Monday through Wednesday from nine until noon. Bob Gardiner opened the meeting but shortly thereafter Irwin Menchel head of Operations took over. The theme of the meeting was "YOU'RE THE TOPS" a tribute to the sales force, but also TOPS was an acronym for a new systems innovation that was being introduced that was going to simplify the tracking of orders in the system intraday and eliminate some of the common errors that popped up continually in the current system. I was vaguely interested, although the salesman who were immersed in order entry six to eight hours a day were very interested and participated enthusiastically in the presentations by Menchel and his assistants. The centerpiece was a component of the new system called "Stars" that tracked and updated salesman on unexecuted orders among other bits of information throughout the day.

After the morning business meetings, afternoons were spent in a variety of ways. I did some horseback riding and hiking in the woods and, one day, even tried my hand at fly fishing, an art I never really mastered although I owned a boat for half my life and loved fishing in saltwater. Rosalie ice skated nearly every day and followed up with time at the pool and spa and really relaxed, as she says one is supposed to do at a resort. I only mention this because, in contrast, I think relaxing is passé. I relax when I sleep.

The breakfasts, the evening dinners, one quite formal and another a great hayride, always with music and dancing, were sweet and magical. The wit, the pithy eye-opening business discussions and the discovery by so many of us that we had so much in common regarding the demands of and our dedication to our work and our families was kind of storybook because of the way I tend to romanticize things. The seriousness of the firm's concern in regard to the new policies and changes to the operating systems all fit and made sense somehow. All of this unfolded to me as if I were reading the gospels for the first time, and it felt like it was a privilege to experience it. Remember, this was like someone handing you a check for $7,500 or $10,000 and saying, "Here, take a vacation." Others may have been, but Rosalie and I were not blasé at all about this. Before long Friday came, we went to a delightful farewell dinner dance and headed back home on Saturday morning.

Quite noticeable, however, during the Wednesday to Friday period of our stay in Sun Valley was the absence of Bob Gardiner. The last time anyone had seen Bob was at breakfast on Wednesday at the wrap-up of the week's business meetings. At six foot five, one got used to seeing Stretch towering over everyone else in the room. In essence, he was easily missed. The joke bandied about was he might be in Ketchum, just down the road a bit from our resort, recruiting the two Dean Witter brokers in residence there. The funny thing about all this was the joke was on us.

On Monday morning, when the 150 odd Pacesetters and the near 100 Reynolds staff executives who were my travel companions got to work, brimming with tales of the great vacation and the fabulous people they'd met and further imbued with enthusiasm for the firm after being told for a week that they were the greatest, in fact "THE TOPS," they were greeted with an audio taped announcement that their beloved Reynolds Securities was merging with another firm. Reynolds Securities was merging with the aforementioned Dean Witter and was going to be called Dean Witter Reynolds Inc. beginning January 1, 1979. After a fashion, Stretch Gardner was indeed recruiting the brokers in Ketchum, recruiting in fact the entre firm of Dean Witter or they us anyway. This news was a shock to say the least and a surprising strange turn of events most especially for the long-time Reynolds people.

Chapter 56

Reynolds and Dean Witter Merge; Whats Going to Happen...?

The remark made that morning that has stuck with me all these years is attributable to Bob London. It was made that morning of the merger's announcement in response to the question: "Does anybody know where Jim Bach is?"

Bobs priceless retort: "He's in Denver and hasn't stopped throwing up since eight o'clock this morning."

To explain the remark perhaps lessens its impact. Bob London, another kid out of operations who became a full-fledged, very much respected municipal bond trader, knew that like so many people in the firm, Jim Bach, if he were to cut himself would have bled the Reynolds logo shade of blue.

For Jim Bach, a veritable disciple of Reynolds, such an announcement took the breath away. It was the equivalent of being kicked in the balls every five minutes for two hours.

For most people though, the first question at a time like this is "What's going to happen to ME?" We fear for ourselves and our livelihoods first. And then we say what's going to happen to the firm, the department, my colleagues, and by extension again, my livelihood/future/family. These are the big questions everyone has on their mind when such things happen. The answers are, for the most part, embedded in what is perceived to be the standing of the partner or board member or manager responsible for the area you work in. Sometimes the decision is made on a legitimate reasoning out of how the firm would be better off, and in others, it's simply a power/political decision or a workout situation that takes a few months to unravel. At the onset, after the announcement, there is a period in which speculation and confusion reigns.

Because Clem and I were responsible for a substantial piece of business (maybe $4.5 million to $5 million in commission and another $1.5 million to $2 million a year net), Clem felt, and I followed his lead without question, that we should know something before the morning was out. The firm, no matter which faction was going to be in charge, would not want to risk having the people responsible for the kind of numbers we produced walk or be lured away by another firm.

We communed a bit and then he went to work, calling around. Eddie Miller ran interference for Clem, picking up all the overflow incoming calls and taking messages. I took calls from in-house, with many of the Sun Valley attendees calling to see if I knew anything. All I could do was reassure people all would be well, and it would be business as usual for the foreseeable future. In the meantime, there was a pile of messages and mail and the residue of being away a week sitting on my desk. I took great comfort that morning in methodically going through it all.

As the morning waned into early afternoon, Clem said he was getting the feeling from his conversations with several people in both firms that we, Clem and I, had not much to worry about. He never told me who he talked to or if Henry was involved in these considerations. All he said was we "shouldn't worry about landing on our feet in the new firm." And further, "We (Clem and I) had a great act in front of about 2000 brokers at Reynolds, and there was no reason to believe, no reason in the world to believe, the new firm would not want to preserve that act and get it to perform in front of 4,500 to 5,000 brokers," which was the rough estimate of what the combined sales force would be, give or take a few hundred.

For me, that was enough for the present, but by late in the afternoon of that fateful Monday, it was confirmed Clem would continue to manage the UIT operation in the new firm. It appeared we were saved.

This was October 1978, just shy of ten years since I had walked through the door into the craziness (or so I thought) of Eastman

Dillon's P&S/Order Room, and now I was working for a major firm, making very decent money, traveling the country, and transacting multiple millions daily. Now all of a sudden my firm merges, and the financial news headlines are full of the firm's name. It was around this time that I began thinking, "I could write a book about what I've seen these past few years."

******

Dean Witter was already in the Merrill Lynch Unit Trust Joint Account, just as we were, but only for the underwriting of corporate bond and preferred stock unit trusts. They (Dean Witter) had dropped out of the Paine-Webber MBF account and now sponsored their own municipal trust known as the Dean Witter Municipal Bond Fund, which was assembled by a fellow named Dave Press and marketed by a Wall Street old-timer named Frank Cullum and his young assistant, Betty Vetel, while a kid by the name of Leo Ricci helped with the operations.

Later in the week, Clem told me to be on the lookout for a call from the manager of Dean Witter's Tampa, Florida office, a fellow named Haskell Adler. He had my name, and I should expect his call. We were in the middle of selling the most recent corporate income fund (known as CIF), and coincidently, there happened to be a large order in Adler's office that could not be filled with Dean Witter's allotment. I guessed Frank Cullum had communicated this to Clem. Dean Witter had sold out their allotment, and Merrill would not give them any additional units because when a deal was hot, they, Merrill, felt the sponsors and underwriters were entitled to a full day to sell out their own units before giving up part of their own allotment to other underwriters or selling group members.

"They missed their shot when they gave an inaccurate indication of how many they could sell on the day the deal came," went Merrill's logic. "Why should we give up our sales to them?"

Around two thirty, the expected call came through from Adler, asking that we put aside some units for him. I said certainly, of course, and filled him in on the pricing and assured him he had the units firm until five o'clock that day and to call me either way toward the close about the status of the order. The sales commission was $25 or $27.50 per unit on long term CIFs, which amounts to a pretty substantial trade as the order was something over $100,000 worth. It's silly, but the number 167 pops into my mind as I write this. It could have been 127 too. Whatever, it made no difference. Either one is a substantial order with a commission of at least $3,000. Adler was totally familiar with the basics and, I thought, displayed the professionalism I was used to when dealing with branch managers, even perhaps a little extra formal in keeping with the circumstances. In less than an hour, he called to say the trade was done and thanked me for the help.

The experience soured somewhat when I called over to 130 Liberty Street where the Dean Witter offices in New York were located to actually execute the transaction that would send the units over to Dean Witter. The number I called got me to Leo Ricci. I introduced myself and was greeted by this idiot with a stream of invective telling me they didn't need anything Reynolds Securities had to offer and they were doing fine on their own. "We don't want you to call any of our branches either," he said.

"What an A-hole," I thought, so I got my business out of the way and kicked the dust of this encounter off my heels.

Related to this incident was a meeting with a friend of my brother-in-law's, which turned out to be a harbinger of future events. This fellow worked in Dean Witter's Commodity Margin Department. Jerry was his name. We met at my wife's brother's house purely by chance one Saturday afternoon, a few weeks after the merger was announced. Once I expressed we, that is myself and my firm, were looking forward to the merger, that we probably would do a pile of business as a team and we were a very good firm, this fellow very bluntly and angrily let me know it was his impression Reynolds was a "low-pay second-rate firm." Then, after referring to us several times as a "a shit firm," added, "Everyone on the Street knows Dean Witter was in the process of getting rid of all the dead weight at Reynolds, and all Dean Witter wanted was the branch offices and the salesmen. Everyone else could take a long walk off a short pier."

I never react well to this kind of rudeness. I knew also this kind of talk was born out of the fact that many people would lose their jobs because there was so much duplication especially in operations, which luckily, I was no longer in. But such behavior always nonplussed me. I could never find a glib retort to such outright ugly confrontational invective. Although after this second encounter, I began to wonder about the quality of the meeting of the minds Henry and Clem were having with their counterparts in the Dean Witter crowd? I was very busy though and didn't get much time to talk about it to Clem, who now, a few weeks into the merger, was spending a lot of time with Henry. I mean, sometimes as much as half the day. Eddie and I had to handle all the phones, the new issue business, and the swaps. Merger or no merger, the beat went on. We came in early and went home late.

Chapter 57

Settling Scores, I Guess

Apparently, Henry was someone to be "dealt with" as far as the Fixed-Income Management at Dean Witter was concerned where a few old enemies resided. There was also, I thought, a measure of secretly held umbrage at Reynolds. Perhaps the word *enemy* is too strong, but there was someone (possibly more than one) at Dean Witter Henry had crossed swords with at one time or another. The one I knew about was Bob Tygh (pronounced Ty) who ran the corporate bond operation at Dean Witter. I didn't know exactly what the problem was between Bob and Henry. Both had lived in the town of Babylon, Long Island, and had at one time been Long Island Railroad travel buddies and possibly members of the SSBC before Henry moved to Plandome on the North Shore. It was rumored they had a falling out of some kind. Whatever the story was, Tygh was designated to head up Corporates at the new firm, and he showed up in our offices at some point to stake out his territory. Certainly, this appeared as an affront, but it was true to Dean Witter style. In-your-face confrontational—that was what I had experienced.

Jim Duncan, a leading institutional salesman at Reynolds, perhaps the leading institutional salesman at the firm, and a close friend of Bill Devlin, was a friend of Tygh's, so there were many tales told I'm sure, especially related to Henry's management style and methodically logical approach as opposed to swashbuckling (Henry called it "cavalier") management style applied in some of the other shops on the Street. Another thing that may have rubbed Duncan the wrong way was Henry's attitude toward, and his perceived treatment of the now retired Bill Devlin who as we mentioned was a close friend of Jim Duncan's. In Devlin's final year, there were several of what Clem called "fond farewells" for Devlin given by various groups in the bond community. On several occasions, Henry had had to endure (my word) a measure of crude innuendo (at these affairs) delivered in the speechifying of several members of the SSBC. I was sure this was partly because Devlin probably complained about Henry to his buddies, many of whom had had confrontations with Henry over the years and one or two that Henry had actually fired from Paine Webber. Clem mentioned to me on several occasions that Henry had tired of going to these fetes and was annoyed at having to contribute to them as well.

The elephant in the room that was totally ignored by Duncan was Bob Gardiner and Tom Staley had hastened the exit of Devlin by seeking out and bringing Henry Arbeeny into the firm. Most of this was inferred to me by Clem, whom I believed because he was in a unique position to know all this stuff. Clem was a confidant of Arbeeny and, at the same time, a charter member of the SSBC with Jim Duncan and Bill Devlin and the extended gossipy grapevine, which Clem was tuned into.

Henry's progressive management style, new to much of Wall Street, that had dramatically increased productivity and improved firm/employee/departmental relations at Reynolds (probably at Paine-Webber as well) was important but not enough to get him into the management of the new firms fixed-income division. The Old Guard, of which Bill Devlin, Bill Kondratuck, and even Al Bianchetti, the current head of Dean Witter Municipals were part of, through their own reputations for integrity and prudence and in some cases ruthlessness, could keep their departments on a short chain. But the newer crowd, Clem's generation, oddly enough and unlike Clem, had less and less respect for their firm's money, and there was a faction of this crowd at Dean Witter.

"So we lose a couple of hundred thousand here or there. That's the business. And when we make money, which is most of the time (so they thought), nobody complains. Look at all the commission we produce, which was a somewhat positive point in the bond departments favor but could not fully compensate for, nor explain away losses."

The world was changing, however. Had changed. The firms that had gone out of business and the merged firms had reduced the players. Interest rates and inflation were trending higher, increasing risk to nosebleed levels for the players left standing, and the deals were getting bigger and more numerous. The operations problems of efficient delivery and receipt of securities that had driven Goodbody and so many other firms into the ground were not as bad, although there were still plenty of operations flareups.

Henry saw the markets simply as an entity to be exploited and less as a fraternity. True, the deep science of municipals, indeed the art of municipals and even the camaraderie of the municipal community, was important, but running the business by putting the old-boy network before the firms well-being was not Henry's style. After all, at Goldman, Merrill Lynch, Solomon Brothers, and Lehman to a large degree, the business was managed with great prudence. Cavalier attitudes toward risk was not tolerated. In those places, the firm came first, and the whim of the trader and salesmen was second. The sales forces were pushed hard and closely managed to produce the orders to justify the risk taking. Prudence in the commitment of (the firms) capital was insisted upon, and inventory controls and daily reporting and striving for a respectable bottom line every month within a business plan was paramount. Proceeding with a hit-or-miss attitude, regardless of how much commission was being paid into the branch office system, was unacceptable.

Perhaps there were other reasons for Henry not fitting in. I think many of the people who had worked for Henry over the years did not like Henry, and it wasn't just because of his unbending nature and his being a tough taskmaster. I'm convinced they were turned off by his high moral standard. Henry's disapproval (although quiet and held closely) of the drinking, general debauchery, and crude social behavior of this crowd was resented by them. Henry was very by the book and straitlaced to a fault. This was a crowd that let down their hair in front of one another, and of course, Henry never did. Testament to this, as I have mentioned, was Henry's remark to me on several occasions when I was privately critical of this one or that one. "Look, you don't have to invite these fellows into your home. All you have to do is do business with them."

After a while, as we got into November, it became clear in the new firm, Henry would have nothing to do with the management of fixed income. That is, nothing to do with their trading or underwriting or the management of the personnel that administered to them. Perhaps that was decided early on, although it wasn't common knowledge until around Thanksgiving or even later. In this territorial dispute, Dean Witter had the clear advantage as it appeared Gardiner did not defend Henry or fight very hard at least to put Henry in charge. It was also true that the institutional and volume side of the business was a lot bigger at Dean Witter than it was at Reynolds in both municipal and corporate bonds. This circumstance carried a lot of weight and determined which salesmen from which firm would cover the major accounts in the merged firm. It was also true Al Bianchetti who ran municipals at Dean Witter was viewed as a highly competent and highly respected member of the municipal bond community. It would have been a truly prescient decision by Melton and Gardiner to put both Henry and Al Bianchetti in as comanagers of Municipals or all of Fixed Income, but it didn't happen. I'm sure Gardener would have done it if Melton had gone along. It would have saved more than several fortunes of money and a ton of aggravation. The fact is Henry would eventually be put in charge in the mideighties, but that's another book.

Back in the unit trust business, by this time, Clem and I, were marketing and selling at all-time highs. We participated in at least two and sometimes three municipal deals a month, then two corporate bond deals and a preferred stock trust as well. A hybrid of corporate bond and preferreds had been introduced as well, and interspersing these regular underwritings was a series of seven or eight short-term CD trusts and several short-term municipal trusts. Along with Eddie Miller, we managed the secondary and executed more than our fair share of swaps. The capital commitments in these deals were roughly two to three million dollars on the taxable products, three to five million dollars on the tax-exempt trusts, and two or three million on the shorter-term CD trusts. Short term municipal trusts average maturities of 5 years began coming to market every couple of weeks around this time and we could sell whatever we got. I went in for high numbers, 12 to 15 million and got 5 to 7 and they always blew out the door.

As the times were changing in terms of the risk environment, management techniques and the number of firms left standing, as well as who was going to manage what segments of Dean Witter Reynolds, the new firm; Clem and I were changing too. While I continued to learn and see more deeply into the business as a whole, Clem spoke more and more about our evolving into and becoming generalists as opposed to our having been "bond man." The truth of this statement was born out by the fact that we routinely admistered to Corporate Bonds and Preferred Stocks and Municipal Bonds, both short and long term, and several hybrid s like the Corporate Bond/ Preferred Stock Trust and the short term CD trusts. We had left the realm of concern with a single security type and its market. The new additions of reinvestment and monthly income and the requirement to understand and interpret the facts and the nuance of all of these different securities and their maintenance to a demanding sales organization, had transformed us into very knowledgeable securities market generalists. The single securities experts we realized, operated in a vacuum, not really seeing the many different securities in the market place, each with their own differing pricing dynamic, competing for shelf space. Nor did they understand that as markets evolved opportunities in these securities came about to be exploited, which was exactly what our unit trust joint account was very good at. In turn because we were able to interpret the product and investment knowledge and the opportunities to the sales force at large we had developed great credibility and a considerable following in the sales organization, at least at our own firm, Reynolds securities.

Our complete thinking in this vein would not evolve fully for a few years, although it had begun to surface at this time. One thing it did do was put more and more distance between the pure bond guys and ourselves and our understanding that to be continually profitable, one had to be nimble. Being in unit trusts was distinctly an advantage.

The reasons why this "single security specialist vs. generalist thinking" idea was so radical to us is because the complex science of municipal securities and municipal markets is such a singular discipline. After one becomes involved with the municipal science we think we are unique to the world. No one understands what we do and we don't care what anyone else does because we, municipal bond traders and primary market denizens are unique to the world. To put a finer point on it, because Clem and I discussed this so much, I made a joke up about a Municipal Syndicate department writing scales on Monday morning. It wasn't hilarious, but it was funny enough to both of us, and get the point across.

Did you hear the one about the Municipal Syndicate Department writing scales on Monday Morning?

A stock trader pokes his head into the Municipal Bond Department and says, "It's a brutal morning. The Dow is down four hundred points."

Not a single head rises. The bond guys are scribbling away at their scales.

Around noon, one of the retail salesman from the branch stops by to pick up some research and says, "It came over the tape that North Korea captured a US frigate in the China Sea, and the market is worse than ever, down another three hundred points from this morning and it's not even one o'clock yet. They say a couple of firms will go down for sure."

Again, not much of a stir at all from the Municipal crowd.

At three, someone shouts over the squawk box that a magnitude 8.8 on the Richter scale earthquake has occurred under the San Andreas fault, causing a major portion of Southern California to separate from the mainland.

Just then, one of the guys writing a scale looks up and says, "Ya think Toms River is a 4.40 in '06 or a 4.35?"

That was the municipal crowd, five one-hundredths of a percentage point of yield on an obscure New Jersey credit was more important than all the other markets and the world falling apart all around them.

******

On January 1, the merger/takeover was consummated, and the two firms became one in terms of their billing and accounting systems. The Fixed-Income Division of Reynolds Securities residing on the tenth floor at 120 Broadway had been gutted. What remained under the aegis of Henry Arbeeny was the Unit Trust Department and the GNMA Department, which consisted of two people, Sandy Rafael and JoAnn La Rocca, plus an operations person. Everything else, Municipal Trading and Syndicate, Corporate Bonds, and all the salesmen and municipal syndicate research people and secretaries, moved to Dean Witter's headquarters at 130 Liberty Street.

Clem, Henry, and I, on the other hand, were joined by Frank Cullum who had been working the UIT business at Dean Witter, Dave Press the buyer and administrator of the Dean Witter Muni Trust, and the two secondary market traders/service operatives, Al Stevens and Ola Reopel. Our secondary trader and service operative, Ed Miller, had taken the test for the New York City Police Department and was slated to train at the academy, so he took a layoff. We also retained our wire room with our old friend Kaye Foster who managed it with Jackie Johnson and a young Hispanic fellow, Danny, a runner and filler in at the machines, along with five operations people. The Reynolds Securities Fixed-Income Division, a department of fifty people under Henry Arbeeny was now reduced to less than fifteen persons, including operations, and had become unofficially the Unit Trust/GNMA Department. The firm didn't even bother to make room for us at their headquarters at 130 Liberty Street but left us behind instead on the tenth floor in 120 Broadway where there was so much empty space that you could sometimes hear an echo. We were probably better off there, away from the turmoil, rumor, rancor, and innuendo that ran rampant in the offices and halls at 130 Liberty, all of which were par for the course in many offices of the firm after the merger.

Chapter 58

The Predictable Aftermath

The final result was that in almost every way, the dominant firm was Dean Witter, both in the product departments and in operations. People either knuckled under to save their jobs if they could or wanted to or left the firm. Many people I knew in operations, from Irwin Menchel and Tom Gambaro who had managed the Reynolds side, to the many junior and senior clerks in places like Dividends, Stock Record, and Cashiers (the Cage), simply pulled up stakes and left. Those who stayed were subject to the rudeness and ruthlessness of the Dean Witter operations crowd that began with Bob Flanagan, their leader, who headed Operations down to the lowliest Dean Witter clerk who got the benefit of the doubt over any former Reynolds employee.

Discrimination against former Reynolds employees existed even to the point where their employee numbers that had different prefixes than former Dean Witter employees. Reynolds employee numbers began with the number seven while Dean Witter employees numbers began with the number eight. Perhaps this was just the way it was. I really can't say. Necessary for some logical administrative/regulatory/insurance/benefit-related reason with no ill intended, which however no one has ever heard articulated. Yet because of the many personal disputes and behavior and attitude of so many in the Dean Witter crowd, former Reynolds employees felt the different prefix amounted to being a target on their backs.

In any case, in the months and even years to come, the Dean Witter operations crew became a gang that couldn't shoot straight and a group that Andrew Melton, the chairman and co-CEO of the firm, had to answer, apologize for and defend ad nauseum. Whether it was true or not, after a while, one got the feeling that intentional or otherwise, Gardiner hung Melton out to dry on this point because it was his (Melton's) man Bob Flanagan who took over the back office operation completely and shut out the clearly more capable (to the Reynolds crowd, brokers included), professional, and forward-thinking Irwin Menchel and company. For nearly two years, the Operations Division couldn't get out of their own way. Every few months, Melton would put out another "apologia" to the sales force and the firm at large, making amends for an endless number of computer "glitches," a word heretofore unknown to me. The memos relating to long delays on corrections, statement pricing, and general incorrectness in the processing of business from delays in dividends and commission payouts to new account openings. What went largely unmentioned but hung thick in the air was the rude and surly nature of the operations staff that the branch offices encountered every day.

Adding insult to embarrassment, on occasion, a former Reynolds employee pulled Flanagan's (and presumably Melton's) feet out of the fire by saving the day. For example, it was rumored that in the first or second month of the merger, the firm duped or duplicated (processed twice) a dividend payment dump or a portion of it. On the fifteenth of the month, when stocks paid their dividends, perhaps tens of thousands of entries are processed crediting many millions of dollars of dividends to the firm accounts. The result of this duplication then was an account that was supposed to receive a separate dividend from three different stocks received those dividends twice—six entries in their account instead of three and twice the money. Apparently the firm paid out something like $19 million instead of $9.5 million. Such an event is a communications, employee, and public relations nightmare, not to mention a logistical quagmire. In this case, a Reynolds guy, a programming expert whom some called a genius, was called upon to fix it and did so by finding a way to reverse the entries soon after the disaster occurred, saving the day. Not to say a Dean Witter employee might not have eventually fixed it, but it did fall to a "Reynolds guy." If anything, such events made Dean Witter operations personnel even more belligerent than they were before.

The Reynolds Securities Unit Trust Department was an anomaly among Reynolds departments in that we still had our manager, Henry Arbeeny. The only change was that Henry now reported to both Bob Gardener and Andrew Melton. Clem's prophetic prediction, made to me within hours of the announcement of the merger had came true. He had said to me at about noon that day, "that" the unit trust departments "act" at Reynolds, performed before 2000 brokers would be just as good when performed before the 4500 brokers of Dean Witter Reynolds." This prediction that our comprehensive and enthusiastic, full service operation would get a chance to remake itself in the new firm had indeed hit the ground running on Jan 1, 1979. Clem and I both liked the brokers, had no problem answering the same questions over and over again and were deeply convinced that the securities we sold were good for broker and investor alike. There was no reason to believe either that Henry would not continue to be his most effective self as well. It may be redundant to say it but we were reasonably sure that no department was as effective as we were in communicating with the sales force.

Chapter 59

The New Unit Trust Department

The folks who came over from the Dean Witter side to work in Unit Trusts were an older, more settled crowd than one might have encountered in most firm's Unit Trust Departments on the Street. Frank Cullum was a very nice man—a cheerful man, in fact—in his midsixties perhaps and a veteran of nearly forty years or more on the Street. Frank was very well respected at Dean Witter and had up until just a few years before been a principal at Lowie & Co., a small firm taken over by Dean Witter in the early seventies.

Frank's experience as a salesman included the introduction of preferred stocks and their tax exempt attributes, which were altogether new and untested at the time he did it. Frank brought preferreds to the savings banks in New York City and Brooklyn in the fifties and sixties and made a killing, as they say. He was very much unintimidated by the merger or having landed among Reynolds people. I was sure he felt both Henry and Clem were very accomplished and honorable fellows. This was helped along by the fact that his brother-in-law and daily travel companion, Larry Fel, was number two and eventually became the head of the Lehman Brothers' Municipal Bond Division. The municipal community was very small, and if there was anything to indicate that Clem and Henry were rotten apples, Larry would have informed Frank early on, but this was obviously not the case. In some way, I came to feel several years later that Frank had experienced the underhanded and frankly often dishonorable nature of the Dean Witter crowd in New York when Lowie and company was taken over. It should not be forgotten that Frank was a practicing

Catholic and was pretty turned off by dishonorable behavior in any way. Although he never expressed it directly, it was plain he saw the unfairness in the way many of the people from the Reynolds side had been treated, and he did everything he could to smooth the way for Clem, Henry, and myself in making inroads with the former Dean Witter sales organization, especially in California, where Frank had some influence.

Al Stevens and Ola Reopel were also Wall Street vets who very quickly became comfortable with the Reynolds unit trust group at 120 Broadway, recognizing the cordial and respectful welcome by Henry, Clem, myself, and in fact everyone on the floor including the operations group and the wire room. Dave Press was a different story. He was in his mid- to late thirties, and I'm sure he felt he landed among the enemy. There was not much wiggle room for him, however, because the firm's management had chosen to give Henry UITs and GNMA's and nothing else, and Dave Press was the Dean Witter unit trust buyer and assembler so he had no recourse.

Our attitude and devotion to service and doing the job right was indeed fully agreed upon and matched by Frank Cullum who sat with Clem and myself in New Issues and Ola Reopel and Al Stevens who handled the secondary and or resale market for unit trusts at Dean Witter and now took the task over for the new firm. In a word, we meshed beautifully. As for our operations backup, on day one a veteran team of Reynolds Securities operatives were on the job. I had no say in any of this, although I knew several of them through previous contact or reputation. One had managed a small department, another ran the vault and the other three were senior clerks. There wasn't anyone in this group who might have been considered anything less than a senior clerk or a veteran of the firm. I dare say their salaries as senior clerks and long term employees might have precluded their being taken on in lower level/routine duty positions in operations, first because they were formerly Reynolds and secondly because of the sea of clerks available at much lower salaries. I became sure after a while that Irwin Menchel had reached out to Henry arranging the transfer of these individuals so they could arrange new positions for themselves in relative calm with their salaries intact. In this way Irwin could help out a few loyalists while Henry recruited a top-flight operations crew. They're names bear mentioning if only because they were instrumental in the departments early success.

They were Ray Urbig, the manager of the group who had managed Reynolds Buy in Department and Mike Brown who was manager in charge of the securities vault. Manny Rodriguez who I didn't know and a great fellow named Sid whose last name escapes me. The strikingly beautiful and very efficient Lilly Thompson from P&S joined this group as well. I had known known Lilly since joining the firm myself in 1970 and while she might not have enjoyed senior Clerk status, as you can imagine the phones ran hot in this little group and with Lilly's help in picking them up a great deal of order was preserved. Both this operations group and the front end were backed up by the wire room run by Kaye Foster, whom I had hired in what seemed a century ago. On the whole we were a great veteran crew who didn't miss much.

One of the reasons for our new success was in fact the many niggling operations problems the sales force was experiencing and the revival of a technique I had used to ingratiate myself when I first joined the bond department. I became, at that time, a sort of a fixer because when Devlin or Kondratuck asked for help in researching a personal problem like a late dividend payment or an incomplete entry in their account, I helped them resolve it. On a departmental level, I helped get some bonds unregistered or checked the vault for the verification of certain securities in the house. In all cases, I would simply make a call to the back office department in the firm that I thought might be able to fix it—Stock Record, the Cage, or DECAB. Some problems took a bit longer to resolve than others, but in the end, every situation got resolved. Little did I know then how valuable my back office experience would prove to be in the future.

Several months after the consummation of the merger nearly every broker had two or three operational problems hanging and a few that might cost them a client. While I couldn't advertise the top-notch operations crew we had in our department, when I did hear some inkling of frustration from a broker regarding (nor was I above hinting that I knew a few fixers) an operations problem I would give out the name and number of one of our guys. After a while I didn't even mention that my contacts were in our department although I often added.

"By the way, keep this quiet. These guys are busy and can just handle so much."

Our crew was so efficient and knowledgeable that no problem was too obscure or complex. Sometimes all they had to do was point the caller in the right direction by giving them the phone number of the individual who could fix the problem. The reality of it was they loved doing these small favors, especially for brokers from the Dean Witter side, because it gained respect for all the beaten down Reynolds souls and was great payback to the organization that had rejected and dispossessed them. The effectiveness of this helping hand as a sales technique in getting a foot in the door with a somewhat ill-tempered sales force was big. After some small problem was fixed, it would always get back to me or Clem or Frank that whatever it was that Charlie Jones from Pasadena had called them about had gotten fixed or that it was just a misunderstanding or whatever. The next step was to follow that notification up with a call to the salesman in question to say, "Hey, Charlie, how's everything? Ray Urbig mentioned to me that screw up is fixed. You okay with it?"

"Oh, man, where did you get that guy from? I got his name and number written in magic marker on my hand. I hope it never comes off. What a go-to guy."

"Good, good, I'm glad. Happy to help. Have you looked at the latest offering of…?"

You had three minutes to sell the guy on something, but in reality, I didn't have to sell anything. The ice was broken. The quid pro quo was in place. I had established myself as a professional or at least a comrade in arms. Times were not easy and fixed income was what was selling, and brokers' generally listened to almost any story or sales pitch related to a fixed-income product with few exceptions. It was simply a matter of engagement, getting a guy to listen to you for a few minutes more to talk about a sales idea, and the type of client or prospect to direct it to. We engaged everyone who called us in sales conversations of this kind, and when a sale was made in a former Dean Witter office that was not a particularly ardent seller of the product, almost always another broker or two got wind of us and gave us a call with a question or two. Without the municipal bond regional offices helping us market, this kind of engagement was all we had other than notification of the branches through the wire system.

Two months into the merger, there were minefields and problems everywhere in the field and in the back office. Where there was duplication in the field—for example, two branches in a city—one had to be combined with another and someone, one of the managers, had to step down, perhaps go back into production, which amounted to starting all over again as if you were a trainee. Others in the operations staff of the offices would have to leave or be let go. These are not pleasant things to have occur to friends and workmates. There's a natural tendency to feel and stick up for and defend ones friends and coworkers. Some people went quietly into the night, and others put up a stink or fight for what they felt was right. Then there were those who had been handpicked by Melton and Gardiner to manage key areas of the firm, sales management and regional management, at the highest levels who had to be fired although too often too late in the game, leaving heaps of wreckage and ill will behind. I refer especially to Alan Snyder, a Gardiner protégé, and Bob Pennington, a very well-respected regional manager from Dean Witter's Southwestern environs. It was sometime down the road from the coming together on January 1 but the story was that these two couldn't get along. They openly bickered and insulted one another until they were both told to leave, were in effect fired.

On the operations side, there seemed to be many personnel and job-related disputes that were unfairly adjudicated contributing to continued rancor and mismanagement getting in the way of fixing the problems in the system caused by the bringing in of an additional 1,500 to 2,000 brokers. The better system might have been the Reynolds system and incorporating parts of it into the Dean Witter operating system, although I never heard anything conclusive on the subject.

The overall dysfunction trickled down into the behavior and the attitude of the troops on the Reynolds side who were asked to be quiet about being treated not just scurrilously but unfairly as their managers lost their positions and people who didn't know what they were doing advanced and effed things up. All of this had to be endured while getting work piled on under the threat of losing their jobs.

I want to attribute much of the bad operations problems to the Dean Witter side because I knew Reynolds people tended to bend over backwards to get the job done and generally seemed to be more civil and less high and mighty or vindictive. However, understanding human nature leads me to believe there was sabotaging on both sides of the merger. Although in my heart of hearts, I find it difficult to believe a Reynolds employee would do deliberate damage. Conversely, I don't feel the same way about Dean Witter employees. So many things went wrong in the merging of the two systems that finally and eventually, several years later, I don't remember if it was two or three years into the merger, Melton's loyalty to Bob Flanagan must have ran out. A new director of operations, Ed McLeod, was brought in. He was neutral in his outlook politically with only one agenda, getting the job done, which resulted in things finally being put right although the task was not completed until the mideighties.

Chapter 60

I Digress: My Part and The Ugly Sheet

After my sophomore year in high school, it became necessary for me to go to summer school. I was changing out of the academic math and science curriculum that included geometry and trigonometry and getting into the business-oriented classes because I couldn't cut the higher math. I simply could not fathom these subjects. I just wasn't a studier. If I didn't get something on the first or second shot, I didn't have the inclination to work at it until I did. There were too many other things going on in my life. I had a part-time job in a supermarket, a girlfriend already at sixteen, and I was deeply into books at the time, with not a lot of care for much else. Sometimes, if the whim took me, I would play hooky for a day, riding the subways to finish a book. When I couldn't learn how to get along in geometry, I simply cut out after the class before it until I was caught and then my benevolent guidance counselor, Mrs. Edelstein, changed my curriculum.

In any case, it became necessary for me to take some business-related courses to fill in the void in the GD that I would eventually earn. I did so at Erasmus High School in Brooklyn, taking two courses that summer, one of which was "Business Writing Skills" taught by a fellow of forty years or so whose name I've forgotten but whose brash demeanor I remember vividly.

He was in the habit of wearing outfits that might be considered shocking. He showed up one day wearing a yellow shirt and a pink tie with huge black polka dots. I thought he was trying to impress the many pretty girls in the class even more than male students were. I didn't care for his sense of humor either, for example he would yell the word "SEX" when the class got noisy or unruly…It usually got our attention and had the desired effect, but I disapproved of it. In any case I thought the guy was an ass who wanted to appear cool to his students. I went to school in Manhattan and was used to much more reserved teachers and a different sort of class decorum. He was a joke because he thought he was so cool, but the kids thought he was a jerk. We simply accepted him; played along as he was in authority over us.

One of the class assignments was to write an introductory letter about oneself to a prospective employer. I did and handed it in, and it was marked and returned a few days later by the teacher as he strolled up and down the aisles of the classroom, quipping about each one as he handed them to students. He approached me from behind and handing me my paper he said loudly, "Pasquale, Pat Scida, I, I, I LOVE, LOVE, LOVE, ME, ME, ME, BLAH, BLAH, BLAH!"

I can't remember that paper or what was on it for the life of me. I can't remember any premeditation either in writing the paper in the way it was described by this teacher in his comments. I do remember the embarrassment I felt at the moment he made those comments and, afterward, the lasting effect it had on me. That cringing moment has been frozen forever in my memory in a way that made me very conscious of my behavior in terms of being boastful or self-promoting.

Now twenty years later, my idealism and sense of wonder at the world had resurfaced. I still had many doubts about myself, but I had broken free, allowing myself to realize my abilities and capabilities. Being capable is one thing; knowing one is capable and relying on one's wits and intelligence under pressure is another. I had proof now. Had I not received approval from my superiors and peers and had something to show for it? Some position, money, and material gain from work and then as well from God and life too. He had rewarded me with a loving, caring, and capable wife, a son and a daughter, and a home. I had tried perhaps to express my view of the world and how

I believed one must behave and be like from a dream or fantasy of mind in that crudely written summer school resume. About a year or so after Henry joined the firm, I began to rely totally on instinct. Henry's approval and trust in me had no doubt activated my confidence to act and react to whatever situation was at hand, letting whatever was inside me to come out at will. I let my actions, my work and my attitude speak for me.

I am competitive by nature and strived always to win in every situation. It is also very Italian to put our "ideal" forward and make *la bella figura*, the beautiful form. The ideal is to put our best foot forward in everything we do. I had seen this in my mother and sister in their cooking and baking, in my father in his woodworking and cement and plastering work and making wine, and on a higher plane, in the few years I worked for the couturier Rossino Angela. These experiences showed the taking of great pride in the persona showed publicly, and so my personification of *la bella figura* was to let my kindness, sincerity, helpfulness, gentlemanliness, enthusiasm, selflessness, intelligence, creativity, worldliness, gregarious nature, creativity, and generosity speak for themselves and on occasion my naivete' and even my outright stupidity and ignorance at times. I fully admit this because one learns, unfortunately, that sometimes realism defeats idealism, and in our "ideal," we often appear to others as fools. The trick is not to appear this way too often, and when you do, not to care. We are all human. In any case, the trick is to do all this with a pure heart because the world on occasion makes fools of us all.

I say all this because I believe I was a big part of this new department's persona, the way it hit the ground running, how it played to its public, and the newly formed sales force of the new firm of Dean Witter Reynolds. In those years in that firm, there was a good deal of despair, strife, problems, mistakes and aggravation. It was my mission to play out the barefaced notion that we were going to succeed. Not only our department but the firm. Not only me but everyone in contact with me. In effect that there was no way we were not going to be successful. I treated everyone with respect and good cheer and every situation and problem they brought to me with serious consideration.

"Fix this, get that, do that, bring that sale in, and let's get to the next thing. We're gonna do this thing," could have been my motto.

I take nothing away from Clem who felt and tried to act the same way. The problem was he couldn't help showing that he was a bit worried, a bit uneasy. It was his nature.

Sure, of course, I may have been the unknowing, unseeing dupe, thinking and going through life as though it was peaches and cream, not realizing (at the time anyway) the ruthless nature of the goings on one or two or three pay grades above me. Perhaps I was Henry and Clem's useful idiot. At times, I came to feel it was deliberate on Clem and Henry's part to make sure I was not privy to the mean-spirited negotiation and power struggles going on between the Dean Witter and The Reynolds factions in the firm. My sunny outlook was to remain as unsullied as possible. It was my job to keep up the morale of anyone and everyone I came in contact with. I was perfect for the part. It was easy. I had come from $4500 a year in late 1968, to something near to $50000 a year in 1979. I was on top of the world, why shouldn't my reality be filled with both enthusiasm and optimism?

In our shop, by mid-February, we were busy as hell. In our former permutation (Reynolds Securities), the Municipal Bond Department's regional offices helped us in getting reads on what the firm could sell. We no longer had that support in the field. We had to get reads on what was likely to get sold or what demand was like in the sales organization ourselves in the minefield just described. The firm was larger, the numbers were bigger, and the risk factors more critical. I had a good feel for handicapping what sales would be from the former Reynolds side of the sales force and chipped in and backed and filled as the Dean Witter crowd began to get interested and as Frank Cullum began to regularly engage the Dean Witter side. It was dog's work morning to night, but we took the story to them, to the brokers on the phones, on the wires, and on what became known as the "ugly sheet."

Ugly sheets were an about every-ten-day, all-office, all-branch, all-broker single sheet, single-sided distribution penned in black magic marker by yours truly. My old buddy from my DECAB warehouse days had survived the merger and was still in charge of in-house printing and distribution. A pouch or package of material went out almost every day to every branch, and Sam printed our stuff and sent it out for us.

Ugly sheets were standard 8 ½" x 11" and, on occasion, legal size. They were called ugly because often the lettering was haphazardly and crudely done, although I suspected that was exactly why they were paid attention to. Ugly sheets announced several deals and promoted a sales idea or two. They might illustrate a formula for calculating taxable equivalent yield or had a few bond market definitions on them. There was a caricature from a Merrill Lynch ad of a man being slammed against a wall by a huge hand that had the word TAXES printed on it in capital letters. I had that image printed as a lightly colored backdrop on the paper on which I announced municipal deals. They were quite effective and I suspect many were sent to the public. A broker in our Memphis office, a transplanted New Yorker named Ira Berlin, called me once and said these missives, my ugly sheets, reminded him of the hand written list of specials on the back of diner menu. Most importantly however, there were phone numbers, our 800 number and our names, Clem Schaefer, Frank Cullum and Pat Scida, thus empowering any broker who saw one of these sheets to call us and get the lowdown straight from the horses mouth. Ugly or not and with all the internal crap and backbiting going on in the firm, I initiated these sheets on my own, bolstering the promotion and success of our department, informing the sales organization and bringing in a boatload of business.

Chapter 61

Philosophies, Conflicts, Fixes

I don't think Andy Melton had any personal animosity toward Henry, although I do believe that he had a problem with unit trusts or perhaps "bond funds" in general. Maybe it was that he didn't think the business was worth all the attention it received, or the attention Henry wanted Andy to give it, or that somehow it was tainted because of the way its yield was calculated. The yield question was a suspicion that was thought to have been planted by the bond purists. In any case Henry gave me an assignment in the early months of the merger that was an attempt to give Andy an idea of the size and scope of the "bond fund" business. Using an industry source called Ibbotson's Directory I was to call every bond fund, mutual fund and UIT and note as many facts as possible about them i.e. title, size, size one year ago, objective, ratings structure, maturity structure, ratings structure and limitations, management fee, load, expenses, method of yield calculation and so on.

I think we learned more than we expected to and that the task was a more daunting one than expected. It was so laborious that I had to get off the sales desk for a couple of hours every day to make these calls. Any inkling to the firms I was calling that I was from a rival firm and I wouldn't have gotten the time of day from them. Clem thought the report was one of Henry's intellectual fancies and saw no value in it, but of course he never expressed this to Henry although he castigated me continually for my daily moving off the desk to work on it. At the same time Henry regularly badgered me because he thought it was taking too long to complete. Finally, one morning, when Clem was meeting with Henry, I got past Angela and stood in the doorway until I was noticed and said.

"Look guys, about this report. A dog can have only one master. Somebody's got to back off, you two should talk about it."

Clem was angrily open-mouthed and Henry looked a bit confused but they must have worked it out as I was left alone for about ten days to finally complete the report. The thing was pretty straightforward as to most of the facts although I fudged many of the yield calculations (methodologies) because they varied so much at the mutual funds. There was dividend yield divided by an average price and or current price, there was trailing yield and current yield and then there were various explanations about how and why yield couldn't be calculated. I believe Henry added an addendum to the report explaining the lack of a comprehensive formula to calculate yield in the mutual fund industry. The report was sent not just to Gardner and Melton but to the entire board. Unfortunately, I never kept a copy, and the number of bond funds outstanding escapes me, certainly in the billions but nowhere near what's out there today but I think it compiled the formidable sum of about forty billion dollars in bond funds outstanding at the time; not big by today's standards but sizable for the time.

Whether Henry proved his point to Andy regarding the relevance of bond funds or unit investment trusts may have been a moot point because the business (UIT) seemed to have a mind of its own as we shall see. In any case the philosophies of the two firms were parallel to a large degree. Dean Witter, like Reynolds wanted to sell lots of securities to retail investors and high net worth individuals. Dean Witter in the person of Andrew Melton wanted to sell many more millions to institutional investors which is perhaps the Merrill Lynch model i.e. do both. In any case the feeling was that if that kind of firm (both a retail and institutional powerhouse) could be built than the investment banking business would also pickup with its fat fees. Of course, the trick was to build that kind of business.

While I go on and on about fixed income and unit trusts as if they were the center of the universe, I'm sure there was a lot more on the collective co-CEO's (Gardiner/Melton) minds than us. These times in the financial services industry might be considered as the end of the Middle Ages and the beginning of the Renaissance. About the time of the merger, Andrew Melton purchased for something more than a million dollars a money market fund from Standard & Poor's known as the Intercapital Liquid Asset Fund, a visionary move if there ever was one. A well-known mutual fund industry operative by the name of Charles Fiumefreddo who managed the fund came to Dean Witter with it. Today, money market funds are legion, but in the budding mid- to late seventies, the most well-known was the Reserve Fund, which was independent and had been for many years the only money market fund in existence. If you wanted to be in it, that is if you or your client wanted their money in the Reserve Fund, you had to transfer the client's cash to the fund. In effect, the client's money left the house. Shipping a clients money out of the house and having them get separate statements from the Reserve fund was not something a firm or a stockbroker liked to do.

In addition to the phenomena of the money market fund, a seminal event was the introduction in 1977 by Merrill Lynch of their Cash Management Account or CMA. It's a sure bet that Melton and Gardener both realized the asset-gathering value of the money market fund and the importance of a brokerage firm morphing into something akin to a savings bank. They might have realized as well that the money market fund was to become the canvas upon which the new and future all-encompassing brokerage account would be painted upon. It's not hard to read into the acquisition of Intercapital, another reason for merging the two firms. Putting together a 5000 plus stockbroker sales organization was the mechanism for piling up a heap of cash in the Intercapital Liquid Asset Fund. It also proved the wisdom behind spending a million dollars to acquire the fund. Dean Witters version of Merrill's CMA Account would however take a while to materialize.

The firm progressed in its first merged year, growing amid a sea of contentious backbiting, argument, and anger. We were fortunate that our Unit Trust Department and the GNMA Desk were located several blocks away from the firm's headquarters at 130 Liberty Street where all the battling occurred. The rooms at 120 Broadway may have been half darkened and empty, but they were quite cheerful. Perhaps Dave Press, the buyer and assembler of the Dean Witter Municipal Trust, walked around with glum face, but there was no way to fight the good humor of those around him, which rubbed off on him despite his troubles.

The new firm, some 4500 brokers and their clients, collectively held several hundreds of millions of dollars' worth of unit trusts that needed constant service in terms of quotes and liquidations. The secondary desk, in the persons of Al Stevens and Ola Reopel, were busy all day. Interest rates had been rising for some time, and municipal bond unit trusts that had been sold in the 5.5–6 percent range moved to the 6.5 percent range in 1978 and were approaching the 7 percent level in the spring of 1979. Those fives and sixes were at deep discounts to their eventual maturity value, and unlike new issues, there was no wait for income to commence being paid. They literally flew off the shelf when they were available, and the tax-swap business was vibrant to say the least. I can't fully remember the progression of hiring on the secondary desk, but it wasn't long before there was a third and a fourth person servicing the aftermarket for UITs.

The new issue business, while less labor-intensive, thrived as well with no letup in underwriting. Early on, Henry decided to discontinue the Dean Witter Municipal Trust solely underwritten by Dean Witter Reynolds because a ten- or twelve-million-dollar deal sometimes took three to six weeks to sell, and in any case, it appeared as though the stronger unit trust sales organization was the two-thousand-broker former Reynolds sales force who were very much endeared to MIT. When an investment product is available over an extended period like the Dean Witter Municipal Trust, the sales force sees no urgency and they tend to work on it when the need arises. When it opens for sale and closes in a day or two, like the Municipal Investment Trust, a sense of urgency develops that spurs sales. Then there was the risk and the staffing factor; I think both Henry and Clem felt or came to the conclusion that the well-oiled cookie cutter Merrill machine adept at the rapid fire issuance of a variety of deals while adequately managing the risk, was the way for us to go. It would take years to build such an operation on our own at Dean Witter Reynolds. Our relationship/partnership with Merrill Lynch was just too big an asset to relinquish. Yet another rational for closing down the Dean Witter Municipal Trust was the near one hundred branch offices in California that for the most part, wanted California state bonds because of the high rate of taxation there and because that was what they had been doing forever. There is a subtler point to make in that a Dean Witter Reynolds underwriting of a California Municipal Bond Trust might have encountered strong resistance from the municipal bond department. A Merrill Lynch underwriting could be complained about but not stopped. In fact, California Municipal Bond head, one Gene Cornelius, railed about the inadequacies of municipal bond unit trusts for years. It wasn't long before the Municipal Investment Trust Fund California Series became a regular attraction to the new firms California sales force.

It's an understatement to say that we were busy. There was a natural pickup in business in all the trusts, so the capital commitments were larger in a market that was a little more volatile than we'd seen before. There was a higher volume of phone work because of the amount of salesman we were covering with lots of questions to answer from brokers who had not been involved with the investment before then. We conferenced called branch offices a good deal and there were plenty of meetings regarding policy and how we were going to handle and approach the future. As interest rates continued to rise the shorter maturity intermediate term unit trusts of twelve to fifteen years in maturity became popular. The shorter maturity of these bonds made them less vulnerable to price deterioration in a rising interest rate market while they delivered near and sometimes more than eighty percent of a long term trusts yield, certainly not a big give up. Soon we introduced intermediate term trusts made up of exclusively New York and/or California municipals. In truth the intermediate term idea was a good reason to call a client, i.e. shorten maturity and still earn a competitive yield. The investor might sell something they already owned raising money to invest in the intermediate term trusts which would have an overall effect of decreasing the maturity of their portfolio or add new money. Intermediate term trusts sold well and the California intermediate term trust particularly awakened the western crowd. A good friend of ours Dean Kois, now moved over to Dean Witter Reynolds Municipal Bond Department was an institutional salesman who had a knack for turning a phrase. When we mentioned the intermediate term trust to him he said.

"Well, you're supposed to buy the intermediate term trust."

We liked it and began to use the phrase often in our conversations and I think I even put it in a little blurb of mock client/broker dialogue on an ugly sheet. When we started hearing this phrase being repeated back to us by the sales forces it was a kind magic moment. It was the equivalent of knowing that we had made some inroads, they were listening after all.

Chapter 62

Coup de GNMA

Around May of 1979, Merrill Lynch announced that the account was going to underwrite a GNMA unit trust. Government National Mortgage Association pass-throughs are bonds secured by pools or bundlings of fifteen- or thirty-year residential home mortgages. Their payment of interest and repayment of principal is insured, meaning if the homeowner(s) default on the mortgage(s), the government pays the investor; thus, they are guaranteed as to (both) principal and interest by the US government. GNMAs are one of the earliest efforts by Congress to spur home ownership (and the economy) through the stimulation of lending by savings institutions. Their investment quality was unquestionable because of their government guarantee. Unlike normal bonds, in which one receives semiannual interest payments and then full payment of principal at maturity, GNMAs pay interest monthly, along with incremental payments (return) of principal. In effect, the GNMA investor becomes the holder of the underlying mortgages, receiving interest on the remaining balance of the portion of the loan he owns as well as small incremental payments of the loan's principal. The investor assumes the role of the bank holding the mortgage. The term "pass-through" is used in reference to GNMAs because the income is said to pass through a paying agent from mortgagee to the investor.

GNMAs were considered a sophisticated investment in the late seventies and perhaps not suitable for the average investor because of their relative complexity, meaning the unorthodox way in which income and principle were paid, notwithstanding this GNMAs were in fact considered by many a good and prudent investment for the average investor. They were very competitive in terms of their yield, and again, most importantly, they were "US government guaranteed and rated AAA." The biggest obstacle however keeping the average investor away from GNMA's was its $25000 minimum purchase rule. A GNMA UIT would remove this barrier, bringing a high quality, high yielding investment to the very people who needed it the most.

Henry was a big advocate of GNMAs, hence the creation of a GNMA Department at Reynolds shortly after his arrival. In Clem and Henry's history as well is a little-known anecdote from the early seventies about an attempt to underwrite a GNMA unit trust, the first ever. I call it an attempt because although the deal got sold, after a fashion, it was a flop. I wasn't there, but here is Clem's version of the story. Henry at Paine-Webber was the lead sponsor and protagonist of the deal. Ironically, Clem from Reynolds was a principal underwriter as was Dean Witter who had assigned Robert Chamberlain, Princeton graduate and long-time head of Municipal Research at Dean Witter, as point man on the underwriting. A week or two before the deal was scheduled to come to market, a meeting was called by Dean Witter and held in a conference room at Dean Witter's headquarters. On the appointed date of the meeting, Henry at Paine-Webber had several millions sold (under three million anyway). Clem at Reynolds had about $750,000 sold and thought he could go to a million plus easily. Bob Chamberlin at Dean Witter, on the other hand, brought an entourage and cast of supporters to the meeting and announced that he hadn't sold bond one and brought forth a list of reasons why the deal was unsellable and should be canceled.

Bob Chamberlin was a bright guy although many might have termed him a stuffy, blustery, Princetonian snob, easy to make fun of, and someone who often hid behind an intellectual cloud of BS. Henry read Bob's pronouncement as an excuse for not doing any work on the deal and thus, as the saying goes, "ripped him a new one" right there and then, publicly and caustically. It was a scene Clem recounted to me several times, I guess because it impressed him so, remarking especially about the viciousness of Henry's devastation of Chamberlain and the shame and embarrassment of the latter. That

GNMA deal, while it did come to market, went into receivership shortly thereafter. The underwriters refused to stock it or make a secondary market for it. One called a fellow named Joe Pogeo at US Trust for an evaluation whenever a client needed a quote or needed to sell. Of course, knowing this story, I couldn't help but wonder what Bob Chamberlain may have had to say about Henry at the time of the merger.

The GNMA trust that was coming to market in late spring of 1979 was announced with an approximate yield of 8.25 percent. Clem was very enthusiastic, as was Henry, and it didn't take long to get the feeling that something special was happening. A short and concise (fifteen minutes maximum) conference call-tutorial-sales presentation was developed by Clem who was a master at such things. The presentation was then given by myself and Clem countless times in the ensuing weeks on conference call after conference call to as few as three or four brokers to fifteen branch managers on a regional conference call or ten or twelve branch office conference rooms with who knows how many brokers listening.

Good conference calls, introducing new and somewhat complex ideas, need the symmetry of a clear introduction and beginning, a middle, and an equally clear summation. It must be delivered enthusiastically with suggestions as to the kind of client who might be interested in the product and a sales idea or two. A poorly given call causes attention to drift. Most importantly, the call could not be longer than fifteen minutes, twenty at the very most, including a few questions and answers or, again, you risked losing the audience's attention. The best result you could hope for was the meetings you had just addressed continued after the call. If a couple of guys were sanguine about the ideas presented and their potential opportunity, it tended to get the ball rolling in the office. Getting it right the first time was very important. Flubbing a question or in some way appearing not to know something or being unable to explain a particular point or crucial piece of information was embarrassing and difficult to recover from. We were also going before a large group of brokers, many of whom didn't know us from a hole in the ground, namely the Dean Witter crowd, and we didn't want to make a mistake.

Lucky for us, we had a great yield of 8.25 percent that was government guaranteed and far and away better than clients could get in the bank and the income would be paid monthly. There was a design here that fit a specific need. A good, even impeccable, quality investment with a high interest rate and even higher cash flow. Someone in the field jokingly made the remark on one of our calls that this was an investment for "moneys that their clients would not show them," money that was kept in banks in CDs exclusively. Frank Cullum and I immediately co-opted the remark. The idea behind the remark was very potent and spurred sales. Brokers put their mothers and grandmother's money into it. Money that had never seen the light of day would go into the GNMA fund at 3 percent higher than it was earning in the bank. Interest and principal would be reinvested monthly and grow at obscene levels. We were also in a time when something new was needed, something that would have no question of working, especially for our firm, Dean Witter Reynolds, which had been continually beset by problems, feuds, computer glitches, and failure of expectations.

Shockingly, several days before the deal came to market, we went into Merrill for twenty million dollars' worth, a number no one would have believed possible six months before. The biggest municipal trusts rarely got past thirty million dollars for the entire account. The biggest corporate and preferred stock deals were fifteen to twenty million. Here, Dean Witter, a mere 25 percent of the joint accounts sales force was in for twenty million on our own. When the deal was priced, it totaled one hundred million dollars and yielded 8.43 percent. We sold seventeen million of the twenty we took down on the first day and the remaining three million dollars flew out the door before ten o'clock the following morning.

Whatever one might call it, this underwriting at Dean Witter Reynolds was an eruption, a cannon shot and a line drive home run up the power alley. The Unit Trust Department, not Syndicate, not Fixed Income, but Unit Trusts, had proved the sales capability of the new firm. Unit Trusts had proven, as it were, what Andy Melton and Bob Gardiner had known or dreamed in merging the two firms. We had reached out with an idea, and with the tools at hand, the phone and the wire system and written a huge ticket. A twenty-million-dollar transaction producing five hundred thousand dollars in commission and ultimately more than three hundred thousand net. The deal had three weeks advance notice and was executed over two days.

Like any business owner, a CEO closes out the month, gathering together every scrap of profit available. I wonder how often Andy Melton and Henry talked to each other and if Andy ever called Henry around the fifteenth of the month to get a read on what might be coming through to the bottom line on the twenty-second or twenty-third. I don't know the answer to these gloating questions. Perhaps it was Gardiner who called Henry about such things.

How ironic that this sideline of a business that might have been seen as an opportunity to marginalize Henry, not necessarily by Andy but perhaps coaxed surreptitiously by the fixed-income guys who had Andy's ear; had become a major source of revenue and somewhat of a pearl from the point of view of the sales force. It was one of the few places in the firm where you got a straight answer, and the business was processed relatively error free. Contrast this with rising interest rates, making life very difficult in the straight fixed-income business. Rumor had it that in order to be in the black, the Municipal Bond Department used an accounting gimmick that added back the commissions paid out to the sales force, a pretty neat trick.

There may be much more to be said in this venue. Maybe Henry should have become head of the Fixed Income Division in the new firm. Perhaps a good deal of money might have been made had events gone that way. More likely a good deal more money might have been saved considering the treacherousness of the markets. But it didn't happen that way, and we moved on. At least I did, not really realizing or thinking these thoughts until many years had passed.

Chapter 63

Six Million or Seven? Ten, Twenty. That Is the Question

I was not a trader who put a price on one or two or five million of bonds two or three times a day, buying and holding for a day or a week and risking the firm's dollars coolly and calmly. That wasn't me. My blood would curdle with every twist of the market. I took risk, but it was a more calculated risk, pitting a sales force against a prospective underwriting. It was easier than trading yes, but I have seen them go wrong and it can get ugly. I witnessed Kondratuck with a Port of New York Authority Deal in the late seventies and an earlier Puerto Rico Electric in the early seventies. Clem was at a breaking point in the mid-seventies with a Con Ed deal. One of Clem's buddies was in the Con Ed deal with him, and they greeted each other with a hug and a kiss on the cheek. When I offhandedly made a remark that in my family, when some guy kissed another guy, it usually meant one or the other was going to die. Clem went white. Who knows what was in his mind?

I didn't consider myself in the category of a trader. As a matter of fact, I didn't have a name or any official title for what my job was except that I was by this time an assistant vice president consulting on four or five and sometimes eight- or ten-million-dollar commitments three or four times a week. I don't think I ever really analyzed what I was doing or where I was in the pecking order of the firm, much less the department or what horizons or opportunities lay before me. I was just there and happy to be there thrown together by the prevailing winds and forces prevalent in the financial markets and the contractions in the securities industry. I was having fun really, making money, achieving impossible feats, privy to high level decision making, always operating at a high level, working with amazing people, and exercising my mind with as much enthusiasm and vigor as an Olympic pole vaulter or an NFL pro.

While I was immensely fortunate, grateful in fact, to be working with such men as Henry, Clem, and Frank Cullum, by many, I was considered an equal partner to them—to Clem and Frank at least. It never phased or dawned on me that I should have been weighing my prospects and the future strategically. That was never my thing. Years later, I ran into guys who told me they had planned their lives in writing and in detail in their last years in college. I couldn't believe such statements at first because it was simply not part of the culture that I was brought up in. When we brought that twenty-million-dollar GNMA deal home, I was having so much fun and felt so fortunate that I just never gave the idea of what my future might be a second thought. A fellow once took me aside and asked me who I thought the Unit Trust Department was. I didn't know what he was talking about, and after pressing me a bit unsuccessfully, he changed the subject. He was implying I think that I was The Unit Trust Department, that my persona was the driving force of the department. Very flattering I guess but after lunch I went back to the office and never gave the conversation a second thought.

I think of the three of us—Clem, Frank, and myself—I had the largest capacity for outright work, picking up phones, dispensing answers and in turn making calls, taking down official information such as the announcement of new issues, and turning that information around to the branch office system. I also formulated what our commitments would be on all new issues. In the five years or so that Clem and I had been together, I had developed an intuitiveness in this regard that proved to be right most of the time, if not on almost every deal we did. I tracked the ticketing and sales of every deal hour by hour, moment to moment even. Neither Clem nor Frank at the time was interested in the clerical nature of sorting and compiling the ticket flow. Kaye Foster in the wire room received copies of the orders, sorted them and brought them to me throughout the day. I rifled through them and tabulated them, mostly in my head, often jotting down rough totals. There seemed to be a rhythm to it all. The volume of indications of interest, then the real orders, incoming calls, communication with Merrill, yield projections on upcoming issues and how they were received by key salesmen in the field, among other things. Somehow I became adept at interpreting and transforming this documentation and feel for the tempo of the moment and transforming it into consistent and accurate sales projections on most deals, so much so that I simply owned the job. Then again I also had an abiding faith in the new sales organization that never failed to back me up. These were not market calls per se although monetary loss could be incurred when and if the market went against you. Getting it right however, maximized the use of the capital at our disposal and minimized possible loss in turbulent markets. And if anything, 1979 through the early 1980s were possibly the most turbulent and treacherous fixed income markets of the twentieth century and when one considered the volume of underwriting—perhaps of any century. Accurately predicting sales so that they matched or slightly exceeded what we went in for and our eventual allotments was the goal on every new issue. Achieving this goal, protected our profitability on all levels. What was the use of underwriting a million or two more if it dragged the deal out, compromising otherwise in-the-bank earnings and profitability?

By the end of summer 1979, new issue volume was incredible compared to the business we were doing the year before. The GNMA Trust had been a breakthrough in terms of absolute volume of course, however, the addition of the Dean Witter sales force and its response to Unit Trusts in general had driven the volume of sales to heights we never could have imagined, at least that's the way I felt. Volume increased to thirty-five to forty million dollars a month and easily surged to forty-five to fifty million a month depending on how the deals fell in and as yield levels adjusted higher. GNMA's alone accounted for twenty million a month. Between all sources of revenue from new issues; sponsors accumulation profits, sales credits paid into the system, leftover earnings after expenses both delivered in later months when each deal was settled and closed out and what remained in our own accounts after sales credit payout, we had become a fifteen million dollar gross revenue operation, if not more, with net before expenses to the firm being at least half that.

Remember if sales credit payout to our sales force was a million dollars a month the firm paid out to the salesman less than 50 percent of that, but again that was before firm expenses.

When a new issue closed out, a vacuum was created that would clean up any loose inventory in the secondary market and leave a vacuum there as well. Before long I began to take an additional five hundred to a thousand ($500,000 to $1,000,000 worth) units more than I needed on some new issues so that I could dump them into the secondary market a week or two later to Al Stevens and Ola. Al called it helping them to keep the lions at bey. Any monetary loss on these was easily absorbed because of the overall volume we were doing.

The increase in the volume of sales of new issues at Dean Witter Reynolds increased the percentage of our participation on an issue by issue basis and therefore entitled us to a larger share of the joint accounts profitability. Naturally Henry and Clem immediately turned to Norman Schevey at Merrill to renegotiate our participation levels in the account to reflect our new production levels. For example where we were formally selling twelve percent of a twenty two million dollar municipal bond issue we were now selling fifteen percent of a thirty million dollar issue and even higher percentages on California municipal trusts.

Needless to say these numbers were welcomed by Gardner and Melton. Henry would mention "Andy's" reactions to them every so often. A more demonstrative appreciation of them occurred one Friday afternoon at about three when Clem, Frank and I slipped out to have a drink. I think Frank was going to take a week off so we popped down to the Parlor Car and Caboose for a quick one to wish him well and ran into Stretch in the lobby of 120 Broadway where he still had an office. Smiling broadly Gardiner walked directly into our midst and put his arms about Clem and Franks shoulders and then reached out to me. An amazing moment really because Stretch's magnetism was infectious, sincere and warm all at the same time. I think he jokingly asked who was minding the printing press or some such thing. It was over in two minutes and the funny thing is that it had a dampening effect on our mood for a while. Sometimes and at the oddest moments the magnitude and weight of what you are in the midst of becomes very real, maybe some other emotion was afoot as well. Running at a near fifty million a month clip was pretty serious and high level stuff. In contrast to these numbers I was earning as I have said something less than $50,000 a year and quite happy too. Maybe it should have been more but I wasn't bothered. First of all a few short years before I was earning half that working eighty to ninety hours a week at three different jobs and now approaching the end of a year at this level of business year end couldn't possibly be a disappointment.

On a further personal note, during the 1978-79 period the house became too much for my mother in law. She worried over a broken shingle or a bit of rust on a wrought iron stair rail. When Rosalie's father was alive, he fixed everything quickly treating every little problem with emergency room status. With me she had to wait a weekend or two if I got around to doing things at all and she was unused to talking to workman. There was a storm I remember when a piece of the roofing was blown away. When we got the roofer down and got an estimate of $200 to patch up the roofing, I had to turn him away because she thought the price was too high. We offered the solution of buying the house, she agreed, and we arranged a way to go forward. Between our meager savings account and a cash injection by my mother in law Helen and a $2000 offering from my brother Dom, we put together a down payment and enough cash reserves for the closing costs, and so, we bought the house on Magee Place. Helen then moved in with us and slept in my daughters room. We cleaned and painted and got a tenant for Gramma Helen's apartment upstairs in less than two months. Not strictly legal but common practice. We then finished the basement with studs and drywall including the ceilings and paneling and electrics with a full bath and a sitting room for Gramma Helen.

It was an astounding passage of events especially because, had Rosalie not been working part-time (Thursday, Friday nights and Saturday's) at Suburbia Federal Savings and Loan in Garden City and banking her salary, we never would have been able to get a mortgage application. In those days if you didn't have a savings account it was often very difficult to get your hands on one. My thinking at the time about money and personal finances was still hand to mouth in a way but with no cause for worry. There was no big sum in a bank account and there were plenty of bills including a couple of credit cart balances and department store charges, but there was plenty of cash flow from salary and rent and Rosalie's part time work, and always a year end bonus to look forward to. So when we talk about money on a personal level, for that time, it was no issue for us, for me anyway. The job was providing adequately, we owned our own home and had a couple of cars in the driveway. We were holding our own and being as responsible to all our obligations as we could. If anything, I was somewhat overwhelmed by our good fortune, me, the cockeyed optimist who always thought so positively. I started teaching CCD in 1979 at St. Anthony's and doing some football and hockey coaching in an effort to give back.

Chapter 64

Who Are These People? You Have a Family!

Going to junior high school at age thirteen introduced me to a new peer group who lived closer to our parish church, St. Lucy's, on Kent between Park and Flushing Avenues, seven or eight blocks away from where we lived. All of these new friends were of Italian decent, many Calabrese even, whose grandparents were born in the same region of Southern Italy my own parents were from. The only difference being that my parents were about the same ages as the grandparents of these new friends and my parents had been born in Italy. My father regularly attended the eleven o'clock high mass on Sundays at St. Lucy's and I often went with him walking through the neighborhood where my new-found friends lived. It wasn't unusual on these occasions to encounter a few of these boys along the way. One might shout from across a street.

"Hiya Pat, where ya goin?"

"Nicky, what's up? Were goin to the 11 at St. Lucy's."

"Hey, seeya tomorra."

Or another one or two might run up to us and say, "Hey, Pat. This your dad?"

"Hey, Anthony. Yep, this is Papa." I didn't know the word dad as it was never used in our house. It was always Papa or Mama. It was even strange to say the word dad.

"Yes, this is my father, Mr. Scida."

My father was quite stoic, he was also kind and polite and always smiled upon these fellows.

On one of these Sundays, after a few more than raucous greetings, he asked, "Who are these people?"

"My friends, Papa, from junior high school," I said. His reply said much and wore many outfits and, in a way, stayed with me for the rest of my life.

"What do you need all these friends for?" he asked most sincerely. "You have a family!"

Yes I did, and I do have a family. I loved and cherished them and shared their world, but none of them shared mine. The events I routinely participated in at the office between seven in the morning to five or six in the afternoon each day, could certainly be termed larger than life to most of the people in my social and family circle as they had once been for me. I had become used to them by this time, by the late seventies, accustomed to thinking in terms of personal commitments worth multiple millions of dollars and having a daily life that regularly and readily digested material about the credit markets that spoke in terms of hundreds of millions and often billions of dollars. Besides these, routinely picking up a hundred telephone calls a day, making twenty or twenty-five more, adjudicating a couple of disputes, clarifying a legal issue, and then explaining said issue to an outraged branch manager or broker or lawyer or all three. Advising and participating in the decision making on any number of situations with a monetary value of a thousand to a hundred thousand dollars, all as easily as ordering a ham sandwich, as easy as Bob's your uncle, the English say.

After six though, there was a private life, an obligation to go home, a life to go back to every night and to live and function in. Another world. A different psyche to put on. The psyche of where one comes from and what it dooms you to be in the world. The world of personal life and wife, children, mother-in-law, immediate and extended family, life events, possessions, lawns and garages, endless discussion, decision making, disagreement and arguing. A real world of ham sandwiches and Uncle Bobs. This world might question whether the seven in the morning to six in the evening world I inhabited during the day was indeed a real world at all because real people in our circle did not deal in or believe anyone else dealt in millions. Certainly, members of my social peer group would question it and probably decide that it wasn't a real world to them at all.

Was the home world dull compared to the average fifty million dollars of sales world my colleagues and I presided over monthly, the market risk, the intensity of competition, workload, and problem solving? Where was my ego drifting during those two and a half weeks when my partners and I contrived to personally speak to several thousand Dean Witter employees and tear off a twenty-million-dollar piece of business? Who could I discuss those two weeks with, and have expectation of having a casual and rational conversation. No one really. Certainly not my close relatives. I can just imagine the conversation.

"How's work?"

"Really busy."

"No kidding, doing what?"

"Well in the past two week we pulled off a $20 million dollar sale."

"Really! Of what, and anyway how much is twenty million."

"Bonds, Ginny Mae's."

"They have girls names? Do you make a lot of money."

I didn't know anyone in my social circle that was in Wall Street or Finance, not at the time anyway. Not the coaches in Pee Wee Football or roller hockey where my son played or the guys at the East Rockaway Anglers Fishing Club where I was a member or any of the guys at the marina where I kept a boat or even at church, although that might have been the place as I had noticed once one of our parish priests, a Jesuit, reading the *Wall Street Journal*. In any case, even if there was some understanding soul at these places, there was little time spent with these folks doing or talking about anything other than what we were doing there. The fact was I didn't make friends easily. My father's Italian ways about why you need friends and keep acquaintances at a distance when you have a family, though confusing to me when he uttered them, had obviously left some residue.

Besides the home-based activity of children's pursuits—Pee Wee Football, dance lessons, scouts, gymnastics, and any available moment to run away from it all and go fishing—there was always something waiting to happen. Home projects, for example, as simple as keeping up with the lawn, shrubs, and general maintenance of the property. A landscaper was out of the question as far as we were concerned, they were for rich people. In any case us Italians did our own gardening chores, it was in our blood. On a holiday weekend we might have a barbecue, but more often than not it was a sideshow to my putting in a new kitchen floor or painting the living room and dining room. The funny thing was that Clem looked at me as if I had two heads when I told him I'd spent half of Saturday or an extended weekend painting.

Then there was the extended family, a sister and a brother in Brooklyn with five and four children respectively and three aunts, to whom my mother had devoted a portion of her life and her soul. One of them never married, and the other two married well into their fifties. All were childless, and we, my siblings and I, were sworn to care for them, with nearly my mother's last dying breath, until their dying day...or ours. Truth be told, she felt being unmarried for so long, with no children to live or suffer for, her sisters were poor unfortunates who would never truly understand life or the world.

"You have a family," my father had said, and so did my mother, in her own way and we, their children, took it seriously.

My wife's mother lived with us and was no great burden at all. In fact, she was, in many ways, a remarkable woman, whom I have come to greatly respect. Still, in all, she was always a presence. Rosalie had two brothers One of whom had two children who married and began to have children of their own in the mideighties, while my own siblings had children doing much the same, and so the inevitable endless stream of family events that included holiday gatherings, numerous weddings, anniversaries, birthdays, communions, confirmations, graduations, and wakes. We went to them all.

At any of these events, there was no way I could explain what I did for a living. My uncle Lou happened to be in earshot at some family gathering when one of my cousins whom I hadn't seen in a while asked if I was still working on Wall Street. As I continued chatting with my cousin, I overheard Uncle Lou say, "Plumbers and electricians, even goddamn lawyers and accountants, at least you know what they do, but nobody knows what the hell those bastards on Wall Street are doing."

Nor could I let on the kind of money I was making. Although when people looked at the car I was driving, never a new one at this time but always a late model, or the clothes my wife and I or our children wore, there was an inkling of prosperity, I guess. On one of those occasions, I got into a little tiff with a fellow who was a big union proponent. He accused me of selling out to "the big guys" who exploited people like him.

"What big guys?" I said.

"You know, the Big Guys."

"What big guys?" I said again, moving to the next room because I had to avoid an altercation. Not physical of course. There would be no arguing with him about something he could never understand.

"Come onnnn, you know what am talkin' about. The big money guys. Don't think am a fool. You're in wit dem."

I delighted at his shock when I mentioned to him some years later that that my sons education at Georgetown was costing me in the neighborhood of twenty to twenty-five thousand dollars cash a year.

Once, at a Christmas Day dinner at my sisters, a mob scene in the eighties, I was asked by someone if the rumors about Christmas bonuses on Wall Street were true. He proceeded to ask me outright what kind of bonus I had received that year. Stupid me, I thought he knew a little about my world. When I told him I had received a twenty-thousand-dollar bonus (it was actually fifty thousand), he became visibly upset and questioned what I could possibly be doing to receive such a bonus. Years later, I explained how I had worked into the position I held. Imagine if I had told the truth. I never explained to him that my boss probably received two hundred thousand dollars that same year.

My wife was the first one in line when it came to having little interest in what I did for a living. I used to joke about trying to discuss a major gain or loss or a big sale I'd just helped to consummate during dinner. Often, she wouldn't even acknowledge what I was talking about with a comment or question. Instead, the conversation would always be steered to anything from the children's latest exploits (or misdemeanors) to the upward advancement in the price of the very roast we were consuming or the problems of autism she was dealing with in her position as a special education aid in the Oceanside School System. This was not on purpose or deliberate. My day-to-day exploits, what I did for a living, was one thing. What was really important was the "family" and "the business of the family"—the children, our parents, the house, our finances, the extended family, and the events therein. Yes, the money was good, but the job needs to stay on the job. It's good, work hard, make money, but don't talk about it too much. It's bad luck. I understood perfectly. I had a family. My father had told me so.

Years later, when I read Herman Wouk's great novel about life inside and outside the synagogue, I thought of myself as a sort of the Italian or at least the Italian-American version of "Mr. Inside, Mr. Outside." I had one persona at work on Wall Street and another at home with my family in Oceanside, and that was that. There was no changing it.

Chapter 65

Upheaval
Another New/Old Investment

In the next few years an unprecedented rise in inflation and interest rates would devastate the world economy. Wall Street and the banking system in the United States would struggle to stay abreast of wildly fluctuating markets without sinking into oblivion. Eventually several Wall Street firms would merge or be bought outright by larger American corporations. But before that an unprecedented transfer of assets began in the United States. With inflation rising over 15 percent and interest rates on certain fixed income securities approaching these same levels corporations required a massive supply of cash to weather the inflationary storm. Borrowing at these rates for the long term would lock in enormous liability for 8 to 15 years into the future so they went to the major commercial banks for short term loans. The banks in turn went to, or perhaps realized that brokerage firms with their innovative product development skills and massive sales organizations could help supply the cash that Americas, indeed many of the world's corporations needed to borrow to tide them over in this inflationary blip (hopefully) in the world economy. I just happened to be in one of those brokerage firms at the time with the guys I have introduced you to over the past couple of hundred pages.

Much of the financial news in 1979 was taken up by the rise of inflation and the ensuing and inevitable rise in interest rates. When the future portends a higher cost of living, higher prices of goods and services, the cost of borrowing money, reflected in interest rates, also rises. Higher interest rates may be described as a sort of "defense mechanism," the extraction of a premium in the form of a higher rate of return to compensate for a possible loss of principal if a sale of the debt is forced. Higher interest rates during inflationary periods compensate the lender for "opportunity lost" during the interim of the loan, due to the probability that inflation and interest rates will continue to rise in the future. Inflation in effect is the diminishing of the value of money; what costs a dollar today costs a dollar and ten cents next year. Thus, in periods of rising inflation the interest rate market assumes that the dollars loaned out today will be worth less when the loan is paid off. In inflationary times interest rates rise to compensate for the devaluation occurring between the time the money is loaned, and to the time it is repaid. The opposite is true when inflation expectations decrease as the market competes to pay a lower rate because of the probability of lower interest rates in the future and the likelihood that the value of the loans made today will increase in the future.

With inflation on the rise as autumn approached, three and six-month treasury bills rose above 9 percent eventually going over ten percent before year end. At the same time, branches of American banks (Chase, Chemical, Bank of America, etc.) located on foreign soil, mostly in London, were borrowing money through the issuance of three- and six-month Certificates of Deposits or CDs at 9–9.5 percent. It was a strange anomaly, ironic and hard to believe as we look back on it now, that then the branches of these same chartered American banks located on American soil, were prohibited by the Federal Reserve under the rule known as Reg. T to issue CDs at a rate higher than 5 percent. The CDs issued in Europe were sometimes called Eurodollar CDs, a general term that refers to US dollars deposited in European (foreign) banks. At first, only American banks with London offices were issuing these CDs, but later, American banks with offices in Japan began to issue them as well. To put a finer point on it some of the major banks in Europe and Asia had been allowed charters by the Fed to conduct banking in the US and so the foreign offices of these banks that had been chartered in America also began issuing Eurodollar CDs. The Federal Reserve had no jurisdiction over these foreign offices of American Banks or the CDs they awarded.

Now as to the product development aspect of this wealth trans-
ference we have previously alluded to. Some years before, around
1976–1977, rising interest rates led to these same banks, London
branches of American banks, issuing CDs in the in the 9–11 percent range. Norman Schevey at Merrill had taken advantage of that
event by bringing to market a series of eight trusts whose underlying portfolios were composed of these CDs. The investment was
called the Corporate Income Fund Short Term Series. The details
of these CD trusts were quite simple to understand and not very
different from other unit trusts, but somewhat difficult to feel
comfortable with, because they changed the CD game as we shall
see. The main point, the crucial point in all this talk about CDs
and CD unit trusts is that that no matter where they were issued,
in Europe or Japan or how they were packaged, as Certificates of
Deposit issued by banks chartered by the Federal Reserve in and
of the United States they were insured, in effect guaranteed by the
Federal Deposit Insurance Corporation aka FDIC. So the higher
yielding euro-dollar CDs issued by foreign offices of American
banks had the identical FDIC guarantee that you got in the states
on CDs that couldn't yield more than five percent: that were man-
dated not to yield more than five percent.

Thus the joint-account purchased these Eurodollar CDs in
one- to three-million-dollar blocks. A 0.75 percent (three quarters
of one percent) sales charge was added on to the price of the underlying CDs, while the income payable was diminished by less than
$1.25 give or take a penny or two per thousand dollars of principal
to mitigate trustee expenses (portfolio maintenance, weekly pricing,
and postage). The sales charge and portfolio expense diminished the
average yield of the portfolio by about 100 to 125 basis points, (1-1
¼%) give or take a few basis points, based on the size of the trusts
among other factors.

Again, as a rule the yields of the CD's in underlying portfolios
of these short-term trusts were diminished by 1.0 to 1.25 percent
after the application of sales charges and expenses. The dramatic
decrease was caused by the amortization of the .75% sales charge
(roughly $7.50) over a six month duration and the diminishing of

the income by $1.25 per thousand dollars of par value to allay the previously mentioned expenses.

Structurally, a thirty-million-dollar portfolio composed of ten three-million-dollar blocks of CDs, each issued by a different bank, when placed in a trust, created 30,000 units or shares of beneficial interest in the portfolio. These were sold in thousand-dollar increments at approximately $1,007.50 plus accrued interest calculated to the settlement date of the transaction. Ownership of units at maturity entitled the holder/investor to 1/30,000 of the portfolio's income (after expenses) and $1,000 of principal per unit held.

Several characteristics of the trust bear further explanation in that at first glance they may be confusing and the cause of some misconceptions. The first is attributable to a kind of trick of the mind. A six-month investment yield of 10 percent has an income of fifty dollars. Investors at first glance often make the mistake of thinking it should be one hundred dollars, forgetting that the calculation of yield is based on the income of the security as if it were paid annually, meaning that earning fifty dollars over six months is earning at the rate of ten percent annually.

The most notable difference from buying bank CDs directly as opposed to this CD unit trust was the change in the format of the securities liquidity. If you wished to cash in a bank CD from a local bank, you received a diminished income but got your full principal returned. The opposite was the case with the CD unit trust. You received market value, which was higher or lower than you paid plus the full interest earned per day held to the settlement date of the sell transaction, meaning if the income was $48.75, the daily interest was around $0.27 per day ($48.75 divided by 180), per unit. Thus, if the investor sold and settlement day was the hundredth day out of the 180-day term, he received $27 per unit owned plus whatever the market value of the CD was, depending on whether interest rates had risen or fallen during the period the investor held the security. Unlike the bank and the standard operating procedure at banks investors had to hold the CD Trust for its entire duration to maturity to be made whole in regards to principal.

When these first CD unit trusts were brought to market in 1976–1977, my recollection was we sold about a million to a million and a half on each in our shop. Most of our sales were in the Midwest and done through institutional salesman who were very savvy and didn't have a problem with the idea of a brokerage firm selling bank CDs. On the other hand, the public at large and the brokers who served them in our firm at least were not too interested. We didn't push it too hard because there were other fish to fry at the time. In addition, there were some political problems regarding the coverage of the New York City and New York state branches, and Henry had asked Clem and, by association, me and Carlos Rodriguez to service these branches for Municipals as well as unit trusts until he could build a team to do the job and so we backed away.

While we were knocking the cover off the ball at mid-year, as we approached the final quarter of 1979, past events and the deteriorating market seemed to be catching up with both investors and brokers. Many were battle weary from the collapse of prices in municipals due to the New York City/state/Puerto Rico/WHUPPS Crisis and the general upward march of inflation and interest rates that severely diminished portfolio valuations for all fixed income investments. It was deemed that a new product was needed to hold investors over, until the inflation storm passed. It was thought as well that American investors would leap at the chance to invest in unit trusts composed of CDs, especially since the rates were so high and the prohibition of the issuance of CDs in the United States anywhere near the rates of those being issued by the London offices by European banks. With this in mind, Norman Schevey at Merrill decided to resurrect the Short-Term Corporate Income-Fund Product that had been sold with modest success earlier in the decade.

There were however, certain…business/profit loss considerations to be discussed with the joint sponsors before the resumption of the underwriting of these short term trusts. Profit margins were very thin on such a short-term instrument, especially the first one of its kind in nearly three years, in which the lawyers and the accountants had to get up to speed anew. In any case, the expenses associated with bringing this deal were the same as any long-term issue. The only way to make any money on it was to build it big. Schevey had to get the major sponsors to come on board for a large deal. I didn't have much input on this one for several reasons. The first of which was that on this particular deal how much we were going for was to be an executive decision made on the Clem/Henry level. I was, however, on the conference call Norman conducted with the sponsors explaining that with no portfolio accumulation profits to speak of on a six months maturity CD trust, the only way to cover expenses and to earn a few dollars a unit was to underwrite fifty million or more. As Norman explained the proposed deal, the confidence of the group was bolstered by the FDIC-insured nature of the underlying CDs, the short six-month maturity, and of course, the projected yield of 8–8.5 percent and possibly higher yield, since six-month Eurodollar CDs in Europe were currently being issued 9.50 to 9.75. We have already mentioned a rule of thumb that after application of sales charges and maintenance fees, CD trusts came to market yielding approximately 1.25 percent less than the yield of the underlying securities in the portfolio.

The CIF Short-Term Series 9 was expected to come to market around September 15, well after the Labor Day weekend. The weekend, actually the Saturday after the conference call with Norman Schevey, I helped my bother clean out a basement of a building he owned in Queens, and the following Monday, I collapsed with muscle spasms in my back and was hospitalized for ten days. So as I lay in hospital in pain and in traction, drugged up half the time, I had to listen to Clem on the telephone every other day and during the couple of visits he made to the hospital.

"Why we could hold the damn thing to maturity if we had to," he said in jest.

It was not in our business model to bring deals and invest in them for the duration, but everyone got the joke.

"Not to mention the projected yield that was now pegged at a solid 8.5 percent."

Unbelievable really for six months. The view was the deal couldn't miss, and it was decided by Henry and Clem that Dean Witter Reynolds would take ten million of the fifty million dollars being underwritten.

"Eight and one half percent for six months!" Clem said over and over again. "They're gonna eat it up! Dammit, I might even buy some for myself."

We started prepping for conference calls, but just a few days later, my back went out as I mentioned. Here I was in hospital for ten days, then home for almost two more weeks flat on my back most of the time, recuperating and miserable over the fact that I wasn't going to be in for the glory on this one. I could sell this one with my eyes closed and a hand tied behind my back, and dammit I wasn't going to be a part of it. I even thought of asking Clem to let me do some conference calls at home, but my wife talked me out of it, seeing it as not only a ridiculous suggestion but also as childish.

"Grow up," she said. "You'll be in on the next one."

As it happened, despite announcing the deal three weeks in advance and after ten days of intense promotion and conference calls into the branch office system, the deal fell on its face. Presale orders came to less than a $1 million and didn't reach $1.5 million on the first day of pricing in our shop and somewhere between $5 and $10 million at Merrill whose commitment was $30 million plus of the 50 underwritten. Months later, we could see that several problems and general circumstances held the deal back. One was the deeply embedded perception in investors' minds, and many brokers as well that something wasn't right about buying CDs through a brokerage firm. The separation (by law) of banks and brokerage firm business operations (as defined by the Glass-Steagall Act of 1933) was much more apparent then than it is now, and as a matter of fact, it no longer exists. This became a major sticking point and would take time to overcome. Further, this lack of credulity was born out in the investments form of liquidity which brokers and clients hinged upon, that they would not be able to be made whole for six months if they needed the money.

"CDs are *always* able to be cashed in without loss, isn't that true?"

Then, once the final prospectus began to be distributed, a problem arose from the fact that there were 9.5 to 9.75 percent CDs in the portfolio but the yield of the trust was only 8.19 percent, what happened to all that yield. As mentioned earlier, in longer term trusts sales charges and expenses diminished the yield of the underlying securities by 20-30 basis points at most (twenty to thirty one hundredths of a percentage) so there wasn't much difference when the yields of the underlying bonds were compared to the trusts yield. But in the short-term trusts, there was very little time to maturity, very little time or duration to amortize the effect of the sales charge upon the income. A point not easily explainable or understandable. The term duration while it may have been in use in academia or in public and corporate finance departments was not as commonly in use at the time and not a term generally known to the public.

These objections might have been overcome in a different time, but there was an ill wind blowing, and the public psyche was marred and distracted by many problems. The Ayatollah Khomeini in Iran had taken over one hundred hostages and was still holding many of them and the oil embargo was in full swing and about to cause a recession, if it hadn't already begun. In addition, the shine was off the apple for a while now as much of the fixed income that had been purchased in the last two or three years was underwater. All of these events, situations, and phenomena had a general cooling effect on investor enthusiasm. Under these circumstances an investment composed of Eurodollar CD's could wait awhile.

By the time I got back to the office, the deal had lingered about ten days with very little inventory having moved out and then the inevitable happened, the market fell out of bed. New six-month CD's were now being issued in the 10-10.25% range and at some of the banks whose CD's were in our portfolio 10.5%. The remaining balance of the trust, CIF Short Term Series 9, was eventually priced in accordance with the market, resulting in a markdown of near fifteen dollars per unit. With the balance (ours) now somewhere around six thousand units (six million dollars), the markdown totaled something shy of a hundred thousand for us and near half a million at Merrill.

I'm sure it was quite embarrassing for Henry (and Clem) to have to go management with this defeat in hand. Not that it didn't happen. It's just that it was our first bloody nose after a long stretch of being lily white. In any event, Melton and Gardiner were getting this kind of news all the time. The grapevine told us the municipal bond and corporate bond departments were operating in this same market atmosphere and were getting pretty beat up too. For me, personally, it was true that I had dodged a bullet, but at the same time, I felt crappy about it. I should have been there to take the blame with my coworkers. Just a quirk of fate caused me not to. When I got back, I just saddled up and did my best to get the remainder of the deal sold. By now the yield was near 8.75 percent and we thought could very easily go over the 9 percent mark even though near a month had gone by of the trusts 6 month maturity. After a few days of encountering resistance I began to get a little testy: especially after I discovered a couple of brokers in one of the Florida offices who were doing about thirty or forty thousand dollars' worth a day. When they both said that they were simply mentioning the short term trust as a side-bar to every client they spoke to and about every third or fourth bought it. Essentially it was selling itself when I heard this story from two very savvy guys in Hallandale. I became convinced that it was downright ridiculous that brokers couldn't find money for; in fact couldn't become wildly enthusiastic about a security that had a five (now) month maturity, was yielding near 9 percent, was FDIC insured and paid them $4.00 for every thousand dollars' worth sold. After a while I took to partly sarcastically and partly humorously scoffing at brokers who resisted selling the CD Trust.

"Okay, I'll call you when something better than this comes along. Yeah right!" Or, "If there was ever a hanger in the side pocket, this was it, and you can't make the shot." Meaning, "What could be easier to sell than this, near 9 percent for five months and FDIC-guaranteed to one hundred thousand dollars? Am I crazy, or are you?? It may shock the reader when I say I cannot remember how that deal finished. One part of me makes me thinks the deal sold out but what actually happened I think is that Merrill bought all units back from the underwriters and sponsors and held the units for the 5 or so months till maturity, thus avoiding calamitous losses indeed. I'm sure they settled the deal and divided the losses or gains when the underlying securities matured. An easy decision when you think about it because there was such a short term to maturity.

Chapter 66

The Regional Sales Co-Coordinators

A story often told by Clem about Don Regan, the former chief of staff for President Ronald Reagan and one time CEO of Merrill Lynch, was about one of Regan's staff who brought him a list of the top ten sales offices on a particularly large underwriting. The idea being that the firm should give this group some special recognition, award, or gift. Regan, in a fit of anger, tore the list to shreds calling loudly for a list of the bottom ten offices shouting, "We should fire those bastards who call themselves branch managers and close the offices."

When we were Reynolds, Clem and I had lots of help from the regional municipal departments in getting the word out and collecting indications of interest in our new issues. The Regional Municipal offices gave us good penetration into the sales force. With the firm twice as big now and Municipal Bonds a completely different department, the regionals were sorely missed. It became obvious that without some presence representing unit trusts in the field that we were missing a good deal of business. A presence in the field acting as an authority of the New York Department and a promoter of the product was required, not just to represent the department, but to do the wrangling; the follow up work, calling branches to announce new issues and then calling back for indications of interest, to answer questions, to arrange conference calls, to periodically visit branches.

That we needed a more targeted delivery of the information on new issues and better feedback as to what sales might ensue was unquestionable. I think there might have been some consensus that if there were some committed voices in the field, CIF 9 might have gone better because by the end of 1979, it became apparent that the product was quite viable. If there were some influential presence and sales effort in the field, the deal might have had some additional velocity. The departments need for regional representation was presented to management and it was agreed upon that we could begin to build a regional sales organization. There was already structure for this in the east, which was a remnant of the Reynolds Equity Syndicate (new issues of stock) Regional Sales Coordinators group. These were stockbrokers (with their own books of clients) very familiar with the new issue market for stocks who canvased the branches in their locales (South Florida, North Florida, New England, the Mid-Atlantic, etc.) announcing new issues, answering questions, and gathering reads on interest and the probability of sales, and occasionally traveling to the branches promoting sales.

Having these individuals in situ so to speak would be much cheaper than hiring and training six or eight people in New York to do this job. The regionals would be paid for this work with 1.5 percent (net) of the commission generated in the offices they covered in sales of newly issued unit trusts, about an annual payout of $225,000 over the entire firm at the time. If a million dollars in sales commission was generated in their regions, unit trust sales coordinators would earn fifteen thousand dollars net where a New York operative might command a salary of thirty thousand dollars or more, not counting benefits. In the West, it was left to the firm's regional sales management to pick candidates for the job. Toward the end of 1979, after they were all named, we began working with them day to day, and the four o'clock Monday afternoon conference call was resurrected, which was, in effect, a weekly business meeting in which attendance was obligatory. Shortly thereafter, a meeting began to be arranged to take place in the spring of 1980 in New York.

Such meetings had become routine to Clem and myself since Henry had held several of them at Reynolds with the Fixed Income Division. The guys from the West Coast began arriving on Tuesday and were all in by Wednesday morning. They spent most of their time in the office hanging around the New Issue and Secondary Desks and, as time allotted, had private meetings and luncheons with Clem, Henry, and Frank who was quite familiar with the West Coast fellows. The East Coast guys came in by Thursday and required less "special handling" in that they had experience in this vein, the approach to the sales force, protocol with the branch and regional managers, and how the added expenses of phone, secretarial help, and perhaps hiring an assistant would be handled, and so on. Clem and I knew the East Coast guys because we had been doing business with them for a while and Clem had even lectured the training classes of a few. At around two in the afternoon on Thursday, the entire group was ferried out to Harrison House in Great Neck while several of us headed home to get our cars and get to the meeting by six thirty for cocktails.

There are several recollections I have of this first meeting of the Unit Trust Regionals, one of which has little to do with the business. I recount it here simply because I have never forgotten it. The fellow who'd been named sales coordinator for the greater San Francisco area and Northern California was called Don Anderson. A week or two before he came out to New York, he asked me if I would show him the subways when he got here. I don't think I took his request very seriously. I thought it was a joke. In fact, a lot of guys like to play the country bumpkin, deprecate themselves in some way, often just to trap the unsuspecting dude from the big city although that's more of a wise guy Georgia redneck move. I said, yes, of course, and forgot about it, but he mentioned it several times and again in the office and at dinner on Wednesday evening. I suggested to him that there were two or three subway lines within close walking distance of his hotel, the Americana, and that he could just take one of those downtown.

"Oh no," he said. "I can't do that."

No matter how I explained to Don as to what to do or how I tried to hook him up with one of the other guys to come downtown on the subway, he refused.

"I don't want to go down into a hole in the ground with someone who isn't a New Yorker. I need an experienced guide. Please, I really want to do this before I go home."

Finally, I gave in and told him to take a taxi in the morning down to 120 Broadway around seven, and I'd meet him in front of the building. He was there at five minutes to seven when I got there. Don was about thirty-five or forty, had a sturdy athletic build, a fair complexion, and a full head of sandy- to reddish-colored hair. He was a very nice guy, quite personable, conversational, and enthusiastic. There was a certain zest for life about him, and I had enjoyed working with him on the phone for the a few weeks we'd been in touch, and now in person, he was different than a lot of guys I knew and easy to be with.

We crossed the street moving away from 120 Broadway and stood for a moment in front of the popular Japanese restaurant called Kabuki a few steps up off the street, and proceeded a few steps down past the equally popular Chop House and then further down a longish flight of steps into the Wall Street Station of the Interborough Rapid Transit System (IRT). I popped a couple of tokens in the turnstile and we took a post by a girder, looking at the station from its extreme northern end. As a train roared past us into the station, I watched Don's knees bend slightly, his shoulders hunch round, and his hair blow this way and that. In reflex, he put one hand to his head to hold down his hair and the other to a side pocket of his jacket to keep it from flapping up in the wind, which had no effect on the other side of his jacket or collar or tie for that matter. He looked confused, and at that moment, I wished I could draw. A caricature of him would have made a great cover for the New Yorker. The train had obviously surprised him with its rush of wind and deafening roar, but he was smiling, happily I thought, and fully engaged and delighted with the experience as if he were on a ride in an amusement park.

The elated rush Don got from the physical sensation of the train crashing through the station was soon tempered by mouth-open surprise as he watched some three or four hundred people, maybe five or six hundred or more, get off the train and crowd the exits, slowly funneling out, and then just a minute or two later, after that train emptied and pulled out, the drama began all over again. After three or four of these, he said, "Where do they come from, where do they live, all these people?"

A silly question I thought. "Everywhere, Don. Well, not every-where," I explained. "Everywhere in New York, the Bronx, Riverdale, White Plains, Queens, Connecticut even, basically anyplace north of Thirty-Fourth Street. Then at Thirty-Fourth Street, the Long Island crowd comes in from the east on the railroad, and a lot of them take the train downtown too."

After watching these three or four trainloads get dropped off, he noticed with great surprise that between trains arriving from uptown, the same thing was happening on the other side with the equally large crowds of commuters, if not more arriving from Brooklyn. When I explained where these additional folks were coming from his awe seemed to be increased as if some great secret had been revealed to him. By a bit after seven thirty, I had answered most of his questions about where Wall Street's workforce resided around the city and its surrounding suburbs. Finally, we turned to leave, and I explained, perhaps as if I was explaining to a child, that the greater metropolitan area, which included Southwestern Connecticut and Northern New Jersey, was home to twenty million based on a book I'd read a few years back and maybe twenty-five million by now. That without this elaborate underground transportation system, it would be impossible to move all these people or have this economy.

Don then said something like, "That's easy for you to say. You're from here. That crazy train smashing into the station every few minutes, one from either side to you, is just another animal in the forest, and all those people getting off and the thought of them doing it all over again at five o'clock is…is…" he trailed off for a moment as if exhausted from the observation and then con-tinued. "I don't know what it is except that there's nothing like it in California. Coming here and seeing this, to me, is better than if I went to the Statue of Liberty or the Empire State Building. I'll never forget it," he said, pumping my hand now, smiling broadly, and asking more questions. I realized when I recalled this incident and began to write about it that it was after all still the seventies when I went down into the subway with Don. There was still some naiveite and sense of wonder in us.

It's true that New Yorkers are blasé about the staggering environment they inhabit. My out of town cousins from Massachusetts always wanted to go to a Broadway show or go to the Empire State Building or visit The Statue of Liberty while most of the family that lived in New York City were not impressed. At 34 years of age I had not yet been to a Broadway show or to the other places mentioned. I had been however a sort of denizen of the subways in my teenage days and Don had touched that lever in me that morning. I kept thinking "too bad we had to go to work." I might have taken him to the places I'd discovered when I roamed the subways playing hooky from high school---the vast yards and machine shops in Coney Island and Pelham Bay in the Bronx, the lofty elevated lines at Smith and Ninth Street in Brooklyn and Astoria in Queens, the Fourteenth Street Canarsie Line where pushers crowded people into the cars. Then there was the last stop on the BMT Line in Coney Island where conductors and motormen passed the time between assignments shooting pool at a regulation sized table. The money shot though were the local stops along Eighth Avenue, my favorite being the Eighty First Street Station of the Independent line, where you get off to visit the Museum of Natural History. Here you encountered the A train, the Eight Avenue express, ten steel cars filled with several thousand people sixty feet underground, in all its power and glory barreling its way up from fifty ninth street to one hundred and twenty fifth street in Harlem. Here, to me, a sixteen-year-old kid, was all of New York in one thunderous experience. The Giants, The Yankees, Wall Street, Broadway, Coney Island, The Planetarium, The Empire State Building and The Statue of Liberty all rolled into one. The A Train thundering its way uptown, with a mighty earth-shattering noise and wind, shaking and blowing away everything around it.

Though I tried to resist it, Don had kind of stopped me that day, put me into a reverie that was at once quite pleasant and alternately annoying because it countered my routine and my work. I decided by about eleven that morning that I was going to relax and enjoy the visiting fireman, let up on the phones and the deskwork, hang out with Don, and take a few guys out to lunch at noon. Clem was a little pissed and said something about it too. I was astounded. I had to remind him, tell him, that we had guests. It was a special time, and I'd be neglecting our visitors if I didn't neglect the phones, which he finally accepted. I would have to work with every one of these guy's day to day, and I wanted to get to know them face to face. Jeez, lighten up, and let the operations people fill in as we planned. It was time to socialize. There would be plenty of time in the future to slave away at the phones.

Chapter 67

The Talks

If there were any other notable incidences at this inaugural meeting of our newly formed national sales team, one might have been Henry's "drop-dead money" speech, given on Friday morning, in which he explained that he, in the positions he'd held up to this point in his career, had earned his "drop-dead money," certainly something he might have been thinking of when he was busted down to being the manager of the Unit Trust Department from being the head of Fixed Income at Reynolds. Presumably, this was the money he could depend on if he had to walk away from Wall Street and from his job. The inference being that here was the opportunity for everyone in the room, especially the new Unit Trust Sales coordinators to earn theirs, to earn their "drop-dead money." The second was the premier performance, but very sketchily planned routine, that Clem and I had given, in bits and pieces a hundred times before and would give a hundred times thereafter, which was at once a casual Q and A about the unit trust product line and at the same time a very serious and detailed overview that covered every nuance and detail in depth, including basic sales ideas, features and benefits, markets, and the idiosyncrasies of the underlying securities we packaged. It lasted near three hours, starting before lunch and ending around three. There was a lot to get across. As the risk of boring the reader a bit were going to get into some detail.

Full disclosure was necessary, so that these fellows could know what they were getting themselves into. The bright side was that a Regional Sales Co-Ordinator could earn an additional twenty to thirty thousand a year, the equivalent of sixty to a hundred thousand in commissions, and possibly more, from a captive audience with no prospecting or opening new accounts or any of the headaches of client relationships. However, there was also a vast body of knowledge to digest and the responsibility to service at a minimum four or five hundred brokers and another entity to be responsible to, several actually, for one New York and if it came to that their own regional manager.

A substantial portion of this segment of the meeting was taken up with product information, how it worked mechanically within itself and how it acted in the investors account. There were also several relationships these fellows would have to develop that needed to be touched on. It had been mentioned on several occasions by both Henry and Clem that we had to make sure everyone knew what they were getting themselves in to. The new West Coast crowd needed this instruction the most, while the more assured (and established) East Coast group could group could use the review. It would be their job to stay in touch with branch managers for example. This was somewhat informal, nonetheless they had to make contact with branch managers once or twice a year, more if there were problems or situations. When this Regional Sales Coordinator job was taken seriously there were plenty of reasons to stay in touch with branch managers that could improve production considerably. I would say that half the group would simply put the information out there, go through the motions and take whatever sales turned up while the other half pushed every lever they could. This was partially true in the east where sales of unit trusts were naturally more prolific, although time would eventually catch up with the slackers.

In terms of relationship development besides the branch manager there had to be regular contact with a branch office sales coordinator; someone in the office who regularly sold the product and kept in touch with the department because he or she had to. It was natural then for other salesman in the branch to ask this person a question if they had some interest in unit trusts or some inquiry about them. It was his name then, that would be given to our Regional Rep by the branch manager to stay in touch with.

This individual dubbed the branch office sales coordinator, was our regional coordinators's contact in the branch would be required to mention what was going on (with the product) at weekly branch meetings, to collect indications of interest in the branch and to stay in touch with his branch manager on a hot deal or with any difficulty or important policy changes and so on. Again, it wasn't a terrible burden because this fellow was usually a regular seller of unit trusts and he had to keep up anyway. Often the more enhanced contact usually improved his performance in the products sales. There was no express compensation other than if a specific inquiry came from a phone call to the branch or if a lead came through this fellow got it. Some branch managers would set aside monies for a mailing or a product seminar for these office coordinators as a reward for their service to the branch.

Along with this PR contact as I call it with branches there was a protocol regarding the announcement of new issues and the taking of indications of interest. If we had a new municipal trust announced on Monday at 2 PM with indications of interest required by noon on Tuesday, the regional sales coordinator or his assistant or secretary was obligated to make calls to his branches and get back to us within this time frame. Individual branch and a total regional commitment was required. It wasn't a guessing game although if you did it for a while you got good at it; but more often than not each branch had to be called with the announcement and the details and had to tell you how many units they thought they were going to sell. In a typical region of 20 branches that was 40 calls, depending on how you got your guys to respond. If your branches were trained to respond to messages sent over the wire they might do so accordingly, if not you had to make the calls. All this might have been overwhelming for the run of the mill broker, but the group before us were a seasoned lot. Most of them made a decent if not a high level of income and were very well-organized and already had or shared full-time secretaries or administrative assistants who would help with the phone work. There was also provision for the UIT department to pay some stipend to the branch for clerical support, use of space and phone usage. While you couldn't put a piker in this position, it wasn't that difficult to master either. I think between Clem and myself and on occasion Frank Cullum coming into the conversation, we did a better than adequate job of getting across what life would be like day to day between New York Unit Trusts and our newly formed Regional Sales Group and the branches they served.

Other topics were thrown out onto the floor as well. For example, a major sticking point brokers have with investments like bonds and unit trusts has to do with statement pricing. Even if there is no market movement a unit trust investment with an initial cost of $1015.00, that had a 3.5% sales charge will be valued at $980 on the investors next monthly statement. Investors bristle at this, interpreting the loss as bad advice or poor market timing on the brokers part or in extreme cases as having been fooled or cheated. Brokers in turn have trouble overcoming this objection or explaining this phenomenon away. This may be because they have some guilt about the fact that most of that 3.5% is commission. Clients on the other hand, don't realize how unfair their angry indignation is. Such securities are invested in for the long haul, however their initial cost is accessed in the short term. If a broker explained the investment properly (even though clients may not listen to these mentioning's of long term and amortization) the investor should understand that the charges will be ameliorated over the ten or twelve-year term of the investment.

On more occasions than we might think, greed is at work on both sides of the transaction. The broker is greedy for the commission the sale will bring. This is understandable, and it is the reason why client "suitability" for any investment must be established before making that investment for the client. The investors greed on the other hand takes the form of elation at the prospect of earning such a high yield and thus he is not listening or fully engaged in listening to the facts about the long-term nature of the security, the cost of the security in monetary terms or market risk. Brokers often take advantage of this non-engagement, thinking they can explain away this stuff later and often get away with it. Selective hearing on the part of investors regarding risk and cautionary provisions is a well-documented and a notorious hazard in the business. This is why taking notes on the specifics of client conversations has become a requirement in many firms.

The sales charge covers the cost of putting the investment together including accounting and legal fees, commission and profit. Some brokers overcome this objection or put this answer in more practical and perhaps more combative terms by asking if the client questions his grocer as to the underlying profit on a head of lettuce or a container of milk. Further did the client question his Mercedes dealer on the 15% drop in value of his MX 300 the day after he drove it off the lot. Whether they knew it or not, we knew that bringing up these topics went a long way toward giving these fellows a way to answer these questions themselves once they got back and up and running as proponents of the firm's investment products. The more they were able to answer these questions in the field, the less we would have to in New York.

Someone said, "You guys are Ham and Eggs." And then, when can you come out on the road in my region?" That statement was a commitment to the job and a signal that we had accomplished our objective.

Yes, we were, we did ham and egg it. Despite on and off petty disputes and differences of personality and opinions, Clem and I were a great and talented team. We played off each other in a way that was both enthusiastic and knowledgeable and at the same time serious and sensible, as well as light and humorous, in any case as light and humorous as one could be discussing such matters. Yes, there was a lot of detail and because of all this detail the one thing that was important to make clear (especially for the new-comers) was that we had their backs, that we would back them up when times got tough and that we knew what we were doing and could handle any situation that might arise.

It might have appeared rehearsed, but it was not. We had near four years of sitting next to each other to develop our "act" as Clem called it. If anything, we had briefly talked the performance over, but it was something or akin to what we did every day in the office. Perhaps Clem had planned how it would flow because he knew I usually deferred to him and picked up on his cue. Later when we talked over this session we felt that our mission had been accomplished. We had begun to impart a vast body of knowledge that would be ongoing; we had stimulated further conversation among the group that brought their collective talent and knowledge out into the open to be shared and perhaps most important left the definite impression that the department in New York especially the three guys out front driving the bus so to speak knew what they were about. I got the distinct impression as well that Henry was immensely pleased with our presentation. There was an almost palpable warmth that emanated from him toward myself and Clem and the entire group actually. At least I felt that way.

By the time the meeting was over I was exhausted and so were my colleagues. Clem, Henry, Frank and myself had been "on and up" since Wednesday or Thursday although I think the others might have been more measured in how they were involved emotionally. The never-ending listening, talking, making notes and compiling of an endless "to do" list had worn me out, while eating and drinking much too much had taken its toll as well. I went home, rested up on the weekend and went back to work loaded for bear on Monday.

Chapter 68

Short Term CD Trusts Take Over

By the spring/summer of 1980, we would be doing at least one deal a week of short-term CD trusts, running at a volume of ten to fifteen million dollars a week. To be sure, we continued underwriting all the other products—municipals, GNMAs, and corporates; however, at 50–75 percent of our normal capacity even though they had hefty yields. Yields in the corporate market, for example, showcased in our Corporate Bond Long Term Series that had looked good at 9.5 percent less than a year ago, were now deep under water with the current trusts yielding near 12 percent. Notwithstanding these increased yields and previous underwritings valued lower, unit trust offerings were very competitive. Each underwriting captured the highest yields during the time frame we underwrote, while other forms of packaging bonds (mutual funds) with yields that were amalgams of previously bought lower yielding securities, could not compete.

Where the joint account combined couldn't sell ten million dollars' worth in the first week of the existence of Short Term Series 9, back in the fall of 1979, we were now doing fifty million dollars' worth a week and sometimes seventy-five million. In 1980, we would underwrite between sixty and seventy short-term CD trusts producing enormous revenue. A $75 million deal, of which we sold on average $12 million worth and sometimes $15 million, would produce about $1.50 per unit net for the department in our accounts and $4 per unit in sales commission, of which more than $2 was recovered by the firm. At this point in time, every week, from short-term trusts alone, the firm collected something more than $40,000, annualizing at $2 million a year from short-term securities alone, and this was just the beginning and a low point.

Early on it was decided that we would have to familiarize stockbrokers and investors on the methodology of the yield calculation for the short-term CD trusts. It may be shocking for us to realize that for many investors and stockbrokers alike, yield is a phenomena taken for granted. Taken for granted of course except in cases where it appears to be specious, as it did in the case of our CD trusts. The tendency then is to shun the investment rather than to try and wade through its logic which is admittedly often a daunting task, for the novice or non-professional.

The yield calculation offered for CD trusts was quite simple and understandable and proved correct in every case. After we calculated it for brokers a hundred times a day for six months, it finally became common, acceptable knowledge, and was a major breakthrough in its contribution to sales. So here it is. The yield calculation that launched the sale of thirty billion dollars' worth of securities, most of which was transferred from local banks to brokerage firms and never returned.

Income - Premium X 365 ÷ 182

Public Offering Price

For example:
61.35 - 7.25 X 365 ÷ 182

$$\frac{61.35 - 7.25 \times 365 \div 182}{1{,}007.25} = 10.77\%$$

The equation reduces the investment income by the premium paid over par ($1000), then multiplied by 365 to annualize the calculation (yield is an annual expression) and then divided by 182 to introduce the investments actual duration (maturity) and finally divided by the public offering price. The introduction of this calculation and continued demonstration of it was immensely important to the legitimization of the investment. It made clear that the sales charge of 0.75 percent was adequately accounted for in the calculation of the yield.

Nearly every short-term CD trust that came to market was advertised somewhere. The *New York Times* or the *Wall Street Journal* or both carried quarter page tombstones and occasionally a full-page ad. Merrill was not shy about this advertising or the money it cost the joint-account because it wasn't just about advertising investment banking, underwriting deals, profits and commissions. It was about gathering assets from other institutions and developing and captivating an audience that had still more whopping amounts of money at those same institutions just waiting to be put into utility stocks, GNMAs, or municipals. You get the picture. Periodically, every second or third deal, the ad was placed in ten or twelve major city newspapers like the *Philadelphia Enquirer, Miami Herald, Cleveland Plain Dealer,* the *Chicago Tribune,* and so on. These ads were like thunderclaps resonating with brokers, branch managers, bankers, and brokerage firm managements across the country. Our clients would see the Dean Witter Reynolds name and a New York address under an advertised yield. Many brokers reported to us that the ads were often a claion call to their own clients who would call them and ask "What's this" or "Why haven't you called me about it?"

The same happened at the other firms in the deals. Clients of firms not in the deal would call their brokers about it too and ask them to find out about it. Bank clients would call their bankers and ask why they couldn't offer a CD with this kind of yield. Believe me, trying to explain the Federal Reserve's Regulation T prohibitions on banking institutions just didn't cut it. Who knows what the banks were thinking, but one remark stuck in my mind, which was sort of disgusting but close to the distress many were feeling. Somebody said Robert Foman the reportedly stern and volatile CEO of EF Hutton, has a goiter every time he sees one of these ads. I used to think EF Hutton might have petitioned Norman to get into the deal, but apparently, they never did. Some time later E F Hutton became a very good dealer client of ours who had been cultivated by Peggy Brennan. Dealer clients bought units from us at discounts and sold them to investors through their sales forces.

The CIF short-term CD trust ads gave a phone number for each firm in the deal and an address for those investors who were inclined to fill out a coupon and mail it in instead of calling. We all thought that allowing the advertising agencies call center to take our calls from these ads would cause too much delay during which the investors' "ardor" might cool. We also felt that many of our calls might inadvertently or otherwise go to Merrill. To create a more timely response, meaning that our firm would respond to a telephone call with a telephone call, we decided our New Issue Desk 800 number would be inserted into the ads. We took the calls in the office, logged them in a notebook, and turned them around almost immediately to local branch offices. No help from computers in those days. We used Rand McNally Road Atlases to find our closest branch to the caller's location and gave the lead over to the branch manager of that office. Sometimes if we knew a broker in an office was doing a lot of our product, we'd give him or her the lead on the QT. Needless to say leads, the names of potential clients, the names of people who call in about investing are very valuable. So we tried to handle these leads judiciously. Sometimes we'd go to the trouble to find out who the branch office unit trust coordinator was and give it to him or her, or give it to the regional coordinator to give the lead away or keep it and work it to try to close it themselves. Responders to the ads who didn't wish to call circled the brokerage firm of their choice on the ad, filled out the blank, and mailed it in. These we began to receive about eight to ten days after the ad was placed.

The ad agencies sent us several hundred 8.5" x 11" copies of the ads printed on glossy paper with the coupon at the bottom showing only our name. We turned these around piecemeal for a while to selected brokers, and later got the printers to make them to the tune of a hundred thousand every two weeks and we distributed them all around the country to be used as flyers and mailers.

By the summer of 1980, I had taken to staying late two or three nights each week until closing to six and sometimes later. I was working at a furious pace, and I used to cool down a bit during this time before taking the train. On most nights, I caught a very convenient train that left Penn Station at six thirty, getting into Oceanside about seven twenty, and although a little late, it was far from the crowds that packed the subways between five and six. I liked to relax and linger a bit after the phones slacked off. Sometimes I stayed even later just to get my desk and thoughts in order for the following day, using the time to clear all the crap I accumulated—firm memos, operations notices, articles I had read or wanted to read, scraps of paper with notes on them, and on and on. I was a pack rat, always in fear of throwing away some important piece of information. On these evenings, the calls from people responding to the ads continued to trickle in, and as I was there, I'd pick them up. On one of the nights, around six thirty, I had a conversation with a prospect that went something like this:

"Pat Scida, Unit Trusts"

"Is this Dean Witter?"

"Yes. I'm sorry, yes, this is Dean Witter. Are you calling about the ad on—"

"Are you in Cleveland? If you are, you're working late?"

"No, sir, I'm in New York, working late as you say. Why do you ask?"

"It's always good to know who and where you're talking to."

"I can agree with that."

"Can you answer a few questions about this short-term thing in the papers?"

"Sir, if you give me your name and number, I'll have one of our representatives call you at a convenient time."

"No, no, never mind. That's exactly what I don't want."

"Well, sir, I don't understand."

"I don't want to get into a situation where someone invites me downtown or offers to come out to my house to see me to sell me something or hustle me. I want to decide on my own without being pushed. Is this thing any good?" he said then in a half angry, half incredulous tone. I started to laugh then, and he said, "Young man, I don't think this is a joking matter."

"Nor do I sir, nor do I, but let me suggest again that we have several offices in the Cleveland area that have been there for a long time with a long list of clients who might recommend them. There are many highly experienced customers' men in those offices, and I can put you in touch with one of the branch managers if you like."

"Why can't you answer a question or two before we do that?"

"Because I'm more of an internal marketing and sales operative than a customers' man who deals with individual investors. Stockbrokers have the training to deal with the public."

"Can't you make an exception in this case? Please?"

Now I'm warming up to the guy and I'm a bit curious, so I say, "Okay, why not."

He went on to ask why such yields were not available at the local savings and loan in West Shore, Ohio (a suburb about twenty miles west of Cleveland), or any of the major banks in the greater Cleveland area for that matter. He asked if it was true as some bank employees had told him Merrill Lynch was deliberately misstating the guarantee of the CDs and misrepresenting the banks. He wanted to know what the charges were and had other questions. which I answered as best I could. We were on the phone for fifteen or twenty minutes and parted very amicably, talking about the Cleveland Browns who were a pretty hot team at the time. The next day I called the branch manager of our Cleveland office and briefly filled him in on the lead. He shifted me over to a broker who he felt would be able to handle a somewhat "high maintenance" prospect. A few weeks later this broker called me with regards from the investor who had now become his client.

The investor, it turned out, had about five months earlier received a pension settlement from JC Penny of nearly $175,000, which had to be rolled over within six months of the date it was received or it would become taxable income. He was so afraid that he was going to be swindled and so confused as to whether he should invest in stocks or bonds or both that he hadn't done anything with the settlement at all except deposit the check in his bank account in a six month CD. It turned out both the bank and his former employer had given him papers about the possible tax liability, but he had not actually understood what was at stake. He was frozen by his inability to make a decision and get some advice, and he had avoided conversation about the money he had received with anyone, not even an attorney or an accountant who would have steered him to a broker anyway. Had he not put himself in the hands of an experienced stockbroker, it would have cost him dearly.

The ad campaign on the Corporate Income Fund Short-Term Series run by Merrill Lynch with and for the Joint Sponsors was in itself a prospecting campaign and a good one with an enormously attractive and beneficial investment to investors who might have kept their money in the bank at 5 percent when they could keep it with us, just as safe at 10 percent plus while paying a modest fee that was well made up for in the yield. It was as simple as that. This ad and the security it represented and the many that would follow, were a catalyst in the movement of many billions of dollars of capital out of the banking system in the United States and into its brokerage firms. Later brokerage firm money market funds like Intercapital Liquid Assets and cash management accounts, like Merrill's CMA Account and later Dean Witters AAA Account would be the devices that firmly held on to this money after its transfer. In fact in 1984 Clem and I at Dean Witter Reynolds would introduce and market a $20 million Issuance of CD's of the Greenwood Savings and Loan in California (a Sears owned bank) at a yield of 14%. That would be just 2 weeks after Merrill Lynch underwrote and marketed the first brokered CD ever. We continued to market CD's in unprecedented amounts side by side with unit trusts throughout the eighties. What I'm saying is that in my opinion the migration of capital caused in part by our Corporate Income Fund Short Term CD Trusts and the advent of the money market funds took so much money out of the banking system that the banks finally had to turn to the brokerage firm community to raise money. As I have said often as well; that story is one for another book.

As 1980 wore on, the yields on our Short-Term CD Trusts continued to rise as did the yields on all fixed income securities. By the late summer/early fall weekly sales were in the $30-35 million-dollar range at Dean Witter on deals reaching $125 to $150 million in total size. This was a weekly event and living with it was a heady experience. The trickier commitments were at what I called the corners, i.e. the .25, .50 and .75 or the 1/4, 1/2 and 3/4 points along the scale 10.25, 10.50 and so on. As interest rates rose through these points that investors and brokers had been watching and mulling over as to when to invest, they made decisions, especially when a move to one of these points was close or actually went over it. I willed myself to become a student of this phenomena and I could feel it just by the temper of the telephone volume. I had also become close to the buyers of the underlying securities in these deals at Merrill. Particularly because Clem was a close friend of Larry Keating, a Rockville Center resident and member of the South Shore Bond Club and perhaps the father of the modern corporate bond business. Keating, the buyer of the CD's that were in the short term portfolios, as well as all the corporate and preferred stocks for all the taxable portfolios. Larry was in his mid seventies at the time, quite forceful and robust and very fond of Clem, who he looked upon as a protégé from their previous associations. Larry was a Rockville Centre resident and member of the South Shore Bond Club and had been a partner at Goodbody. At one time, the fifties through the sixties, Larry and the afore mentioned Bill Marlin, another of Clem's mentors might have been considered the founders of the modern corporate bond industry. I attended weekly luncheons at Harry's with Larry and Clem and sometimes Bob Volpe one of the marketing and service operatives and perhaps my counterpart at Merrill. In this way we kept up with markets, the general warp and woof of the underwriting and legal side of the operation and the gossip at Merrill. Beside this it gave me and Clem an ongoing inside view of what the thinking was at Merrill as to future deal size, the constraints they were dealing with on the regulatory side especially with the SEC and the Fed who were both trying to find a way to limit the underwritings.

The new year 1980 began with yields in the 10 to 11 percent range and would end in the 14 to 15% range. When the handles changed, meaning when we went from 11.9 % to 12.05 or 12.95 went to 13.10 percent it was, as the saying goes a "fuggeddaboudit" moment. A near insanity broke out in the sales organization that was a struggle to control, to get ones arms around. It seemed to grip everyone at times in one way or another. It was a feeding frenzy in the sales force which was my concern. I learned to be calm about it, by holding back several millions of dollars of inventory. If I was awarded $32 million, I'd say I got only 28 or 29 to everyone, Clem and Henry included until somewhere in the spring they figured it out. This allowed me to adjudicate problems that occurred in the ticketing process too numerous to mention: system jam ups, wire operator errors, closing down ticketing abruptly and on and on. The fact that the world was coming to an end was Clem's problem, his and Henry Kaufman's and Al Wojinower's, nicknamed Dr. Death and Dr. Doom. These were Wall Street analysts at Solomon Brothers and First Boston who weekly predicted some form of financial Armageddon meltdown. I didn't know enough, I didn't look at it intellectually or historically, I just held back several millions of dollars in inventory as I said, and made nice to everybody after the deal closed and in so doing kept the wolves at bay and remained sane enough to meet the challenge of the next deal.

I was aware that what I was asking for at these yield points or surges in sales were often milestones in our takedowns. I lobbied Clem constantly keeping him apprised of what was going on for two reasons. Clem being conservative to a fault was the tougher one to convince that sales were going to match my proposed commitments and secondly because I relied on his input with Norman at Merrill to get me the inventory. In the end Norman was the final arbiter. It was a weird dance we did because we were at eighteen percent of the underwriting profits of these deals and we wanted it to stay that way. If I didn't sell out my commitments and returned units to Merrill too often because I couldn't sell them, I put that eighteen percent in jeopardy. I pushed hard and I think I was lucky, but at the same time I believe I saw and understood the phenomena of the time that some may have missed. That we were in a new time, that there was a capacity for sales at Dean Witter Reynolds that had not been tapped yet and that we'd gotten a glimpse of in the GNMA deal. That capacity and capability was now combining with a new willingness for money to leave savings accounts and banks and the fact that at this point our product was the link. It was better than anything the bank could offer, and the advertising and the 20000 brokers represented by the joint account out there selling and explaining it to the public every day was unmatchable. The banks were simply helpless.

I mentioned instincts earlier, certainly I relied on them because to say this period was anything short of rapid fire is an understatement. Short Term deals every four or five business days with four or five others (municipals, corporates etc.) always open and/or closing and another taking its place: systems breaking down, questions from the field, from Henry, hiring new people, conference calls, writing marketing material, gathering indications of interest, sales training appearances and on and on. Toward the end of 1980 we were traveling at the thirty to thirty-five million dollar a week level on CD trusts with rollovers of previous trusts to contend with in addition to new sales in addition to the fifteen to twenty odd millions of Municipals, Corporates and GNMA's we were selling. Remember GNMA's were at the 13 percent level, Municipals at 13 to 14 percent corporates at 16 percent. At some point in 1980 we began to suggest to brokers that they suggest to investors to convert some of the proceeds of maturing CD Trusts into municipal or Corporate Bond unit trusts.

What can I say at this point? I was a guy who had been banging out dents a decade before in a body and fender shop. I was Joseph the Israelite buried in a well in a hole in the ground and ten years later guardian of the granaries of Egypt. I was Indiana Jones just going along with the story, making it up day by day, figuring out how I was supposed to act.

Chapter 69

New Digs and Continued Chaos

Toward the middle of 1980, amid enormous success, on multiple levels; profitability, volume of sales, popularity in the sales organization, multiple successful introduction of new products into the sales organization, we moved to new quarters in 130 Liberty Street on the twenty-seventh floor. They were newly constructed offices on the west side of the building with a great view of the Hudson River. The new issue and secondary desks were side by side and split by an eight or ten foot ramped entryway. Together, they totaled about thirty workspaces that were bathed in light most of the day but rarely got direct sunlight. It was a very comfortable place to work in because whenever you walked in or got up to stretch your legs, you got a great view of the river, New Jersey, and Watchung Hills. Just after we moved, a new hire, Peggy Brennan, joined the New Issue Desk. Henry asked us to hire her. She was a friend of Angela Cincerelli, Henry's secretary, and had been a secretary herself for some of the Reynolds salesmen before the merger. She wanted out of the new municipal setup. Another new hire was a fellow called Hugh McPartland. Hugh, a former institutional salesman on the equity side, had been hired to develop a dealer sales operation. Interestingly enough, when Hugh left, Peggy took over and made a great success of dealer sales.

The unit trust regional coordinator group had gradually fallen into a routine as it got comfortable with the day to day flow of information and communication with their sales forces and us in New York. We had several new hires on new issues and the secondary desk and had a new telephone system installed as well. All of this gelled by the third quarter of 1980 with volume regularly reaching $60 million a week and sometimes more. I stopped being concerned with logging in weekly and monthly totals because the individual components of the volume, were overwhelming. A long term corporate deal with an astounding yield announced in the middle of getting indications and ticketing an upcoming $250 short term trust. On the same day toward four in the afternoon, a California Municipal Trust is announced, compelling the desk to turn west and announce the deal, set it up on our books, inform the coast, besides putting prices into the system for the two or three live deals that were ticketing and selling. By November $250 million short term trusts were coming every four to five days driving volume to unspeakable levels; remember we were now accommodating rollovers of previously underwritten trusts, plus new money which drove volume and profitability to nearly unspeakable levels.

As we were not automated, the "paper" trade-ticket volume was enormous. Stack upon stack of trade tickets were brought in from the wire room after being ripped off the machines to be sorted by issue and counted. Average ticket size was fifteen thousand dollars, so there could be thirty-five hundred to forty-five hundred trade tickets to be sorted and totaled and noted in a typical week. There was no mechanized sorting of tickets or order in which they were received. A particular problem were orders for longer term trusts and secondary market orders getting mixed in with the overwhelming preponderance of CIF Short Term order tickets. Despite these handicaps getting this sorting and tabulating process done in a timely fashion every day, hourly even was important for obvious reason i.e. estimating sales, formulating takedowns and knowing when to cut off ticketing. So, we answered phones, sorted and counted and answered still more phones, constantly mulling over and discussing commitments and being swept away emotionally by the ever changing higher yield expectations.

I used to run downstairs to the lobby for coffee and a Danish or a jelly doughnut two or three times a day, sugar and caffeine kept my energy up and my temper in check. One afternoon around three, in the middle of a raucous week I ran into Stretch Gardiner and

Dave Cariseo. Both were cordial and Stretch asked what going on. Because Dave was a bit of a rival of Henry's I decided to let them know. Normally I would have said same ole same ole and that would have been that, but I felt like jazzing them up a bit and in any case, everything I said was true.

"The ticketing is wild and sometimes surges, backing up the system and sometimes causing it to shut down. The problem is that in the past couple of days the yield levels have jumped more than a 1/4 of a percent from 13.30-35 to 13.60-13.70, more than 25 basis points so I think the deal were supposed to do on Friday will be cut off and done Thursday. We'll fill it and then just start taking orders for the next one.

"Why?" They asked, captive now to the story.

"Well at this rate the deal could go to 300 million, we've never been in that range before. I'm not sure but I think the logistics of buying the deal change when you get up that high. I think Merrill is worried the market might back away from these levels. It's just too confusing to try and communicate these fast changes in yield to the sales organizations not to mention the risk, better to fill this deal quickly and start anew on Friday."

Now this all came to pass in a thirty second ride up the escalator and another minute or so elevator ride to the 27th floor at which point I got off and in three minutes I'm back on the phone with half the Danish gone and a cigarette burning in my ash tray. Ten minutes later someone yells.

"Pat, Clem and Henry on 28." Whatever? So I pick up the phone and after hello and what's going on, Henry says,

"What the hell did you do to Stretch and Cariseo?"

"Nothing really, I just told them what's going on here, maybe I pumped some drama into it. Man! News travels fast around here."

They passed Henry's office coming back from lunch, your Stretches' hero of the week." Clem said.

"They can't believe you weren't jumping out of your skin." Henry said.

"That's because they couldn't see inside his head," Clem added.

"Just another day in Mayberry." I said.

"Your doing great Scida," says Henry, and then to Clem with the sound of his voice trailing away, "speaking of heads I thought Dave's was going to expl…." Click.

Just as it was back when I was a comparison clerk at Eastman Dillon in 1969 it was kind of primitive by today's standards to be tabulating paper orders by hand, but again, in 1980, there were no desktop computers, not on our desks anyway, much less an intranet that connected the firm's communications systems. Bunker Ramo was static, nonfluid information. We tested several ideas and theories. Clem experimented with a theory about weighing tickets and taking a reading by weighing twenty to fifty tickets like a cashier weighs pennies or quarters to get a count at the end of the day. I used to try to read sales by measuring volume of sales over ten-minute, twenty-minute, and half hour intervals, collecting and tabulating all orders received within certain time frames and taking an average or multiplying to gauge what sales might be at one- and two-hour intervals. Neither theory proved to be a solution nor in any way a viable or trustworthy method to avoid counting and totaling the actual paper tickets. The grapevine was the better gauge, the sense you got from the sheer volume of tickets coming in, the volume of phone calls, communications with the regional sales people and conversations with key brokers. I got this because it was what I did and it didn't make much difference if I was off a few million because sales velocity was so high that Merrill would eat up any overage or as I did in most cases I would hold a million or two until the next deal and then dump the overage into the secondary market to Al Stevens who sold them off in a flash anyway. If some loss was incurred it was minor and meaningless and negligible because overall the money we were earning was overwhelming.

Chapter 70

Underwriters Distribution Control

Time literally flew by in 1980 because so many things were going on. Deal after deal came and went printing a higher yield than the one before. The market was fueled by huge increases in money supply measured by M1 and M2 statistics announced weekly portending still higher inflation. Dr. Doom and Dr. Death, economists and market gurus Henry Kaufman of Solomon Brothers and Al Wojinaur of First Boston continued to predict the end of the financial world and economy at least once a week in the newspapers. Through all of this we toiled day after day. After lengthy petitioning of management, we began meeting with a group from the systems and programming division of operations to devise a program, an application of some kind, that would automate our ability through the wire system to more easily tabulate sales and distribute inventory into the sales organization, and also give us an automated capability to electronically price and execute the business. Clem knew in his bones this was possible and, he and Henry had fought for these considerations against a Dean Witter crowd that was resistant and reluctant to help us. But that wasn't my job, and I really wasn't privy to what they were doing other than having some peripheral knowledge of the subject and some of the political machinations that Clem let me in on.

The first delegation sent to discuss our needs was a group of young fellows who seemed to want to dictate to us what they were going to do before we even got a chance to introduce what we felt our needs were or even explained the way the product and our business operated. I was part of this meeting and was told to keep quiet and let Clem handle the first bit of communication. In a meeting in which Clem and I thought we were going to be listened to about the business we were in, it seemed as though we were being told what our options were and that any systems we might need would not come on line for at least a year. It seemed to be a brushoff. We came out of the meeting quite skeptical as to the abilities of these guys but we came to the conclusion that it was more of a case that we didn't seem to be speaking the same language. A few days later, a second shorter meeting had similar results. A week or two passed without any news or comment about systems and then one afternoon, late, around four or so, Clem came out to the desk and said I had to meet with someone regarding the development of a new automated ticketing system.

"When?" I said.

"Tonight. We really need to talk to this guy,"

"Sounds like a pretty quick pitch to me. Jesus, Clem, how long have you known about this?"

"It's offline. Henry just set it up through Gardiner, and he thinks it's a stroke of luck for us. He's a formers Reynolds systems guy, and you have to give it a shot."

"Me?"

"We, I said."

"No, you said you!"

"Yes, but I meant we."

"Okay," I said, scratching my head. "Who is this guy?"

"His name is Henry Schlanger. Ever heard of him?"

"I think so, vaguely," I said.

Around five fifteen, with the day wound down, the office emptying out, and me wanting to wind down, Schlanger arrived, and Clem and I went into the conference room where we introduced ourselves. I remembered his face from my days in DECAB at 2 Broadway. I never knew what he did, but in subsequent years, I learned of his intimate and vast knowledge of the firm's systems. The story was he could write programming, install it, tweak, and test it as well, and probably better than most. Most importantly, he understood the brokerage side of the business and could translate its practice into his work, an art form at the time much less prevalent than it is today. That anything and everything was programmable was much less generally understood or believable at that time. To some of my friends from the Reynolds organization, Henry was a legend, a little wacky, nonetheless a legend.

One couldn't tell if Henry Schlanger was forty-five or sixty-five, even though he had a full head of silver hair, combed neatly with a lock or wave that curled forward and sort of bounced up and down impishly as he walked. He wore thick rimless glasses and appeared to have large clear and always smiling (or surprised looking) eyes. He might have been a sort of cleaned up Albert Einstein with eyes of a lighter color and a neater coif. He was slight to me but might have had a medium build. He had a penchant for light colored suits, often plaids. He loved to have fun and laughed breathlessly and eccentrically at jokes, repeating the punch line with a joyous near maniacal look on his face. He was widely learned in many subjects, very aware of current affairs and, much to my liking, thoroughly schooled in classical music which he said he loved to play as loud as possible on a very expensive stereo system. He was born and raised in the heavily Jewish Lower East Side, had a son from a first marriage, and was rumored to once having had a nervous breakdown. He was currently married to a much younger second wife and had a young daughter, Sarah I believe, whom he idolized.

It was also rumored that it was Henry Schlanger who saved the firm terrible embarrassment and probably countless dollars lost early in its newly merged life by reversing a duplicate payment of an entire months dividends worth more than ten million dollars. Doubtless this is one of the incidents contributing to the Schlanger legend. Everything described about him, except the fact that I had seen him around before, was learned or observed subsequent to that first meeting Clem brought me into, a meeting by the way, the bastard (Clem that is) snuck out of not more than three minutes after it began, a meeting that shortly became somewhat unpleasant, which of course Clem knew would happen beforehand, that's why he left.

Schlanger had placed a wooden stool about eight feet from a grease board at the front of the conference room and mentioned casually something about needing information about unit trusts. I knew the reason I was there had to do with systems development as Clem mentioned, but Henry did not explain or elaborate. He just stood between the board and me with a yellow pad in one hand and a red pen in the other, and after maneuvering me into this little set up, he said something like, "What is a unit trust?"

"It's a closed portfolio of securities."

"Like a mutual fund?

"Yes, somewhat similar but different."

"How?"

"They (unit trusts) are finite and separate portfolios of securities that function independently on their own."

"So are closed-end mutual funds."

The questions were asked with a great intensity of interest and almost as if it was an interrogation in which my intention would be to deceive him. Perhaps it was my imagination, but I do remember it to be an uncomfortable encounter.

"Yes, but closed-end mutual funds have management and expense fees and can be enormous. Most unit trusts are closed off at twenty or thirty million, and they trade and travel through the firm more like an individual security rather than an investment company, but they are definitely an investment company."

"Meaning?"

"Meaning? Meaning just what I said. Unit trusts are an investment company, but they tend to act like or live in the firm like the security they are composed of."

"Meaning?"

Meaning that they live in the firm like their underlying security might live in the firm. For example, a municipal unit trust can be registered in an investors name and be delivered, It has an annual income and can be tax swapped like a bond and used as collateral for a loan or margin. A GNMA Unit Trust acts like a GNMA it has a…"

"I got it, good. Now where do they come from?"

"What's that supposed to mean?"

"The unit trusts you distribute, sell here in the firm, where do they come from?"

"Heaven."

"Heaven!" Maniacal laugh, weird throaty noise, sound of slobbering. "Heaven." And then heaven repeated again with a question mark inflected, and then again with an eastern European accent and then calming down. "No kidding, heaven. Ha-ha. Securities created in heaven. Are they divine?" Laughing again. "Pretty good, huh? Divine. Ha-ha. Get it?" Things lightened up a bit, but Schlanger went back to the intense questioning. "Seriously now where do we get them in heaven?"

"Well, we are part of an organized group, a syndicate of firms, who 'sponsor' the construction and incorporation of 'investment companies' called unit investment trusts. Merrill Lynch is the leading sponsor who initiates the accumulation of their portfolios of securities, which the members finance according to their percentage participation in the syndicate. The securities are usually bonds of different classes purchased and then legally formed into an investment company that is represented in many ways—by legal documentation and by prospectus and registration with the states securities boards and the SEC. Then certificates of beneficial interest, which are the actual evidence of the security and their collective income…"

"Okay, okay, good. Now when and how is the security introduced into…?"

"Well, when a deal is announced, we…"

It took about a half hour to get to this point and we went on for at least another hour, maybe an hour and a half, until near eight o'clock when we finally quit with a cryptic and minutely detailed timeline of a typical deal outlined on the grease board. In addition to this, Schlanger's yellow pad was filled with fifteen or twenty pages of alternately filled or scratched out or heavily underlined observations of every miniscule twist and turn the unit trust security might take within the firm's trade processing and accounting system during its life as a new issue. By this time, we were both a little tired, and my attitude toward Henry had become a little skewed. On the one hand, I liked him. He was terrifically knowledgeable and intelligent and funny. Despite the wild look in his eyes, I thought he was okay, but I had been tempted more than several times during the interview to bash him over the head with the wooden stool I was sitting on. He was pushy, distrusting, and borderline sarcastic. He had an annoying penchant for asking the same question over and over and then a few minutes after he had already gotten the answer twice, he asked the question again.

Oddly enough, this meeting was the beginning of a great relationship and friendship with Henry. Not just with me but with Clem as well. It was never a personal relationship where we visited outside the office, but nonetheless, Henry Schlanger who seemed uncomfortable being with most people was very comfortable with Clem and myself. Perhaps partly because we were Reynolds people but also because we saw Henry not through what he appeared to be but for what he was. In a word, a terrific, thorough, and selflessly hard worker, a great practitioner of his art and work, and a very, very decent man. In later years, he explained to me that in interviews such as our first encounter and in extended additional interviews about such business procedures, people often lied or simply made things up when they didn't know the answers to his questions. They felt they were being tested or that they would appear foolish if they didn't know an answer. Thus, he had resorted to a carping interviewing style that proved the facts from several different directions and hence the belligerent tenor of our first meeting. He also spoke of the terrible treatment he encountered at the hands of Dean Witter management at the outset of the merger. Like many however, he prevailed while many Dean Witter personal faded.

What came of these meetings and Henry's eventual programming was the implementation of a system that was already operating in the firm processing the business of equity syndicate. It was known as UDC or Underwriters Distribution Control. For whatever reason, the Dean Witter side did not wish to have the system adapted for another product (read that as a competing product, unit trusts, or those guys from Reynolds).

In any case, when UDC was adapted for our use, which turned out to be a relatively easy transition, it allowed us to control our inventory electronically through the wire system in a way that could produce responses in the branches through allocation and pulling back unsold inventory. Whenever we did this, the system sent a printed wire communication to the branch detailing our action. This activity would of course both signal and produce sales velocity. For example, we would, at the outset of an underwriting, award a branch one hundred units, of which they might use (sell) twenty with eighty remaining. If the issue was selling well, we might pull back fifty of the remaining eighty, which would tend to signal the branch to get moving in the ticketing or sale of the remaining 30, implying of course that the remaining thirty might be pulled away as well.

Of course, we could query the system at will as to what sales were up to the moment. The Underwriters Distribution Control came on line for unit trusts in late 1980 early 1981, a great Christmas gift that relieved an enormous burden, although we often strained the capacity of the firm's systems. We added enormous volume of order flow, information traffic and tabulation from our business that often brought the system down, causing it to freeze sometimes for hours that could put us in the same pickle we were in when we didn't have it. But those early kinks were well worth it because we were running, between all products, between five and seven deals all the time. It would take a while but eventually the firm would iron out the kinks in the program.

One day, Andrew (Andy) Melton, appeared in the department. Clem wasn't around and neither was Frank although they may have been in their office off the sales and trading floor. Melton was around five foot ten, white haired with chiseled unsmiling serious features and an erect marine like posture. The department was full-on busy; pandemonium with every soul in the room on the phone and still more ringing. First, he looked out over the river and New Jersey on the far shore. He turned and observed the mayhem of activity in the room although he made no eye contact with anyone. Again, he turned toward the view for a few moments, seconds maybe, turned again, and walked out briskly. Later Clem came in, and before I could say anything, he said he'd heard Melton was in the department. I tried to make an excuse for not talking to him saying it was a complete surprise and that he came in and went out in under four minutes. Clem said not to worry about it. He probably preferred it that way.

A day or two later, Henry Arbeeny was in the department and pulled a chair over to sit between me and Clem, and I mentioned Melton was in.

Arbeeny replied, "He was impressed. He said we had quite a group down here. What did you do say to him?"

I said, "Didn't Clem tell you? Not a word. He was here about three minutes and didn't really look like he wanted to be approached, so I let it go for a while and he was gone."

Henry said, "Yes, that's his way."

The holidays passed, my bonus was very satisfactory, close to $50,000 if I remember right with the promise of a raise on my anniversary in April. Sometime in the latter half of January, we all went uptown one night for a Christmas party given by Henry. These were subdued affairs, dinner parties really in restaurants uptown on the East Side somewhere, in a private room or a closed off corner, almost like a family party and, again, always subdued and dignified, the kind of party and night out you'd expect from Henry.

Chapter 71

Uneasy Times

Clem never liked or shall we he wasn't a big Christmas or New Years fan. On the other hand I liked to take a few days off between the two Holidays and leave early on Christmas Eve and New Years eve because there was always family stuff going on which was OK with him. Clem usually came out of his year end holiday funk around January 10, but this year was different. He was always on edge and upset about the political state of affairs in the country as well as its economic woes. He abhorred Jimmy Carter and was happy that Ronald Reagan was elected and that the hostages had been released, but again his views were very pessimistic about everything, the economy, the country and most especially the firm. While he didn't reveal much about what upset him about the firm, he spent a lot of time with Henry who was privy to many of the inner workings of the firm and things that went wrong especially in the fixed income division and other risk areas. Henry could paint a pretty ugly picture of things while constructing a plan with which he could save the day. The problem with cluing Clem in on the challenges and difficulties the firm faced and Henry's ideas on how to solve them was that Clem focused in more of the problem than the proposed salvation.

Of course I don't know this to be true absolutely, but Clem had to be sourcing his bad feeling about the firms future from somewhere and that's my best guess. You must remember that Clem was a student of the market and the market at this time was a disaster. Long term investment grade municipal bonds were approaching the 15% yield level and Corporate's 17%, while long term US Government

Issues were in the high 14% range. Half or at least a third of the dealer book, the brokerage firms that had been in existence when Clem got into the business had disappeared. Many had morphed into other firms, none the less, they had too and were out of business. Guys who had been high flying traders in the sixties and seventies were driving taxis and Clem knew a few. So for some these times could feel like the end of times.

I on the other hand blissfully bumped along, concerned and serious but optimistic and enthusiastic as always. We were more organized and more efficient than ever before thanks to the installation of UDC. Still enormously busy, but controlling the mayhem adequately. By mid January yields on CD Trusts were above 15%. A new trust came about every four business days and our commitments regularly to $45- $50 million. On the day a short term trust came to market we could be holding $60 to $65 millions of inventory and even though the inventory was flying off the shelves these numbers rattled Clem. He was constantly in fear of some market meltdown or financial crisis that might erupt and hurt us badly. On the other hand, every CD deal sold out as fast as it came and at times our allotment of $50 million wasn't enough to stem the demand. Because interest rates had continued to rise the shine was off the apple regarding the surge in sales in longer term investments we'd seen in the fall of 1980. The CD trust was the only game in town now. I though that because of this we had less to worry about as the longer term inventory was diminished but it wasn't enough to cheer Clem up. It was clear that he had other things on his mind.

By the middle of March yields on CD Trusts had come near 16% and would exceed that and make a run at 17% in mid to late April. By this time we had done several three month deals at 18%. Ironically at this crucial moment Clem had scheduled a much put-off swing through California with Frank Cullum. Our California Regional Unit Trust guys had wanted him to come out for a while now to visit some of their branches and he was very interested in meeting the firms western regional Managers who were very close to Frank. I knew, I could read his body language, which told me he didn't want to go, but he'd put it off for so long that he had to.

By this time Clem's theory that some enormous calamity was going to befall the country or the economy or both led him to sell his Dean Witter Reynolds stock a week before the tip. I'm sure it was a substantial holding given that he was a senior vice president, with lengthy service to the firm and earning great money over the years. I think the price of the stock was around thirteen or fifteen. I can't remember what the price of the stock was at the merger although I believe it was substantially higher. I also think that had he not been planning this extended trip to the coast he might have held on longer.

Upon Clem's return, he was somewhat frazzled from jet lag and the fact that he had ran into many managers and stockbrokers who seemed (to him anyway) too casual by half about their work and their assessment of the times. He was particularly both appalled and amazed at the manager of our La Jolla office who was the leader of a local rock band that played around the area on weekends. To Clem, this was the height of frivolity, and he came home feeling that we were doomed as a firm, a conclusion that corroborated his decision to sell his stock. He said to me once, referring to Southern California, "All these young, blue-eyed, blond-haired, good looking, young people living in one of the most beautiful places that God ever created really don't have a clue."

I hardly knew what to say about his commentary on the West Coast offices of our firm. I kind of understood his feelings in a way and how he could feel that they were a little naive and maybe a little spaced out, but I couldn't take it as seriously as he did. He was in his early fifties and a generation ahead of me. It was common of his a generation back from me to look on mine with a little disdain. He inferred that he encountered some marijuana use, and this was a bad sign. I talked to these guys all the time. They were in my age group and seemed okay to me, although the use of marijuana never came up. The truth was that I heard many of these remarks in passing. I was too busy to weigh all these observations and nuances seriously.

Chapter 72

A Hundred Million? You're Out of Your Mind

By this time, the spring of 1981, when one of our ads appeared with a new milestone in yield, we were having as many as 150,000 glossy 8.5" x by 11" copies made of the ad for use as a mailer and prospecting vehicle. We did one printing a month of the most recent ad and kept a listing of those brokers who had requested them. Sometimes the printer shipped them for us, and at other times, we had them delivered to the office and shipped them ourselves. They would be piled up in boxes of five hundred, and Peggy, Clem, and I, and whoever else was available, would repackage, address, and ship them between picking up phones. You can imagine the time and effort it might take to administer to this sales effort beside all the other things going on. Imagine as well the impact of the distribution of these flyers to the public.

One broker in Chicago, Jim Phillips, would order as many as fifteen thousand and pay the newspaper sellers at various stations of Chicago's commuter rail system to stuff each newspaper they sold with a copy. In Jim's case, we personalized them with his name and phone number. His sales and new account openings justified this kind of investment.

On the Friday at the end of the first week in May, I put an indication in for fifty million dollars of Short-Term Series 119 slated to come at a yield of 16.9%. We were awarded the fifty or something very close, and when the deal priced on Tuesday, we were completely sold out by midday. Another deal was quickly announced at something over 17 percent for Wednesday, and I went in for another sixty million and was given only forty-five or something near that. I was pissed, feeling I got ripped off because Merrill, who had overwhelming demand, filled some of it with the ten million they failed to give us. This was an underestimation of the public demand for the product that produced a backlash of complaint in the firm because there were so many unfilled orders when we had to pull back inventory from UDC much sooner than we usually did.

But there was no time to breathe because on Thursday morning, Merrill announced another deal, Series 121 for the following week with indications of interest due on Friday. That was good because the sales organizations were on fire, clamoring for a new deal, and getting them working on it, would stem their complaining about the last one.

The approximate yield for series 121 was pegged at around 17.4 percent. I immediately began making my rounds of calls only to find astonishing and unbelievable demand for this next deal. Each of my regional guys themselves had orders for several hundreds of thousands' worth from their own clients let alone their home branches. Every office that was home to one of our regionals had a million plus in orders for this deal. Flagship offices like Chicago, Atlanta and San Francisco as well as several of our New York offices indicated that they had multiple millions in orders. The regions were bringing in indications of five to as much as eight million dollars. Indications of interest have to be taken with a grain of salt, but the calls and conversations I was having were all pointing to a feeling I already had in my bones. I turned to Clem about ten thirty on Friday morning and said, "Look, boss, we can do a hundred million here. I've never seen anything like it."

"You're out of your mind!" He shouted. "You're fucking crazy! Where do you come off telling me this, giving me a number like this? Do you realize what you're asking for? Do you even know what the words one hundred million really mean?"

When I tried to explain, he didn't want to hear it. Even though sales had matched or exceeded takedowns for weeks on recent deals since before year end, he just couldn't accept these numbers. He was so preoccupied with anxiety about the future, and the way he went on and on, it appeared to me at least he had not gotten over the cavalier behavior and lack of seriousness of our West Coast brethren in the face of what he thought was impending disaster. I, on the other hand, was disturbed about his not going to Merrill to carry out my complaint about our allotment on the last deal. I didn't know how much got back to Norman through my contact, Ilene McCormick, and while I might mention something to Norman if I ran into him by chance, calling him to complain was out of the question. He was a nut job to begin with, and he might flare up and do something rash that I didn't want to be responsible for. Clem was close to Norman, he could have done it, but he was just too preoccupied by his demons or being obstinate or both.

"You did ninety million dollars in short-terms this week and another $15 million of the other stuff. You're never satisfied. Be happy with it. And besides, they're gonna announce another deal after this one. Now take another look and give me a more reasonable number."

Maybe I didn't have a true conception of what a hundred million dollars was, but that had no bearing on the issue at hand. This was my read and I stuck by it, and if I use the vulgar form, forgive me. I put it in writing in a short memo copied to Frank Cullum instead and told him where he shove it. I would not go back to the drawing board as Clem had requested. He didn't like it, and I was annoyed and was starting to push back. I wanted some respect. I had been engineering deal after deal, sellouts for months and years in fact, and all Clem had been doing was breaking my chops over every single one. I said earlier that we rarely fought over commitments and we didn't but Clem always questioned me always asked questions about how I came up with numbers. Ninety, even ninety five percent of the time I put in what I had what I had decided upon. But I was getting tired of the questioning. It began to feel like he didn't trust me. Where the hell did he think I got the numbers out of my a__? Underneath it all, my respect for Clem was eroding. In any case, Clem took it to Henry Arbeeny, which was, from a management point of view, the right thing to do. With this size commitment, it was right to kick it upstairs a notch and see what the big boss says. He had to, because I had put it in writing. If we got it really wrong it would be his fault then not mine.

Apparently, Henry suggested that they check with Merrill to ask them what they were thinking, which was what Clem should have done in the first place before he took it to Henry and before he wound me up. I have no way of knowing he didn't, but the fact that he disappeared for the better part of that Friday afternoon told me he was with Henry, working things out. At around four that afternoon, I left and went home to my family which was my usual thing on Friday. I would stay late any other night and in fact I often popped in early on Saturday or Sunday morning for a few hours to get my affairs straight, but I never stayed late on Fridays and Clem knew it.

I would have loved to be in that room when they called Merrill to know exactly what was said. However, it was reported to me on Monday morning that Clem and Henry had negotiated a $101,500,000 participation in the deal that was to be 20 percent of the entire underwriting. That I was right was great vindication, although I thought ill of it and was angry about the whole situation. I felt I no longer owned it. It had become a committee decision now. Clem wanted me to be jumping for joy. "You got what you wanted," he said.

"FUCK YOU," was my thought. I probably was being selfish in a way, not taking the time to think that this was a totally out of the ordinary situation as it was a commitment near twice as big as any I or we had ever made, although it was plain that this was an inevitable turn of events. But there was no time argue or to think on it anymore. Once we knew the commitment was going to be $101 million, we had to make sure it got sold.

The way pricing on these deals occurred was on the morning of the day the deal would be offered for sale to the public, in this case Tuesday on May 12, 1981, a preliminary offering price based on the previous days market (May 11) was announced publicly. On that day, all the legal documentation contained in the final prospectus and the numbers were summarily reviewed and approved by the SEC in form and format and printed in the issues final prospectus.

A new price would be assessed then based on that days market, (the twelfths) and orders in hand are then processed at the twelfth's evaluation. On this occasion, the preliminary offering price came through on the morning of the twelfth consisting of the elevenths evaluation. In effect what the price per unit would have been had the trust come to market on the eleventh, $1,007.50, plus accrued interest to yield 17.39 percent. The ticketing system was so overloaded that it went down some time in the midafternoon that day with the last reading taken around two in the afternoon indicating that forty-one million dollars and change was sold. Not good news because we had sixty million to go. But you don't panic. The system was bound to get jammed. If orders averaged twenty thousand dollars, it would take five thousand orders to bill this deal, and the fact was that average order size was more in the twelve- to fifteen-thousand-dollar range.

When the pricing came through that afternoon at around three thirty, we went into shock. This trust CIF Short Term Series 121 had come at what might be called the very bottom of the bear market for interest rates, at the very moment of the market turning positive. The price came in at $1,012.50 or thereabout, a full $5 increase in its dollar price and a yield of 17.21 percent. Price changes of 70¢ or 80¢ either way were a frequent occurrence, but a $5 rise and a decrease in yield of 18 basis points (18/100 of a percentage point) was a major move to the upside—very big and very noticeable. The yield 17.21 percent was a still a king's ransom in terms of a six-month investment. However, investors would have the right of refusal if they felt used in any way or if they felt misled.

We hung around the office until near nine that night, but the system never came back up to give us a read on the day's final sales. We went home consoled by the fact that the market had given us some protection, five hundred thousand dollars' worth of protection in fact, if the deal was not sold out to a respectable degree.

What had happened? Over the past 6 business days our joint account alone had gone in for two deals in the $250 to $300 million-dollar range and this last one, series 121 was something over $500 million. Who knows what other sources were lending to these banks. In any case for this slight drop in interest rates to occur the corporate demand to borrow from the banks we were lending to had to have fallen away. The banks demand to lend money had slackened, borrowers thirst for money had been slaked and so interest rates fell, hence the increase in value of our trust. As a matter of fact, this week was the very turning point in the market. A crescendo of sorts within which demand for money reached its peak and fell off, market psychology turned somewhat positive, and yields decreased, at least in the short end of the yield curve.

The next morning, a system inquiry from the previous evening put on my desk around eleven o'clock the night before by Kaye Foster showed that seventy-one million dollars had been ticketed and processed sometime during the night. There were hundreds upon hundreds of calls regarding the price change but very few requests (less than five hundred thousand dollars' worth) for cancellations. The deal sold out in a few days, and early the following week, Series 122 was announced at a yield of around 17.05 percent. This announcement of the subsequent deal at a lower yield transformed a mildly restive sales force to an elated one, at having gotten in on the biggie.

For my part, maybe I was small-minded in some ways, maybe there was no maybe about it. I never had any training that prepared me for the affairs of the kind I was now involved in except the hands-on experience of doing the work these past five years. The extent of my formal education in finance was a high school economics class. No matter. I got this one right and got no credit for it.

Chapter 73

Events Unfold

The significance of this underwriting and of the entire week's events were not lost on me, and I understand that the reader may think me completely daft and that I was not roaring back to the world around me about how great I was. I wasn't dead, but the feeling that I did not own that deal remained. I felt Clem, and then Henry, had appropriated my views and my decision making and had made them their own.

Before I became angry about it though, I was sad. Not woe is me so much as a bitterness that after all this time, what was a milestone in my career and certainly a milestone in the history of the firm would not be recorded in some way and that this special event would not be remarked upon as something having to do with me. I then focused on the fact that I was also denied the duty that had been mine on almost every new issue we'd participated in for the past two years and more. I made the call. I had made the call to Merrill on almost every deal to say we wanted ten million, we need fifty million, we need six million. I told myself that if I had made the call for the one hundred million, at least it would have been recognized at Merrill that I had had something to do with it. Not this time. As it stood now, the decision had been made above my head.

These thoughts seethed in me. I was angry and gave Clem the cold shoulder and, after a while, was terribly disappointed over the fact that Henry had not called. How rotten people could be, especially when one considered the numbers, which amounted to nearly a million-dollar gain overnight. Between the price swing, the sales credit production of four hundred thousand and what would be left-over from the take-down and the underwriting expenses were accounted for. Four hundred thousand dollars roughly in sales credit, of which the firm kept near two hundred fifty thousand plus another seventy-five to one hundred thousand of earnings in the sponsorship account, which would come in a month or two. There was no one in the office to talk to, secrets can't be kept under such close working conditions anyway, so I just chalked it up. I would reconcile myself to my feelings in time, and in some way, my attitude would change and that was all I could do. I could stand up for what I believed, but I was not confrontational as many in my business were, as Clem was in fact. I was not so direct or given to show-down, so I would swallow my feelings—eat them, as I often did.

On another level, writing this memoir and going over my career has made it clear to me that whether or not some people thought elements of my background, personality, ethnicity, or anything else about me made me ill-suited for my position, perhaps underneath it all, I thought the same of myself. It's clear now it can take a lifetime to find out who we are and who and what we have been to feel secure in our own skin and act in such a way as to not really care what others may think and to live in the world and not in our minds.

Some few days later, maybe a week or a bit more after the hundred million had come and gone, Henry walked into the trading room holding something I realized after a few moments was a magnum of champagne. When I looked at him, he was smiling broadly (which he did not do often) and looking right at me. A moment or two passed and then Clem and Frank came in and began signaling and shushing the office down with raised arms and loud voices to quiet down, to end their phone calls, so everyone could hear Henry address the department.

He began by stating that the department was having a great year, and this was no mean feat considering the market climate. On behalf of the firm and himself, he wanted to thank everyone for their dedication and hard work. He then singled out the New Issue Desk for the banner week it had had earlier in the month and the extraordinary achievement of having successfully completed a hundred-million-dollar-plus commitment, the largest single transaction in the firm's history to date and a near $1 million-dollar net profit. After giving some details, he announced Pat Scida had made the call and the commitment, and I was being made a vice president effective immediately and gave me the appointment in writing dated just a few days before. Everyone applauded, the cork was popped, a drink was poured, and a buffet lunch was brought in.

I later learned from Clem and Henry at lunch the following Friday that when they called Norman over at Merrill, he immediately confirmed the number I had submitted was right on, and we, Dean Witter Reynolds, were selling 20 percent of every short-term deal for months now. With the next one (series 121) slated for upwards of $500 million, my $100 million was, again, right on the money. Then it was decided that we would take $101,500,000 worth of the deal, slightly more than 20 percent, which as was said the largest single transaction done to that date at Dean Witter Reynolds.

All my rancor and vengeful thinking receded, forgotten, as pain often is. I had been an AVP since 1976 or 1977. Today, officerships come down the pike in droves and are expected steps in the right of passage of young execs on the rise. They seemed to come along more infrequently in my day. For me to have become a vice president of a major corporation was at once enormously important, considering I had achieved it despite having none, absolutely none, of the qualifications most of my counterparts had, which included education and pedigree, and at the same time was almost a nonevent for precisely the same reason although it took me a while to understand it. I hadn't needed the education or the pedigree, or the recognition of my family. It was enough that I had the ability, the chops to get me there.

The very next week the interest rate markets began a march in the other direction in the beginning of what was to be a near two decade rally, with a few bumps along the way. Eventually my appointment to Vice President got posted in some firm documents and the gist of the magnitude of what had gone on in our shop got around in New York and in the field. I got some notes and phone calls here and there but life in the moment is the way of Wall Street, there was no time to rest on or even think about my laurels. Early in 1982 though, there was a reminder and it was a bell ringer. The firm awarded me a major advance in salary, and a bonus sufficient enough to pay all our bills with enough left over to buy a house on the beach in Point Lookout New York.

Epilogue

I would continue to work at Dean Witter Reynolds through its take-over by Sears in 1982 and subsequent spin off and finally its merger with Morgan Stanley in the late 90's. I retired from Morgan Stanley Dean Witter in May of 2001. During those 20 years interest rates fell from 10 to 15 percentage points depending on the investment examined. I would witness and participate in many more introductions of new investment products and the ongoing transfer of assets out of the nations traditional savings institution and into its brokerage firms. All of those events in my future would take place amidst a continuing Wall Street backdrop replete with many more dislocations of capital, market crashes, merging firms and a continuous, if not choppy bull market for stocks and bonds that continues to this very day. A continuous flow of new players and work partners was never in short supply either. None of these later times and events or the persons that inhabited them, remain as indelibly impressed on my mind as those I have chronicled here. My sincere hope is that these scribling's have entertained and enlighten my readers.

Appendix
Fixed Income/Bond Market Primer

Introduction

Various details and jagged disconnected fragments of detail related to the Fixed Income Securities Industry and The Bond Markets are scattered throughout this book. It seemed important after putting together a hopefully cohesive manuscript, that we put one foot in front of the other in an orderly description of how it works.

The Bond Market

The Bond Market is conducted by Wall Street Brokerage Firms and Investment Banks, and participated in by investors who may be as familiar to you as the owner of your local dry cleaners or as remote as your State Teachers and Municipal Workers Pension Fund, or the administrator of Allstate Insurance's investment division. Bonds are a savings and investment vehicle used by a broad spectrum of individuals and institutions. The ownership of a bond constitutes the holding of a loan that entitles the holder to receive periodic payments of interest, and a payment of principle at maturity from the borrower. Bonds are generally liquid and negotiable through brokerage firms in the so called secondary market.

Bonds, also known as Fixed Income Securities are loans made by corporations, municipalities and countries. The lenders are the previously mentioned investors. The market sets interest rates on these loans based on many factors, notably credit quality and maturity, i.e. the length of time to the loans repayment date. Rating agencies such as Moody's and Standard and Poor's determine credit quality through extensive research into how likely borrowers are to make timely semi-annual interest payments to bondholders and eventually pay off the loans principle at some pre-determined future date. From this research, a shorthand grading system (A, AA, AA3, BBB1 etc.) is published and regularly (monthly) updated for use as a credit rating guide. Other factors such as supply and demand and economic conditions, i.e. the rate of inflation and economic trends play a major part in the determination and formulation of interest rates.

In practice, interest rates are determined day to day by investor willingness to lend at any given moment. For example, if investors are not willing to buy (invest in) AAA-rated prime quality bonds at 6%, their interest rate rises until a purchase point is reached, 6.25, 6.45 and so on. Conversely, aggressive investing at 6% will drive the rate of interest down, (5.9% 5.75% etc.) Typically, bonds are issued in units of $1000 of principal value, also known as par value at maturity, with the minimum purchase being $5000. In general bonds are differentiated from stocks because they have a maturity date (due date) upon which they go out of existence, a payoff or principal value of $1000 payable to the holder on that date, and a fixed annual payment of income from their point of issuance to their proscribed payoff date. Common stocks have no intrinsic principal payoff value or set annual income payment. Because of this known payoff value and date, bonds are considered a safer more conservative investment than stocks.

Issuers of Bonds

To function as the populace expects them to, large sums of money are required by sovereign nations, states, counties and localities to maintain law and order and the seats and facilities of government. Further their political and municipal subdivisions need ready supplies of capital to provide basic human requirements such as clean water, ease of movement, adequate housing and healthcare among others. Large corporations and institutions such as banks and other commercial enterprises require enormous sums of money as well to conduct business in the present and to secure their capability to function in the future. The access to, and the ability to borrow these monies is provided by the Bond Market which Wall Street presides over, governed by a vast body of Federal and State Law, rules, customs and precedents. In the United States, the major borrowers or issuers of bonds are:

The Federal Government

— The US Treasury Department which issues Treasury Bills, Bonds and Notes and US Government Agencies securities, examples of which are The Federal National Mortgage Association (FNMA) and The Tennessee Valley Authority (TVA) among others.

Income from US Treasury Bonds although federally taxable is exempt from state and local taxes. Income earned from US Government Agency Debt is taxable.

States and Cities

— Municipal Bonds are issued by every state in the Union and every major population center from the City of San Francisco California, to Erie County New York, to tiny Ephrata, Pennsylvania.

For investors who meet certain qualifications the income earned from Municipal Bonds is exempt from Federal Income Tax and may be free from state and local taxes as well.

Corporations

Corporations such as IBM, Bank of America, Reynolds Aluminum, American Airlines to name a few are major borrowers among many, many others.

In modern times, it is fair to say that the publics ability to shower with clean water, pay for their coffee at Starbucks with a credit card or safely commute to work and otherwise be protected from harm wouldn't be possible were it not for the Bond Markets and Wall Street.

Basic Terminology

Bill and Sally James have accumulated savings of 8 or 9 thousand dollars which is kept at the local bank. When Sally's grandmother passed away they inherited $15000 dollars which they deposited with the nine thousand already at the bank. Twenty thousand of the twenty-four they invested in a 5-year CD paying 3 ½ % annually. Sometime thereafter Bill and Sally see an ad in the newspaper about a new issue of $100 Million of IBM bonds paying 5% annually for 10 years, an investment that will provide them with considerably more income annually than the bank CD they currently have. They decide to remove $20000 from the bank and invest in the IBM bonds. The written confirmation of that purchase provides them with the basic information and details of their investment. The confirmation and the definitions of those details are noted below.

The Confirmation

Trade Date 6/20/2017 | Settlement Date 6/25/2017

You Bought
20000 IBM Corporation (AA1) @100 $20,000
CPN 5% YTM 5%
12/15/ 2027-Dated Accrued Int. 27.78
6/15/2017, JD15
Call 12/15/2025 @101

Amount Due
$20,027.78

The confirmation states the obvious points and details of their investment which are explained in detail below.

Trade Date.............................The date of the transaction.

Settlement Date............The date the transaction must be paid for.

You Bought.........The activity the confirmation is reporting, buying

20000...............The principal value of the investment at maturity.

IBM Corporation...The Corporate Name of the borrower or Issuer

@100.................Bond prices are quoted at 1/10th of actual value
thus a price of 100 is $1000, (101 ½ would be $1015.00 and
97 1/4 is $972.50 etc.)

5%..................The annual rate of interest that will be paid to the
investor. 5% per $1000 or $50 per $1000 principal value.

YTM 5%............The rate of return to the investor earned from
payments of principal and interest compounded at the stated
yield and rate.

12/15/2027.........The bonds maturity upon which it will make its
final interest payment and pay off its principal value to its owner.

Dated 6/15/2027...The date from which interest on the bond begins
to accrue.

JD15...............Bonds pay interest as a rule semi-annually, JD 15
notes that the holder Will receive a $25 payment of interest (per
bond) on June 15th and December 15th each year for a total of
$50 or 5% annually. (JJ would denote January and July, AO
April and October etc.)

Accrued Interest...Bonds generally accumulate or accrue interest on a
360 day-annual Schedule or 1/360 th (.1389 cents) of their stated
coupon rate and pay at intervals of 180 days or roughly six months.
Bond holders are entitled to the interest earned during the time
they hold them. In this case the brokerage firm has held the securities (the bond) from their 06/15/2017 dated date to the date upon
which Mr. and Mrs. James take ownership on settlement date 6/20
2017 or 10 days @.1389 cents per bond per day on 20 bonds.
.1389 X 10 X 20 or .1389 X 10 =1.39 X 20 =$27.28. This Accrued
interest paid to the previous holder will be remitted to Mr. and
Mrs. James when they receive their first income payment.

Callable...............12/15/2025 @101...Just as mortgagers have the right to re-finance loans because interest rates have gone down, so do bond issuers. This note states that IBM may call in or redeem these bonds on December 15, 2025, two years prior to maturity at a price of 101 or 1010, $10 more than their value at maturity.

The Markets
Primary/ New---Secondary/Previously issued

Regardless of Issuer and within each issuing category, US Treasury, Municipal or Corporate, the markets for each of these is divided into two separate though dependent disciplines. The Primary Market which underwrites and prices new loans, often referred to as new issues, and The Secondary Market through which investors can sell and buy previously purchased bonds. When an investor purchases a newly issued bond he is buying it from the firm's primary market division and when he sells it he is selling it through the firm's secondary market division. Just as one buys a new automobile from a dealership, one may purchase a used car from a different section of that dealership, namely it's used car division. The new car lately come from the factory is priced to the current market for materials, labor, accessories and markup. The used car's value will be determined however from the close consideration of the year it was manufactured, its mileage and repair history, visible damage and so on. The market concept for automobiles New and Used and that of Bonds, Primary and Secondary, while not one in the same, are conceptually similar enough to make a good comparison. New Cars are newly made from the factory as Primary issues are newly created from very recently made loans purchased directly from the issuer. Used cars are purchased from previous owners as bonds in the secondary market are purchased from previous investors. Used car values are generally diminished in so far as their characteristics differ than new cars, mileage, years in use etc. A major difference between the valuation of a used car and the valuation of a previously owned bond is that in the case of bonds their value is not based on their years in existence. Their value increases or decreases based on whether the market for interest rates is higher or lower today than it was when the bonds were originally issued. Read further for a better understand of this phenomenon.

The Future Calendar of upcoming new bond issues is published in newspapers and can usually be found in Mondays edition of the Wall Street Journal or New York Times. More detailed versions appear on the so-called wire or electronic news services and trade papers. In the primary market, the US Treasury might borrow 40 to $60 Billion dollars in various maturities in a single week once each quarter. In that same week in the Municipal Market, Oklahoma or Michigan may be scheduled to borrow seven hundred million dollars each and/ or the Tri-Borough Bridge and Tunnel Authority of NYC might borrow a billion dollars; yes, a billion. Add to this The Watchung New Jersey Downtown Restoration District borrowing $1.625 Million, $39 Million Las Cruces New Mexico Water Purification District and 30 or 40 issues and more of 5 to $500 million each, around the country. During the same week IBM and Boeing might come in for $500 million each of 10-year bonds. Typically, any borrowing done by The US Treasury for two years or more is conducted on a quarterly schedule while shorter term borrowing occurs week to week. The Municipal and Corporate Calendar of offerings is a week to week schedule although announcements are made weeks in advance.

The ever present and ongoing Future Calendar of upcoming loans, listing untold billions of dollars of borrowing coming to market weekly and the Wall Street/Bond Market mechanism that brings it to a satisfactory end on a week to week basis can be characterized as a miracle of modern capitalism. The Investment Bankers, i.e. the underwriters, traders, analysts and investment advisors in the new issue divisions in Wall Street firms who run for their lives before the Future Calendar to make sure it gets done might characterize it as a steamroller or juggernaut never more than a foot or two away from their coattails.

The Secondary Market

This New Issue or Primary market could not be sustained, could not exist, without liquidity; the ability to readily convert previously issued securities into cash. This liquidity is provided in and through the Secondary Market conducted by the Wall Street Brokerage community which is a vast worldwide network. It is perfectly understandable that Bill and Mary James, mentioned previously, who purchased $20,000 worth of the IBM 5% of 2027 bonds might want to sell their bonds prior to maturity for any reason whatsoever; to buy a house, take a trip, education expense, whatever? If they could not, the risk of removing monies from a bank to buy bonds would be much greater, probably prohibitive. In fact, the secondary market is not just maintained for Bill and Mary's twenty thousand IBM's but also for Allstate Insurance's ten or twenty or thirty, even hundreds of millions of dollars of bonds that must be liquidated when disasters strike, such as earthquake' and hurricanes. The secondary market is maintained for the millions of investors who for some reason may wish to liquidate their investment prior to its stated maturity and for the many buyers who are in the market to purchase these "used" if we may apply that term, but still viable securities.

Pricing-Primary Markets

US Treasury Bonds....

The issuing entities of bonds have differing though similar pricing methodologies in their primary markets. In the US Treasury Market, the various consumers i.e. investors, banks, insurance companies, pension funds, mutual funds, credit unions, foreign governments, brokerage firms: submit bids to the US Treasury as to what level of interest would be acceptable to themselves or their clients. Of course, these bids must be reasonable and in line with current market conditions. Shortly thereafter The Treasury awards the bonds to the bidders. Much of the bidding is competitive, so bidders who are not in the range of the consensus of interest rate applications must accept the rates of return set as final, or pass. With some exceptions, all bonds are issued at par or $1000 maturity value, paying income semiannually.

Municipal Bonds

In the municipal market two separate bidding methodologies may be applied. In Competitive Bidding, a syndicate or group of brokerage firms meet and decide on a rate structure based on current market conditions and the previously mentioned parameters such as credit ratings, recent financial news about the municipality and investor receptivity to the name of the issuer as well as any orders that might be on hand. The bid is submitted to the issuer at an appointed date and hour. Syndicates are formed to spread risk and several competing syndicates may submit bids which include the charges and expenses related to the underwriting. The syndicate submitting the lowest NIC or Net Interest Cost to the municipality is awarded the right to remarket the issue to its clients.

A second methodology, the Negotiated Sale is used in the new issue markets for municipals, especially when an issuer wishes to borrow substantial amounts of capital of one or two long-term maturities. For example, $400 million maturing in 2050 or 2060. This is a widespread practice, in the case of raising capital for the purpose' of building power plants or the construction of Housing, Turnpikes or Water Treatment facilities. In the negotiated sale, a single syndicate is formed which, and over a specified time frame (several days) submits price (yield/ rate of return) ideas to its clients. If substantial orders result or the issue is oversold, the yields can be reduced somewhat saving the issuer interest cost. Conversely, if orders do not materialize, yields are raised, increasing interest cost, until an orderly flow of buyers (investors) is secured. Once the yield is set the bonds are issued at the rate of return and price negotiated.

Corporate Bonds are issued almost exclusively in the Negotiated Sale format.

Pricing in The Secondary Market

A major problem that confronts both the stockbroker and the investor is understanding how prices are arrived at when investors choose to sell their holdings of bonds. There is a tendency to feel that pricing is arbitrary because often the prices received, real prices are lower than routine monthly statement evaluations. The answer to this lies initially in understanding the pricing mechanism and secondly fully realizing that finding a real buyer at a firm price for your bonds is a much more rigorous task that takes into consideration the lot size you are selling, the payment of expenses such as commissions, overhead, market risk and general market conditions. Monthly statement evaluations on the other hand are simply generalized evaluations and as a rule do not take into consideration the critical factors mentioned. The comparison may be made to selling a used car whose pricing will be discounted by every scratch and little dent the evaluator can find as well as the mileage and the cost of remarketing expenses i.e. any clean-up, refurbishment or servicing of any kind, in addition to any future commissions to be paid. As we shall see the key to understanding pricing in the secondary market is revealed in an understanding of the pricing of new issues.

The Interest Rate Scale

The interest rate Scale is a table or schedule of interest rates drawn up by bond market underwriters to be used as a pricing mechanism and guideline. The following scale was submitted and accepted by the fictional Blossom County on a $40 Million Dollar Loan in the Municipal Bond Market. It can be said that in general these mathematical notations i.e., coupon rates, yields to maturity, dollar price* and maturity dates can be used as a guideline in the valuation and pricing of similarly rated bonds of similar maturities in the secondary market for the purposes of liquidating previously issued bonds. Let us identify the details and then explain the phenomena of pricing.

*In bond market parlance, the dollar value of a "point" is $10 thus 3/8 is $3.75, ¼ is $2.50 etc.

$40,000,000 Blossom County, Anystate
Rated AA

Amt	Mat.	C/R	Pr.	YTM	Spread	T/D	Commission/DC
$1000	8/01/2016*	2.5%	100	2.5%	3/8	3/16	1/8
$1000	8/01/2017	2.6%	100	2.6%	3/8	3/16	1/8
$1000	8/01/2018	2.65%	100	2.65%	3/8	3/16	1/8
$3000	8/01/2019	3.00%	100	3.00%	5/8	3/8	1/4
$3000	8/01/2020	3.10%	100	3.10%	5/8	3/8	¼
$3000	8/01/2021	3.20	100	3.20	1	7/8	¾
$3000	8/01/2022	3.30	100	3.30	1	7/8	¾
$3000	8/01/2023	3.50	100	3.50	1	7/8	¾
$3000	8/01/2024	3.65	100	3.65	1 1/4	1.0	7/8
$3000	8/01/2025	4.2%	100	4.20%	1 ¼	1.0	¾
$6000	8/01/2030	4.65	100	4.65	1 ¾	1 ½	1/1/4
$10000	8/01/2035	4.95	100	4.95%	3.0	2.5	22.50

*Interest paid semiannually on 8/ and 2/1

To understand what we are looking at let's examine one of the maturities, the bonds maturing in 2025

$3000	8/01/2025	4.2%	100	4.20%	1 ¼	1.0	¾

Of the $40 Million Blossom County is borrowing, $3,000,000 will mature in eight years on 8/01/2025, paying at a rate of 4.2% ($42.00 interest per year per $1000 borrowed) priced at 100 (par) or $1000 to the investor providing them with 4.2% yield to maturity. The immediate cost to the municipality of borrowing this maturity alone is 1 ¼ points ($12.50) or 1 ¼% per $1000 borrowed totaling $37500 (thirty-seven thousand five hundred dollars.) This cost may be viewed and compared to the closing fees incurred in the securing of a mortgage and are separate from the interest cost to the borrower. The takedown and commission columns indicate how that cost, also known as the "spread" is divided up between the syndicate members.

The $12.50 cost per bond is deducted from the amount borrowed. The municipality will have borrowed $3 million but receive only $2,962,500 for the 2025 maturity reflecting the deduction of borrowing costs.

"Price and Yield"

The yield or the interest rates designated by the underwriters of/ for Blossom County to bondholders on the day of the underwriting and quite possibly for the entire week during which the underwriting took place is a measure of and a proxy for the pricing AA rated municipal bonds throughout the US with some minor considerations taken. Demand for Blossom County bonds and any current "normal" economic conditions in the state or county or the level of taxation in the state are essentially negligible. During the week Blossom County borrowed this $40 million AA rated municipal bonds of any state or county across the country of these same maturities must be priced to the same yields as Blossom County, give or take five, to twenty-five one hundredths of a percentage point, based on local economic conditions, local taxation and or demand as has been mentioned.

This fact relates directly to how previously issued bonds are priced in the secondary market. The interest rate or coupon rate of the bond being liquidated is compared to what it would cost to borrow today for that bonds credit rating and remaining life to maturity. How do we make these comparisons? Where does this data come from? Remember we said that new loans are being priced every day according to current economic conditions, supply and demand, credit ratings, maturity etc. In effect, the Blossom County scale is a pricing mechanism for AA rated bonds being liquidated in the secondary market. How?

Valuation

Let's say I bought a AA rated bond in 2005 when interest rates were much higher, with a coupon rate of 5 ¼ % maturing in the year 6/15/2025. It's now 2017, the bond still has 8 years to go and I want to sell it. If you look at the bonds maturing in 8 years on the AA rated Blossom County scale you will see that they are priced to yield 4.2 percent, a full percentage point less than my bonds. Based on what we have just noted, a trader must price my 5.25% AA rated bonds to yield 4.2% or the current rate for AA rated 8-year maturity bonds. The resulting dollar evaluation would be 107.70 or $1077.00, $75 per bond more than what I paid. The reason for the high price is that the coupon rate or annual income of my bond greatly exceeds the current market rate. My bonds warrant a higher price, and their buyer will pay a premium for the higher than current market rate of $52.50 annually to their 2025 maturity. To put it more simply the current bond is paying $42.00 a year, my previously issued bond is paying $52.50 a year, the market says that extra income of $12.50 a year is worth $77.00 more per bond. Note that if you amortize the $77 premium over the 8 years left to maturity the buyer of my bonds is paying $9.63 a year for the extra $12.50 in income he will collect annually.

Now, let's say the reverse were true, that the 20-year bond purchased in 2015 had a coupon rate of 4.2 % and todays rate was 5.25%. What would be the price of 4.2 % coupon bonds be in a 5.25 %. current rate environment. The resulting dollar evaluation is 93.09 or $930.90*, nearly $70 less than the purchase price. The reason for the lower evaluation is that the market (investors) require a discount, a monetary compensation for holding a lower than current market bond to maturity.

Expenses

The final component of a secondary market sale or liquidation is expense. In the Blossom County interest rate scale, there is a column noted as "spread." Spread is the term given to the expenses incurred in remarketing or reselling the bonds to another investor and the expenses incurred by the brokerage firm, i.e. commissions to be paid, market risk, overhead and so on. While these costs may be considered nominal individually, they can sometimes add up to $40 or more per bond. In the secondary market these costs and expenses are born by the seller. First the cost of commissions, both a nominal commission to the seller's broker and a larger though also nominal commission to buyer's broker. Add an additional fee for risk or holding on to the bonds for a week or two depending on how long it may take to find a buyer. These combined expenses are called the "concession." In this case for the 5 ¼% eight-year bonds a $5 a bond commission is paid to the selling broker; a $10 commission is proposed for the buying broker and a $5 risk and remarketing fee is assessed totaling a $20 concession is paid by the seller and comes off the top of the market valuation. Thus, the valuation of $1077.70 becomes $1057.70. Still not bad in the sense the investor is selling at a premium. It's a sort of double whammy for the seller at the discount as his bid evaluation sinks even further being hit hard by the combined market and expenses. It should be noted that in a stable and upward trending market (lower interest rates and higher prices) the commission values and risk assessments that are applied may be termed moderate. Conversely in a downward trending market (higher interest rates and lower prices) these applications will become more severe.

Lot Size…

What most effectively reduces these expenses is "lot size." A ten-bond lot will command a better evaluation and lower concession than five bonds and twenty-five bonds an even lower concession and possibly a higher yield evaluation. Expenses begin to become negligible when lot size reaches seventy-five to one hundred thousand dollars of principal value, because these larger lots are more marketable to a wider range of professional buyers. Expenses are often a difficult pill for investors to swallow, but one must think and understand how the world turns. The valuation of an automobile three days after leaving the showroom can be down as much as fifteen percent. Typically, the cost of the purchase and sale of a home between closing costs and commissions can be a minimum of $20,000 for the most reasonably priced unit and these costs are typically born by the seller.

Finally

Considering all the above explanations and illustrations there are three key points to bear in mind regarding the secondary market for bonds, the market in which an investor may liquidate his current holdings:

1- all previously issued bonds are priced to the current market (loans being made today) conditions based on their characteristics ranging from length of time to maturity, credit rating, market conditions, supply and demand and lot size.

2- as interest rates rise the value of previously issued bonds fall and the opposite is true; when interest rates fall the prices of previously issued bonds rises. Note that the relationship of bond yields to bond dollar prices is known as an "inverse ratio." Though the meaning of the term as applied to the bond market is a simple concept, it can be confusing because in conversation, the terms used to describe market activity can be misleading. For example, when bond market operatives say the interest rate market is higher, they mean yields are falling and are lower and when they say interest rates are higher the dollar value of bonds is decreasing. Thus the "inverse relationship" of bond yield to bond dollar price. When yields rise dollar prices fall, when yields fall dollar prices rise. To put it another way when interest rates decrease the prices of the bonds you own rise, when interest rates are higher the prices of the bonds you own are lowered.

This price to yield relationship begs us to understand the further and practical application of the relationship of bond yield to dollar price.

For example, let's say an investor pays a dollar price of 97.5 or $975 per bond for a block of bonds yielding 4.5%. When calculating the dollar value of 97.5, placing the maturity and settlement date in the bond calculator and the yield of 4.5% the bond will calculate to a dollar price of 97.5. Using the same maturity date and settlement date and putting in a dollar price of 97.5 the bond will calculate to a yield of 4.5%.

3- expences will always be deducted from market evaluation.

Taxation and Interest Rates

The income from Corporate Bonds is fully taxable and must be reported to the federal and state income tax authorities. The income earned from US Treasury Securities is exempt from state income tax but fully taxable federally. The income earned from Municipal Bonds however is exempt from both Federal Taxation and some state and local taxation. This interconnectivity of Finance, Government and Politics i.e. the theory, methodology and political expediency of exemption of taxes on income from loans made to government entities is traceable to pre-Victorian England and the Civil War period in the United States. For whatever reason, social upheaval, need for public works, or good business sense, it became expedient to wave taxes on the income earned from loans deemed to be made for the public good. Undoubtedly the purpose of the waver of taxation was to incentivize the lender (the investor). The first instance of exempting income from loans to the Federal Government in the United States was during the civil war. Before that there is a long history and tradition of The British Crown waving taxation of income earned on loans made to it by its counties and boroughs.

As mentioned credit quality and length of maturity among other factors affect interest rates. Taxation, the way in which the income from the three issuing entities are taxed also effects their rate of return or the hierarchy in the range or spectrum of interest rates among the issuers of debt.

For example, today AAA rated long term Corporate Bonds may be priced to yield 6% while long term US Treasury Bonds might be priced to yield 5.6% with long term AAA rated municipal bonds yielding 4.8%. What accounts for this disparity or interest rate range among these securities? Corporate Bonds tend to be the highest yielding securities of the three classes because as far as credit quality is concerned, corporations are fallible, they can go out of business. Additionally, income earned from corporate bonds is fully taxable by Federal and State Income Tax Authorities.

Next in the spectrum of interest rates are US Treasury Securities that are rated AAA and guaranteed by the US Treasury and US Government which have never failed to miss a payment of interest or principle. Thus, their interest rates tend to be lower than corporate bonds. Secondly while the interest from US Treasury securities is taxable by Federal Income Tax authorities, it is exempt from taxation by state income tax authorities. This tax-exempt benefit places additional downward pressure on their rate of return since the benefit of state tax exemption compensates the investor somewhat for their lower yield. The slight mathematical interest rate adjustment on US Treasury Securities due to state tax exemption is much more apparent in municipal securities because their incomes exemption from federal taxes delivers a bigger benefit to investors.

On municipal securities, federal taxation amounting to as much as 35% may be waved. Add to this the waver of as much 10% state tax. These exemptions from state and federal taxes deliver a tremendous boost to the value of the income earned from municipal bonds. Hence the market in keen observation of these factors lowers the yield of long term municipals in this case dramatically in the example given, 6% for Corporates, 5.6% for US Treasury's and 4.8% on Municipals.

Taxable Equivalent Yield

The yield of a municipal bond is often interpreted or recalculated into a more practical expression for investors known as "taxable equivalent yield." Taxable equivalent yield is the taxable yield an investor would have to earn to equal the benefit delivered by the tax exempt municipal bond. The calculations below are done in consideration of an investor with a marginal federal tax bracket of thirty percent. A second calculation considers an investor in the thirty percent marginal tax bracket plus an additional five percent state income tax for a combined thirty-five percent. The formula is Tax Exempt Yield, the 4.8% arrived at above divided by 100% minus the investors tax bracket:

Example 1.

$$\frac{4.8}{100\% \text{ -}30\%}=6.85\%$$

Example 2.

$$\frac{4.8}{100\%\text{-}35\%}=7.35\%$$

-In example number 1 we see that the taxable equivalent yield of a 4.8% municipal bond equals 6.85%, .85% higher than the highest corporate bond yield in the hierarchy of interest rates presented.

In example number 2 when a state income tax is added to the federal tax bracket we see an even more advantageous result with a taxable equivalent yield of 7.35%.

At this writing by the way there were only 7 states that did not have a state income tax. They were Alaska, Florida, Nevada, South Dakota, Texas, Washington and Wyoming. Lower grade (AA, A) but still eminently investment grade securities will have nominally higher yields and will deliver commensurately higher taxable equivalent yields.

While we note that the tax exemption of municipal bond income is a great benefit to wealthy Americans it is equally noteworthy that lower interest rates in the municipal bond market caused by the non-taxation of income provide a cheaper source of capital for municipalities than is otherwise available, which may be deemed a benefit to society in general. The market interest rates on municipal bonds are lower precisely because their income is exempt from federal taxation. More precisely were it not for tax exemption the municipality borrowing $250 million dollars payable in 2047, say for the purpose of infrastructure repair, would be borrowing, as in the above example at 6% instead of 4.8%; a savings of $12.00 per $1000 borrowed annually for 30 years ($360) times 250,000 or $90 million over the life of the loan.

The market rates shown do not reflect current market rates in any way shape or form. They are used for illustrative examples only. Current market rates may be higher, lower or the same as these are simply coincidental with no relation to the illustrations presented here.

Fixed Income or Bond Surrogates

Many investors for a wide variety of reasons are reluctant to invest in individual bonds be they municipal or corporate or even US Government bonds. Individual securities to many investors are unwieldy in terms of minimal sums to invest, market timing, the many nuances of credit quality, liquidity and irregularity of income payment among other concerns. These investors instead count on investment vehicles that are surrogates for direct investment in bonds. These vehicles are professionally managed for investors or care taken for investors for a fee so that for example the ministrations and perhaps even the frustrations of the liquidation process described above may be avoided. The three most notable surrogates or alternative means of investing are Mutual funds, Unit Investment Trusts and Exchange Traded Funds. These are vehicles or containers in which the individual securities are placed and managed based on guidelines, rules and regulations enforced by law, industry principle and custom. To be sure each of these investment vehicles have distinctive characteristics, features, benefits and risks. Each investor and investment advisor are cautioned to make inquiries about their suitability before investing. Lastly in general with some exceptions the tax treatment of the income thrown off by these vehicles is treated as if the investor were investing in directly in the underlying security.

Summation

One can go on and on in detail and nuance regarding the bond market. Hopefully in this brief primmer we have addressed the particulars, enough at least for the reader to have a solid grounding in what bonds and the fixed income markets are all about.

About the Author

Pasquale "Pat" Scida was born in Brooklyn, New York, to a Southern Italian immigrant family in 1943. After finishing high school, he worked as a grocer's clerk, shipping clerk, and auto body mechanic with brief stints at the Fashion Institute of Technology, New York University, and Fordham. He married Rosalie Scigliano in November 1968 and, in December, took a position as a Wall Street clerk for eighty-five dollars week. Eventually rising to the position of senior vice president and director at Morgan Stanley Dean Witter, he retired in 2001. Mr. Scida has two children, Pasquale "Pat" III and Nancy, and four grandchildren, Ellena Rose, Sophia Joan, Pasquale "Pat" VI, and Adelina Grace. He resides on Long Island and continues to write.